University of
Bedfordshire

LEARNING AND TEACHING MATHEMATICS

Learning and Teaching Mathematics: An International Perspective

edited by

T. Nunes
Institute of Education, University of London, UK

P. Bryant
University of Oxford, UK

Psychology Press
a member of the Taylor & Francis group

Psychology Press Ltd., Publishers
27 Church Road
Hove
East Sussex, BN2 2FA
UK

British Library Cataloguing in Publication Data
A catalogue record for this book is available from the British Library.

    ISBN 0-86377-454-7

Typeset by Gilbert Composing Services, Leighton Buzzard, Beds.
Printed and bound in the United Kingdom by Biddles Ltd,
Guildford and King's Lynn

Contents

Contributors

Dr Guida de Abreu, Dept. of Psychology, University of Luton, Park Square, Luton, Beds LU1 3JU, UK.

Professor Alan J. Bishop, Faculty of Education, Monash University, Clayton, Victoria 3168, Australia.

Professor Peter Bryant, Dept. of Experimental Psychology, University of Oxford, South Parks Road, Oxford, UK.

Professor Erik De Corte, Center for Instructional Psychology and Technology, University of Leuven, Vesaliusstraat 2, B-3000 Leuven, Belgium.

Dr Regine Douady, IREM Paris 7, CP 7018 Tour 56/55, 3ème Etage, 2, Place Jussieu, 75251 Paris CEDEX 05, France.

Professor Herbert Ginsburg, Dept. of Human Development, Teachers' College, Columbia University, New York, NY 10027, USA.

Dr Koeno Gravemeijer, Freudenthal Institute, Tiberdreef 4, 3561 GG Utrecht, The Netherlands.

Dr Giyoo Hatano, Dept. of Human Relations, Keio University, Mita, Minato-ku, Tokyo, Japan.

Professor Celia Hoyles, Mathematical Sciences, Institute of Education, 20 Bedford Way, London WC1H 0AL, UK.

Professor Carolyn Kieran, Dept. of Mathematics, University of Quebec at Montreal, C.P. 8888 Succursale Centre-Ville, Montreal, Quebec, Canada H3C 3P8.

Dr Sandra Magina, Centro das Ciências Exatas e Tecnologia, Pontifícia Universidade Católica de São Paulo, Rua Marquês de Paranaguá, 111 São Paulo, S.P. CEP 01303–050, Brazil.

Professor Richard Noss, Mathematical Sciences, Institute of Education, 20 Bedford Way, London WC1H 0AL, UK.

Professor Terezinha Nunes, Child Development and Learning, Institute of Education, 20 Bedford Way, London WC1H 0AL, UK.

Professor Anne-Nelly Perret-Clermont, Faculté des Lettres, Séminaire de Psychologie, Université de Neuchatel, Espace Louis-Agassiz 1, CH-2000 Neuchâtel, Switzerland.

Dr Geraldo Pompeu Jr., Depto. de Matematica, PUCCAMP, sn 112 km, Rodovia SP 340, 13100 Campinas SP, Brazil.

Professor Lauren Resnick, Learning Research and Development Center, 3939 O'Hara Street, University of Pittsburgh, Pittsburgh, PA 15260, USA.

Professor Maria Luisa Schubauer-Leoni, Faculté de Psychologie et des Sciences de l'éducation, Université de Genève, 9 route de Drize, 1227 Carouge, Switzerland.

Dr Leen Streefland, Freudenthal Institute, Tiberdreef 4, 3561 GG Utrecht, The Netherlands.

Professor Gerard Vergnaud, Groupement de Recherche Didactique, CNRS, 46, Rue Saint Jacques, 75005 Paris, France.

Professor Lieven Verschaffel, Center for Instructional Psychology and Technology, University of Leuven, Vesaliusstraat 2, B-3000 Leuven, Belgium.

About This Book:
A Brief Overview

Most of us can think back to the time when we were in school and picture what our mathematics lessons were like. For us, in particular, learning mathematics was practising a series of techniques to try to master them and using the same techniques over and over again in a series of problems. Although we grew up in different countries, our mathematics lessons were in a way very much the same: mathematics was a collection of rules about how to set up numbers, how to expand or simplify equations, how to demonstrate theorems, and our task was to learn how to use these rules to solve the problems we were given. If this sounds boring to you, that is because it *was* boring. But much has changed in people's thinking about mathematics since our days in primary school. Many people concerned with mathematics education see mathematics learning and teaching as a significant part of the social construction of intelligence in which pupils and teachers are engaged at school. The chapters that are collected in this book were chosen to illustrate this process of social construction of intelligence in school from different perspectives.

The first section includes chapters that connect mathematics and intelligence. In these chapters, Piaget's definition of intelligence is implicitly used: intelligence (but note, *one form of intelligence only!*) and mathematical reasoning are the same because both are ways of solving problems in an adaptive, not arbitrary, and coherent fashion. These chapters analyse what one must consider in order to understand better the nature of mathematical concepts (and, consequently, intelligence). The second section includes a series of chapters that deal with the assumption that intelligence is constructed. The development of different conceptions in mathematics is discussed, showing that we can assume neither that children's knowledge of mathematical concepts is already programmed in the human brain or that it is simply a copy of the adult knowledge: children face difficulties and go through intermediary steps in the process of construction of mathematical conceptions which would not be expected if knowledge were simply innately programmed or copied from the environment. The third section focuses on the idea that this construction is socio-cultural. The definition of "mathematics" itself constitutes a socio-cultural idea and children have to construct a social representation of mathematics. But this is not all: they also have to rely on cultural tools to represent number and space and they draw on their environment for this construction. The impact of socio-cultural environments on learning is the central theme of section three. The last section considers the evidence that much of the social construction of intelligence that we are interested in takes place in school. Therefore the design of teaching and learning experiences, and the way that teachers and pupils relate to each other in their roles in school, are central issues in studies of the processes involved in the social construction of intelligence.

The chapters in this book comprise a unique collection of papers. The contributors are from different backgrounds—developmental psychologists, social psychologists, and mathematics educators—and from different countries. Some of these differences are clearly reflected in the sorts of questions that are examined, in the style of writing, and in the nature of the evidence considered central to the arguments. These differences, we think, make for an unusual theoretical and methodological richness. However, this variety does not lead to contradictions: often the same theoretical constructs are used in different papers, and this gives the reader the opportunity to reflect on these constructs in distinct situations and from a variety of points of view. For these reasons, we believe this to be a valuable collection of papers, which offer new ideas both about research and about the practice of mathematics learning and teaching.

T. Nunes and P. Bryant

MATHEMATICS AND
INTELLIGENCE

Research on children's mathematical learning has flourished in recent years. The amount of information that we have on children's understanding of basic mathematical concepts, like number, addition and subtraction, is now truly formidable. So is the volume of work on children coming to terms with more sophisticated ideas and techniques, in algebra, for example, and geometry. There is also an astonishing range in the kind of data that researchers have produced. Some of it comes from experiments, and some from classroom observations. The widespread use of computers in classrooms has not only influenced teaching methods but has also been a source of new information about children's mathematical ideas. In addition there has been a refreshing and exciting move to look at children's experiences and their mathematical activities outside the classroom, and this interest in informal mathematics has added to the need for cross-cultural research, as children's informal mathematical experiences vary widely with the environments in which they happen to find themselves.

It takes no great insight to see that much of this information is interesting and valuable, and that a lot of it is quite surprising. But we need to make sense of it and that, in our view, is impossible without a theory. So we begin this book with a theoretical section and our aim is to offer you, from the start, a theoretical framework to organise and comprehend the rich data that will follow in the remaining chapters in this book.

1

Of course, the authors of the chapters in the three later sections all have theoretical explanations for the data that they present, but each of these necessarily takes the form of rather specific hypotheses about the particular topic that the chapter tackles. The individual chapters set out to explain, for example, how children understand different word problems and learn about proportions, or how they coordinate spatial and numerical ideas in order to understand the measurement of time, or how to get unmotivated youngsters to consent to be taught about the properties of arithmetic operations. Each chapter is concerned with a particular aspect in mathematical development. But to do these chapters justice we need a broader picture as well: we need to understand what these different aspects of mathematics have in common. Our aim in this section is to paint that broad picture.

What kind of theory do we need? Theories of mathematical development vary in several ways, but one of the most central differences concerns what counts as mathematical knowledge. The two chapters in the first section approach this very central issue. Both Vergnaud and Nunes use a dynamic view of mathematical knowledge: it involves reasoning, solving problems, understanding the necessary relations between aspects of a given situation (or a variety of situations). In short, mathematical knowledge is a form of intelligence and needs to be distinguished, as Piaget (*The psychology of intelligence*, 1947) pointed out, from other forms of behaviour. To say that mathematical problem solving is intelligent behaviour might seem a platitude but it has implications for what we seek to explain when we are concerned with mathematics, what counts as data about mathematical knowledge, and what can be left aside because it belongs to a different domain of human behaviour—perhaps perception or memory. The view of mathematical knowledge as intelligence excludes from the set of observations to be explained, for example, comparisons of numerosity that can be accomplished perceptually or the mechanic memorisation of addition and multiplication tables through repetition. For example, it has been found in some studies that 7×8 and 8×9 are the least often remembered multiplication facts. However interesting (or boring) this may seem, it is not a central question to be explained by theories of mathematical reasoning. These theories would rather attempt to explain why some children can figure out the answer to 7×8 if they are told what 7×7 is, whereas other children don't even dream that this latter knowledge may help them figure out what 7×8 is.

Unlike Piaget, however, the two chapters in this section devote a great deal of attention to the question of representation. The central role of representation in contemporary theories of mathematical reasoning involves the implicit or explicit recognition that mathematical knowledge is not simply a question of a child's development in interaction with the physical world but also a matter of interactions in the social world: mathematical knowledge incorporates the systems of signs and ways of speaking and reasoning that are characteristic of mathematics as a cultural endeavour.

The connection between representation and the socio-cultural nature of mathematics is stressed in different chapters in this book, but we will refer to three issues more specifically here. In the first chapter, Vergnaud considers the distinction between schemes, on one hand, and concepts on the other, a distinction that he anchors on the way in which knowledge is represented. He characterises schemes as knowledge-in-action and, in this sense, a personal form of knowledge. Whereas this personal knowledge is essential, he argues that it is not sufficient for mathematics to exist as a science: science is made of texts and schemes are not texts. He suggests that mathematics as such requires the explicitation of the knowledge that is functionally available through schemes and that this explicitation is accomplished through external representations. The significance of socially communicable representations resides for Vergnaud not only in the cultural construction of mathematics but also in the personal process of making schemes into objects of thought, thereby changing the status of the knowledge for the individual.

In the second chapter in this section, Nunes discusses the role of representations from a different but not incompatible perspective, starting from the concept of mediated action. The concept of mediated action plays a central role in Vygotsky's theory, because he uses it to distinguish between "higher" and "elementary" psychological functions, in the same way that, in Piagetian theory, the emergence of representations allows children to go beyond the "here and now" and gives birth to the first intelligent actions. Nunes explores this role of representations by stressing that thinking is carried out through representations, and not directly through actions on objects or situations. In this process, not only the represented objects and situations but also the structure of representational systems have an impact on thinking; representations, as the objects for thinking, enable their users, but also restrain what they can do in particular ways. Differences between ways in which the same situations can be represented are viewed as playing a fundamental role in thinking. For example, the process of compressing or expanding representations is important both in pre-school children's reasoning and later on in algebra. Young children may understand well that a double block represents two sweets but find it difficult to deal with the notion that a single coin can represent two pence. What they can see in the extended representation they may not recognise when given the compressed representation. When considering results in the domain of algebra, Douady (Chapter 15) discusses a similar issue: a product of squares might more easily be recognised as such when presented in its expanded forms, for example, $(x + 3)$ $(x - 3)$, than when it is presented in its compressed form $(x^2 - 9)$.

The third chapter which relies on mathematical representations to make the connection between personal and cultural knowledge is by Schubauer-Leoni and Perret-Clermont (Chapter 11). They stress the role that conventional representations play in the distinction between two sorts of knowledge, which they refer to as operational thinking and mathematical reasoning. The latter, they suggest, is a social and cultural construction of a particular type, whereas the first relates to invariants in objects and situations, even if they can be mastered through social interaction.

Finally, the first section also introduces the idea that mathematical concepts cannot be viewed in isolation from each other. They form "conceptual fields", in Vergnaud's terminology, and the inter-relations between the concepts in a field are essential for pupils to be at home with mathematics. Vergnaud's notion of conceptual fields is akin to the notion of cognitive structures but there is a major development in his proposal: whereas cognitive structures are typically analysed on the basis of abstract (or syntactic) relations, Vergnaud's analysis of conceptual fields is firmly grounded on semantic relations, considering the distinct sorts of situations that must be mastered within the same conceptual field.

In short, the two chapters that compose the first part of this book characterise mathematical knowledge as a form of intelligent activity that relies on specific forms of representation. In order for the representations to have meaning and be functionally available during problem solving, they must be connected to schemes and concepts. Different representations for the same situations shed light on different aspects of the situations. The development of interconnections between different representations and situations allows students to have a clearer grasp of the conceptual fields as they progress through their mathematics learning in school. Finally, the use of external, socially shared representations seems to be an important move in making mathematical knowledge more explicit. Explicitation is a necessary step in the construction of mathematics as a science and is therefore also a major goal for mathematics teaching in school.

1 The Nature of Mathematical Concepts

Gérard Vergnaud,
CNRS, Paris

INTRODUCTION

The Nature of Concepts

It is certainly obvious nowadays, for most psychologists involved in research on mathematics education, that the psychological definition of a concept cannot be reduced to its mathematical definition. The paradox comes from the fact that mathematicians normally strive to be precise, complete and parsimonious when they write definitions, whereas psychologists try to understand how concepts are progressively shaped, by different kinds of situations and competences and by different kinds of linguistic representations and symbols. There is a lot of redundancy in this process, whereas a definition is supposed to be non-redundant.

Mathematicians consider that one is supposed to derive all the properties of a concept from its bare definition. But this hides the fact that a definition takes place in a system of concepts and true propositions without which this derivation would be impossible. Therefore it is misleading, even in mathematics, to consider that the properties of a concept are self-contained in its definition.

When studying the learning and development of mathematical concepts in children, one is struck by the fact that the recognition (or the discovery) of different properties of the same concept does not always take place simultaneously but often covers several years. This is true not only for the

5

concept of whole number, which has been extensively studied by psychologists, but also for additive and multiplicative structures, for algebra, geometry or calculus.

The thesis that the psychological definition of a concept cannot be reduced to its scientific definition is not specific to mathematical concepts, but it is in mathematics that one finds the biggest gap between the knowledge as expressed by scientists, and the knowledge underlying children's and adults' ordinary competences. This gap is so large that some mathematicians consider that there is no mathematics in what children learn or what the person-in-the-street does; in contrast, some anthropologists consider that real mathematics is the mathematics used by people in their usual activities, and that school mathematics is of little relevance and may even be useless.

Such a schism is damaging both from a theoretical and from a practical point of view. There is little hope of attaining a sound understanding of cognitive processes if one does not try to understand the relationship between the knowledge that underlies ordinary competences and the knowledge that is involved in science. There is also little hope of improved teaching unless schools are seen as places for learning what is useful for ordinary life as well as what science consists of. It is the schools' duty to make that connection.

To study and understand how mathematical concepts develop in children's minds through their experience in school and outside school, one needs to consider a concept C as a three-uple of three sets:

$$C = (S,I,R)$$

S: the set of situations that make the concept useful and meaningful.
I: the set of operational invariants that can be used by individuals to deal with these situations
R: the set of symbolic representations, linguistic, graphic or gestural that can be used to represent invariants, situations and procedures.

This definition, if applied to the concepts of number, to addition and subtraction for instance, means that psychologists and researchers in mathematics education should endeavour to characterize and classify the large set of situations for which these concepts and operations can be useful to students. It also means that they should try to identify the different invariants involved in the schemes used by individuals to master the different aspects of these situations, even though most of these invariants may be totally implicit. Finally a comprehensive definition of a concept cannot ignore the immense part played by words and symbols in the recognition and selection of the relevant mathematical objects, of their properties and relationships, and in the progressive elaboration of differentiated explicit conceptions.

It is my obligation to explain these views, as the concept of scheme and the concept of invariant are not commonly accepted concepts in the scientific community of mathematics education, and the relationship between signifier and signified, i.e. between symbols and symbolic operations on the one hand and conceptual meanings and operations on the other hand, tends not to be fully understood.

The Nature of Mathematics

To discuss the nature of mathematics is another challenge, for this is a controversial topic. Since Plato and Aristotle many questions have been raised about the empirical or non-empirical roots of mathematical knowledge, about intuition and formalism, about the nature of mathematical proofs, about the relationship of mathematics to logic, or about the possibility of proving the consistency of mathematics.

It is not the purpose of this chapter to deal with such high-level epistemological questions, but one cannot simply ignore them, because researchers and teachers have their own views. For instance, many mathematicians and teachers think that mathematical activity consists of discovering timeless truths, totally independent of culture and other disciplines like physics or economy, whereas others stress the relativeness and historicity of mathematical knowledge. One finds some echoes of these controversies in the debate among psychologists concerning the innate or non-innate character of some principles concerning the early development of whole numbers and counting (Baroody, 1992; Briars & Siegler, 1984; Gelman & Gallistel, 1978), or in the Piagetian thesis that physical knowledge would derive from empirical abstraction (isolation of the properties and relationships of external objects) whereas logico-mathematical knowledge would derive from reflective abstraction (isolation of the properties and relationships of the subject's operations).

Another important problem concerns the part of symbols in mathematics. The inflation of symbolism over the last four centuries has had much influence on the way mathematics is viewed. For instance, many teachers and parents view mathematics as a language, rather than as a domain of knowledge. This nominalistic conception has strong implications for teaching, especially on the kind of competences that teachers expect from students.

Final Introductory Remarks

There are several ways to approach the problem of the nature of mathematical concepts empirically. The most widely accepted is the historical approach. In fact the history of mathematics and science does shed an illuminating light on the relationship between the emergence of new concepts and the kind of questions, practical or theoretical, that these concepts are supposed to answer. It was an essential goal for Piaget to offer a complementary approach: the psychogenetic or developmental approach, which tries to understand the nature of mathematical concepts through the study of children's cognitive development concerning quantities, classes, relationships, space, combinatorics, proportion, chance etc.

One must never forget, however, that such an enterprise requires both a sound psychological as well as a sound epistemological point of view. Epistemology can be psychologically naive and psychology can be epistemologically naive. Psychology teaches us that most of our knowledge consists of competences, in which concepts are often implicit. Epistemology teaches us that mathematics is made of specific concepts which have their own functions and their own difficulties and traps. For instance the difficulties and properties of the concepts of function and variable are different from the difficulties and properties of negative numbers.

Therefore, a sound psychological and educational approach to the nature of mathematical concepts requires on the one hand that these concepts be traced to students' competences and in the way students progressively master mathematical situations, and on the other hand that these competences be analysed carefully with the help of well-defined mathematical concepts and theorems.

A fair theory of reference for knowledge requires both the idea that mathematical competence has to do with some class of situations, and the idea that mathematics, as a scientific discipline, provides us with the explicit concepts and theorems that we need in order to analyse those competences. This is not a matter of concern for many psychologists, unfortunately. On the ground that the mathematics taught in school is not a sufficient framework for analysing children's mathematical competences, some researchers invent idiosyncratic and ad hoc descriptions without thinking of the possibility of describing these competences in precise mathematical terms. A good example can be found in the way additive and building-up strategies are commonly described in proportion tasks, without any reference to the isomorphic properties of the linear functions, which make these strategies easily understandable from a mathematical point of view:

$$f(x + x') = f(x) + f(x')$$
$$f(n) = f(1) + f(1). \ldots + f(1) \text{ (n times)}$$
$$f(nx) = f(x) + f(x). \ldots + f(x) \quad \text{(n times)}$$
$$f(nx) = nf(x)$$
$$f(nx + n'x') = nf(x) + n'f(x')$$
$$\ldots$$

The theory and the examples that follow are intended to offer a simple and comprehensive view of the conceptualizing process by which students progressively understand what to do and how to proceed in mathematical situations, and what mathematical sentences and symbols mean. The main theoretical problems to be dealt with concern:

- The relationship between the representation needed for mathematical procedures and the representation contained in words, diagrams and symbols.
- The long-term process of conceptual development in a given domain.
- The emergence of new concepts and the change of their cognitive status.

THE THEORY OF CONCEPTUAL FIELDS

If one accepts that the psychological approach must be developmental, social, cognitive and epistemological, it is then possible to outline a research agenda. Here are some central issues:

- Which categories of situations offer occasions for children and students to form mathematical concepts, at school and outside school? How can we analyse the hierarchical complexity of these situations and classify them?
- Which procedures are used by students to face these situations? Which ones are successful, or unsuccessful? Under which conditions? Which implicit concepts and theorems does each procedure rely upon?
- Which procedures are taught? Which ones develop rather spontaneously? What do teachers, parents and peers do to help students?
- Which words, sentences and symbolic expressions are used by subjects to communicate and comment upon what they do or what they understand, to accompany, generate and control their operations of thought and procedures, and to represent the objects and relationships involved?
- Which kinds of situations, never met outside school, should we introduce into the classroom to make certain mathematical concepts meaningful?

The Example of Symmetry

The concept of symmetry can be involved in a variety of situations. These situations do not require the same kind of activity, and the sentences that can be expressed are not always the same.

Children's experience of symmetry is very important (probably even in the case of blind children) as most animals and manufactured objects are symmetrical (furniture, houses, tools). Moreover from an early age, children are invited to draw pictures and geometrical objects like borders; they may be invited to continue the drawing in Fig. 1.1, or complete the one in Fig. 1.2.

FIG. 1.1.   Type of border that young students may be asked to continue.

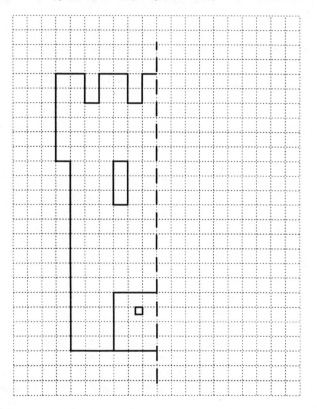

FIG. 1.2.   Kind of drawing that 2nd and 3rd graders may be asked to complete.

In the example of the fortress, 8 or 9-year-olds can already grasp important properties of symmetry, for instance:

- two symmetrical shapes (battlements; windows) look alike, even though some of them may look inverted;
- two symmetrical dots are equidistant from the axis.

The measure of lengths and distances is made rather easy owing to the fact that the sheet of paper is squared. The task also requires very little cognitive work on angles, as all of them are right angles: therefore there is no opportunity to measure angles or to wonder about the conservation of angles.

In completing the figure, children also develop perceptuo-gestural competences, the use of the ruler, the precision of the drawing (where to start and stop, how to draw exactly on the lines of the squaring). They can also use different relationships like "same as . . . on the other side", "symmetrical", "as long as", "same distance".

Finally the teacher may help children at different points:

* clarify the goal to be reached: give a simpler example, show quickly what the final drawing looks like and hide it, use some verbal explanation;
* demonstrate technique, for one part of the drawing;
* draw children's attention to some property of symmetry by asking questions, pointing at some element, or wording some invariant property.

In the example shown in Fig. 1.3, which is commonly offered to 11 and 12-year-olds in France (6th graders), the properties of symmetry used are a lot more complex and therefore the procedures to be used more sophisticated:

* the angles are not right-angles;
* the axis is oblique;
* there is no squared paper;

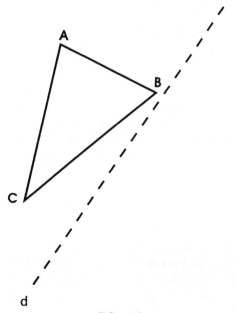

FIG. 1.3

- one may have to use such tools as the straight edge, the projector or the compass; and the ruler may be used not only to draw straight lines but also to measure lengths;
- angles are conserved but the orientation is not;
- the summits are necessary and sufficient elements for the figure to be defined and transformed; whereas in Fig. 1.2, lines or shapes (a crenel for instance) can be used as elements.

Symmetry offers us a good example of the enrichment of the ingredients that must be put together to generate a behaviour like drawing the symmetric figure of another figure. Several other tasks are also relevant: for example the identification of the axis of a symmetrical figure, the recognition of several symmetries in the same figure, the identification of the smallest module that can be symmetrised, translated or rotated to generate a pavement, and so on. These tasks stand at different levels of complexity.

The activity involved in the situations illustrated by Figs. 1.2 and 1.3, is organized. This organization is not restricted to one figure, for instance the same organization works for a whole class of type 2 figures. But it does not work for type 3 figures, which are more complex. In other words the scheme needed to deal with type 3 figures is hierarchically more complex than the one for type 2: in the sense that subjects who can accomplish the task for Fig. 1.3 can also usually succeed with Fig. 1.2; but not the inverse.

Definition

A scheme is the invariant organization of behaviour for a certain class of situations

Comment

A scheme is a dynamic and functional totality; the organization of behaviour must be considered as a whole (totality); it takes place over a certain period of time (dynamic); and it is aimed at achieving something (functional).

Analysis

Although it is a totality, a scheme is a combination of different kinds of elements:

- goals and expectations;
- rules to generate actions according to the evolution of the different variables of the situation and therefore rules to pick up information and check;
- operational invariants: to grasp and select the relevant information (concepts-in-action) and treat this information (theorems-in-action);

- inference possibilities (there are always *hic et nunc* inferences when the subject is facing a task; a scheme is not a stereotype but a universal organization; it is relevant for a class of situations and not for one situation only).

Symmetry is both perceptual, and operational. This offers a first idea of what concepts may be: empirical and pragmatic. But the goal that the subject wants to reach and the coordination of concepts and theorems in coherent systems are also essential aspects. Concepts do not derive purely from empirical regularities. They also derive from questions about the reasons for such regularities and about the existence of unpredicted events, such as the failure to reach the expected goal. Empirical regularities are not a self-sufficient source of inquiry, of relevance and truth. In the case of symmetry for instance, the question whether the placement of the summits is a necessary and sufficient operation to draw the symmetrical figure, is not purely empirical. Nor is the question of deciding what is conserved and what is not conserved purely empirical.

Operational invariants underlying behaviour are the essential source of concepts. But language and symbols also play an essential part. In the case of symmetry, words and sentences are important. The conceptual status of such expressions as "the same shape", "the same distance", "the length is conserved", "the angle is the same but inverted" is obviously different. I have selected below the four sentences concerning symmetry to show how different the linguistic and conceptual levels may be. For each of these sentences, a short comment points out the most striking character of the new sentence, in comparison with the preceding one. A true sentence is a theorem.

1. *The fortress is symmetrical*
2. *Triangle A'B'C' is symmetrical to triangle ABC in relation to line d*
3. *Symmetry conserves lengths and angles*
4. *Symmetry is an isometry*

In sentence 1, "symmetrical" is a unary predicate and the argument is the whole figure. One can symbolise it by the formula $S(F)$.

In sentence 2, ". . . symmetrical to . . . in relation to . . ." is a three-termed predicate, and the three arguments are: triangle A'B'C', triangle ABC, line d $S(A'B'C', ABC, d)$.

In sentence 3, "symmetry" is a substantive and has become the argument of the sentence. There are two unary predicates: "conserves lengths" and "conserves angles" $C_1(S)$ and $C_2(S)$.

In sentence 4 both "symmetry" and "isometry" are substantives and arguments. They are connected with each other by a binary predicate $R(S,I)$ which happens to be an inclusion relationship $S \subset I$.

One can follow the transformation of the concept through the four sentences and see the different conceptual levels through its different linguistic aspects:

- the move from the status of "adjective" to the status of "substantive";
- the move from one-argument predicates to three-argument and two-argument predicates (from unary properties to several-termed relationships);
- the move from singular *hic et nunc* objects (the fortress, triangle ABC, line d) to objects that represent a whole class of transformations (symmetry, isometry).

Mathematical concepts are involved both in schemes and in sentences. They may be involved in simple tasks and schemes like the scheme needed to complete Fig. 1.2, or more complex schemes like the one needed for Fig. 1.3. They may also be involved in different level mathematical sentences.

To complete Fig. 1.2, students need some concepts-in-action like those of shape, length, distance, measure (with simple units), and theorems-in-action like the following:

- any part on the right is at the same distance from the axis as the corresponding part on the left;
- it has the same shape and the same lengths.

Different rules of action follow:

- start from the axis towards the right, count the squares and check the number against the number of squares on the other side;
- go up or down, count the squares, and check the length of a certain line against the length of the corresponding line on the other side.

It is clear that such rules of action are not theorems, as their function is not to be true but appropriate and efficient; but they rely upon implicit theorems, which I call "theorems-in-action". Theorems-in-action are "held to be true propositions", even though they may be totally implicit, partially true, or even false. They say something about the world of objects and about truth, whereas rules of action do not. Rules of action are also propositions, most often implicit, and inevitably laconic. They say something about the appropriateness of the subject's action, not directly about the world of objects.

Concepts-in-action are not true or false, but only relevant or irrelevant. At the same time there are no theorems without concepts and no concepts without theorems, as it is the function of concepts to be involved in theorems.

The words used in mathematical texts have the important function of labelling the operational invariants underlying schemes; algebraic symbols also have this function. It is the function of both lexical and syntactic components of natural language to contribute to the transformation of operational invariants into explicit concepts and theorems; and therefore to change the status of knowledge. We have seen with sentences 1 to 4 that the status of explicit concepts can also be changed. The use of high-level concepts usually goes with such linguistic operations as the process of substantiation and with the increasing complexity of predicates and arguments.

The Two Main Conceptual Fields of Ordinary Arithmetic: Additive Structures and Multiplicative Structures

The concept of number cannot be isolated from its functions and properties. Numbers are used to count discrete quantities and measure continuous magnitudes, compare them, combine them additively or multiplicatively.

Addition is the first essential characteristic function of numbers. To classify objects, one needs only qualitative labels like names and adjectives, to compare and order them, one needs only comparative labels like the alphabet or some ordered parts of the body. It is only because one needs to combine quantities and magnitudes and find the measure of the whole, knowing the measures of the parts, that humans invented and developed the concept of number.

One cannot be surprised therefore that psychologists and education researchers have devoted important major efforts to understanding how young children progressively give up counting-all procedures and use either number facts or counting-on procedures; how they progressively understand counting as not only recalling a series of ordered words in correspondence with a set of discrete objects, but also as adding one unit each time, and building therefore a sequence of sets included in one another. The measure of a discrete set is called its "cardinal". It is the first measure that children master from the point of view of its additive properties, even though they may also have been interested in comparing lengths, volumes or weights during the same period of their early mathematical experience.

Therefore one must consider as essential the cognitive development from procedures that do not involve the addition of cardinals (like counting the whole after having counted the parts), to procedures that involve such additive operations, (like counting-on from the cardinal of one part as many units as there are elements in the second part, or recalling a number fact). This behavioural criterion of the recognition of the additive properties of numbers can be expressed as an equivalence theorem:

$$Card(A \cup B) = Card(A) + Card(B)$$

It is equivalent to count the parts and add the cardinals, and to count the whole.

This is not, of course, the only interesting step in the early development of the number concept, but it is as essential as the Piagetian conservation theorem or the principles investigated by Gelman and Gallistel (1978).

Today one needs a more diversified analysis of concept development than was usually considered useful 50 or even 15 years ago. The main reason for this is the diversity of situations that make a concept meaningful, the diversity of schemes and operational invariants that can be used to master these situations, and the diversity of words, sentences and symbolic representations that can be used to communicate about them and represent them.

Additive Structures

Additive structures provide us with a striking example of the diversity needed for the analysis of mathematical concepts, because addition and subtraction are needed in a variety of situations, for which the cognitive task depends on the kind of relationship involved and the kind of unknown one has to calculate.

The union of two sets that results in the binary combination of two cardinals offers the possibility of only two classes of problem: find the cardinal of the whole, knowing the cardinal of the two parts (addition); find the cardinal of one part knowing the cardinal of the whole and the other part (subtraction). The correspondence between the arithmetical operation needed and the structure of the task (represented in Fig. 1.4 with different symbolic systems) hides the fact that, for many other relationships, the correspondence between the arithmetical operation and the structure of the task is not one to one.

The other primitive relationship in additive structures is the state-transformation-state relationship in which there are not two but six different classes of problems, among which two only require addition while four require subtraction.

The arrow diagram (Fig. 1.5) is more congruent with the unary character of this relationship than the equation symbolism. Whether the relationship is symbolised or not, the most difficult task is the "find-the-initial-state case" (Carpenter & Moser 1982; De Corte & Verschaffel, 1987a; Nesher 1982; Riley, Greeno, & Heller, 1983; Vergnaud, 1976). This difficulty is conceptual, as the canonical scheme needed is the inversion of the transformation, and the application of the inverted transformation to the final state. This scheme relies upon a theorem-in-action which makes it necessary to differentiate clearly between four different concepts-in-action: the initial state, the final state, the direct transformation and the inverse transformation. Two different symbolic representations (among others) can make this theorem-in-action explicit (Fig. 1.6).

The second representation, which uses functional notation, cannot be used at the elementary level, whereas the arrow-diagram is rather easily understood by 7 to 10-year-olds, (provided one fills it in with numbers, not with letters). Symbols help children to understand relationships, concepts and situations. They may also raise obstacles when they are too abstract or even inadequate: for instance the Euler-Venn diagram is very useful to represent the union of sets

There are 4 boys and 3 girls at the birthday party. How many children altogether?

ADDITION

Peter needs 8 francs to buy a miniature car. He has 3 francs. How much does he need?

SUBTRACTION

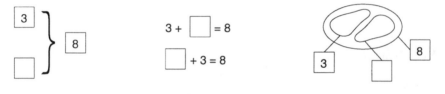

FIG. 1.4

but it cannot represent negative transformations. Teachers who try to get students to use Euler-Venn diagrams for all kinds of addition and subtraction relationships make the situation worse than by using no symbolic diagram at all.

The comparison relationship (*John has 12 marbles, Daphné has 18. How many more has Daphné?*) also offers six categories of problems, very similar in structure to the state-transformation-state categories (Riley et al., 1982; Vergnaud 1981, 1982).

It is not so well recognized by researchers and teachers that, on top of these three elementary relationships (part-part-whole; state-transformation-state; comparison) stand three other important additive relationships:

- the combination of transformations, such as:
  John has played two games of marbles. In the first game he has won 6 marbles; in the second game he has lost 8 marbles. As a whole, has he won or lost marbles? How many?

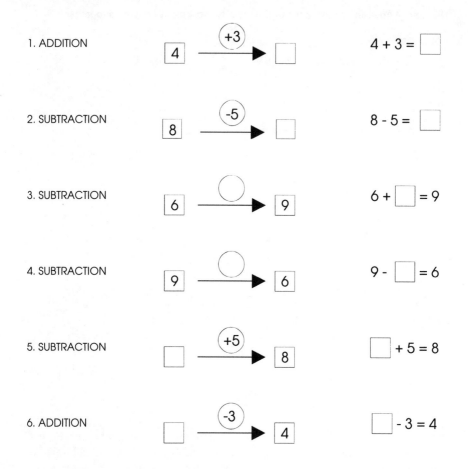

1. ADDITION — 4 →(+3) [ ] — 4 + 3 = [ ]

2. SUBTRACTION — 8 →(-5) [ ] — 8 - 5 = [ ]

3. SUBTRACTION — 6 →( ) 9 — 6 + [ ] = 9

4. SUBTRACTION — 9 →( ) 6 — 9 - [ ] = 6

5. SUBTRACTION — [ ] →(+5) 8 — [ ] + 5 = 8

6. ADDITION — [ ] →(-3) 4 — [ ] - 3 = 4

EXAMPLES

Case 1: John had 4 miniature cars. His grandmother offers him three more. How many miniature cars does he have now?

Case 4: Fred had 9 marbles. He plays a game of marbles. He now has 6 marbles. What has happened?

Case 6: Joan has just given 3 francs to her little sister. She now has 4 francs. How much did she have before?

FIG. 1.5

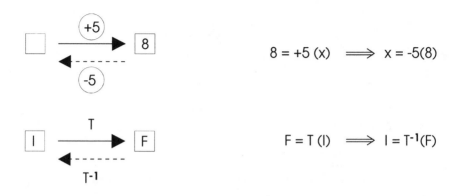

$$8 = +5 (x) \implies x = -5(8)$$

$$F = T (I) \implies I = T^{-1}(F)$$

FIG.   1.6

- the transformation of a relationship, such as:
  Stephanie owes 6 francs to her sister Connie. She gives her 10 francs, for Connie to buy a book. What is the new situation now?
- the combination of relationships, such as:
  Arthur is 6 centimetres smaller than Connie. John says he is 2 centimetres taller than Connie. How much is Arthur smaller than John?

Their common character is that each of the three elements can eventually be negative, whereas in the part-part-whole relationship no element, neither the cardinal of the parts nor the cardinal of the whole, can possibly be negative. In the state-transformation-state analysed above and in the comparison case, only one element can be negative.

Many researchers think that elementary school students are not concerned with these relationships. This is a misleading opinion because many children are interested in combining transformations (a win of 4 and a loss of 7 outcomes in a loss of 3), in understanding and combining debts, and in combining and decombining all kinds of relationships. This is true even for young children in some familiar situations.

The consequence is that it is possible to widen the variety of problems of addition and subtraction that can be offered to children in the classroom, especially if one considers that each of the six elementary relationships mentioned above (see Fig. 1.7) can itself be combined with each of the others and with itself.

PART-PART-WHOLE

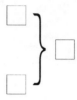

STATE-TRANSFORMATION-STATE

REFEREE-COMPARISON-REFERENT

COMBINATION OF TRANSFORMATIONS

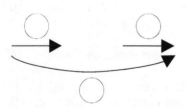

COMBINATION OF RELATIONSHIPS

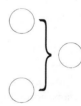

TRANSFORMATION OF A RELATIONSHIP

FIG. 1.7. The six fundamental additive relationships.

It is also possible to increase the variety by changing the task. One can offer tasks in which students have to generate the questions, or explain their solution to other students, or understand the equivalence of two different procedures, or sort out relevant and non-relevant information (as is usually the case in real situations).

Multiplicative Structures

The variety of problems involving either a multiplication or a division, or a combination of such operations is also very large. But this problem-space is structured differently from the additive one. The reason is that most multiplicative relationships are not ternary but quaternary. Even the simplest multiplication (how much money do I need to buy 5 cakes at 4 francs each?) does not involve three numbers but four, as can be seen in Fig. 1.8.

The only elementary example of ternary multiplicative relationship is the comparison relationship: *John has 24 miniature cars. Connie has 4. How many times more has John?*

Most multiplicative problems are simple or multiple proportion problems and therefore there are at least two different kinds of quantity (two variables) involved. In the comparison case, there is only one. Nevertheless the comparison relationship is essential, as it is probably the most natural way of analysing proportion, at least for primary school students.

In the example above, one can extract three different relationships (see Fig. 1.9):

a binary commutative combination $4 \times 5 = 5 \times 4 = \boxed{}$
a vertical unary operation: start from 4, multiply by 5
a horizontal unary operation: start from 5, multiply by 4

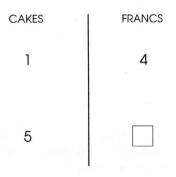

FIG.   1.8

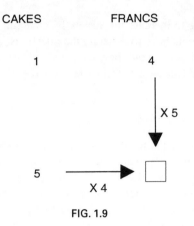

FIG. 1.9

These three ways of reading and treating the information are not conceptually equivalent and cannot be explained to children as easily. As far as the binary combination is concerned, the main obstacle is that it is difficult for children, who see numbers as quantities; to understand why multiplying 4 francs by 5 cakes gives francs and not cakes.

The vertical unary operation (start from 4, multiply by 5) has a clearer meaning, due to the fact that ×5 can be seen as a scalar operator (a pure number, with no dimension) extracted from the comparison relationship: 5 cakes is five more than 1 cake. The implicit reasoning is that the price of 5 cakes is also 5 times more. A scalar operator (five times) applied to 4 francs gives francs. This reasoning is possible only because there is a theorem-in-action underlying it— the price of 5 cakes equals 5 times the price of 1 cake:

$$P(5) = 5\,P(1)$$

This theorem can easily be connected with the additive property of the linear function:

$$P(5) = P(1 + 1 + 1 + 1 + 1) = P(1) + P(1) + P(1) + P(1) + P(1)$$

Therefore there is a natural way for young students to move from addition to multiplication.

The horizontal unary operation cannot be explained so easily to 8 or 9-year-olds as starting from 5 cakes and arriving at a certain number of francs, the operation ×4 corresponds to the constant coefficient between the two variables. The dimension of this coefficient is a quotient of dimensions francs per cake. Above all there is no way of explaining how the result of multiplying 5 by 4 may consist of 5 + 5 + 5 + 5, as the addition of 5 cakes four times gives cakes, not francs.

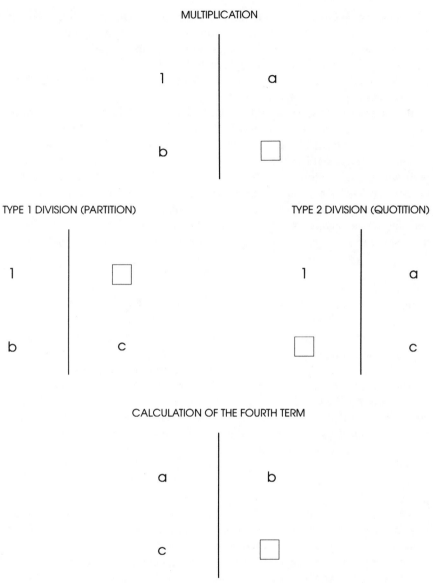

FIG. 1.10.   Different columns represent different quantities or magnitudes.

This primitive obstacle of multiplication can be traced in much older students, when they have to solve more complex problems. As this chapter is supposed to be synthetic, I will not develop here extensively the different structures that can be found when analysing problems and students' procedures (see Fig. 1.10).

It may be enough to recall that there are four main classes of simple proportion problems and that the complexity of each of these four types of problems varies a lot when the numerical values change (large numbers, small or large scalar ratios, small or large constant coefficients, decimals, fractions numbers smaller than 1), and when the domain varies (prices, production, consumption, speed, geometry, density etc.

It is now well known (Lesh & Landau, 1983) that students use a wide variety of procedures to deal with these problems, among which those relying upon the isomorphic properties of the linear function are probably the best mastered.

The only point that I would like to stress is the importance of facing students with double and multiple proportion at the secondary level, and even at the elementary level for some simple cases. The main argument is that double proportion is essential for conceptualizing the measure of space (area, volume) and for understanding most topics in physics. Formulae cannot be fully understood if they are not analysed as multiple proportion expressions:

$$V = L \times W \times H$$

Volume is proportional to Length when Width and Height are held constant; and similarly to Width (or Height) when the other two variables are held constant. It is conceptually important for students to understand the difference between the product of two variables in double proportion tasks, and the product of one variable by a constant in simple proportion problems.

The conceptual field theory provides a framework for the understanding of the relationship between the situations offered to students and the different cognitive tasks that they may have to deal with, the concepts-in-action that are relevant to select the information, the theorems-in-action that are necessary to compute the adequate rules of action and expectations, and the different wordings and symbolic representations that can profitably be used to make the structure and procedures explicit at different phases of the students' learning process.

The analysis of the conceptual field of additive structures shows that different concepts are involved: measure, part, whole, state, transformation relationship, unary and binary operation. It also shows that the concept of directed number is essential, even for young students (increase, decrease, so much more or less than etc.). This does not mean that students can easily understand all the properties of directed numbers; some of these properties are difficult even for secondary school students. But there is no reason to prevent younger students from understanding easy properties, such as (+5) and (−14) being equivalent to (−9) (*a win of five and a loss of 14 is equivalent to a loss of 9*), or the reciprocity between (+ 5). and (−5) in comparison relationships (*A has 5 more than B → B has 5 less than A*) or between a direct transformation (from the initial to the final state) and the inverse transformation (from the final to the initial state).

Similarly the conceptual field of multiplicative structures involves such concepts as those of proportion, scalar ratio, rate, linear and multilinear function, linear combination, dimensional analysis. The concepts of fraction and rational number are also involved in such relationships as those of the part-whole, part-part, constant proportion. But most of these concepts and theorems remain totally implicit for students, or only partially explicit. Words and symbols change the cognitive status of concepts-in-action and theorems-in-action.

ELEMENTARY ALGEBRA AND FORMAL CALCULATIONS

Algebra is an important step in the learning of mathematics. Not only does it require symbolic calculations in a sense and to an extent never met before by students, but it also involves new concepts and new theorems. The concepts of equation, formula, function, variable, and parameter are not arithmetical concepts but algebraic ones, and the same is true for the concepts of a set of numbers, group or vector-space. Historically the identification of such sets as the set of natural numbers N, the set of directed numbers Z, the set of rational numbers Q, the set of real numbers R, or the set of complex numbers C, is tightly associated with the development of algebra.

At a certain stage, students have to understand that negative numbers are solutions to equations such as $a + x = b$ when $b < a$, and that rational numbers are solutions of equations such as $ax = b$ when a is not a divisor of b. A natural way to introduce directed numbers to elementary and early secondary school students is to associate them with transformations or relationships. This way of considering "algebraic" numbers makes it possible for students to see the connection between arithmetic and algebra, and offers them ways of putting natural language problems into equations or interpreting the results of the treatment of equations.

In fact, the main difference between arithmetic and algebra is that algebra uses a formal detour where arithmetic would use a sequence of intuitive choices: the choice of the relevant intermediary unknowns and calculations.

Formal calculations must not be confused with formalism. There is practically no mathematics, and there is certainly no algebra, without some kind of formal calculation. The mastery of a domain goes through many phases, among which the axiomatized and formalized phase is the last one. The danger of formalism for mathematics teaching is that the connection between natural and intuitive reasoning and formal calculations is not made.

As a matter of fact, the connection is not straightforward. For instance the minus sign may have several meanings:

- a decrease   *Peter had 18 sweets, he eats 4 of them*

$$18 - 4 = \square$$

• a difference   *Jane is 9 years old, Paul is 5. How much older is Jane?*

$$9 - 5 = \square$$

• a complement   *There are 7 children at Daniel's birthday party. 4 of them are boys. How many girls are there?*

$$4 + \square = 7 \Rightarrow$$

$$\square = 7 - 4$$

• an inversion   *Paul has just received 15 francs from his grandmother. He now has 27 francs. How much did he have before?*

$$\square + 15 = 27 \Rightarrow \square = 27 - 15$$

The mathematical power of algebra is partly due to the polyvalence of signs and symbols, but this polyvalence raises difficulties that cannot easily be overcome by students. The multiplication sign in algebra is an operation on and with numbers; but those numbers refer to quantities and magnitudes of different kinds, such as ratios, rates and constant coefficients. In other words the formal character of algebra hides the fact that the same symbols may cover very different mathematical objects and operations, and that algebraic calculations convey important reductions and equivalences, which are not usually made explicit.

Among the new concepts involved by algebra, those of function and variable are essential. Any number (or magnitude) can be considered as a function of other numbers. Therefore it is not enough to consider letters and numbers as unknown and known quantities; they are also variables, and the relationship between variables can be inverted, combined, and decombined. There lies the epistemological root of algebra.

In this chapter I can only deal with a few major ideas about mathematical concepts and the conceptualizing process. One must recognize that algebra deeply modifies the cognitive status of arithmetical concepts. This change does not consist only in the use of algebraic symbolisms but also in the identification of new mathematical objects.

TOOL-CONCEPTS AND OBJECT-CONCEPTS

Psychologists have discussed, on many occasions, the change of status of concepts in the course of cognitive development. Among others Piaget mentions the process of reflective abstraction, and Vygotsky proposes the idea that algebra is to arithmetics what a written language is to speech, or what a foreign language is to the mother language, because in all three cases a reflective process takes place. Douady (1991) uses the words "tool" and "object" to characterize the change of status of mathematical concepts. I find these words particularly suggestive because they express the change from concepts and theorems which are useful for action to theorems organized in explicit systems. This is not an all-or-none process that would involve all the consituents in a given conceptual field at the same time. For instance, the change of additive concepts from tools to concepts is different for measures or states, for transformations or comparison relationships, and for the concept of directed number. In mathematics, concepts usually emerge as tools. The first properties that children can grasp are the simplest ones. But repeated use of these tools, their familiarity and awareness of their part in reasoning, transform these tools into objects, even though they may be quite abstract. For instance, the concepts of function and variable are naively used as tools in proportion tasks, and conceived as mathematical objects in algebra.

I have also already mentioned the way the concept of symmetry changes from its original status of unary predicate to the status of three-argument predicate, and then to the status of a substantive. Substantiation and symbolization play an important part in the transformation of conceptual tools into objects.

CONCLUSION

The understanding of the process of conceptualizing is essential to our understanding of what a concept is. This is what both the historical approach to epistemology and the developmental approach to students' learning teach us. The analysis of the way in which situations and problems are treated by students is at least as enlightening as the way in which they talk about mathematics. The concept of scheme is essential to any theory of cognition because it articulates into a unit both its behavioural and representational features: rules of action and operational invariants. Schemes are at the heart of cognition, and at the heart of the assimilation-accommodation process. The strange thing is that the centrality of this concept to cognitive psychology is hardly recognised by any researchers today. In mathematics, there exist many algorithms. Algorithms are schemes. Like schemes, algorithms are composed of goals, expectations, rules, operational invariants and possibilities of inference. Not only are they functional but they are also effective, in the sense that they enable the subject either to reach a solution in a finite number of steps or to show that there is no solution. Non-algorithmic schemes are not that safe and secure: they are efficient, not effective.

The theoretical importance of schemes comes from the fact that operational invariants are more or less adequate: the relevance of concepts-in-action and the truth of theorems-in-action are essential conditions of the efficiency of schemes.

Representation through words and sentences changes the status of concepts and theorems. The process of explicitation is difficult, but explicit concepts and theorems enable students to objectify their knowledge and discuss its appropriateness and validity. Science is made of texts; schemes are not. Mathematics as a science would not exist if there were no schemes and algorithms to make it functional in action, but it would not exist either if there were no words and theorems to make it shared and debatable textual knowledge.

2 Systems of Signs and Mathematical Reasoning

Terezinha Nunes
Institute of Education, London

The aim of this chapter is to explore the idea of mediated action in the context of mathematical problem solving and its implications for our understanding of the development of mathematical concepts in educational settings. To begin, I wish to justify the need for the notion of mediated action in mathematical reasoning and the consequences that this notion has for understanding what mathematical knowledge is. In the second section, I will discuss different studies which highlight how systems of signs affect pupils' problem-solving activity. In the final section, I will suggest some of the educational implications of this theory and further steps in the investigation of the way systems of signs affect mathematical reasoning and learning in school.

WHY DO WE NEED THE IDEA OF MEDIATED ACTION WHEN DISCUSSING MATHEMATICAL KNOWLEDGE?

According to Luria (1979), all higher mental functions are mediated by systems of signs. Without such mediation, we would be basically restricted to what our unaided organism is directly capable of. But there are innumerable actions that we carry out every day that we cannot carry out without tools, both physical and mental. These actions are in a sense so common that the fact that they surpass our organic capacities no longer impresses us. We can fly, we can lift up tons of weight, we can see microscopic particles, we can solve complex equations in a very short period of time at the touch of a button—to list just a few examples. If we can stand back just for a minute, we might be filled with wonder, until the sceptic observes that it is not *we* who are doing all this but the aeroplane, the crane, the microscope, the calculator etc. It is the tool, not the person. However, what the sceptic fails to realize is that *we cannot understand human actions if we exclude the tools that humans use from their system of activity.* The concept of mediated action stresses exactly this: in the course of history, cultures have developed tools that enable us to act, perceive and reason beyond our natural limits. Bateson (1972; p.459) proposed a most illustrative example:

> Suppose I am a blind man, and I use a stick. I go tap, tap, tap. Where do I start? Is my mental system bounded at the handle of the stick? Is it bounded by my skin? Does it start halfway up the stick? Does it start at the tip of the stick? But these are nonsense questions . . . The way to delineate the system is to draw the limiting line in such a way that you do not cut any of these pathways in ways that leave things inexplicable.

It is instructive to consider briefly the example of a very simple mathematical activity which is also clearly mediated action: counting. In order to count adequately, as Gelman and Gallistel (1978) have pointed out, we need to: (1) establish a one-to-one correspondence between unique counting words and the objects that are being counted; (2) maintain the counting words in a fixed order; and (3) use the last word to represent the number of objects in the set. As simple as this activity may seem, it cannot be carried out without the mediation of a numeration system: a system must be used if we wish to keep the words in a fixed order. Most 7 or 8-year-olds in many cultures could easily count to one thousand, if they chose to, and produce one thousand counting labels in a fixed order. This marvellous accomplishment (which we take for granted) is only possible because we rely on a system that allows us to generate rather than actually memorize the words in a fixed order. Once the structure of the oral counting words is understood, the user of the system can produce counting labels which he/she has never heard. In this case, the structure of the system enables the user to go beyond the limits of his/her natural memory.

But counting is often not an action in itself but rather a tool for solving a problem. If there are many marbles in a jar and we want to know just how many, we count them. We can count and find out how many marbles are in a jar even if we could not tell the number of marbles in the jar just by looking— that is, we can overcome our perceptual limitations with respect to numerosity. When we use counting as a tool to solve a problem, we as users decide what sense to make of the tool. However, the sense of culturally developed tools is not obvious: it is culturally constructed and socially transmitted. A stick is nothing to the blind man if it is not incorporated in his system of orientation when he walks down the street. There is in our culture a tradition in its use which is socially transmitted but still must be reconstructed by individuals as they incorporate the use of a stick into their system of orientation.

The same is true of counting systems. The use to which they can be put has to be reconstructed by children as they learn to count. It has been demonstrated, for example, that young children who know how to produce the sequence of numbers in counting may not know how to use counting sensibly to solve a problem. Sophian (1988) asked 4-year-old children to observe a puppet counting and judge whether the puppet was counting in the right way to answer the question posed by the experimenter. Two sets of objects were placed in front of the puppet and sometimes the question the puppet had to answer was which set had more objects whereas on other trials the question was how many objects altogether. Clearly the puppet had to use different ways of counting in order to answer the different questions. However, most 4-year-old children did not judge correctly whether the puppet had done the right thing when counting to answer these two different questions: although able to count, these children did not make the same sense of the counting system that we as adults make. Thus mediated action involves a culturally developed tool and a user who can make sense of it, using it to solve problems.

A second reason why we need the idea of mediated action to understand mathematics learning is that the system of signs that enables the actor also shapes the activity in significant ways. The highest number that can be produced by a subject who has mastered the counting system in his/her environment is not simply determined by the counter's memory skills but by the system. Counting to a thousand is not a very difficult task in our system; actually, we can count on indefinitely. However, there are non-base counting systems that are finite; this means that their users cannot count on indefinitely. Lancy (1983) described several such systems in Papua-New Guinea. These counting systems use the names of body parts as number words. The body parts are taken in a systematic order and this enables the users to keep the number words in a fixed order. However, because the system does not have a base and is not recursive, the system is finite—and so also is the counting ability of the user. Other cultures have developed numeration systems that enable their users to continue counting on indefinitely through recourse to a base and iteration.

A third aspect of the notion of mediated action is that, because the use of mediators is not obvious, they must be understood in the context of the cultural practices where they are used. This aspect of systems of signs has been most clearly recognized in the domain of literacy studies by the seminal work of psychologists such as Scribner and Cole (1981) and anthropologists such as Street (1984). The analysis of literacy has shown that, although the reading of words can be described in terms of psychological operations of thought or processes that are somewhat general, the reading of texts is not completely described by these operations. Texts have a meaning in the context of the literacy practices to which they belong. This is quite easy to bring home to a literature student who can pronounce the words but not grasp the meaning of a scientific text, or to a physicist reading a psychology book. The aims of the text, the structure of argumentation, and the implicitly accepted views are essential elements of a particular literacy practice. When we learn to read in primary school, we cannot be said to have mastered written language once and for all. What literacy practices we master will depend on what we use written language for in the course of our life in and out of school. There is also some evidence for the need to understand mathematical signs in the context of particular mathematical practices; this evidence will be discussed in the third section of the chapter.

To summarize: the concept of mediated action is fundamental to the understanding of mathematical reasoning. Mediated action in mathematics implies the use of systems of signs, the sense of which needs to be learned in the context of cultural practices. In the next section, differences between systems of signs and their use will be discussed in the context of children's problem solving in mathematics.

VARIATIONS IN SYSTEMS OF SIGNS AND THEIR IMPACT ON CHILDREN'S REASONING

In this section, two types of variation in systems of signs will be discussed, both of which affect children's problem-solving activity. The first section deals with the process of compressing representations and the second deals with the question of partial versus complete representation.

Compressing Representations

Children can draw on different tools to mediate their problem-solving activity; in other words, the same concept might be represented in different ways. For example, when trying to solve an addition problem—such as "Mary had 3 mint sweets and 2 orange ones; how many sweets altogether?"—children might use 3 fingers to represent the mints and 2 to represent the orange sweets, and then count all the fingers. In this case, the representation is extended: each sweet is represented by one finger, all fingers are counted. But the children might represent the mints just by the word "three", put up 2 fingers to represent the orange sweets, and count "four, five". In the second case, the representation of the mints is compressed: the child does not need each object to be represented by a sign, the word "three" stands for the whole lot.

In the following sections, variations in children's performance that relate to the issue of compressed representations in different types of problem will be discussed. Examples from different topics in mathematics will be used. The discussion of compression of representations is concluded with considerations that indicate that compressing a representation may actually create a new domain or a new way of thinking about the represented situation.

Understanding the Concept of Unit With Different Representations

The idea that units can have different values is a complex one and also a very important idea in mathematics. It is central, for example, to the understanding of numeration systems with a base, where we count units of different values, such as ones, tens, hundreds, thousands etc. Young children seem to be able to grasp this idea of units with different values in some circumstances and not in others: the more compact the representation of value, the more difficult it is for the children to use the concept of unit.

Frydman and Bryant (1988), for example, demonstrated that clear differences between the components of a double unit facilitate children's performance in a sharing task when they have to take unit-value into account. In one task, the children were asked to share some pretend sweets to two dolls in a way that would be fair—that is, the recipients would each receive just as much to eat. The difficulty of the task was that one of the recipients liked her sweets in double units whereas the other liked her sweets in single units. Thus, sharing on a one-for-you one-for-me basis would not work. Most 5-year-old children were successful in this task and could take the unit value into account: they would give two singles to one doll while giving one double to the other. In contrast, most 4-year-olds did not succeed when the two units forming the double-sweet were of the same colour. They were able to succeed, however, when each unit in the double was of a different colour. In this case, they would give a double to the doll who liked doubles and a single of each colour to the doll who liked singles. The explicit distinction between the two types of units helped the 4-year-olds to find a method for keeping the amounts constant even when the units were of a different size (for more information, see Bryant, Chapter 3).

Recently, Wang (1995) demonstrated further the impact of representation in this type of task by asking 5-year-old Taiwanese children to share fairly both sweets and coins to two dolls. The sweets were in either doubles (in only one colour) or singles, as in the study by Frydman and Bryant. The coins were either worth 1 dollar or 2 dollars. Thus, mathematically the children had the same task. However, the representation of value was different across tasks: whereas the units in the sweets task were distinguishable, the value of "two" was represented by a single coin in the task of sharing money. The children carried out the sharing by placing the objects into boxes so that no feedback from the results of the distribution was obtained as the children did the sharing. The children's performance differed significantly across situations. The majority of the children succeeded in the sweets task, where representation of doubleness was explicit, but only about half of the children succeeded in sharing the coins fairly.

Another study that illustrates the significance of the process of compacting representations for understanding mathematical concepts was carried out by Kornilaki (1994). Kornilaki asked 5-year-old Greek children to solve a series of missing addend tasks. In these tasks, the children were told that a girl had a certain sum of money—for example, 5 drachmas—in her wallet and then got some more money—say, 4 drachmas—from her grandmother. The children were asked how much money the girl had now. The significant characteristic of this task, which distinguishes it from a simple counting task, is that the first addend is hidden—the children cannot see the 5 drachmas that are inside the wallet. They can only see the 4 drachmas given by the grandmother, which are placed on the table.

Kornilaki (1994) observed that children approached this problem in different ways (and confirmed earlier observations by Steffe, Thompson, & Richards, 1982, about similar problems). One group of children *counted only the visible objects*: they counted the wallet as "one" and the remaining coins one by one, coming up with a wrong answer. In this example, this group of children would produce the answer "five". A second group of children said all the count-words up to the value of the hidden addend as they pointed to the wallet and then went on to count the remaining coins. These children, who were *counting their motor acts* up to the value of the hidden addend, were able to obtain the correct answer to the addition problem. It must be noted that, for this group of children, verbal representation was not sufficient to stand for the hidden coins: imaginary pointing at the hidden coins was a necessary support for them to solve the problem correctly. A third group of children did not need to point to the wallet but still *went through the sequence for all the counting words* for the hidden addend and then went on to count the visible drachmas and succeeded in solving the problem. Finally, a fourth group of children simply *counted on* from the value of the hidden addend and they also succeeded. These different performances show a progression in the process of compacting the representation of the hidden addend. When counting only visible objects, nothing can be represented by a sign, all the elements must represented by an object. When counting motor acts, the pointing gestures (or, in some cases, the children's own fingers) represent the objects but the representation is still spelled out, the drachmas are represented one by one. When producing the sequence of counting words, the elements are still represented one by one but there is no need to have an element in correspondence with the words: the words are in and of themselves sufficient representation. Finally, when counting on, a single word, "five", is used to represent the whole set. This is a most compact representation.

Kornilaki found a clear relationship between children's progress in this process of representation and their success in another task, which investigated their ability to compose a sum of money using coins of different values. In this second task (originally described in Carraher, 1985), the children were asked to carry out pretend purchases, and pay for the items using, for example, 10 drachmas and 1 drachma coins. In one example, the children have two 10-drachma and five 1-drachma coins and are asked to pay 13 drachmas for an item in the shop which they chose to buy. Although all the children could count out 13 drachmas when asked to do so using 1-drachma coins, only about one third of the children could pay 13 drachmas by using one 10-drachma and three 1-drachma coins. The relationship between their success in this task and the type of representation they used in the addition task with a hidden addend described earlier can be examined in Table 2.1. It is rather clear that, as children become able to use more and more compact representation in the addition task, they are also more likely to succeed in combining units of different values to form a single value.

In brief, the representations offered to children in problem situations have an impact on how well they can solve the problems. Young children seem to work better with extended rather than with compact representations of values when solving problems.

Representing Values With Letters

Children's preference for extended over compressed representations can also be observed much later, in their initial attempts to use letters to represent unknown values. I asked two pairs of 10-year-old children (Nunes, 1992) to solve a problem and later write instructions that could be used by a friend to solve the same problem. The difficulty with writing the instructions, they were told, was that the friend would have the same words in the problem but different numbers. Thus they could not use numbers in their instructions to the friend: they should use letters to represent the numbers, and tell the friend what the letters were supposed to mean.

The children had no difficulty in understanding this task. However, their representations clearly differed from the sort of representation that would most

TABLE 2.1
Number of Children Using Different Strategies in the Addition Task and Their Performance in the Additive Composition Task

| | | Strategy in the Hidden Addend Task | | | |
		Figural	*Motor*	*Verbal*	*Count On*
Additive	Fail	12	7	2	0
Composition	Pass	0	1	5	6

From Kornilaki (1994).

likely be chosen in a mathematics lesson for this problem. The children used an extended representation of the relations in the problem and required a larger number of letters to produce the instructions. For example, one of the problems was: "There are 98 books to be distributed between two classes in one school. However, one class has more children and will receive 16 more books than the other. How many books will each class receive?". The message produced by one pair of children read:

> Call the number of books *a*. Call the extra books that one class will receive *b*.
> Do *a* minus *b* and you will get *c*.
> Call the number of classes *d*.
> Divide *c* by *d* and you will get *e*. Add *b* plus *e* and you will get *f*.
> Your answers are *f* and *e*.

This is a very good production, arrived at after much checking and improving on the instructions. When asked to write the message using arithmetic signs, the children produced a list of meanings for the letters, similar to the above, and the following sequence with arithmetic signs (capitals and small letters are maintained here in the way they were used by the children):

> $A - b = c$
> $c \div D = E$ 1 answer
> $E + B = F$ other answer

This message clearly differs from the traditional representation that this sort of problem would receive in algebra classes: if *a* is the total number of books, *b* is the number of extra books, and *c* is the number of classes, $(a - b) \div c$ gives the number of books for the smaller class and $c + b$ gives the number of books for the larger class. Whereas the pupils' message contains six letters, in a more canonical representation three letters would suffice. The children used a new letter to represent each value in the instructions; for an adult, (a–b) can simultaneously stand for the values, the operation, and the result, whereas the children create separate symbols for the values in the operation and the result.

This extended message was then given over to a second pair of 10-year-olds, who were asked to use it in order to solve the problem. The message was considered quite clear by this pair of decoders, who had no difficulty in interpreting it and solved the problem correctly. Their good performance in this extended message contrasts strongly with the errors often described in the literature for exactly this type of problem when it is presented to children in algebraic representation. Although further research is still needed, it seems that children prefer an extended form of representation to a compressed one both in producing and interpreting problem-solving formulae that contain letters.

What is Involved in the Process of Compressing Representations?

If we now reflect on several examples of mathematical representation, it is clear that compressed representation is often used even without our awareness of this compression. The place value system, for example, uses compressed representation: instead of writing $100 + 20 + 3$ we write 123; the tens and ones are re-written over the zeros. But many children produce either fully extended representations (100203 for 123) or partially extended representations (10023 for 123) before producing compact ones (see, for example, Nunes & Bryant, 1996; Seron & Fayol, 1994; Silva, 1993).

Other examples of compressed representation are: $a + a + a + a$ can be compressed into $4a$; $a \times a \times a$ can be compressed into a^3; $a \div b$ can be compressed into the fraction a/b, which represents both the operation and the numbers simultaneously.

One of the advantages of compact representations is that they can be connected to two meanings at the same time. For example, $y \times y$ is an extended representation of y^2. Although these two ways of representing the product of a number multiplied by itself mean the same thing, the compact representation y^2 is more immediately connected with two operations, multiplication and exponentiation. The advantage of this compression is clear if we have to find the value of y from y^2: The representation y^2 is much more easily connected to the idea of square root than the extended representation $y \times y$.

Thus the process of compressing representations seems to open the way to a new set of relationships to be understood by connecting the compressed representation to new operations. It is useful to think of what operations are applied when we compress a representation, in order to consider the difficulties involved in the process. Compressing the extended representation of sets in problem solving—that is, $(1,2,3,4,5) \rightarrow 5$—means replacing counting by addition because a single word, "five", represents all of the elements added together. Compressing $(a + a + a + a) \rightarrow 4 \times a$ or $4a$ means moving from addition to multiplication. Compressing $(a \times a \times a) \rightarrow a^3$ means moving from multiplication to exponentiation. Compressing $(a \div b) \rightarrow a/b$ may involve going from whole numbers to fractions, and consequently having to deal with a new type of number.

This analysis indicates that compressing representations must therefore be rather difficult for pupils. However, this difficulty does not appear to be clearly recognized in mathematics teaching. The evidence reviewed in the previous sections suggests that extended representations are preferred at initial points in learning and therefore it might be advantageous to start to work on new concepts with extended representations. But the analysis of conceptual relations indicates the advantages in the use of compressed representations and thus the need to cope with the move from extended to compressed representations in mathematics instruction.

Complete Versus Partial Representation.

When children are given concrete materials as manipulatives to solve problems, they are usually given enough materials to re-enact the solution to the problem. For example, if a teacher is introducing the idea of multiplication, she might give the children a large number of blocks to be used as pretend-sweets, and ask the children to figure out how many sweets altogether in 4 bags with 5 sweets in each. The children can easily create 4 groups of 5 sweets, each group representing the contents of one bag, and then count out the sweets. It is, however, possible that the children learn relatively little about *multiplication* from this activity. They might think about their activity as counting and need not see anything else in the situation. If they already know how to count, they do not have a problem to solve.

A small change in the problem-solving environment might make a lot of difference. If the children do not have enough blocks to produce an extended representation of the objects, they might have to develop a schema of the situation where a group becomes a unit of representation, and can therefore represent the other groups. Although to an adult this might seem so trivial a change that it is not worth considering within an instructional setting, the change is not trivial for children. Not all children who can solve the problem with a full set of materials will succeed if they only have a partial set. We (Bryant, Morgado, & Nunes, 1991, in Nunes & Bryant, 1996) carried out a study with 8 and 9-year-old children, who were asked to solve a series of multiplication problems. The children were randomly assigned to one of two conditions: either they had enough materials to re-enact the problem and could count all the sets—*complete sets condition*—or they only had part of the materials, so that they could build a partial model of the situation to think about it but not solve the problem by counting—*incomplete sets condition*. In this incomplete sets condition, for example, they might have had 12 yogurt cups, which allowed them to form 3 groups of 4, when they would have needed 20 to form 5 groups of 4 (having been asked how many yogurt cups altogether if you have 5 packs with 4 cups in each). They could partially represent the problem and, if they used this partial representation to form a schema of the whole problem, they could solve it correctly—for example, by imagining the remaining two groups or by using two of the three groups twice as referents for adding. The results of this study showed that 8-year-olds solved significantly more multiplication problems in the complete sets condition than in the incomplete sets condition. That means that some of the 8-year-old children can succeed in solving multiplication problems if they can use an extended representation and count the elements one by one, but not if they must develop a new schema of the situation, where the units to be dealt with are groups (see also Steffe, 1994, for similar observations).

Among the 9-year-olds there was an interaction between problem difficulty and condition of testing (complete versus incomplete sets of materials). In the simple problems, they could easily use the incomplete sets to form a schema of the situation and work out the answer. However, in the more difficult problems, they succeeded more often when they had the complete sets, although all of the problems were multiplicative. For example, in one of the more difficult problems, the children were asked how many different-looking outfits could be formed with 4 T-shirts of different colours and 6 pairs of shorts. In the complete sets condition, the children had 4 miniature T-shirts and 6 shorts cut out in coloured paper. In the incomplete sets condition, the children only had 2 T-shirts but did have the 6 shorts. If they reasoned that, for each T-shirt, they could have 6 changes of shorts, giving 6 outfits per T-shirt, they could develop a schema of the situation and thus just imagine the remaining T-shirts. But most 9-year-olds could not develop this schematic representation of the situation in the absence of the whole set of T-shirts. They did significantly better when solving the problem in the complete sets condition, although this is by no means a simple problem for 9-year-olds even if they have the whole set of materials.

In another study, we gave children incomplete sets of materials to solve area problems (only the relevant aspect of the study is described here; for a complete description, see Nunes, Light, Mason, & Allerton, 1994), which are consistently shown in the literature to be difficult for children. The first problems involved finding the area of two rectangles; the children had 20 one-square-centimetre bricks to measure with, but both rectangles had larger areas than this. The latter problems involved calculating the area of more complex figures, such as a U-shaped figure that could be decomposed into rectangles and a parallelogram. We wanted to find out whether the children could, in this environment of limited sets of materials, discover a multiplicative formula for the area of the rectangle. With insufficient bricks to cover the figures and count the bricks, we expected that a schema for the situation might be developed. The children worked in pairs (there were 16 pairs in grades 4, 5, and 6 each).

Results showed that 80% of the responses to the simple rectangle problems were correct. Despite our attempt to prevent solutions based on counting, some children used the bricks until they ran out, tried to mark with their fingers the portion of the area already covered, and moved the bricks on to cover the remaining portion of the figure. Thus only about half of the children who solved the problem successfully (39% of the total number of pairs) obtained their solution using multiplication. Their multiplicative formula was "number of bricks in a row times the number of rows" of bricks that could be fit into the rectangle. The most encouraging result in this study, however, was that the majority of the children who invented a multiplicative formula for the area of the rectangle also used the formula adequately for the parallelogram: 30% of the total number of pairs of children did so (but note that 50% of the responses were correct because some children still managed to move the bricks around and count). This result is encouraging because finding the area of geometrical figures is often difficult for children of this age level. A comparison group from the same classes, who solved the same problems using a ruler, showed significantly poorer performance (only about 30% correct responses both for the rectangles and for the more complex figures) despite the fact that all the children had received instruction previously on how to calculate the area of the rectangle from linear measures. The results of this experiment indicate that solving a problem in an environment where an extended representation is not readily available might promote the development of a schema for the situation. This schema is likely to be a compressed representation that allows the pupils to attend to new relationships in the situation. In this particular example, the children seem to have developed a multiplicative notion of area (number of bricks in a row times number of rows) and at least some of the pupils constructed a distinction between height and side, necessary for the solution of the area of the parallelogram.

In short, representations become the objects on which we act when we solve problems. The operations we carry out on extended representations may be different from those we can carry out on compressed representations. Extended representations may allow for counting, for example, when compressed representations require other operations. Although the problem might be the same across problem-solving environments, the type of reasoning required might differ when different means of representation are available in the environment. Having only an incomplete set of objects to represent a situation makes a difference for children's reasoning: with full sets of materials, the whole situation can be re-enacted when problems are solved, whereas with partial materials the children need to develop a schema of the situation, and then operate through the schema. Incomplete sets of materials may be an effective way of provoking the compression of representations at least in some situations: this seemed to be the case in addition problems with an invisible addend and in multiplication problems where only a sub-set of materials was made available to the children. But further research is clearly needed before firm conclusions can be reached.

This section discussed how different representations change the problem-solving environment for the children. The next section examines how the same system of signs might have a different sense depending on the cultural practice in which it is embedded.

THE CONNECTION BETWEEN SYSTEMS OF SIGNS AND DIFFERENT PRACTICES IN MATHEMATICS

When children first learn the signs + and −, these signs are used to indicate operations on natural numbers. When solving a problem presented orally, for example, the children will learn that they need to listen to the whole problem before they can choose which operation they will use. This way of making sense of the signs + and − contrasts with the practices in the mathematics classroom when directed numbers are involved. For example, two numbers preceded by the minus sign are to be added, not to be subtracted from each other, and pupils have been observed to make many mistakes when working with directed numbers even in simple situations (see, for example, Bell, 1980). The studies presented in this section investigated the hypothesis that at least some of the pupils' errors might not result from their lack of understanding of the properties of directed numbers but from the confusion that results from the changes in the meaning of the plus and minus signs.

In a first study, I attempted (Nunes, 1993) to separate out the pupils' ability to reason about directed numbers from the difficulties they had with the signs by manipulating experimentally their use of the written signs + and −. It was hypothesized that, if a significant portion of the pupils' errors had resulted from the change in the meaning of the signs, pupils who solved the problems orally, and therefore did not use the signs + and − in the representation of the problem, would perform significantly better. The study thus involved asking pupils to solve a series of directed number problems after the pupils had been randomly assigned either to a problem-solving environment where paper and pencil were not available or to an interviewing condition where they were asked to first write down the information and then solve the problems. The participants in this study were 72 Brazilian pupils in grades 4, 5, and 6 (grade 5 pupils having just received instruction on signed numbers). The values used were all simple tens (e.g. 40, 30, 20) to minimize issues related to arithmetic; the important question for the problem solver was whether to add or subtract the numbers. All problems related to gains and losses of a hypothetical farmer in his different types of harvest, a situation that was familiar to all subjects.

Pupils in the oral condition performed significantly better than those assigned to the written condition. An analysis of the errors displayed in the written condition suggested the existence of a conflict between the two written arithmetic practices that the pupils had learned in school. This conflict involves (at least) two major rules. First, in written arithmetic taught before directed numbers, signs stand for operations and children are taught that they need to carry out different operations separately. They should not, for example, add and subtract using a single algorithm. When directed numbers are introduced, signs no longer stand for operations because two negative numbers can be added or a positive number can be subtracted from a negative one. Second, when subjects use the plus and minus signs to represent an operation they cannot write down the sign for the operation after the presentation of the first figure in the problem but only after the second figure has been presented. At such an early stage in problem presentation, the subjects cannot yet know which operation they will need to carry out and must wait for further information to know what the sign ought to be. In contrast, when signed numbers are introduced, the signs should be used as each number is written down—the number is itself signed.

Typical errors in directed number problem solutions in the written condition are therefore expected to be of two kinds. One type of error consists in failing to write down whether the first figure in the problem is positive or negative. Because pupils reason that they need to wait until they decide which operation they will be carrying out, they write the first number without a sign. A second type of error involves carrying out the operation indicated by the sign regardless of whether two debts are presented consecutively. This would result, for example, in subtracting a negative number from another rather than adding them. These were, in fact, the most common types of error observed when the pupils' written production was analysed (Nunes, 1993).

In a second study (Nunes, 1993), the possibility of changing pupils' sense of the plus and minus signs was analysed again through an experimental manipulation. The pupils solved the same series of directed number problems twice, once in the oral mode and once with the problems presented to them in written form. When the problems were presented in writing, they were given a particular meaning: they were described as notations produced by an illiterate farmer about his profits and debts with different crops during one season. Because the farmer was illiterate, he used a + to indicate his profits and a – to indicate his losses. Thus the problem presentation involved an explicit attribution of a different meaning to the signs and included the notation in the context of a different practice, divorcing it from the school practice. It was expected that this change in context of problem presentation would significantly change pupils' responses, because they would no longer draw on their school approach.

Results showed that, in this study, pupils' performance did not deteriorate as a function of the use of the written signs: there was no difference in their performance across oral and written presentation. On the other hand, pupils' performance in the written condition was better than the performance of the pupils from the previous study in the written condition, whereas there was no difference between performance in the oral condition across the two studies. The ease with which pupils' performance was changed suggests that they did not need to learn anything new in the written condition: all that was necessary was to connect the problems to a different practice of arithmetic.

LESSONS FROM THE ANALYSIS OF MEDIATED ACTIVITY FOR THE MATHEMATICS CLASSROOM

Often when mathematics teaching is discussed, the focus of discussion is exclusively on the invariants of mathematical concepts. There is little doubt that invariants are central to mathematical concepts. If there were no invariants in problem situations, deduction would not be possible. We can calculate the size of a part on the basis of the knowledge of the size of the whole and the sum of the other parts because the part-whole relations are assumed to be constant. We can deduce that one set is larger than the other by knowing that they stand in different ratios to a comparison set because the correspondences are taken to be constant. "Every notion, whether it be scientific or merely a matter of common sense, presupposes a set of principles of conservation, either explicit or implicit" (Piaget, 1965, p.3). However, what should not be overlooked is that invariants must be constructed by the problem-solvers themselves, and that this construction is influenced by the way the problem is represented. For example, if pupils are given manipulatives to solve a multiplication problem; they can solve the problem by acting it out. If asked: "How many biscuits in three packages of biscuits with five biscuits in each package?", they can form three groups of five blocks, each block representing a biscuit, and count the whole lot of blocks. They will succeed but they might not have reflected about the multiplicative invariants in the situation: all they had to do was to count. Their schema of the situation does not involve anything related to multiplication. The step to formalization, as Hart (1986) termed the connection between practical problem solving and its mathematical representation, might be a large one indeed for the pupils in this situation. All the children did was to count the bricks but what they were asked to write down as a mathematical representation is a multiplication sum.

How can we, then, create an environment in a mathematics classroom that will stimulate the children to produce a different schema of the situation, where multiplication is a significant aspect? The studies that I have discussed indicate a possible route. If the children were only offered incomplete sets of materials—for example, three packages and about 12 bricks—the partial but extended representation would have to be complemented by the use of words or numbers, which are compressed representations. The incomplete sets could allow the children to start acting out, to find a path for the reasoning, but then extend this path mentally. This extension might not develop in one shot. We observed, for example, in the study of multiplication problems that children who worked with incomplete sets tried to use the same sets twice, moving one set along as they kept track of the number of sets, or even pointed repeatedly at an empty bag until they counted out the number of yogurt cups. Like the pre-school children in the hidden-addend problem, the school children who solved multiplication problems with incomplete sets of materials compressed their representation over a series of steps.

Similarly, in the area problems, some children tried to use the same bricks repeatedly but others extended the pattern discovered with the bricks into a symbolic schema that allowed them to calculate the area. When the pupils invented the formula "number of bricks in a row times number of rows", they were expressing the pattern they had observed with the bricks but extending it to a general approach. They were also on their way to inventing the idea of height, which in the parallelogram is an imaginary line: it does not coincide with the side of the figure but with the "number of rows" in the children's formula. It is likely that this formulation in terms of "number of rows" plays an important part in children's interpretation of the formula for the area as "height times width" rather than "side times side".

The implications from the research I have presented in this chapter are provocative. Different invariants can be constructed in a situation depending on how the situation is represented. Problem-solving environments may include different representational resources, influencing children's problem-solving efforts in significant ways. An important aim of mathematical instruction might be to lead pupils to compress their representations in such a way that they realize the new operations that become possible with this compression without losing sight of the old ones. But I wish to stress that the evidence on which I drew to come to this formulation is still rather scarce. Much more research is needed on the steps involved in compressing representations, on the role of incomplete sets of materials in provoking the development of a schema of the situation, and on how these difficult transitions can be managed in the mathematics classroom.

II

THE DEVELOPMENT OF MATHEMATICAL UNDERSTANDINGS

In the introduction to Part 1 we discussed an important difference between diverse approaches to the analysis of children's mathematics and followed the view that mathematical knowledge is a form of intelligence. The chapters collected in this section deal with a second significant difference between theories of mathematical development: it concerns the emphasis that they place on the child's own contribution to this development, and the form that they claim this contribution takes.

There are some extreme, all and none, views on this question, but we can dismiss them reasonably quickly. It is plainly absurd to claim that children somehow provide their own mathematical knowledge for themselves without much help from the environment around them, though some claims have been made about infants' and children's knowledge at very early ages (Gelman & Gallistel, 1978; Wynn, 1992). The idea cannot work because there are very well documented instances in which children take a sequence of ordered steps—spread over several years—towards understanding some basic mathematical concepts. If mathematical understanding were innate, one would not expect children to have to go through a series of earlier stages in which their understanding of some mathematical idea is not just incomplete but rather takes a different form before they achieve a full understanding of the idea in question.

Number and counting are an example: as shown in Bryant's chapter in this book (Chapter 3), children produce number words in an impressively proficient way several years before they have a full understanding of what these words mean or how to use them. They have to learn some important things about these words and it takes time. Another instance, to be found in the opening chapter by Vergnaud, is the developmental change from "counting all" to "counting on". When children begin to add two quantities and before they know by heart the simple addition facts, they adopt a curiously long-winded, though correct, strategy for addition. Even though they know the number of both addends (for example 5 in one pile and 3 in another) they insist on counting first one pile and then the other. It takes more than a year for them to see that there is a more economic way of doing the addition, which is to start with the number of one addend, preferably the larger one, and to count on from there. Vergnaud's entirely plausible contention is that this development has to wait for the child to appreciate the relation between part and whole in addition, and that this too takes time: so the understanding of addition does not come all at once, and the understanding of multiplication and of multiplicative relations takes even longer and involves many more steps. For example, the chapter by Singer, Kohn, and Resnick (Chapter 6) shows that young children seem to be able to make proportional judgements on a perceptual level long before they can deal with proportions numerically, even though the numbers concerned are well within their grasp. One can argue whether or not the earlier judgements are genuinely proportional, but they can be viewed as a step on the route to a full understanding of proportions and it is hard to see how these steps would be needed by a child whose understanding of proportions is innate.

Piaget would almost certainly have been happy with all three of the examples that we have quoted, and was himself responsible for charting the steps that children take over several years towards essential mathematical concepts, including conservation, cardinal and ordinal number, and additive and multiplicative relations. Yet he also argued for a considerable contribution on the part of the child to his or her own mathematical development. But there are two differences between Piaget's theory and a theory of innate mathematical structures. One was his argument that the child's contribution was not the possession of innate knowledge, but the construction of mathematical knowledge for himself or herself. The other was that the child managed this construction in tandem with the environment: thus the child's experiences in the environment are also important in Piaget's theory, though he stressed the child's informal experiences rather than the instruction that the child receives from teachers, parents, or even from more experienced friends.

We need to make two points about this enormously important idea of the construction of mathematical knowledge. The first is that it is almost certainly right, and the second is that it is almost certainly not completely right. We shall adopt it as part, not as the whole, of the theoretical framework for this book.

We think the notion right because it accounts for the pattern of the child taking a series of discrete steps towards different aspects of mathematical knowledge, each step a closer approximation to the concept in question and each step leading to the next. The idea about construction explains these sequences; we find that no other ideas can explain these sequences as well. The only other serious alternative suggestion that has been made is that children show only limited understanding at first because of limitations in their capacity to process information. In particular, limits in their "working memory" have been mentioned. But the research on this explanation has concentrated on children doing straight sums, which is a very limited way of looking at mathematical understanding, and it does not seem possible that this purely quantitative speculation (working memory is said to increase with age) could account for the clearly qualitative changes that we have mentioned or for other qualitative changes in mathematical understanding, which have been documented in profusion.

The idea of construction works a great deal better here, although there are grounds for thinking that it needs refining. The notion of "theorems in action" introduced by Vergnaud is a case in point. Vergnaud argues that children in the intermediate stages have definite ideas, which can be identified on the basis of the pattern of their responses to different problems, but which would not show up in answers to questions about what they are doing (one of Piaget's main sources of information). So, for example, the change from "counting all" to "counting on" that we have already mentioned demonstrates, according to Vergnaud, that children have a definite understanding of additive relations as the merging of two wholes, but not as involving part-whole relations.

The underlying notion of construction seems a good one, but it cannot, we believe, account for all mathematical changes. The reason lies in the nature of mathematics itself. Mathematics embodies certain universal truths, but it is nevertheless a cultural achievement and its nature does vary considerably between cultures. The decimal numeration systems and the place value system are cultural inventions. They are so widely used, so much part of our basic mathematical instruction, that we easily forget that they are a comparatively recent invention in the history of mankind and that even now not all societies have adopted them. Measurement systems vary as well as counting systems and are cultural inventions; for example, the idea of using movement at a constant speed around a full turn in order to measure time is a fascinating cultural invention, and one that causes a lot of problems for children, as Magina and Hoyles (Chapter 5) show in their research. It is clearly difficult for children to think of the size of an angle as an indication of an interval of time, especially because the angle they need to consider is not a visual figure but the figure that is imaginarily formed by the minute hand at the start and at the end of the interval. And, of course, the list of other cultural inventions such as calculus and trigonometry is very long indeed. It would be impossible to expect each child to re-invent these inventions, but that is what he or she would have to do if mathematical knowledge were just the product of the child's own constructions in informal interaction with his or her environment.

It is no coincidence that Piaget had little to say about cultural inventions and concentrated instead on children's understanding of the logic that underlies mathematics. His research analysed the most basic aspects of logic and thus it was possible in principle to suggest that children construct these necessary logical principles for themselves. But they could not reinvent the cultural inventions.

The main impact of these tools, in our opinion, is to provide effective ways of representing (and thus of solving) mathematical problems. Children's success in solving mathematical problems is not just a matter of whether they are capable of doing the sums. Slight differences in the wording of a problem have a striking effect on whether the children can find the right solution to it, despite the fact that the actual mathematical manoeuvre needed is exactly the same in both versions of the problem. The evidence for this is amply described in the chapters by Vergnaud and by Nunes in the previous section, and by Verschaffel and De Corte in this section (Chapter 4). (The third section too is largely concerned with this same question, but from a cultural point of view.)

So we conclude that any theory about children's growing understanding of mathematics has to account for at least two factors. One is the learning of invariants: the second is the acquisition of cultural tools and the way in which children represent mathematical problems and how these representations affect their solutions. These themes interweave and interact, but they need to be unravelled if we are to understand what children themselves understand about mathematics. The chapters in this section provide many details of this story. Each deals with particular invariants, each describes cultural practices which sometimes help and at other times actually hinder children's mathematical understanding, and each gives us specific instances of the pervasive importance of children's representations of the problems that they are given.

INVARIANTS

The invariants discussed in these five chapters are all basic to mathematical understanding, but some are simpler than others and the result is that the chapters cover quite a wide range of ages—from the pre-school period when children, quite slowly, become acquainted with the principle of one-to-one correspondence and its relation to number, to the last years in school when they are taught about functions.

It takes time, as we have said. The gap in time between children beginning to count and achieving a reasonable understanding that number is a basis for comparing quantities is striking (see Chapter 3 by Bryant). Young children also have clear difficulties at first with the relationship between parts and wholes, and thus with the understanding of the additive composition of number. These difficulties are demonstrated beyond a doubt by children's reactions to the different word problems (they do much worse in problems that involve part-whole relations than in ones that do not) described in Chapter 4 by Verschaffel and De Corte. Their conclusion about the difficulties that young children have with part-whole relations and the hindrance that this causes to their understanding of the additive composition of number echoes Vergnaud's analysis of the developmental change from counting all to counting on. It is worth noting that in both chapters the authors draw our attention to the fact that children's understanding of addition and subtraction is not an all-or-none business. Young children understand adding as combining early on, and apparently long before they go to school (see also Chapter 3). They have learned some of invariants when they begin to be taught arithmetic: others come later.

It takes children about two or three years at school to grasp the essential invariants of additive relations, but when they have finally done so, they still have a long way to go with multiplicative relations. Children's initial difficulties with multiplicative relations are very well documented: there is no disputing the fact that children up to the age of 10 years or so often have great difficulty with quite straightforward tasks involving proportion, probability, area and division. The mistakes that they make in these tasks and their tendency to produce additive instead of the correct multiplicative solutions are striking and consistent. But, in contrast to the work that we have just mentioned on additive relations, the conclusions drawn from research on multiplication has tended to be of an either-or nature:

either they do not understand multiplicative relations, or they do. Chapter 6 by Singer, Kohn, and Resnick tells a different story.

These authors argue that there are two ways of solving proportional problems: one is a direct and perceptual way, while the other involves an explicit calculation of the two quantities involved. With judgements of crowdedness, a perceptual judgement rests on a rough impression of the relative distance between objects in a given area, and with judgements of density in relation to floating, perceptual comparisons are based on the immediate impression that the child (or adult) gets from "hefting" the object. These perceptually based comparisons are proportional in the sense that they result in correct proportional judgements in some situations. However, there are other situations that exclude perceptual judgements and demand explicit calculation, and here young children, who do well with perceptual judgements, are often at a loss.

Singer, Kohn, and Resnick conclude that they have identified two stages, and that one eventually leads to the other. Children who can form perceptual judgements about proportion eventually combine this ability with their new-found knowledge of number and of computation, and as a result become able to make explicit proportional judgements based on the two quantities involved.

This conclusion receives some support from work by Spinillo and Bryant (1991) who also found that young children can make proportional judgements in some situations but not in others. These authors attribute the developmental difference to a change from relational strategy applied to part-part comparisons to a part-whole strategy which makes a complete range of proportional judgements possible; it is not at the moment clear whether the same interpretation could be made about the Singer, Kohn, and Resnick results.

In all these examples, the plausible assumption has been made that one stage leads, in a causal sense, to the other. The experiences that children have with perceptual judgements . or part-part judgements of proportion and with sharing, lead in the end to a full, quantitative understanding of proportion and division. One of the future jobs of work on mathematical development must be to establish whether this assumption is right. It probably is, but if it is not then the significance of the earlier stages of multiplicative understanding would be greatly diminished. We still need to know.

REPRESENTATION

The theme of representation takes two forms in this section. In one form it is used as an explanation of some of the children's mathematical difficulties: they make mistakes because they represent mathematical problems in the wrong way, usually because the circumstances conspire to make them do so. In its other form we see how children learn to represent one quantity by another.

The first point is quite straightforward. Not all of young children's mathematical errors can be traced back to their lack of understanding of the invariant involved. They frequently produce the wrong answer even when they have grasped the invariant and are in principle able to make the necessary mathematical move. This has been shown to be the case with addition (Hughes, 1986), with inferences and measurement (Bryant & Kopytynska, 1976) and with directed numbers (Nunes, 1993), for example.

Word problems are the demonstration *par excellence* of this other source of errors. Time and again, as Verschaffel and De Cortes's chapter shows, when children are given two problems that, from a mathematical point of view, are the same problem, but which have slightly different wordings, they succeed with one and yet completely fail to find the solution to the other. Some of the cases are very striking. For example, the following two problems are the same from a mathematical point of view, and yet children manage the second version far better than the first:

1. "Pete has 3 apples. Ann also has some apples. Pete and Ann have 9 apples altogether.
   How many apples does Ann have?"

2. "Pete and Ann have 9 apples altogether. Three *of these* apples belong to Pete *and the rest belong to Ann*.
   How many apples does Ann have?"

We agree with Verschaffel and De Corte that the clue to these striking imbalances in children's mathematical answers can only lie in the way that they represent the questions posed to them. The fact that changes in wording, which often seem trivial to the experienced adult, can have such a powerful effect on children's ways of representing mathematical problems to themselves, is of course a salutory warning to teachers and parents and to researchers too. But it also gives research workers a powerful tool for investigating forms of mathematical representation.

The second way in which the question of representation comes up in the chapters in this section is over the question of representing one quantity by another. The question was raised in the first section in the discussion by Nunes of full and compressed representations, and is asked in a different way in the chapter by Kieran (Chapter 7).

Algebra, of course, is the use of the representation of one quantity by another *par excellence*. Carolyn Kieran's chapter demonstrates the extraordinarily interesting path that takes children from thinking that it is simply working out unknown quantities to realising the power of algebra. Two points in her discussion are particularly striking. One is how algebraic formulae can be used to demonstrate general principles, and thus that algebraic problems are not just a matter of working out particular unknown quantities. The second concerns the relation between algebra and functions, and the fact that this relation is usually ignored in mathematics classrooms.

Kieran's exposition of the connection between algebra, and functions and her argument that children should be told about it, stand for themselves. We would like to comment that her point about current teaching practices takes us directly to the question of social and educational influences (which are the main topic of the third section in this book). Here is an awesome example of how an unjustified separation of two naturally related topics can have a very considerable effect on children's views of a whole subject—in this case algebra.

So we end with a causal question, and the comment that causal questions are the ones on which least work has been done in research on children's mathematical development. The various strands in this development are now becoming clear, as the following chapters will show. The next step must be to see exactly what makes development happen.

3 Mathematical Understanding in the Nursery School Years

Peter Bryant
Department of Experimental Psychology, University of Oxford, UK

DO CHILDREN HAVE GENUINE MATHEMATICAL EXPERIENCES IN THE PRE-SCHOOL PERIOD?

It goes almost without saying that young children take part in activities that have the appearance of being mathematical long before they go to school and are taught mathematics. Children of 3 and 4 count, not perfectly but with a tolerable degree of competence, and they share out sweets and divide chocolate with an impressive degree of precision (Frydman & Bryant, 1988; Miller, 1984). They even manage simple additions and subtractions, at least when tangible objects are involved (Hughes, 1986). Are they not laying the foundations of their mathematical understanding in these early years? If they are, then we ought to do our best to see that these foundations are the right ones.

In fact, there are two questions to be asked about these pre-school activities that are so easily dubbed as mathematical. One is whether they really are mathematical, and here the problem is whether the children understand the mathematical significance of what they are doing when they count and share and add and subtract. The other question is whether there is a connection between these informal activities and the child's subsequent success in learning about mathematics at school. This second question is a causal one. We need to know whether the experiences that children have with mathematical activities before they go to school play a role in the mathematical progress that children make in their school years.

It will be one of the main points of this chapter that a great deal more is known about the first of these two questions than about the second. In some ways, this is understandable, for the first question is the prior one. If young children do not understand the mathematical significance of the pre-school activities we have already mentioned (counting, sharing etc.), then the experiences that they have when they do these things are most unlikely to have much impact on the progress that they make in mathematics lessons at school. But if the answer to the first question is positive in any way, then we really need an answer to the second. We cannot simply assume that children's mathematical experiences in the pre-school period, however genuine these are, will play any part at all in their school learning. There may be a conceptual connection between the two kinds of mathematical experiences—informal, preschool experiences and formal classroom ones—but this does not mean that the children themselves will make it. The barriers between informal and formal knowledge have been shown to be quite daunting for children and for adults in other contexts (Nunes, Schliemann, & Carraher, 1993): we need to know whether children surmount them in this case.

COUNTING

In any list of young children's activities that might be called mathematical, counting has the obvious first place. Very early on, usually by the age of 3 years, children begin to count (Fuson, 1988). This counting is more than just a verbal routine, for they count things, such as the number of stairs as they mount them or the number of mouthfuls that they take of something that they are eating. They apply these number words to objects and to actions.

In many ways the extent of their achievement is demonstrated by the initial difficulty of the number system for them. Young children, and particularly young children who are learning English numbers, make many mistakes when they count, and these mistakes are remarkably persistent (Fuson, 1988). One notable characteristic of these mistakes is that they are particularly common with words for the teens and for the decades. This is a phenomenon to which I will be returning later, because it tells us a lot about linguistic factors in learning about mathematics.

Children's early knowledge and use of number words is without doubt the result of patient coaching from other people. We know that parents spend a great deal of time counting with their young children and explaining with varying degrees of success how to count. Here, apparently is a clear example of cultural transmission: the parents are handing on to the next generation their knowledge of a system that was developed a long time ago and was taught to them by their own parents and teachers.

Of course this account of an early introduction to mathematics begs a question, and it is a question that was raised originally by Jean Piaget (1952).

Do young children understand what they are doing when they count? Piaget's own answer was unambiguously negative. For him, young children's counting was a clear instance of children using words without understanding what they mean. They learn the number sequence, he claimed, and they even learn how to apply it to objects and to actions, and yet for many years they do not have the slightest idea of what the sequence means.

Piaget argued that children have to understand both the cardinal and the ordinal properties of number, before they can be said to have grasped the meaning of number words. The cardinal properties of number concern absolute amounts: two or more different sets of objects that have the same number are equal in amount and for every member of each set there will be an equivalent member in the other sets (one-to-one correspondence). The ordinal properties are about relations between different numbers. Children have to understand that the order of numbers in the number sequence is an order of increasing magnitude: two is a greater number than one and three than two, with the logical consequence that three therefore is a greater number than one.

Few people would disagree with these two requirements. Suppose that a child knows that two sets both contain six objects, and yet nevertheless thinks that one of these sets is more numerous than the other. That child would plainly not understand the full meaning of the word "six". Similarly a child who does not understand that six objects must be more than four objects because six is more than five and five is more than four cannot be said to have understood why the number sequence is a sequence.

What made Piaget reach his striking conclusion that children count for several years before they understand the significance of what they are doing? His main reasons were the results of his well known conservation, transitivity and seriation experiments. The conservation experiments convinced him that children do not understand one-to-one correspondence in the pre-school years and therefore have no grasp of cardinality. The seriation and transitivity experiments provided the basis for Piaget's claim that children cannot deal with a series of relations: they are perfectly capable of understanding that A is more than B at one time, and at another that B is more than C, but they cannot coordinate these two pieces of information to reach the conclusion that A is more than C, according to Piaget, and this means that they are unable to understand the number sequence as a sequence of ascending magnitude.

Of these two claims, the first (failure in cardinality) is easier to assess than the second (failure in ordinality), at any rate as far as children's counting is concerned. This is because Piaget's work on children's understanding of seriation and of transitivity was only done with continuous quantities and did not involve counting. On the other hand some of Piaget's work on conservation, and particularly the work that he did together with his colleague Pierre Greco (1962), are directly concerned with children's use and understanding of number words.

In a well known experiment Greco gave children of 4 to 8 years three different versions of the conservation of number task. One of these tasks was the traditional conservation problem, in which children saw two identical-looking sets, judged correctly that the two sets were equal in number, then saw the appearance of one of the sets being altered, and were asked once again to compare the quantity of the two sets. The second task took roughly the same form except that after the transformation the children were required to count one of the sets and were then asked to infer the number of the second set. In the third task the children were required to count both sets after the transformation and then were asked whether they were equal in quantity.

Two of the results of this rather complicated study are important here. Most of the younger children, children younger than 6 years, failed all three tasks, and the important point to grasp about their performance is that in the third task they counted both sets in the final part of the task, arrived at the same number, and yet still said that the more spread-out of the two sets had more objects in it than the other one. They judged that one set with "eight" objects in it was more numerous than another set, also with "eight" objects, and that meant according to Piaget and to Greco that they really could not know what the word "eight" means.

The second important result was that slightly older children tended to get the first task (the traditional conservation problem) wrong and yet were right in the second task in which they counted one set and then were asked to infer the number of objects in the second set. These children therefore judged that spreading out a set of objects alters its quantity (their mistaken judgement in the traditional task) but not its number, in the sense of the number one would reach if one were to count the set.

Piaget and Greco's explanation of these results took the form of a distinction between "*quantité*" and "*quotité*". "*Quotité*" describes the understanding of the children who realise that two sets of objects have the same number, in the sense that counting each one leads to the same number word, and yet think that there are more objects in the more spread-out set. These children grasped the fact that the number words (*quotité*) stayed the same despite the perceptual transformation of one of the sets, and yet did not realise that the numerosity (*quantité*) was also quite unchanged by this irrelevant, perceptual change.

The *quotité/quantité* distinction has received remarkably little attention in recent years, and that is surprising given that these recent years have also seen an upsurge in research on young children's counting. For the most part the people doing this work have taken a more optimistic view about children's understanding of the number sequence. The fact that they have consistently ignored Piaget and Greco's evidence may have been a considerable help to them in reaching this position.

The conclusion reached by Gelman and Gallistel (1978) in their book on young children's counting and by Gelman and Meck (1983) in a later study of children's judgements of the correctness of a puppet's counting provides us with as strong a contrast to Piaget's views as is possible.

Gelman and her colleagues argued that children must grasp five basic principles in order to understand what they are doing when they count, and their main conclusion is that children as young as 2 and 3 years do have this understanding even though they make many mistakes. The name that these researchers give to their own theoretical position is "principle before skills". Children understand the basic principles of counting right from the start, they argue: their mistakes are merely failures to put these principles into practice all the time, and this is a skill that it takes them some time to acquire.

The first three are "how to count" principles. One is the one-to-one principle. Here the requirement is that the child understands that he or she must count all the objects in a set once and once only: each one must be given just one number tag. This is quite a different requirement to Piaget's. For him one-to-one correspondence was about the relationship between members of different sets. For Gelman and her colleagues the one-to-one principle is about how to count one set of objects.

Another "how to count" principle is the stable order principle, which means that one counts in a set order, and in the same set order each time. This principle is the nearest that Gelman and Gallistel get to ordinality, but again their requirement is different from and much less demanding than Piaget's because they are only concerned with the children's appreciation that they must count in a consistent sequence and not with their understanding that the sequence is a sequence of increasing magnitude.

The final how to count principle is the cardinal principle, but despite its name it is a far cry from Piaget's notion of cardinality. In Gelman's terms the cardinal principle involves the understanding that the last number counted represents the value of the set. So a child who counts a set "one, two, three, four" must understand that "four", the last of these numbers, represents the number of objects in that set. The requirement falls short of Piaget's because it concerns the value of a single set and not the relation between sets of the same number.

Gelman's requirements involve two other principles. One is the abstraction principle which states that the number in a set is quite independent of any of the qualities of the members in that set: the rules for counting a heterogeneous set of objects are the same as for counting a homogeneous one. The other is the order irrelevance principle: the point here is that the order in which members of a set are counted makes no difference, and anyone who counts a set, for example, from left to right will come to the same answer as someone else who counts it from right to left.

The main aim of Gelman's research on counting was to show that even very young children understand these principles at the time that they begin to count, and therefore know from the start what counting means. They observed young children counting sets of objects and recorded whether the children always counted the same order and always counted each object once, and also whether they seemed to recognise that the last number counted signified the number of the set. They also asked children to make judgements about a puppet that they saw counting: this puppet occasionally violated the one-to-one principle and the cardinal principle, and the aim of these experiments was to see whether the children could spot these violations. By and large the results of these studies supported Gelman's contention that the children did have some understanding of the three "how to count" principles as these were set out in her model.

So we end up with two entirely different answers to the question "Do children understand what they are doing when they count?", and it is worth spending some time considering what is the nature of this striking disagreement. It is certainly not a dispute about evidence, as the actual research of the two groups took an entirely different form. The fact is that Piaget and Gelman did different kinds of experiments because the criteria that each of them used for understanding counting were also quite different. Piaget opted for ordinality and cardinality, and Gelman for her five principles.

We have already noted that in some ways Gelman's requirements are less demanding than Piaget's, and this means that we should start by considering two possibilities. One is that Piaget's requirements are too strong, the other that Gelman's are too weak.

The first of these possibilities seems much more plausible than the second. Both models, for example, include cardinality, but they treat it quite differently. Piaget concentrated on the relationship between sets of the same number, and it is impossible to dispute his claim that a child will only understand the meaning of the word "six" if he or she also understands that a set of six objects is equal in number to any other set of six objects. Gelman, on the other hand, concentrated on the question of the child understanding that the last number counted represents the number of the set. It is true of course that the child must realise this, but it is also true that a child could grasp the fact that the last number is the important one without really understanding the quantitative significance of this number, at any rate as far as its relationship to other sets is concerned.

There is some striking evidence that young children who count quite proficiently still do not know how to use numbers to compare two different sets. Both Michie (1984) and Saxe (1979) have reported a remarkable reluctance in young children who have been asked to compare two sets of objects quantitatively to count the two sets. They could have counted them and it would have been the right thing to have done, but they did not.

This reluctance to use number as a comparative measure was demonstrated even more clearly in a remarkable experiment by Sophian (1988) in which she asked 3 and 4-year-old children to judge whether a puppet who counted was doing the right thing. This puppet was given two sets of objects and was told in some trials to compare the two sets and in others to find out how many objects there were in front of it altogether. So in the first kind of trial the right thing to do was to count the two sets separately, whereas in the second it was to count them together. Sometimes the puppet got it right but at other times it mistakenly counted all the objects together when it was asked to compare the two sets and counted them separately when it was asked how many objects there were altogether.

The results of this experiment were largely negative. The younger children did particularly badly (below chance) in the trials in which the puppet was asked to compare two different sets. They clearly had no idea that one must count two rows separately in order to compare them, and this suggests that they have not yet grasped the cardinal properties of the numbers that they are counting.

This empirical evidence only serves to underline a conceptual point that Gelman's requirement for the understanding of cardinality was too undemanding. It is in principle possible for a child to understand that the last number counted is the important one and still have no idea about its quantitative significance.

One of the most obvious differences between the two approaches is that Piaget is concerned above all with relations between sets whereas Gelman concentrates on children counting one set at a time. But there is even some evidence about young children counting single quantities that casts further doubt on Gelman's claims that children understand the cardinality of number words as soon as they begin to count. Several studies (Frye, Braisby, Lowe, Maroudas & Nicholls, 1989; Wynn, 1990) have shown that when children are asked to give someone a certain number of objects (Give me five bricks) they often fail to count and simply grab a handful of objects, and the number that they hand over is for the most part wrong. So, even when only a single set is involved, young children do not seem to understand the significance of counting. They may realise, when they do count, that the last number is the important one, but the fact that they do not seem to know very well when to count suggests that they have no idea why it is important. They have not grasped the cardinal properties of the number words that they know so well. Their performance fits the Piagetian picture of *quotité* without *quantité* very closely.

Much the same point can be made about the other two "how to count" principles. Children certainly have to know that they should count each object once and only once, but this is not the only form of one-to-one correspondence that they must understand. Piaget's point that children must also understand one-to-one correspondence between sets if they are to understand the quantitative significance of number words is surely right, and yet this is not part of Gelman's one-to-one principle.

Nor does Gelman's stable-order principle go nearly far enough. Numbers come in a certain order and it is certainly true that children have to understand this. But the reason for the order is that numbers are arranged in increasing magnitude and it is quite possible that a child who always produces numbers in the same sequence realises the quantitative significance of this sequence. Gelman's evidence is no help on this particular point, but much the same goes for the work of other interested psychologists. Piaget's evidence as we have seen is remarkably indirect, as it concerns only continuous quantities and not number, and there does not seem to be any other clear work on young children's understanding of the ordinal properties of number. We simply cannot say whether children understand the ordinality of the number sequence or not.

My conclusions about this controversy about children's understanding of counting are simple. Of the two sets of requirements, Piaget's are better than Gelman's. Children will only understand the quantitative significance of the number words that they learn when they have grasped both the cardinal and the ordinal properties of the number sequence. Most of the evidence suggests that children at first do not understand cardinality and Gelman's own work on the cardinal principle, as she defines it, throws no doubt on this suggestion. Our knowledge about children's understanding of ordinality is much less advanced, but again Gelman's work on the stable-order principle does not in any way show that children understand the ordinal relations in the number sequence. There are good reasons for thinking that at first children are practising little more than a verbal routine when they count.

SHARING AND ONE-TO-ONE CORRESPONDENCE

There are two ways to deal with difficulties that children have with the counting system. We can call one the broad approach, and the other the linguistic approach. The basic tenet of the broad approach is that the young child is incapable of any kind of mathematical reasoning whether this involves number words or not. To take this approach is to argue that children fail to understand the mathematical properties of the counting system because they are incapable of understanding mathematical properties in general. This roughly was Piaget's view and it is still held by a large number of psychologists.

The other approach is to treat children's difficulties with the counting system as problems with number words and no more than that. When a child learns to count he or she has to come to grips with an artificial system that was invented many centuries ago, and has its own structure and also its own quirks and pitfalls. These are described in detail in Chapter 2 by Nunes, and I only mention them here to make the point that children's difficulties with the counting system may be with the system *per se* and not with the mathematical reasoning that is needed to understand it.

If this second view is right, young children should be able to make judgements that are mathematically respectable in tasks that do not involve number words. Mathematical problems without mathematical words are no paradox. For example, any task that requires the use of one-to-one correspondence can be called a mathematical task. Any child who judges that two quantities are equal because each member of one set has an equivalent member in the other set has made a genuinely mathematical judgement.

As we have seen, Piaget argued that young children do not understand one-to-one correspondence, but this was a conclusion that he based mainly on the conservation task and there is at the moment a great deal of controversy about the interpretation of children's difficulties with that task. Nevertheless there is a lot of evidence to support Piaget's claim, at any rate with what I should like to call spatial one-to-one correspondence. If two sets of objects are put side by side it is possible to work out whether each item has its pair in the other set. Of course these spatial comparisons are much easier with some spatial arrangements than they are with others. It is easier to compare two ranks of soldiers in this way than two football teams. Yet there is some striking evidence that 6-year-old children seem unable to use one-to-one correspondence even with displays where it should be very easy to do so. Piaget and Inhelder (1966) and also Cowan and Daniels (1989) have shown that children often fail to use one-to-one correspondence to compare the number of items in two straight rows of counters laid side by side, even when the individual counters in each set are themselves connected by straight lines. Even this blatant encouragement to use one-to-one correspondence often makes no difference to the children's comparisons, which for that reason are frequently wrong.

It would be easy to decide from results such as these that young children have no understanding at all of one-to-one correspondence, but there is at least one good reason for not rushing to this negative conclusion. This is that children often share, and sharing is an activity that on the face of it seems to involve one-to-one correspondence. Three quite separate studies (Desforges & Desforges, 1980; Frydman & Bryant, 1988; Miller, 1984) have shown that when children as young as 4 are asked to share out numbers of things equally between two or more recipients they usually do so, rather successfully, on a repetitive "one for A, one for B" basis. Is this not a temporal form of one-to-one correspondence?

The answer must be "Yes", but then we have to ask the same question that we asked with counting. We have shown that children often count without understanding counting. It seems just as plausible that they can share on a one-to-one basis without any idea why this is the right thing to do. After all sharing, like counting, is a common activity which young children must witness quite often and may very well imitate. They may know that sharing in a one-to-one way is the appropriate action without understanding the reason for it.

Olivier Frydman and I (1988) tried to find out more about children's understanding of sharing by devising a task in which children who share on a rote basis without understanding what they are doing would behave in one way, and children who understand the basis of one-to-one sharing would respond quite differently. We gave the children "chocolates" which were either single or double chocolates: in fact these were plastic unifix bricks, all of the same colour, which could be stuck together. We asked the children to share the chocolates out to two recipients, so that each recipient ended up with the same total amount, But we also told the children that one of the recipients only accepted doubles and the other only singles. So the child's problem was to work out that for every double that he gave one recipient, he now had to give two singles to the other one. We reasoned that a child who had shared on a one-to-one basis in a rote fashion would not be able to make this adjustment, whereas a child who understood the basis for one-to-one sharing would see the reason for changing to a one for A, two for B pattern.

This study produced a very sharp developmental difference. Most of the 4-year-old children did not make the adjustment, and in fact the majority ended up giving the recipient who accepted doubles twice as many chocolates as the recipient who accepted singles. This was because these children continued sharing in a one-to-one manner, which meant that for every single that they gave one recipient they handed out a double to the other. In contrast most of the 5-year-olds did manage to make the necessary adjustment. These children usually gave the double to one recipient and then immediately two singles to the other, and so on. The reason for this difference between the two age groups is unclear to us, but at the very least the study establishes that 5-year-old children have a clear and flexible understanding of the mathematical basis of one-to-one sharing. They know why they do it.

What about the 4-year-olds? They had certainly hit a barrier in our new version of the sharing task, but we still had no idea how formidable that barrier was for them. So in a later study we devised a new version of the singles/doubles task in which we introduced bricks of different colours. Our aim was to use colour cues to emphasise one-to-one correspondence. In this new task each double consisted of a yellow and a blue brick joined together, and half the singles were blue and half yellow. This was the only change, and yet it had a dramatic effect. Nearly all the 4-year-old children solved the problem, and they did so because they could now see how to use one-to-one correspondence to solve the problem. The typical pattern of sharing was to give a double (consisting of course of one yellow and one blue brick) to one recipient and then to give a yellow and a blue single to the other one. They adapted the one-to-one strategy successfully when the one-to-one cues were emphasised. They also learned a great deal from this experience, because later on when we gave the same children the single/doubles task with bricks of one colour only (as in the original experiment) these children did extremely well. They had surmounted the barrier that we identified in the first study, and we conclude from this that even 4-year-old children have a basic understanding of the reason why one-to-one sharing leads to equal quantities. It follows that they do have a respectable understanding of one-to-one correspondence and therefore a basis for understanding the cardinal properties of number.

But do they extend this understanding to number words? We looked at this question in another study. In this we took a group of 4-year-old children who could share quite well, and we asked them to share out some "sweets" (again unifix bricks) between two recipients. When this was done we counted out aloud the number of sweets that the child had given to one recipient, and then asked him or her how many had been given to the other recipient. None of the children straightaway made the correct inference that the other recipient had the same number of sweets, even though they had meticulously shared the sweets out on a one-to-one basis: instead all of them tried to count the second lot of sweets. We stopped them doing so, and asked the question again, But even then less than half the children made the correct inference about the second recipient's sweets.

Thus many 4-year-old children fail to extend their considerable understanding of sharing to counting. We conclude from this that young children do grasp the cardinality of number and yet do not at first apply this understanding to number words.

SHARING AND DIVISION

Our emphasis on one-to-one correspondence in our discussion of sharing is a little unusual, because sharing is typically associated with division in primary schools. In many classrooms and in many exercise books "sharing problems" mean division problems. Teachers use the word "sharing" because it is already familiar, and presumably not at all frightening, to young children, but there is a great deal more to the understanding of division than a knowledge of sharing. To understand division one must grasp the relation between the number of divisors and the quotient. The more divisors there are, the smaller is the quotient. But when a child shares, his or her aim is to ensure that the recipients end up with the same amount, and that is all. The fact that these amounts would be smaller if there were more recipients and greater if there were fewer is immaterial to sharing but is the essential stuff of division. In principle, therefore, a young child might be able to share quite well and to understand the rationale for one-to-one sharing completely, and yet shall have no inkling about the relationship between the number of divisors and the size of the quotient.

Some recent experimental work by Jane Correa, Terezinha Nunes and myself (submitted) suggests that at first children have very little idea about the divisor/quotient relationship even though they share perfectly well. In one study we saw 5, 6, and 7-year-old children and we gave them a task that was designed to test whether they understood that the quotient varied with the number of divisors. We showed the child two groups of toy rabbits (one pink and the other blue) who were our recipients. Sometimes the number of blue and pink rabbits was the same, but at other times there were more of one than the other. For example, in some trials there were two pink rabbits and four blue ones. Then we produced two equal quantities (either 12 or 24) of "sweets" and we shared one of these two sets equally among one group of rabbits and the other among the other group. So, in the example that I have used, each pink rabbit received a great deal more sweets than each blue rabbit. The children knew that we had shared in this way but they could not see our actions or the actual sweets when we had shared them out because these were in a backpack on each rabbit's back.

Our question was whether the children could work out the consequences of the number of divisors. Could they see that blue and pink rabbits would each get as many sweets as each other when the number of blue and pink rabbits was the same, but that each pink rabbit would get more than each blue rabbit when there were more blue than pink rabbits and vice versa?

We found great differences between the three age groups. The 5 and 6-year-olds found the task extremely difficult, particularly when the number of rabbits in the two groups was different. In this more difficult condition the 5-year-old children were as likely to produce a wrong answer as the right one. In contrast the 7-year-old children were right nearly all the time. Moreover the justifications that the children gave for their answers confirmed that for the most part the young children paid very little attention to the number of divisors. Few of them mentioned this factor, while most of the 7-year-olds did.

So it seems that the everyday activity of sharing does not give the child an immediate insight into the nature of division, and as far as we can see the first important steps to a proper understanding of division are taken during the child's first few years at school. Whether this change is the result of the instruction that children receive at school we cannot say, but the idea seems quite plausible to us.

Problems in division take two forms, partitive and quotitive. In partitive tasks the dividend and the number of divisors are given and the problem is to work out the quotient. The task that we have just described is a partitive one because the children knew about the dividends and the divisors and had to answer questions about the quotients. In quotitive tasks the dividend and the quotient are given and the problem is to work out the number of divisors. So, "How much will each person get if I share £20 among 4 people?" is a partitive question, and "I have £20 and I want to share it out in £5 notes: how many people can I give a £5 note to?" is a quotitive one.

In another study we devised a quotitive equivalent of the partitive task that I have just described. Here the children were told about the dividends and the quotients and had to answer questions about the number of divisors. We showed the children that we had two equal amounts of sweets to divide among two groups of rabbits, and over a series of trials we told the children how much the rabbits in each group would get. The child's task was to judge whether the same number of rabbits would be given sweets in each group or whether more rabbits would be given sweets in one group than in other. So, to take two examples, in one trial the child was told that all the pink rabbits would be given four sweets each and all the blue rabbits two sweets each, and in another that all the rabbits in both groups would be given four sweets. (The information about the size of the quotients came in both verbal and visual form: we told the children what they were and we also gave them pictures of each group's quotient.) In both cases the child had to work out whether there would be more recipients in one group than in the other: so, the correct answer to the first example was that more blue than pink rabbits would be given sweets, and to the second that the number would be the same in both groups.

This quotitive task was noticeably harder than the partitive version. Even the 7-year-old group struggled with it. They made many mistakes, particularly with the problems in which the rabbits in the two groups were given different quotients. The reason for the relative difficulty of the quotitive problem, it seems to us, may be that it requires the child to provide more of a structure than the partitive version does. In the partitive task the children could see the dividends and they could also see all the divisors (the rabbits). In the quotitive task they could only see the dividends: they were told about the divisors but could not actually see them.

These results suggest that the rather widespread activity of sharing, which is a commonplace among young children, may well play an important part in their growing mathematical understanding. Not only does it give them their most direct experience of the significance of one-to-one correspondence: it may also be their first serious step towards an understanding of division.

ADDING AND SUBTRACTING

Adding and subtracting are often rather concrete activities and they are a commonplace in any young child's life. The question that we have to ask is whether children understand the nature of adding and subtracting, and the relation between these two operations. In principle the answer to this question need not involve calculations about actual amounts. A child could understand that addition increases and subtraction decreases a quantity and that addition and subtraction cancel each other out without being able to work out actual sums. In practice however, most of the evidence that we have on young children's understanding of addition and subtraction comes from their performance in tasks in which they were asked in one way or another to provide the answer to a particular sum.

A well known experiment by Martin Hughes suggests that slightly older children are quite proficient at using numbers in addition and subtraction problems. However, Hughes also showed that the kind of task that children are given makes a big difference. In some circumstances they add and subtract quite well: in others they do not.

Hughes (1981) gave the 3, 4, and 5-year-old children three kinds of task. One was called the closed box task: here the children were first shown that a box held a certain number of objects, and then the experimenter added or subtracted a certain number of objects. The second was called a "hypothetical" task: in this the children were simply told about additions and subtractions in a concrete situation (either a box or a shop). Hughes called the third kind of task the "formal code" task: in it the children were given verbal problems with no reference to any concrete material ("How many is two and one more?").

The children did rather well in the first two kinds of task which involved actual or imagined concrete material, particularly when relatively small numbers were being added or subtracted, but quite poorly in the formal code task in which no concrete material was used or even mentioned.

This initial barrier between the understanding of a concrete addition and being able to cope with a formal sum is certainly interesting, particularly when one considers whether children will transfer their informal mathematical understanding to the classroom when they begin to be taught arithmetic. But from the point of view of the question about a basic understanding of addition and subtraction, the most important results in the study by Hughes are the positive ones. If young children can carry out simple additions and subtractions with consistent success, surely they do understand the nature of addition and subtraction.

It would be churlish to argue against the importance of these successes, but addition and subtraction are quite complex operations with many requirements. One requirement is to understand the inverse relation between addition and subtraction, a form of understanding that Piaget stressed a great deal. He argued correctly that you must understand how addition and subtraction cancel each other out in order to grasp the additive composition of number.

Very little is known about pre-school children's understanding of the inverse relations between these two operations, and most of the data that we have is negative in the sense that it does not show any understanding of inversion in children below the age of 5 years. Starkey and Gelman (1982) claimed some success with 3, 4, and 5-year-old children in a task, rather like Hughes' box task, in which the experimenter put a certain number of objects in his hand and then both added to and subtracted from this number (e.g. 2−1+1). However the number of objects used in each of these inversion problems was so small that the children could very well have reached the correct solution without ever using the inversion algorithm $(-1 + 1 = 0)$, and in fact the children were as successful in equivalent problems that could not be solved by inversion (e.g. 2+2-1). The question about pre-school children's understanding of inversion is still unanswered.

CONCLUSIONS

I began this chapter with two questions. One was whether pre-school children do understand anything about mathematics before they go to school. The other was whether any mathematical understanding that they build up during this time does help them understand the arithmetic that they are taught when they go to school. But I have spent the entire chapter dealing with the first question. This is not because I think the second question a trivial one. On the contrary it is extremely important: if there are connections between children's pre-school mathematical experience and the progress that they eventually make in mathematics lessons at school, we need to know what these are so that we can prepare children for learning mathematics. The question is also answerable. We know this from studies of reading which, with the use of longitudinal methods and intervention, have demonstrated beyond doubt some strong connections between children's early experiences and their subsequent success in learning to read at school. There is no reason at all why equivalent studies cannot be done with mathematics. Yet, so far as I know, they have not been done.

Until they are, we have to be content with the answer to the other question, whether children do have any form of genuine understanding of mathematics before school. The answers that I have reached in this chapter can be stated very briefly. Young children are quite good at learning to count, but their grasp of the meaning of number words and particularly of cardinality seems very shaky indeed. In contrast they seem to have a good understanding of what is involved in sharing, and particularly of the significance of one-to-one correspondence in sharing. There are signs too that their understanding of sharing allows them to take the first genuine step (the first of many) towards learning about division. Finally they can add and subtract small quantities, but we have no answer yet to the crucial question about their understanding of the inverse relation between these two operations.

They make a definite start before they go to school. They know some things but definitely not everything by the time that they go to school. We must find out now what effect this knowledge has on them when they enter the classroom.

4

Word Problems: A Vehicle for Promoting Authentic Mathematical Understanding and Problem Solving in the Primary School?

L. Verschaffel and E. De Corte
Center for Instructional Psychology and Technology (CIP&T),
University of Leuven, Belgium

INTRODUCTION

Arithmetic word problems constitute an important part of the mathematics programme at elementary school. Initially they had an application function, i.e. they were used to train children to apply the formal mathematical knowledge and skills learned at school to real-world situations. Later on, word problems were given other functions as well: they were thought of as a vehicle for developing students' general problem-solving capacity or for making the mathematics lessons more pleasant and motivating. At present word problems are also mobilized in the early stages of learning a particular concept or skill, i.e. to promote a thorough understanding of the basic arithmetic operations (De Corte & Verschaffel, 1989; Treffers, 1987).

In spite of this long tradition in educational practice the international literature is full of evidence that word problems do not fulfil these functions well. By the end of elementary school many students do not see the applicability of their formal mathematical knowledge to real-world situations (Nesher, 1980); they do not have flexible access to heuristic and metacognitive strategies for attacking non-standard problems (De Corte, 1992; Van Essen, 1991); they have only a weak understanding of arithmetic operations as models of situations (Greer, 1992); finally they seem to dislike mathematics in general and word problems in particular (McLeod, 1992).

Word problems have attracted the attention of researchers too. In the present chapter we review only the work on one-step word problems involving either an addition, a subtraction, a multiplication or a division. Moreover, this review focuses on studies that have been carried out since the late 1970s. By that time, new ideas and methods from the information-processing approach led to the emergence of a firm new research paradigm in the area of elementary addition and subtraction word problems, which resulted in a large number of findings and conclusions. Somewhat later a similar approach towards the study of word problems involving multiplication and division emerged.

The chapter starts with a discussion of the classifications of one-step arithmetic word problems based on the type of problem situation. The rest of the chapter is organized around the different phases that are typically distinguished in mathematical problem solving in general (Schoenfeld, 1985), and in the solution of one-step arithmetic word problems in particular (De Corte & Verschaffel, 1985a): the representation of the problem, the selection and execution of a solution strategy, and the interpretation and verification of the result. Of course, the treatment of all these research topics will necessarily be very brief and selective. For more extensive discussions of the literature on additive and multiplicative word problems, we refer to Fuson (1992) and Greer (1992). The present discussion aims especially at:

- elucidating some similarities and differences between the research on addition/subtraction problems and problems involving multiplication/ division;
- highlighting the problematic relationship between arithmetic word problems and the real-world situations they intend to model;
- analyzing the complex interaction between different kinds of knowledge and skill involved in understanding and solving arithmetic word problems.

CLASSIFICATIONS OF WORD PROBLEMS

Before 1980 research on word problem solving focused heavily on the effects of superficial or mathematical task variables on pupils' problem-solving capacity, such as the number of words in the problem, the structure of the number sentence hidden in the problem (Verschaffel, 1984). In the late 1970s, the focus of the research on word problem solving shifted from superficial and mathematical task variables towards a new kind of task characteristic which had received hardly any attention before, namely the type of problem situation.

Classifying Addition and Subtraction Word Problems

In 1978 Greeno and his associates introduced a classification schema for addition and subtraction problems distinguishing between three basic categories of problem situation: Change, Combine, and Compare problems (Greeno, 1978; Riley, Greeno, & Heller, 1983). Change problems refer to active or dynamic situations in which some event changes the value of an initial quantity. Combine problems relate to static situations involving two quantities that are considered either separately or in combination. Compare problems involve two amounts that are compared and the difference between them. Each of these three basic categories of problem situation can further be subdivided into different problem types depending on the identity of the unknown quantity, and for Change and Compare problems further distinctions can be made depending on the direction of the change (increase versus decrease) or of the comparative relationship (more versus less). Combining these three task characteristics, Greeno and associates distinguished 14 types of addition and subtraction word problems (see Table 4.1).

More or less similar analyses differentiating classes of addition and subtraction word problems have been proposed by Carpenter and Moser (1982), Fuson (1992), Nesher (1982), and Vergnaud (1982). While there is great overlap between these classifications, there are also some differences. Both Carpenter and Moser (1982) and Fuson (1992) proposed an additional category that can be considered as a "mixture" of the Change and the Compare categories from the Riley et al. (1983) classification, namely, Equalize problems, in which the comparative relationship between two quantities is not expressed in a static form (as in a traditional Compare problem), but rather dynamically, such as in "Susan has 8 marbles. Fred has 5 marbles. How many more marbles does Fred have to get to have as many marbles as Susan has?".

A more dissimilar classification consisting of six instead of three basic categories has been proposed by Vergnaud (1982). The first three categories ("Composition of two measures", "Transformation linking two measures", "Static relationship linking two measures") correspond to the Combine, Change, and Compare problems, respectively. The other three are:

- Composition of two different transformations, for instance "Peter won 6 marbles in the morning. He lost 9 marbles in the afternoon. Altogether he lost . . . marbles";
- Transformation linking two static relationships, for instance "Pete owed Henry 6 marbles. He gave him 4. He still owes Henry . . . marbles";
- Composition of two static relationships, for instance "Robert has 7 more marbles than Susan. Susan has 3 marbles less than Connie. Robert has . . . marbles more/less than Connie".

While these latter categories of problem situation are somewhat related to the three previous ones, they are at the same time fundamentally different. For instance, the last example resembles the Compare problem type from the Riley et al. (1983) classification because it also involves a static description of a comparative network. However, contrary to traditional Compare problems, the network involves two comparisons instead of one. One possible explanation for the greater range of Vergnaud's (1982) classification is that it extends to operations with negative integers (see Fuson, 1992).

During the last decade a large amount of investigations have analyzed the level of difficulty of the different types of addition and subtraction word

TABLE 4.1
Classification of Addition and Subtraction Problems by Riley et al. (1983)

Type	Example	Schema	Direction	Unknown
Change 1	Joe had 3 marbles. Then Tom gave him 5 more marbles. How many marbles does Joe have now?	Change	Increase	Result set
Change 2	Joe had 8 marbles. Then he gave 5 marbles to Tom. How many marbles does Joe have now?	Change	Decrease	Result set
Change 3	Joe had 3 marbles. Then Tom gave him some more marbles. Now Joe has 8 marbles. How many marbles did Tom give him?	Change	Increase	Change set
Change 4	Joe had 8 marbles. Then he gave some marbles to Tom. Now Joe has 3 marbles. How many marbles did he give to Tom?	Change	Decrease	Change set
Change 5	Joe had some marbles. Then Tom gave him 5 more marbles. Now Joe has 8 marbles. How many marbles did Joe have in the beginning?	Change	Increase	Start set
Change 6	Joe had some marbles. Then he gave 5 marbles to Tom. Now Joe has 3 marbles. How many marbles did Joe have in the beginning?	Change	Decrease	Start set
Combine 1	Joe has 3 marbles. Tom has 5 marbles. How many marbles do they have altogether?	Combine	–	Superset
Combine 2	Joe and Tom have 8 marbles altogether. Joe has 3 marbles. How many marbles does Tom have?	Combine	–	Subset
Compare 1	Joe has 8 marbles. Tom has 5 marbles. How many marbles does Joe have more than Tom?	Compare	More	Difference set
Compare 2	Joe has 8 marbles. Tom has 5 marbles. How many marbles does Tom have less than Joe?	Compare	Less	Difference set
Compare 3	Joe has 3 marbles. Tom has 5 marbles more than Joe. How many marbles does Tom have?	Compare	More	Compared set
Compare 4	Joe has 8 marbles. Tom has 5 marbles less than Joe. How many marbles does Tom have?	Compare	Less	Compared set
Compare 5	Joe has 8 marbles. He has 5 more marbles than Tom. How many marbles does Tom have?	Compare	More	Reference set
Compare 6	Joe has 3 marbles. He has 5 marbles less than Tom. How many marbles does Tom have?	Compare	Less	Reference set

problems. Most studies involved (a subset of) problems similar to those mentioned in Table 4.1. The overall results can be summarized as follows. Change problems in which the initial quantity is unknown (Change 5 and 6) are typically found to be more difficult than those with the unknown change set (Change 3 and 4), which elicit in turn considerably more wrong answers than problems with the result set unknown (Change 1 and 2). Combine problems with an unknown subset (Combine 2) are more difficult than Combine problems with an unknown superset (Combine 1); the latter have about the same difficulty level as Change 1 and 2 problems. Compared to Change and Combine problems, Compare problems are particularly difficult and within that category, Compare problems with an unknown difference set (Compare 1 and 2) are easier than problems with an unknown compared set (Compare 3 and 4) which, in turn, are less difficult than problems with the referent set unknown (Compare 5 and 6).

However, not all available empirical data fit this summary (see also Fuson, 1992). Some studies found that Change problems with the start set unknown (Change 5 and 6) were solved equally well or even slightly better than Change problems with an unknown change set (Change 3 and 4) (Verschaffel, 1984). In other investigations, the difficulty level of Change 4 problems was equal to Change 1 and 2 problems, rather than to Change 3 problems (Riley et al., 1983). Finally, Compare problems did not always elicit more difficulties than Change and Combine problems (Fuson, 1992), and within this problem category, Compare 3 and 4 problems were sometimes solved better than Compare 1 and 2 problems (Verschaffel, 1984).

These dissimilarities are not in conflict with the overall conclusion that the type of problem situation has a strong impact on the difficulty of elementary addition and subtraction word problems. Rather they suggest that, besides that task variable, the relative difficulty of a particular problem is also seriously affected by a number of other factors, such as the exact phrasing of the problem, the particular numbers used, the testing procedure (collective versus individual, availability of manipulatives . . .), the age and instructional background of the pupils, etc. Therefore, these divergent data raise doubts about the validity of computer models which pay attention almost exclusively to the type of problem situation (De Corte & Verschaffel, 1988; Fuson, 1992).

Classifying Multiplication and Division Word Problems

Although it was suggested in the late 1970s that a similar classification task could be undertaken for word problems involving multiplication and division, systematic attempts emerged somewhat later. Examples of classifications have been provided by Greer (1992), Kaput (1985), Nesher (1988), Schmidt and Weisser (1992), and Vergnaud (1983). In Table 4.2 we present Greer's (1992) classification schema, in which an interesting distinction is made between situations that are "psychologically" commutative and non-commutative. In the latter case the multiplier and the multiplicand can be distinguished, that is to say, one of the quantities involved in multiplication (namely the multiplier) is conceptualized as operating on the other (the multiplicand) to produce the result. With respect to division, that implies that two types of division can be distinguished: division by the multiplier (= partitive division) and division by the multiplicand (= quotitive division). In a commutative situation it is impossible to distinguish between multiplier and multiplicand (and consequently between the two types of division).

According to Greer (1992) this classification is by no means exhaustive. Moreover, as for addition and subtraction, the extension of the concepts of multiplication and division can be continued almost indefinitely to encompass more complex numbers, e.g. decimals, fractions, directed numbers, negative numbers, etc. (For an attempt at such an extended classification of situations modelled by multiplication and division in relation to number type, see also Greer, 1992.)

Contrary to the field of addition and subtraction, the conceptual analyses of multiplication and division situations were not accompanied to the same degree with systematic research on the difficulty of the distinct problem types. The focus was rather on the effects on problem difficulty of the kinds of numbers used. Moreover, the scarce results are difficult to interpret, because of dissimilarities in the classification schemata used by different researchers. There is, however, one clear finding, namely that problems involving "Equal groups" and "Equal measures" (see Table 4.2) are systematically found to be rather easy, while those involving "Cartesian product" and "Measure conversion" seem very difficult (Douwen, 1983; Hart, 1981; Mulligan, 1992).

To conclude this section on classifications, some critical questions need to be raised. A first set of questions relates to the ultimate meaning and purpose of these classifications. Are they intended to capture the whole range of additive or multiplicative *situations* that occur in the real world (see e.g. Fuson, 1992), or do they only apply to the restricted versions of the real world as they occur in *traditional school word problems* (see e.g. Riley et al., 1983)? Do the different problem types merely stand for different *classes* of situations or problems that provide an analytical framework useful for guiding instruction and research (see e.g. Greer, 1992), or do they also represent hypothetical *cognitive structures* which drive pupils' understanding and solving of a particular problem (see e.g. Riley et al., 1983)?

A second set of questions concerns the relationship between the classification for addition/subtraction, on the one hand, and for multiplication/ division, on the other. Why are certain dimensions (e.g. static versus dynamic) only used in the classification schemata for addition and subtraction problems, and other dimensions (e.g. discrete versus continuous quantities) only for

TABLE 4.2

Problem Situations Modelled by Multiplication and Division (Greer, 1992)

Class	Multiplication problem	Division (by multiplier)	Division (by multiplicand)
Equal groups	3 children each have 4 oranges. How many oranges do they have altogether?	12 oranges are shared equally among 3 children. How many does each get?	If you have 12 oranges, how many children can you give 4 oranges to?
Equal measures	3 children each have 4.2 litres of orange juice. How much orange juice do they have altogether?	12.6 litres of orange juice is shared equally among 3 children. How much does each get?	If you have 12.6 litres of orange juice, to how many children can you give 4.2 litres?
Rate	A boat moves at a steady speed of 4.2 metres per second. How far does it move in 3.3 seconds?	A boat moves 13.9 metres in 3.3 seconds. What is its average speed in metres per second?	How long does it take a boat to move 13.9 metres at a speed of 4.2 metres per second?
Measure conversion	An inch is about 2.54 centimetres. About how long is 3.1 inches in centimetres?	3.1 inches is about 7.84 centimetres. About how many centimetres are there in an inch?	An inch is about 2.54 centimetres. About how long in inches is 7.84 centimetres?
Multiplicative conversion	Iron is 0.88 times as heavy as copper. If a piece of copper weighs 4.2 kg, how much does a piece of iron of the same size weigh?	Iron is 0.88 times as heavy as copper. If a piece of iron weighs 3.7 kg, how much does a piece of copper the same size weigh?	If equally sized pieces of iron and copper weigh 3.7 kg and 4.2 kg respectively, how heavy is iron relative to copper?
Part/whole	A college passed the top 3/5 of its students in an exam. If 80 students did the exam, how many passed?	A college passed the top 3/5 of its students in an exam. If 48 passed, how many students sat the exam?	A college passed the top 48 out of 80 students who sat an exam. What fraction of the students passed?
Multiplicative change	A piece of elastic can be stretched to 3.3 times its original length. What is the length of a piece 4.2 metres long when fully stretched?	A piece of elastic can be stretched to 3.3 times its original length. When fully stretched it is 13.9 metres long. What was its original length?	A piece of elastic 4.2 metres long can be stretched to 13.9 metres. By what factor is it lengthened?
Cartesian product	If there are 3 routes from A to B, and 4 routes from B to C, how many different ways are there of going from A to C via B?	If there are 12 different routes from A to C via B, and 3 routes from A to B, how many routes from B to C are there?	A college passed the top 48 out of 80 students... 3 routes from A to B, how many routes
Rectangular area	What is the area of a rectangle 3.3 metres long by 4.2 metres wide?	If the area of a rectangle is 13.9 m² and the length is 3.3 m, what is the width?	
Product of measures	If a heater uses 3.3 kilowatts of electricity for 4.2 hours, how many kilowatt-hours is that?	A heater uses 3.3 kilowatts per hour. For how long can it be used on 13.9 kilowatt-hours of electricity?	

classifying problems involving multiplication or division? There is no evidence that dimensions that are considered as important to addition/subtraction word problems are unimportant to word problems involving multiplication/division, or the reverse.

REPRESENTING ARITHMETIC WORD PROBLEMS

It is generally accepted that a skilful solution process of a word problem starts with the construction of a network representation of the basic semantic relationships between the main quantities in the problem. This representation, which emerges at the end of this first stage, is the result of a complex interaction of bottom-up and top-down processing. Throughout that constructive process of problem representation, different kinds of knowledge seem to play an important role. Three such knowledge types will be highlighted—schemata of problem situations, linguistic knowledge, and knowledge about the game of school word problems—and their role illustrated using the same word problem, namely the following Combine 2 problem:

> Pete has 3 apples. Ann also has some apples. Pete and Ann have 9 apples altogether. How many apples does Ann have?

The illustrations come from a study by De Corte and Verschaffel (1985a; Verschaffel, 1984) in which a set of elementary addition and subtraction word problems were individually administered to a group of 30 first graders three times during the school year. With respect to each problem, the pupil was given a series of tasks, two of which aimed especially at obtaining information about the problem representation, namely retelling the problem and building a material representation using puppets and blocks.

Schemata of Problem Situations

A first kind of knowledge involved in understanding and solving addition and subtraction word problems is schemata of problem situations (i.e. generic, organized knowledge structures of the basic classes of situations that can be modelled by addition and subtraction). In line with their classification of addition and subtraction word problems (see Table 4.1), Riley et al. (1983) developed computer models of the development of the skill in understanding and solving those problems, in which three such schemata are assumed: the Change, the Combine, and the Compare schemata. At the most competent level, the process of understanding a word problem is considered to consist of triggering the appropriate schema and mapping the incoming information onto it by assigning the known and the unknown quantities correctly to its slots. As an example, Fig. 4.1 represents the Combine schema in the form of a generic network structure (Fig. 4.1a), and also the representation of the above-

Problem: Pete has 3 apples. Ann also has some apples. Pete and Ann have 9 apples altogether. How many apples does Ann have?

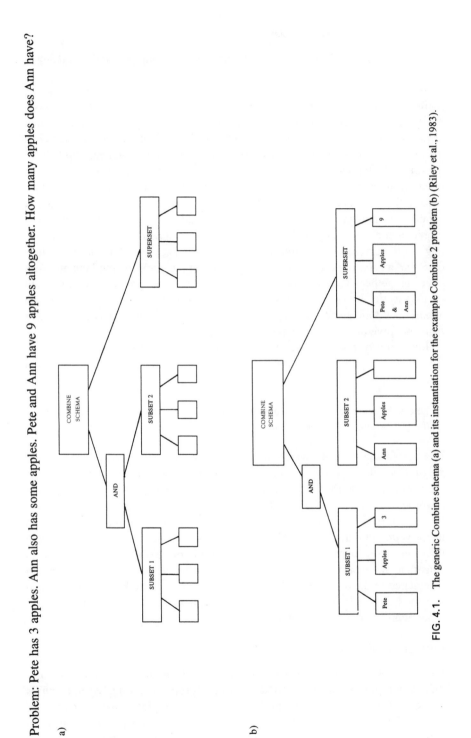

FIG. 4.1. The generic Combine schema (a) and its instantiation for the example Combine 2 problem (b) (Riley et al., 1983).

mentioned Combine 2 problem as worked out in the computer model of Riley et al. (1983) (Fig. 4.lb).

When pupils do not master the generic knowledge about Combine relations represented in Fig. 4.la, they are unable to infer the part-whole relation between the 9 apples that Pete and Ann have *altogether*, and the apples that each of them has *on his/her own*. Indeed, this part-whole relation is not explicitly stated in the problem, and without the corresponding schematic knowledge, pupils have no way to infer the relation between the distinct given quantities, and may therefore interpret each problem sentence separately (De Corte & Verschaffel, 1985a; Riley et al., 1983). In De Corte and Verschaffel's (1985a) study a significant number of first graders who could not solve this Combine 2 problem, constructed a set of 3 blocks and a set of a random number of blocks (e.g. 2) to represent respectively the apples that Pete and Ann have on their own, and a *separate* set of 9 blocks representing the 9 apples that Pete and Ann have altogether. This erroneous interpretation of the problem situation led necessarily to an incorrect answer in response to the question "How many apples does Ann have?"; these pupils simply counted the blocks associated with Ann and gave this number as their answer, in this case "2".

Interestingly, the semantic relations between the two parts and the whole in Combine 2 problems like the above-mentioned example, can made much clearer:

Pete and Ann have 9 apples altogether. Three *of these* apples belong to Pete *and the rest belong to Ann.* How many apples does Ann have?

In a systematic study in which large groups of first and second graders were given Combine 2 problems that were stated either in the standard or in the reworded way, De Corte, Verschaffel, and De Win (1985a) found that the reworded versions of the Combine 2 problems elicited significantly fewer representational errors than the standard ones. Their interpretation is that in many young children the Combine schema is not (yet) very well developed; therefore, they depend heavily on bottom-up or text-driven processing to construct an appropriate semantic representation of a Combine 2 problem formulated in the traditional way. For these children, rewording the problem so that the part-whole relation is made more explicit, facilitates the construction of an appropriate problem representation.

Linguistic Knowledge

Pupils not only fail to understand and represent Combine 2 problems because they do not possess the appropriate situational problem schema. Even if pupils master this knowledge, incomprehension or misinterpretation of a particular word or linguistic expression in the problem statement may prevent them from building an appropriate representation of the problem situation (Cummins,

Kintsch, Reusser, & Weimer, 1988; De Corte & Verschaffel, 1985a; Stern, 1993).

For instance, based on a careful analysis of first graders' retellings and material representations of word problems, De Corte and Verschaffel (1985a) discovered a type of representational error for the above-mentioned traditionally formulated Combine 2 problem ("Pete has 3 apples. Ann also has some apples. Pete and Ann have 9 apples altogether. How many apples does Ann have?") which was not due to pupils' lack of the Combine schema, but to their misinterpretation of the word "altogether" as "each". These pupils seemed to misunderstand the third problem sentence as "Pete and Ann possess 9 apples each" instead of "Pete and Ann possess 9 apples altogether".

Combine 2 problems can be reworded to compensate not only for the lack of the necessary schematic knowledge about problem situations (as in the above-mentioned reworded variant of the Combine 2 problem used by De Corte et al., 1985), but also for misunderstanding the word "altogether", as in the following variant:

> *There are 9 apples.* Three of them belong to Pete. The rest belong to Ann. How many apples belong to Ann?

This alternative reformulation of the standard Combine 2 problem in which the word "altogether" is avoided may yield an even stronger decrease of representational errors than the variant used in the study of De Corte et al. (1985). Although we do not know of any purposeful and systematic comparison of the two *re*formulations of Combine 2 problems, there is some evidence supporting this assumption. In a study with a similar design to the one by De Corte et al. (1985), Cummins (1991) compared traditionally formulated Combine 2 problems with Combine 2 problems reworded in such a way that their surface structure makes the semantic relations more obvious *and* does not contain the word "altogether" (as in the last mentioned variant). This resulted in a rewording effect that was considerably stronger than in De Corte et al.'s (1985) study.

Knowledge About the Game of School Word Problems

We have argued that the first stage of a competent problem-solving process consists of constructing an appropriate representation of the problem situation in terms of sets and set-relations. To arrive at such a problem representation one must possess and apply the necessary knowledge of prototypical problem situations and of specific linguistic terms. However, this construction of a problem representation cannot be understood exclusively in terms of the interplay between the particular text and the person's knowledge about problem situations and linguistic terms. As several authors have argued (De Corte &

Verschaffel, 1985a; Nesher, 1980; Schoenfeld, 1991), the representation of a word problem in terms of the semantic relations between the constituting elements is also seriously affected by the solver's knowledge of the peculiar type of text that a word problem is and of the scholastic context in which it is encountered. This involves knowledge about (1) the intent and role of word problems in a mathematics lesson, (2) the typical structure and wording of school word problems, and—last but not least—(3) the implicit rules, assumptions, and agreements that need to be known when "playing the game of school word problems". Students seem to develop this knowledge rather smoothly as they participate in the culture of solving traditional school word problems (De Corte & Verschaffel, 1985a; Schoenfeld, 1991). But failure to acquire this knowledge may lead to "bizarre" errors and reactions.

For example, in the above-mentioned study of De Corte and Verschaffel (1985a) several first graders responded to the standard Combine 2 problem ("Pete has 3 apples. Ann also has some apples. Pete and Ann have 9 apples altogether. How many apples does Ann have?") in the following rather unconventional ways: one child answered "some apples", another said "a couple", and a third one's answer was "a few". While such answers are not totally incorrect, they are inappropriate in the context of word-problem solving in school. Some other children simply made a guess (instead of a computation with the two given numbers), suggesting that they could not differentiate between a word problem and a guessing game or a riddle (see also Nesher, 1980).

These young and inexperienced first graders' bizarre reactions to school word problems are very similar to those found in adults with little or no experience with school arithmetic in general and with the game of school word problems in particular. For example, in a study of illiterate adults from a remote part of the former Soviet Union, Luria (1976) found that most were incapable of reasoning within the conditions given in a word problem; instead, they slipped back into arguments based on personal practical experience.

Representing Multiplication and Division Problems

The previous discussion of the role of different kinds of knowledge in representing arithmetic word problems was based on research on addition and subtraction. This is not surprising, as the theoretical and empirical work on these word problems focused heavily on the first stage of the problem-solving process. Research on multiplication and division word problems, on the contrary, has concentrated on the subsequent stages of the solution process, i.e. the selection and execution of the appropriate arithmetic operation (Greer, 1992; Mulligan, 1992; Treffers, 1987). However, some preliminary data suggest that the same or similar kinds of knowledge contribute to building an appropriate representation of multiplication and division word problems.

For example, a well-established finding is that one-step multiplication problems are frequently answered by the result of an addition instead of a multiplication with the two given numbers. This kind of error has been documented for several of the problem types mentioned in Table 4.2, such as "Multiplicative comparison", "Cartesian product" and "Rectangular area" (see e.g. Douwen, 1983; Nunes, Light, & Mason, 1993a). Additive strategies have also been regularly found in more complex word problems about ratio and proportion, such as "The candy store sells 2 pieces of candy for 8 cents. How much do 6 pieces of candy cost?". Students employing such a strategy view the relationship within or between the ratios in terms of the difference between terms (e.g. the difference between 2 pieces and 6 pieces is 4 pieces, so the number of cents [8] must also be increased with 4), instead of realizing that it is a multiplicative one (Hart, 1981). While such additive errors may originate from different sources (as we will show later), representational difficulties due to non-mastery of situational problem schemata or linguistic knowledge also account here for a number of them. For example, Douwen (1983) administered to a group of third graders individually a set of one-step multiplication and division problems. As in De Corte and Verschaffel's (1985a) study, pupils were not only asked to solve the problem, but also to perform a number of additional diagnostic tasks, such as to retell the problem and to choose the correct pictorial representation among four alternatives. The following problem elicited a considerable amount of erroneous additive responses: "A shop-keeper has made a stack of cases of cola bottles against the wall of his shop. The stack has a height of 4 cases and a breadth of 6 cases. How many cases does this stack contain?". The analysis of the retelling and picture-choosing data revealed that most of the additive responses (i.e. answering with either "10" or "9") resulted from building a representation of the problem situation as involving one vertical column and one horizontal row of cases rather than as a rectangle.

In discussing the knowledge necessary for understanding addition and subtraction word problems, we also highlighted the role of being familiar with the game of school word problems. Multiplication and division problems typically occur only after pupils have obtained substantial experience with (addition and subtraction) word problems. Therefore, errors due to insufficient knowledge about the peculiar role and format of word problems and about the implicit rules of the game of solving word problems can be expected to occur rather rarely. Indeed, after some years of experience with solving school word problems, pupils in general seem to break the rules of that game alarmingly rarely. In a study by Verschaffel, De Corte and Lasure (1994) 75 11–12-year-old pupils were collectively administered a word-problem test involving multiplication and division problems in a regular mathematics classroom context. Besides standard problems in which the relationship between the situation and the corresponding mathematical operation(s) is simple and straightforward (e.g. Carl has bought 6 planks of 2 metres each. How many planks of 1 metre can he saw out of these planks?), the test contained parallel versions of these problems in which the mathematical modelling assumptions are problematic, at least if one *seriously* takes into account the realities of the context in which the problem was embedded (see problem 1 in Table 4.3). For this latter type of problem, only a small minority of the pupils showed hesitancy or reluctance to perform the simple and straightforward mathematical modelling (e.g. by criticizing the problem statement, by stating a numerical answer that did take into account the realities of the problem situation, or by supplementing their answer with comments) (see Table 4.3). Similar results for 13–14-year-old students have been reported by Greer (1993). Together, these findings convincingly show that considerable experience with the sanitized view of the world as presented and strengthened in current instructional practice, develops in students a strong tendency to exclude real-world knowledge and realistic considerations from their understanding of the problem.

The instructional implication of this finding is that the impoverished diet of standard word problems currently offered in mathematics classrooms, should be replaced—or at least supplemented—by a wide variety of problems that draw students' attention to realistic modelling, so that they do not (implicitly) learn that "if there are two numbers in the problem, the answer will be found by adding, subtracting, multiplying or dividing these two numbers" (Greer, 1992, p.292). As Nunes, Schliemann and Carraher (1993b, p.148) put it: "If mathematics education is going to be realistic, problems will have to be sought that respect assumptions about life outside school".

TABLE 4.3
Answers of 75 Fifth-graders on Two Word Problems with Problematic
Mathematical Modelling Assumptions (Verschaffel et al., 1994)

Steve has bought 4 planks of 2.5 metres each. How many planks of 1 metre can he saw out of these planks?

"8" (either with or without comments)	10*
"10" (without any comments)	55
Other answers (without any comments)	10

John's best time to run 100 metres is 17 seconds. How long will it take him to run 1 kilometre?

"170 sec." (with comments)	2*
"170 sec." (without any comments)	65
Other answers (without any comments)	4
No answer (without any comments)	4

*Only answers marked with an asterisk express any awareness of problematic mathematical modelling.

SELECTING AND EXECUTING THE ARITHMETIC ACTIONS

The selection and execution of an appropriate arithmetic action constitutes the next steps in the solution of a one-step arithmetic word problem. However, these steps can be taken in very distinct ways that differ considerably in terms of accuracy, sophistication, and instructional desirability. Three different ways are discussed:

- Selection of a formal arithmetic operation based on an appropriate initial representation of the problem situation.
- Selection of a formal arithmetic operation based on a superficial coping strategy.
- Solving the problem through application of an informal solution strategy instead of a formal arithmetic procedure.

Matching Problem Representation and Formal Arithmetic Operation

At the highest level of skill, the arithmetic action to solve a one-step word problem consists of the selection and execution of the appropriate formal arithmetic operation (i.e. either an addition, a subtraction, a multiplication or a division with the two relevant numbers), based on the problem representation constructed in the previous stage. For some problem types, this mapping of the problem representation with the necessary operation is rather easy. However, for others, it is a difficult step requiring the simultaneous application of sophisticated conceptual and strategic knowledge and skills.

Addition and Subtraction

The computer models of the development of the skill in understanding and solving addition and subtraction word problems of Riley et al. (1983) referred to earlier, imply that the 14 problem types from Table 4.1 differ considerably with respect to the ease with which the problem representation can be linked to the appropriate formal arithmetic operation. Indeed, some problem representations can be directly mapped on to either an addition or a subtraction with the two given numbers, but others require additional mental rearrangement processes. Take, for example, a child who understands the symbols + and − in terms of a "change add" (e.g. $6 + 8 = 14$ as "6 objects increased by 8 become 14 objects") and a "change take from" meaning (e.g. $14 − 6 = 8$ as "14 objects take away 6 objects becomes 8") respectively (Fuson, 1992), and who is given the following Change 2 problem: "Pete had 14 marbles. He gave away 6 marbles to Tom. How many marbles does Pete still have?". For this child, connecting his representation of that problem in terms of a Change 2 structure to the appropriate formal arithmetic operation, namely $14 - 6 = ?$, is rather easy.

However, for Compare 5 and 6 problems, this mapping seems much more difficult. Consider, for example, the following Compare 6 problem: "Pete has 9 apples. He has 6 apples less than Ann. How many apples does Ann have?". Lewis and Mayer (1987) developed a model which predicts that these problems are solved by transforming them into a Compare 4 and 3 problem, respectively. For example, the above-mentioned Compare 6 problem would be solved after a mental rearrangement consisting of reversing (1) the subject and the object of the relational sentence, and (2) the relational term. More specifically, the Compare 6 problem "Pete has 9 apples. *Pete* has 6 apples *less* than *Ann*. How many apples does Ann have?" becomes the Compare 3 problem "Pete has 9 apples. *Ann* has 6 apples *more* than *Pete*. How many apples does Ann have?". According to Lewis and Mayer (1987), this additional processing of Compare 5 and 6 problems puts heavy demands on problem solvers' working memory. Therefore, they may neglect the execution of the second step of the rearrangement procedure, namely, the reversal of the relational term, which will by necessity lead to a wrong-operation error (e.g. a subtraction instead of an addition with the two given numbers).

The Lewis and Mayer (1987) model has received substantial empirical support from a number of studies using different process-oriented data-collecting techniques including individual interviews and the registration of solution times and eye movements (Hegarty, Mayer, & Green, 1992; Stern, 1993; Verschaffel, 1994; Verschaffel, De Corte, & Pauwels, 1992). For example, Verschaffel (1994) asked 40 fifth graders to solve and retell a set of Compare 3, 4, 5, and 6 problems. As predicted, Compare 5 and 6 problems were retold—both correctly and incorrectly—very frequently as a Compare 3 or 4 problem, while Compare 3 and 4 problems elicited no retellings with the structure of a Compare 5 or 6 problem. Based on the plausible assumption that pupils' retelling protocols reveal their internal problem representation, Verschaffel (1994) interpreted the large amount of such transformations in the retellings of Compare 5 and 6 problems as strong evidence for the Lewis and Mayer (1987) hypothesis that Compare 5 and 6 problems are typically solved by mentally transforming them into a Compare 3 or 4 problem.

Multiplication and Division

Problems involving multiplication and division also differ considerably with respect to the complexity of the mapping between the problem representation and the necessary formal arithmetic operation. However, as is the case for the difficulty level of word problems (see earlier), research on multiplication and division has not so much explored the effect of the type of problem situation on the choice of the appropriate operation, but rather the effect of the number types involved in the problem (Greer, 1992). Results from several experiments using a variety of multiplication word problem types (see Table 4.2), consistently show the multiplier effect: the difficulty in recognizing multiplication as the appropriate operation for the solution of a word problem depends heavily on whether the multiplier is a (positive) integer, a decimal larger than 1, or a decimal smaller than 1. There is robust evidence that pupils are systematically better at choosing the correct operation (from a list of alternative operations) for a multiplication word problem with an integer as multiplier, than when the multiplier is a decimal larger than 1; problems with a decimal multiplier smaller than 1 are still much more difficult. The most frequently observed type of error for the latter two problem types is dividing instead of multiplying the two given numbers. By contrast, the size of the multiplicand has no effect on problem difficulty (De Corte, Verschaffel, & Van Coillie, 1988; Greer, 1992).

To illustrate this multiplier effect, Table 4.4 shows the percentages of correct answers for three problems from a study by De Corte et al. (1988) in which 116 sixth-graders were instructed to choose the correct operation from a set of six alternatives (a+b, a–b, b–a, a × b, a:b, b:a) for a series of multiplication problems.

Several explanations have been put forward for these experimental findings. So far, the concept of an intervening intuitive model probably provides the most plausible theoretical account of children's difficulties in mapping their (correct) representation of the problem to the appropriate formal arithmetic operation when a decimal multiplier is involved (Fischbein, Deri, Nello, & Marino, 1985). According to that theory, each operation is linked to a primitive, intuitive model, even long after that operation has acquired a formal status. Identification of the operation needed to solve a word problem is mediated by these intuitive models. The model affecting the meaning and use of multiplication is "repeated addition", in which a number of collections of the same size are put together. In order that a situation fits this model, the first

TABLE 4.4

Percentages of Appropriate Solution Strategies as a Function of Type of Multiplier (De Corte et al., 1988)

Multiplicand	Multiplier	Problem	% correct
Integer	Integer	Spinach is priced 65 Bfr a kilogram. Ann buys 3 kilograms. How much does she have to pay?	98
Decimal < 1	Integer	One piece of sugar costs 0,4 Bfr. How much would it cost for 60 pieces?	99
Integer	Decimal < 1	Milk is priced at 20 Bfr a litre. Ann buys 0,8 litre. How much does she have to pay?	32

crucial constraint is that the multiplier must be an integer; this restriction does not apply to the multiplicand. For example, it is easy to conceive intuitively of 3 times 0,63—namely 0,63 + 0,63 + 0,63—but not of taking a certain quantity—such as 3—0,63 times. A second constraint of this model of multiplication is that the result is always larger than the multiplicand. In multiplication problems with a decimal multiplier larger than 1, the first constraint of the "repeated addition" model is violated; therefore, such problems will elicit more wrong operations than problems with an integer as the multiplier. In problems where the multiplier is a decimal smaller than 1, the second constraint is violated too; therefore, the chance of a wrong-operation answer is even greater (De Corte et al., 1988; Greer, 1992).

The available research does not provide a clear answer to the question of what exactly distinguishes successful from unsuccessful solvers of those difficult multiplication problems. According to Fischbein (1987), the crucial difference is *not* that successful problem solvers are totally emancipated from those intuitive, primitive models. But successful problem solvers may have (1) greater metacognitive awareness of the nature and causes of fallacious patterns of thinking mediated by these primitive models, and (2) better metacognitive control over these intuitive thinking processes by systematically exploiting resources such as "alarm devices" (see also Greer, 1992). A complementary possibility is that successful problem solvers have access to and can flexibly shift between different models of multiplicative structures (e.g. "repeated addition" and "rectangular area") (Greer, 1992; Treffers, 1987).

Superficial Coping Strategies

A basic assumption underlying the theoretical and empirical work discussed so far, is that errors on word problems are largely due to difficulties in understanding and representing the information in the problem statement and/or mapping the problem representation to the appropriate formal arithmetical operation. However, there is a lot of research evidence suggesting other reasons for errors. Many students do not even *try* to base their selection of the appropriate operation on a thorough analysis and a complete representation of the problem situation. In other words, they simply skip the representation stage and jump immediately into calculations with the numbers in the problem. We will present some examples of such "number-crunching" coping strategies.

A first typical strategy is that the pupil does not read or represent the problem, but simply selects all the numbers contained in the problem and performs either the operation that was most recently taught in the classroom, or the operation with which he or she feels most competent (usually addition) (De Corte & Verschaffel, 1987b; Sowder, 1988). Goodstein, Cawley, Gordon, and Helfgott (1971) presented a group of mildly mentally retarded children with addition and subtraction word problems with and without irrelevant numerical information, and found that their subjects tended to add all numbers including the irrelevant one. Exemplary evidence that this add-all strategy does not involve a careful reading of the problem statement has been provided by De Corte and Verschaffel (1987b). In one of their eye-movement studies, a dozen traditional one-step addition and subtraction word problems were individually administered to a mixed-ability group of 20 first graders. One girl answered all problems with the sum of the two given numbers. (As half of the problems required an addition, her add-all strategy yielded a score of 50% correct!) A closer look at her eye-movement protocols revealed the following very systematic pattern. Each eye-movement protocol started with typical reading behaviour, involving, however, only the first and (part of) the second sentence. As soon as the child's eyes arrived at the second given number, the reading process stopped at once; from then on, the child's eyes shifted between the two given numbers, which is the typical eye-movement pattern for making a calculation involving those numbers.

A second superficial approach consists of using the key-word strategy (Nesher & Teubal, 1975; Schoenfeld, 1991; Sowder, 1988; Verschaffel et al., 1992). In this case the pupil's selection of an arithmetic operation is not based on a global representation of the problem situation, but is guided by the occurrence of an isolated key word in the problem text with which that arithmetic operation is associated. For example, words like "more" and "altogether" are associated with addition, "less" and "lose" with subtraction, "times" and "each" with multiplication. Empirical evidence supporting the existence of the key-word strategy comes from studies that have provided student performance data on collective paper-and-pencil tests in accordance with the key-word strategy (Nesher & Teubal, 1975), but also from individual interviews with pupils motivating their choice-of-operation by explicitly referring to a key word in the problem statement (Garofalo & Lester, 1985; Sowder, 1988; Verschaffel, 1984).

A third category of superficial coping strategy can be paraphrased as "look at the numbers; they will 'tell' you what to do". Sowder (1988, p.228) observed the following comment from a middle-grader who was asked to justify his choice-of-operation for a particular problem: "If it's like 78 and 54, then I'd probably either add or multiply. But if they are 78 and 3, it looks like a division because of the size of the numbers". Apparently, this pupil's choice was again not based on an in-depth semantic analysis of the problem, but on an analysis of the nature of the given numbers from a purely computational point of view (e.g. "which of the four operations yields the 'nicest' or the 'most reasonable' answer?").

A last type of superficial coping strategy consists of looking at cues in the instructional environment in which the problem appears. In a naturalistic experiment in an elementary school setting, Säljö and Wyndhamn (1987) gave 12-year-old pupils different kinds of work sheets containing word problems requiring either a multiplication or a division. The experimental treatment consisted of introducing a strong expectation among the pupils about the nature of the target problems: through headings and instructions on the top of the problem list it was strongly suggested that they were supposed to practice multiplication (while some of the tasks in fact required a division). In the control treatment only neutral headings and instructions were used. Säljö and Wyndhamn (1987) found that the presence of a heading or an instruction which indicated that the problem set entailed multiplication, had a dramatic effect on the choice for that operation, especially among the low-achievement group. A more subtle example of using cues in the instructional environment, observed by Verschaffel (1984), is that of a first grader who succeeded in solving a one-step subtraction word problem involving the numbers 15 and 8, and who responded as follows when asked to explain how he arrived at his correct solution: "I wasn't sure whether to add or to subtract, but finally I decided to subtract because adding would have led to a result larger than 20". Indeed, at the time this protocol was collected, the number 20 was generally considered as the upper limit of the number domain for the first grade of elementary schools in Belgium. In both cases, the strategy chosen relied on the interpretation and application of subtle didactical conventions shared by those who participate in the game of school arithmetic word problems.

One could ask: where do these superficial coping strategies come from? Occasionally, they are more or less directly or explicitly taught. In an analysis of a representative sample of textbooks for elementary mathematics education in grades 1 and 2 in Belgium, De Corte, Verschaffel, Janssens, and Joillet (1985) found one textbook in which the key words occurring in word problems were accentuated by printing them in red! However, more typically, these strategies have been derived—albeit probably implicitly and unconsciously—by the pupils themselves in response to certain features of current teaching practices. A first important feature in this respect is the impoverished and stereotyped diet of word problems currently used, which makes the application of superficial strategies undeservedly successful (see also Greer, 1992; Schoenfeld, 1982, 1991). Schoenfeld (1982), for example, reported that in a widely used elementary textbook series in the US, more than 90% of the problems could be correctly solved by the key-word strategy. Similarly, Säljö and Wyndhamn (1987) note that Swedish textbooks often contain headings that clearly and systematically spell out the nature of the tasks to be performed, so that pupils know what operation to select before they even have begun to read the problems. Reusser (1988, p.337) concluded that "whoever observes students in classroom and homework situations can find again and again how few textbook problems force students to do an in-depth semantic analysis". A second feature is the product-oriented nature of elementary mathematics instruction and testing, which is also reflected in teachers' misbelief that correct answers are a safe indicator of good thinking (Sowder, 1988). Third, there is the premature imposing of the formal arithmetic approach toward word problem solving, by requiring that the pupils must identify as quickly as possible the operation to solve a word problem (as described in the previous section), and, consequently, the premature discouragement of more intuitive or informal solution strategies (see also Carpenter & Moser, 1982; Fuson, 1992; Treffers, 1987).

Informal Solution Strategies

In the preceding subsections it is more or less implicitly assumed that the solution of a one-step arithmetic word problem is reached through selecting and executing one of the four formal arithmetic operations (i.e. adding, subtracting, multiplying or dividing the two given numbers). This is undoubtedly a very sophisticated and efficient solution strategy, at least when the choice-of-operation is based on an in-depth semantic analysis of the problem. However, this is certainly not the only way in which elementary arithmetic problems are effectively solved. Indeed, as will be shown later, one of the best-documented research findings is that before learners are taught this formal arithmetic approach, they are able to invent and apply a variety of informal strategies successfully.

Addition and Subtraction

Carpenter and Moser (1982) have carried out pioneering work about children's informal strategies for solving elementary addition and subtraction word problems. In a three-year longitudinal study they followed more than 100 children from grade 1 through 3. Their results demonstrate convincingly that early in their development children have a wide variety of material counting strategies (based on the use of concrete objects) and verbal counting strategies (based on forward or backward counting) for successfully solving addition and subtraction problems, many of which are never taught explicitly in school. Carpenter and Moser (1982) also found that the situational structure of a *subtraction* problem significantly affects the nature of children's informal solution strategies. More specifically, children tend to solve each subtraction problem with the *material or verbal* counting strategy that corresponds most closely to its situational structure. As an illustration, Table 4.5 gives an overview of the most frequently occurring material strategies for three subtraction problems from their study.

According to Carpenter and Moser (1982), users of these informal solution strategies frequently are not aware of the interchangeability of these strategies and are unable to link them to one single formal arithmetic operation (+ or −). Using a more differentiated problem set than Carpenter and Moser (1982) as well as a more elaborated schema for classifying pupils' solution strategies, De Corte and Verschaffel (1987a) complemented the findings of those authors by

TABLE 4.5
Material Solution Strategies for Three Different Subtraction Problems
(Carpenter & Moser, 1982)

Problem type	Example	Solution Strategy
Change 2	Pete had 6 apples. He gave 2 apples to Ann. How many apples does Pete have now?	*Separating from*: using objects or fingers, the child constructs a set corresponding to the larger given number (6) in the problem. Then the child removes as many objects as indicated by the smaller number (2). The answer is the remaining number of objects (4).
Change 3	Pete had 3 apples. Ann gave him some more apples. Now Pete has 10 apples. How many apples did Anne give to Pete?	*Adding on*: the child constructs a set corresponding to the smaller given number (3). Then the child adds elements to this set until there are as many objects as indicated by the larger number (10). The answer is found by counting the number of objects added (7).
Compare 1	Pete has 3 apples. Ann has 8 apples. How many apples does Ann have more than Pete?	*Matching*: the child constructs a set corresponding to the smaller (3) and a set corresponding to the larger given number (8) and matches them until one set is exhausted. The answer is the number of objects remaining in the unmatched set (5).

showing that: (1) the solution strategies for *addition* problems of children operating at the material and verbal counting levels are also strongly influenced by the situational structure of the problem; (2) for addition and subtraction problems, the type of situation keeps a significant influence on children's *mental* solution processes based on known-fact or derived-fact strategies (see also, Fuson 1992).

As stressed by Fuson (1992), subjects using informal strategies that closely match the problem situation typically do not go through clearly separated problem-solving phases. They do *not* first represent the problem situation, followed by a decision whether to add, subtract, multiply, or divide, and, finally, by carrying out the selected operation. Rather, these children's problem representation and solution process is "a complex, interrelated whole in which the addition or subtraction meaning is taken directly from the problem situation and modelled with entities or counters" (Fuson, 1992, p.251). No wonder pupils operating this way solve elementary addition and subtraction word problems correctly without first writing an appropriate formal arithmetic number sentence, as is frequently required in school; from these pupils' point of view, this is a redundant, unnecessary and even obstructive activity for getting the problem solved (Carpenter & Moser, 1982; De Corte & Verschaffel, 1985b; Fuson, 1992).

Multiplication and Division

A growing number of investigations on young children's solution strategies to multiplication and division problems have recently emerged (Kouba, 1989; Murray, Olivier, & Human, 1992; Mulligan, 1992; Nunes & Bryant, 1992; Treffers, 1987).

The results indicate first of all that before pupils have been instructed in multiplication or division, many of them are able to solve problems involving these operations. For example, in a two-year longitudinal study, Mulligan (1992) analyzed 70 children's performance and solution strategies to a variety of multiplication and division word problems (half with small and half with large numbers) at four interviews spread over the second and third grade. Analysis of individual profiles across the four interview stages indicated that 75% of the pupils were able to solve multiplication and division problems with small numbers before they had been formally instructed in these operations.

Second, these studies have also provided evidence that for these operations too there is widespread use of informal or intuitive strategies prior to formal instruction. Although the solution strategies for multiplication and division problems are more diverse and more complex, the levels of material counting strategies (based on the use of concrete objects), verbal counting strategies (based on forward or backward counting), and mental strategies (based on the use of known number facts), were found to be analogous to these identified for addition and subtraction (Kouba, 1989; Mulligan, 1992).

Third and most compelling, however, is the evidence that—as for addition and subtraction word problems—pupils' strategies tend to reflect the action or relationship described in the problem (Mulligan, 1992; Murray et al., 1992; Treffers, 1987). The next illustration comes from a study by Murray et al. (1992). For a sharing problem such as "There are 18 cookies that must be shared among 3 friends. How many cookies will each friend get?", young children typically drew three icons representing the three friends (e.g. three faces), and then dealt the cookies out by drawing them one by one underneath each icon. A more advanced strategy, which still reflects the sharing structure, is an estimate-and-adjust strategy in which each child is given, for example, four cookies, and then another two. On the contrary to solve a quotition problem such as "How many bags of 3 cookies each can be made up from 18 cookies?", young children typically built up groups of three elements (e.g. three blocks or three dots on a piece of paper) until 18 was reached and then counted the number of groups. A more advanced strategy may involve adding threes (3+3+3 . . .) until 18 is reached, and then counting the number of threes.

In sum, in the early stages of learning the four basic arithmetic operations, children seem remarkably competent in solving word problems involving these operations. They rely on informal solution strategies in which the problem situation is directly modelled, rather than on an integrated concept of each operation and on one economical strategy for solving all problems involving that operation. Interestingly, such situation-dependent informal strategies are not only found in young children (or in adults) with little or no formal schooling in mathematics; they are also observed among schooled subjects (both youngsters and adults) who are solving quantitative problems embedded in daily routines in out-of-school contexts (see e.g. Lave, Murtaugh & de la Rocha, 1984; Nunes, 1992; Nunes et al., 1993b).

However, while these informal, situation-dependent strategies can be very helpful in solving certain problems, they also have their restrictions. First, they are frequently rather inefficient from a computational point of view, in the sense that they may exclude the flexible application of mathematical principles like commutativity, inversion, distributivity, . . . which can make the computational work less hard (De Corte & Verschaffel, 1987a; Nunes & Bryant, 1992). Second, they lack generalizability toward problems with larger and/or more complex numbers (e.g. decimals and fractions), for which an integrated concept of each operation and one general economic solution strategy (e.g. using the algorithm, an electronic calculator . . .) becomes almost indispensable (Fuson, 1992; Nunes, 1992). These unified conceptions and abstract solutions require cognitive steps that make them psychologically quite different from the informal, context-bound procedures described here. Indeed, they require more powerful representational schemata and problem-solving procedures, allowing pupils to loosen the ties between their problem representation, on the one hand, and the arithmetic procedure they generate to identify the unknown number in their representation, on the other (Fuson, 1992; Vergnaud, 1982).

Because of these restrictions, informal strategies cannot be considered as the ultimate goal of mathematics education. But they can play a very important role in the initial stages of the mathematics teaching–learning process as a starting point from which students can progressively and reflectively abstract, and thereby make the transition to more formal mathematical activity. In this process of progressive schematisation, abbreviation, internalisation and generalisation of informal and context-bound mathematics, a crucial role is played by carefully chosen problems, models, schemes and instructional activities stimulating pupils to reflect on their actual level of mathematical thinking. This basic principle underlies many approaches towards (elementary) mathematics education developed over the last few years, but especially the so-called Realistic Mathematics Education of the Freudenthal Institute (see, e.g. De Corte, Greer, & Verschaffel, 1996; Nunes et al., 1993b; Treffers, 1987).

INTERPRETING AND VERIFYING THE ANSWER

In a skilled word-problem-solving process, the execution of the arithmetic operation(s) is followed by a stage in which the outcome is interpreted and verified (De Corte & Verschaffel, 1985a; Schoenfeld, 1985). Interpreting means that the outcome of the calculations is considered within the context of the original problem representation. Verifying typically refers to activities performed deliberately at the end of the solution process to check the reasonableness or correctness of the answer obtained during the execution stage. However, such verification actions may also be carried out earlier, as part of the metacognitive on-line control of all steps taken during the understanding and solution process (Van Essen, 1991). The major outcome from the rather scarce research on this topic is that pupils and students tend to neglect these interpreting and verifying aspects of a competent word problem solving process.

A notorious illustration of students' failure to *interpret* the answer comes from the Third National Assessment of Educational Progress (Carpenter, Lindquist, Matthews, & Silver, 1983) involving a sample of 45,000 US pupils. One of the problems given to the 13-year-olds was "An army bus holds 36 soldiers. If 1128 soldiers are being bused to their training site, how many buses are needed". Of the pupils tested, 70% performed the division algorithm correctly but only 23% gave the correct answer (i.e. 32). Of the remainder, 29% wrote that the number of buses needed was "31 remainder 12", and 18% answered "31". In other words, less than one third of the children who performed the calculation correctly were able to interpret their outcome in line with the meaning of the problem situation; the others totally neglected to make such an interpretation. Accordingly, in their studies about the mathematical modelling assumptions involved in traditional school word problems (see earlier), Greer (1993) and Verschaffel et al. (1994) found that a problem like "If there are 14 balloons for 4 children at a party, how should they be shared out?" is frequently answered with "3.5" without any hesitation or further comment. It can be assumed that when confronted with the same problem in a real-life context (e.g. effectively sharing 14 balloons at a party), none of the children who gave that answer would take scissors and cut in half the two remaining balloons . . . The question arises: why did these students neglect to interpret the outcome of their calculations? The most plausible explanation is again that this is the result of the meaningless and unrealistic nature of the large majority of the word problems given in the maths lessons, as well as of the way in which these problems were analyzed and solved in those classrooms. These aspects of current didactics suggest that making realistic considerations and elaborations about the situations described in school arithmetic word problems is more of a hindrance than a help in finding the correct answer anticipated by the teacher or textbook writer (De Corte et al., 1996; Greer, 1993; Nesher, 1980).

A few researchers have systematically investigated pupils' *verification* actions as part of their heuristic or metacognitive repertoire for solving arithmetic word problems (De Corte & Somers, 1982; Overtoom, 1991; Van Essen, 1991). The available research allows some tentative conclusions. First, pupils do not very often spontaneously verify their solutions of elementary arithmetic word problems. In a study in which fifth graders were confronted with a set of non-standard word problems, Van Essen (1991) found that answers were checked in only 5% of the cases. Second, verification actions are more often performed by skilled problem solvers than by poor problem solvers (Overtoom, 1991; Van Essen, 1991). Third, if verification occurs (either spontaneously or provoked), it is frequently restricted to the correctness of the arithmetic calculations. Checking whether the problem was appropriately represented, whether the correct operation(s) was(were) selected, and/or whether the answer was adequately interpreted, occur much less frequently. Fourth, the application of a possibly effective verification strategy does not always lead to error detection, especially when the error-causing factor is conceptual and not computational. For example, when a first-grader misinterprets the word "altogether" as "each", or when a fifth-grader believes that "multiplication always makes bigger", verification actions will usually not improve their performance. Apparently, the efficiency of verification actions depends on the nature of the error-causing difficulty (Van Essen, 1991).

As several authors have argued (see, e.g. Greer, 1993; Van Essen, 1991; Verschaffel et al., 1994), current instructional practice does not seem to pay much attention to the development of appropriate interpretation and verification actions among students. Such actions will only develop if pupils are confronted with a variety of problems and tasks that strongly appeal to their use. In that respect, one can think of tasks focusing on a variety of situation-bound interpretations of an arithmetic operation, and others that are especially designed to demonstrate the usefulness of verifying one's answers. An illustration is the following task aimed at linking the result of computational work to the meaningful problem situation (Streefland, 1988): "Invent stories belonging to the sum "6394:12", such that the result is, respectively: 532, 533, 532 remainder 10, 532.84 remainder 4, 532.833333, and about 530".

CONCLUSIONS AND FUTURE PERSPECTIVES

Children's competence in solving one-step arithmetic word problems has been a remarkably active and productive area of research during the last 10–15 years. This holds especially for the domain of addition and subtraction word problems, but, more recently, scholars have increasingly turned their attention to the more complex field of multiplication and division word problems as well.

First of all, this research has yielded a categorisation of the different kinds of (word) problems involving the four basic operations. It has also documented the different knowledge components and skills underlying the competence in solving such word problems, thereby attending especially to the role of conceptual knowledge about additive and multiplicative structures in competent problem solving. Moreover, researchers have provided us with detailed and systematic descriptions of the errors that students make and of the difficulties they encounter in the different stages of the word-problem-solving process, due to lack or insufficient mastery of particular categories of knowledge and skill.

We also know much about the rich variety of strategies that pupils employ to arrive at correct solutions on additive and multiplicative word problems, and also about the conceptual knowledge and the cognitive skills underlying these different solution paths. In this respect, we point especially to the distinction between informal strategies based on direct modelling of the problem situation, and a more formal approach in which *the* underlying operation is identified and executed using the formal arithmetic concepts and procedures explicitly taught in school.

Finally, a great deal of progress has been made in identifying the developmental stages that children pass through before they can solve arithmetic word problems in a competent and formal manner, and in unravelling the progressively more abstract and more efficient conceptual structures and cognitive skills underlying this development.

Notwithstanding these accomplishments, there is no shortage of issues and tasks for further research. First, while our understanding of the development of the conceptual knowledge and the cognitive skills underlying competence in solving arithmetic word problems has substantially increased, many questions remain about *how* and *why* children move through this progression and about the influence of environmental and instructional factors on this development (see also Fuson, 1992).

Another limitation of past research is that it has largely focused on the initial and middle stages of the development of additive and multiplicative concepts. Therefore, a general research priority should be to investigate as well the upper stages of the development of these conceptual fields, where the additive and multiplicative concepts extend beyond the domain of positive integers (Greer, 1992; Vergnaud, 1990).

Third, while separate analyses of the conceptual fields of additive and multiplicative structures will doubtless continue, there is a strong need for a synthesis of these two hitherto rather separated bodies of research (Greer, 1992). Such a synthesis should involve both theoretical analyses of the relationships between the conceptual fields of additive and multiplicative structures, and empirical studies in which data are simultaneously collected for all four arithmetic operations.

A fourth limitation relates to the restricted nature of the word problems used until now. In line with current maths teaching practice, researchers have relied heavily on a restricted set of problems, i.e. brief, stereotyped, semantically impoverished pieces of text that contain all the necessary numerical data and end with a clear question that is undoubtedly solvable through one or more arithmetic operations on these numbers. Moreover, these problems are typically administered and solved in the context of a school arithmetic lesson. These textual and contextual constraints raise serious doubts about the generalizability of the theoretical constructs and empirical findings (such as the importance of schematic knowledge of problem situations, students' tendency to employ superficial coping strategies, . . .) towards the use of mathematical concepts and skills in more authentic and more complex problem-solving situations outside school. Therefore, researchers should broaden the scope of their tasks and contexts by not only looking at how pupils solve traditional school word problems in a typical mathematics class context, but also at their activities while posing, modelling and solving complex, ill-structured problems of applied mathematics in more realistic out-of-school contexts (see also Fuson, 1992; Greer, 1992; Nunes et al., 1993b).

Finally, ascertaining experiments that describe and explain existing problem-solving and learning processes *under given instructional conditions*, should be complemented with teaching experiments designed to test the feasibility and effectiveness of recommended new approaches toward the teaching of (applied) elementary mathematics (see also De Corte et al., in press; Fuson, 1992; Greer, 1992).

Of course, researchers have made a lot of research-based recommendations for the construction of new materials and strategies for teaching elementary arithmetic word-problem solving. For example, the classification schemes presented in Tables 4.1 and 4.2 have been suggested as valuable tools for designing a sufficiently rich variety of problem situations to develop in students a broad understanding of the formal arithmetic operations. From the findings about the impact of the type of problem situation, the wording of the problem statement, and the nature of the given numbers on problem difficulty, one can derive valuable suggestions for selecting and formulating appropriate problems at different stages of students' learning process. The findings about children's spontaneous and efficient use of informal solution strategies have been used as an argument in favour of instructional approaches in which these informal strategies are explicitly and systematically used as the starting point for the formation of more abstract and more formal arithmetic concepts and skills. Finally, researchers have argued that effective instruction and remediation in arithmetic word-problem solving requires that teachers have substantial and detailed knowledge about the typical misconceptions and incorrect strategies underlying pupils' errors, as well as good mastery of a repertoire of diagnostic skills for unravelling individual errors.

Meanwhile, the effectiveness and feasibility of these research-based recommendations have already been tested in teaching experiments that range widely in scope, content, and teaching method (see e.g. Bebout, 1990; Carpenter, Fennema, Peterson, Chiang & Loef, 1989; De Corte & Verschaffel, 1985c; Jaspers, 1991; Marshall, Barthuli, Brewer, & Rose, 1989; Willis & Fuson, 1988). There is no doubt that these investigations have yielded interesting building blocks for an integrated and inquiry-based intervention theory of arithmetic word-problem solving. However, here too a substantial amount of work remains to be done, because most of the available intervention studies suffer from one or more of the following shortcomings. First, the teaching programmes were mostly executed in settings that are not representative for the typical classroom setting (e.g. a one-to-one tutorial setting or a researcher working with small groups of children). This raises the question of to what extent these programmes will also be effective when applied by regular teachers under the constraints of a typical classroom environment. Second, most experimental teaching programmes focus on one particular aspect of skilled word-problem solving (e.g. either teaching knowledge about the different types of problem situations, developing links between informal and formal solution methods, or teaching particular heuristic and/or metacognitive skills). However, it has already become clear that simply combining elements of successful teaching programmes does not automatically result in a (more) effective programme (Jaspers, 1991). Third, most available teaching experiments involve only traditional school word problems such as the ones given in Tables 4.1 and 4.2. Future studies should apply a wider variety of problems including less sanitized and less structured problems that resemble more closely the quantitative problem situations encountered in the real world. This broadening of the scope of the problems may have important implications for the content and the organisation of the teaching programmes.

ACKNOWLEDGEMENTS

Partial support for writing this chapter was provided by a NATO Collaborative Research Grant on "Multiplicative structures".

L. Verschaffel is a Senior Research Associate of the National Fund for Scientific Research, Belgium.

5 Children's Understandings of Turn and Angle

Sandra Magina
Pontifícia Universidade Católica de São Paulo, Brazil
Celia Hoyles
Institute of Education, University of London, UK

This chapter describes part of a study that set out to explore children's conceptions of angle and dealt with possible situational influences and to a certain extent developmental questions as well. We probed how children of different ages negotiated meaning within different settings, all of which involved the conceptions or interpretation of angles. Thus, as well as investigating individual and group differences, we sought to explore how far contexts structure practices. Here we present findings derived from one context, where angles were investigated from a dynamic perspective, in terms of turns of the hands on an analogue watch used to represent and measure intervals of time. Before setting out our study and its results, we shall briefly discuss the theoretical foundations of our work and summarise research that has illuminated children's conceptions of angle.

GENERAL FRAMEWORK OF THE STUDY

This work has its roots in Piagetian theory. We are interested in trying to identify children's schemes, as described by Vergnaud (1984, 1987; see also, Chapter 1), for the concept of angle. We wanted to identify the organising invariants of their actions involving angle and turn within situations that we devised. We also acknowledge the failure of Piagetan theory to account for the influence of social and cultural factors on children's developing understanding of mathematical concepts. Thus we consider the importance of analysing mathematical concepts in everyday life (as has been done by

Carraher, Carraher, & Schliemann, 1985; Lave, 1988; and Nunes, Schliemann, & Carraher, 1993b). These authors have suggested that it is possible to identify the invariants of mathematical concepts required for participating in everyday practices and to analyse people's understanding of these invariants in the context of their knowledge of such cultural practices. Within this perspective, our study set out to identify children's understanding of angle by examining the organisation of their actions in a situation that involves some basic invariants of the concept of angle but which we may not immediately perceive as involving angle—the measurement of time intervals through turns of the hands of a watch. More specifically, we looked at children's understanding of how the magnitude of the turn of the hands of a watch informs the child about the interval of time elapsed as the hands go from a starting to a finishing position. We will seek to relate children's performance in these situations to the findings regarding children's notions of angle observed in other contexts. For this reason, we briefly review these findings in the next section of the paper.

CHILDREN'S CONCEPTION OF ANGLE

Research studies of children's notion of angle have identified a range of misconceptions (APU, 1987; Close, 1981; Herschkowitz, 1990). Problems include the failure to recognise right, acute or obtuse angles in orientations other than the standard horizontal/vertical; confusion between the magnitude of an angle and the length of its rays; difficulties in recognising obtuse angles as "angles"; and difficulties in identifying angles embedded in different sorts of figures. In all these studies the questions were presented to pupils as written tests. The impact of the medium of presentation of the tasks on these results must therefore be taken into account. If we reflect on the nature of the misconceptions observed, they intuitively seem to be connected with the notion of angles as "figures drawn on paper". The results of paper-and-pencil investigations strongly contrast with those obtained when children's notions of angles are analysed in the context of LOGO tasks.

In LOGO, the properties of a figure are encapsulated in the steps of its construction by the turtle. LOGO gives a procedural description of structures and relationships. Angles are formed by turtle turns, their position and orientation depending on the starting position of the turtle and its state. Thus we should expect pupils who have experience with LOGO to develop different conceptions of angle from those displayed by pupils who do not have such experience. This hypothesis finds some support in the literature. Noss (1985), for example, compared responses on a paper-and-pencil test of angle conservation and measurement of a sample of children with LOGO experience and a control group, and reported significant differences in favour of the LOGO children in both tasks. In general, pupils who have experience with

LOGO seem to perform on tasks about angles at higher levels of reasoning (according to the Van Hiele levels) than those who do not, although in some studies as much as one year of experience was needed for this advantage to be observed and in other studies no positive effects were found (for a review, see Clements & Battista, 1990).

However, the experience with LOGO does not necessarily wipe out sound conceptual developments in the understanding of angle previously developed in paper-and-pencil contexts. Carraher and Meira (1990) observed that the pupils with LOGO experience who performed better than the controls on angle tasks were those who were able to coordinate their new experiences with angle as turns of the turtle with an imagined system of coordinates which the pupils used as a frame of reference. The system of coordinates used by the pupils in the LOGO tasks was essentially the same as that described by Piaget, Inhelder, and Szeminska (1960), who investigated children's understanding of angle in the context of paper-and-pencil tasks in an era where LOGO was yet to be created. Setting aside the issue of the "efficiency" of LOGO in promoting the development of the concept of angle, it unquestionably offers a context in which it is possible to investigate a different view of angle—namely, a dynamic view of angles as turns rather than a static view of angles as figures.

Another context in which to explore how problems involving angles are approached is in everyday life activities. Unfortunately there is little research on which to draw and little is known as to how any notions of angle are developed when interleaved with cultural practices that take place outside school. Yet if geometry is viewed as the act of appropriating the space in which we live, breathe and move (Freudenthal 1973), then it is reasonable to hypothesise that children's understanding of angle arises at least in part from their own experiences interacting with their environment. There is a multitude of contexts in which children might "bump up" against the notion of angle. We chose to investigate here the use of angle as a turn in the analogue watch.

INTRODUCTION TO THE STUDY

The study was carried out in Recife, a large town situated in the north-east of Brazil. In Brazil schooling is organised in grade levels that are not strictly connected to pupils' ages because of the practice of resitting a grade if a pass is not obtained for all courses in the grade level. We were concerned with children in primary school, comprising the first eight years of education and organised in two levels, the Elementary and Middle Schools. The Elementary School comprises four years and is normally preceded in private schools by one year of pre-school during which children acquire basic literacy skills. The Elementary School is rather similar to an English primary school in that children have only one teacher responsible for all the central subjects in the curriculum, including mathematics. The Middle School comprises four years and covers the period from the fifth to the eighth grade. Children in Middle School are taught by specialist teachers for different subjects.

The study was undertaken in a private school attended by middle-class children. The main reason for working with such a school (rather than a state-supported school) was that there was a reasonable expectation that a well-structured curriculum established by the Ministry of Education (the same as that followed in State schools) would be in place. We would therefore be able to make some assumptions as to when and how the topic of angle would be taught—namely, children in Elementary School would have some contact with the topic of angle, albeit largely in the context of playing with shapes, whereas more formal work including angular measurement would take place in Middle School. The school (unlike a school for upper-class children) has similar educational and technical resources to those of state schools. As far as we could ascertain, the school from which we drew our sample does not see it as their job to teach the children about watches (how a watch works, how to tell the time) and we supposed that most of what the children knew about watches had been learned through their experiences outside school.

Our sample included 54 students, six of each grade level, with the youngest group consisting of 6-year-old pre-school children and the oldest 14-year-olds in the last grade of Middle School. Because of the differences in teaching and curriculum between Elemental and Middle Schools, we felt that a division of the sample into the 30 children from Elementary School (aged 6–10 years) and the 24 children from Middle School (aged 11–14 years) might be useful when investigating any effects of schooling.

Why Watches?

We used watches because of their potential to evoke a wealth of diverse settings and child interpretations. Watches are present in many situations and are quite familiar to the pupils whom we interviewed. Additionally, although digital watches have became popular in Brazil, analogue watches are still used on a large scale and school clocks tend to be analogue rather than digital. Keeping track of time is thus a cultural practice in which children can be expected to be involved in everyday life according to their own understanding of this practice.

A second reason for choosing watches was mathematical. The notion of measuring angles by rotation is an integral part of the way time is represented on a watch. This means that children should have a framework for making sense of rotations on watch-faces and should be able to make predictions and comparisons based on the rotations of watch-hands in sensible ways. Additionally there is a range of signifiers available to represent time on watches arising from different but precise metrics which involve number or spatial knowledge or a synthesis of both. For example, we know that half an hour has elapsed when the minute hand has gone half-way around the watch or when we count 30 minutes using the numbers on the watch-face. The efficacy of the latter approach depends, of course, on an appreciation of the meaning of the 12 numbers on the clock face—that is, the fact that the distance from one number to the next represents 5 minutes and that 60 minutes represent one hour.

Finally, we must mention a cultural feature of the use of language in Brazil that might affect our results. The number 6 is associated with a half-dozen through shopping experiences (for example, a half-dozen eggs are pre-packaged and buying "a half-dozen" is spoken about in natural contexts). The word "half" is also used to refer to the digit 6 in the context of saying phone numbers, in order to avoid the phonological confusion between 3 (*três*) and 6 (*seis*). Thus, one hears expressions like: "my phone number is: two, half, eight, one, half, three, zero" (for the phone number 268–1630). When reading time, the half hour is also signalled as such—for example, 8:30 is read as "eight and a half"—and the minute hand coincidentally points to the digit 6. Thus it becomes a matter of interest how the 6 on a watch-face is viewed by children.

In summary, using watches to tell the time raises many questions that touch on the notion of angle. How do children measure time intervals on a watch-face, do they rely on the numbers or on the spatial measure of the turn of the hands? Do they use the same strategy regardless of the initial time? Are their strategies affected by the physical features of the watch—its shape, its size—as children's notions of angle drawn on paper seem to be? Does the presence or absence of numbers on the watch-face affect their performance significantly? Do different representations of watches such as changes in the medium in which they are drawn and in the units marked on the watch-face influence pupils' responses? And finally, is it possible to identify progress in children's understanding as they grow up and progress through school? How do 6-year-olds differ from, say, 13-year-olds in the way that they construct or compare angles?

The activities designed for this study and the children's performance will be described here (for a complete report, see Magina, 1994).

ACTIVITIES WITH CARDBOARD WATCHES

Different types of cardboard watches were used which varied according to size and shape and the presence or absence of numbers: three watches had a large circular shape, three a small circular shape and three an oval shape. Two of the watches in each set had no numbers on their faces and one did. Each set of watches was coloured differently to assist in distinguishing the pupils' responses. The turns of the hands in the activities were carried out following the clock-wise orientation.

Prediction Activities

Five activities were devised, all of which involved the children in predicting the position of the minute hand half an hour after the time shown on the watch-face. In each case the child was asked to move the minute hand to its position after half an hour and justify his or her response. The activities varied in terms of:

(a) the *exact wording of the questions*. In the first three activities (Fig. 5.1, top) the child was asked to turn the minute hand through half a turn, whereas in the last two activities we asked the child to show where the minute hand would be after half an hour (Fig. 5.1, bottom);

(b) the *starting time* (in activity 4 it was 12:00; in activity 5 it was 12:10);

(c) the *shape* and *size of the watch face* (differences existed in all activities);

(d) the *presence* or *absence of numbers* on the watch-face (there were no numbers on the watches in the first three activities). The activities are presented schematically in Fig. 5.1.

We have grouped the first three prediction activities together because the questions were concerned with the turn of the hand and there were no numbers on the watch-faces. Therefore we expect no interference of children's knowledge of the position of the number 6 for indicating "half". Further, to answer questions about the half turn the children do not need any knowledge of the watch metric nor to know about angle. Thus we expect activities 1, 2, and 3 to be easier than the subsequent ones.

In activities 4 and 5 there are some new complexities. First, there are numbers on the face of the watches and these could have an effect on the children's performance. Second, the questions were now about half-hour (rather than half-turn) and thus knowledge of the watch metric is required. The use of different shapes and sizes of watches can also be a source of difficulty if the children are prone in this context to misconceptions similar to those observed with respect to angle—that is, if they think, for example, that the length of the hands in the watch influences how much time has elapsed. However, if the children understand the watch metric, they should have no difficulty in performing well on these tasks.

It should be noted that activities 4 and 5 differ in a significant aspect. In activity 4 the minute hand will be at 6 after a half-hour whereas in activity 5 it will not. If the number 6 is used by children as a reference (as in 8:30 read as "eight and a half"), activity 4 will be significantly easier than activity 5.

Comparison Activities

In these activities the children were asked to compare intervals of time measured on watches of different sizes and shapes. In the first of these activities, six watches with no numbers on their faces were used. The six

Activity 1:
Starting time: 12:00
Shape: Small circle
No numbers

Where would the minute hand be after it has turned through half a turn?

Activity 2:
Starting time: 12:30
Shape: Large circle
No numbers

Where would the minute hand be after it has turned through half a turn?

Activity 3:
Starting time: 11:45
Shape: Oval
No numbers

Where would the minute hand be after it has turned through half a turn?

Activity 4:
Three watches, small and large, circular and oval, all with numbers on their faces and all showing 12.00 were presented to the child *at the same time.*

Where would the minute hand be half an hour later?

Activity 5:
This activity was identical to Activity 4 except that the watches showed 12.10 as a starting time.

Where would the minute hand be half an hour later?

FIG. 5.1. Prediction activities

watches were presented side by side, all showing a starting time of twelve o'clock (see Fig. 5.2). It was explained that each watch was given to a child to figure out how long he/she had worked on his/her homework. For each watch the hands were turned by the experimenter until reaching the time indicating when the homework was finished: The child was the asked two questions: (a) which child had worked longest? (b) which child had worked the least amount of time?

An analysis of activity 6 allows us to observe whether rotation is the most relevant information for the children or whether other variables, such as the shape of the watch or the distance between the hands in the final position, influence the children's responses. This is especially salient if one considers that the time in one of the watches was changed from 12:00 to 22:00 and the interviewer had to rotate the minute hand 10 full turns in order to accomplish the change.

Activities 7 and 8 involved comparisons of half-hour intervals starting from different times and using watches with numbers on their faces. Activity 7 (see Fig. 5.3) used small circular and oval watches; activity 8 (see Figure 5.4) small and large circular watches. The subjects were again told that the different watches had been used by some children to time how long they had worked for. The subjects' task was to indicate whether or not the children had worked just as long. If the subjects did not recognise the equality (the intervals were always of a half-hour), they were asked which child had worked longer. All subjects were asked to explain their answers.

The new variable introduced in the last two activities is the different starting and ending times. To obtain success in this task, children must take into account the fact that the time elapsed is not only influenced by the ending but also by the starting time. If the subjects only consider the time at which the homework was completed, they will answer that the child with the oval watch in activity 7 and the child with the small circular watch in activity 8 worked longer. If the subjects consider only the shapes of the watches, they

Activity 6: Comparing time intervals.

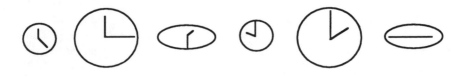

FIG. 5.2.   First comparison activity

Activity 7: Comparing time intervals on small circular and oval watches.

Starting times

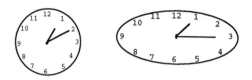

Finishing times

FIG. 5.3. Second comparison activity

Activity 8: Comparing time intervals on small and large circular watches.

Starting times

Finishing times

FIG. 5.4. Third comparison activity

will indicate longer working times for the children with the oval watch in activity 7 and the large circular watch in activity 8.

RESULTS FROM THE PREDICTION ACTIVITIES

The results obtained for the activities concerning a half-turn (activities 1, 2, and 3) show that 6 and 7-year-olds did not do well on any of these tasks. In contrast, only occasional errors were observed among 8 and 9-year-olds. The performance of the oldest children was errorless. Starting point did not have any impact on the pupils' performance in this task where they had to turn the minute hand a half-turn.

However, the picture is rather different when we consider the responses to the questions concerning half an hour, where the metric of time was to be constructed by analogy to that of turns in space. The proportion of mistakes was much higher and even 11-year-old pupils displayed errors. Younger children, who did not perform well in the spatial task of producing a half-turn, had clearly no basis on which to develop the analogy between turns and intervals of time. But although the older pupils, in the age range 8 to 11 years, performed well on the half-turn tasks, they did not seem to use the metric of turns as a basis for reasoning about intervals of time.

A comparison between children's performance in activities 4 and 5 indicates that they were consistent across watches within each activity, even though the watches differed in shape and size. Thus in these tasks the shape of the watch-face had no discernible effect on the response. In contrast, there was an increase in the incidence of errors from activity 4 to activity 5, which might be related to the fact that the interval of a half-hour in activity 4 ended on a half-hour (after a half-hour the watches would show 12:30) whereas in activity 5 it did not (after a half-hour, the watches would show 12:40).

Table 5.1 gives the number of incorrect answers observed in each activity. If children were incorrect in activities 4 or 5 this meant they were incorrect in their responses on each of the three watch-faces; because this was the same error it was counted only once in the total number of errors. Considering that shape did not appear to influence pupils' responses in any of these activities, this information is omitted from the variables cited in the table, which summarises each activity in terms of the two variables of starting time and type of instruction given to the subjects (do a half-turn or change the watch a half-hour).

Age Effects

Analysis of the data cross-sectionally by age indicates a strong trend of performance that improves with age/schooling; children aged 6/7 years had considerable difficulty with all the tasks, children aged 13/14 years produced almost errorless performance and children between 8 and 11 years, while

TABLE 5.1
Number of Incorrect Responses to Half-turn and Half-hour Predictions

	Age Group	Half-turn			Half an hour		(Activity)
		1	2	3	4	5	
		12:00	12:30	11:45	12:00	12:10	(Start time)
Elementary	6	6	4	6	3	6	
School	7	5	5	4	3	6	
	8	0	0	2	0	3	
	9	1	1	1	0	4	
	10	1	0	0	0	2	
Middle	11	0	0	0	1	3	
School	12	0	0	0	0	1	
	13	0	0	0	0	1	
	14	0	0	0	0	0	
	Total	13	10	13	7	26	
	% inc	24.1	18.5	24.1	13.0	48.1	

performing very well on some activities, had a great deal of difficulty with others. These findings suggest a developmental effect, but the age effect cannot be separated from any influences of schooling because these two variables are confounded in our study.

Analysis of Strategies

An analysis of strategies used in activities 4 and 5 was conducted to describe children's ideas about measuring intervals of time with analogue watches. (Activities 1–3 are not of interest here because they deal with half-turns.)

In activity 4 there were very few errors overall. However when we come to activity 5, there was a considerable increase in errors not only amongst the younger children but also the middle age range, and even some of the older pupils made mistakes. Considering together the pupils' responses in activities 4 and 5, we can classify their responses as characterising four types of approach to the measurement of time intervals:

1. *No strategy* was the category that we used when the child gave irrelevant explanations or no explanation for his/her prediction. This was found to be the case for five of the 6-year-olds and for three of the six 7-year-old children. Examples of this type of response are: "It is here because the hand wants to" (6-year-old); "I don't know about hour" (6-year-old); "After half hour the hand must be in a different place" (7-year-old).
2. *Fixed representation of "half"* was a category used when the child seemed to associate the place of half-hour with the position of the number 6 on the

watch-face. In this case the children succeeded systematically in activity 4 but not in activity 5. This type of strategy was found amongst 6 to 13-year-old children. Three examples are: "I have to stop on number 6 because half hour is half, and half is 6" (7-year-old); "Half is in the number 6" (11-year-old); "Number 6 means half, and you asked me for half hour" (13-year-old).

3. *Moving across numbers* was a strategy characteristic of children who began to reason about time intervals as defined by moving across a certain number of spaces on the watch-face. However the children were not sure how to control the number of moves across the watch-face. They resorted to different sort of strategies for this purpose. Some children seemed to attempt to use their response to activity 4 in order to solve activity 5. For example, in activity 4 they had counted from 12 to 6 making the number 12 as the first move. They thus considered that they needed 7 moves in this activity and transferred to activity 5 the idea of jumping 7 numbers to find a half-hour. An example is: "Last time I jumped 7 numbers to stop in the 6 [points to the place of number 6] and I did the same now" (10-year-old); "I counted while I jumped 7 numbers" (9-year-old).

Other children used the number 6 to mean "half" and tried to apply it in this context by moving across 6 numbers on the watch to determine the interval. However, they were not sure whether the starting point had to be considered or not. This strategy is illustrated by this explanation: "I counted 6 numbers and then I put the hand in the sixth [but the starting point was counted as number 1]" (11-year-old).

Finally other children knew that they should move across some of the numbers on the watch-face but did not know how many numbers they had to move across: "To be a half hour it [the minute hand] has to move into 3 numbers" (11-year-old).

4. *Coordinated strategy* was a category that covered responses of children who were able to explain what a half-hour means on the basis of different ideas. They could explain that a half-hour interval is the same as going across 6 numbers on the watch because this is equivalent to 30 minutes or a half-turn around the hour. They also realised that the hand would be in a final orientation where it would form a straight line with respect to its own starting position and that if another half-turn were performed the hand would return to its original position. These children showed that they could consider the rotation and its result in a coordinated fashion. For them there is no question of remembering how many numbers to move across: they can see it because it is a half-turn. All the 14-year-old children and many 13 and 12-year-old children explained their prediction using this strategy: "1 hour is 60, half is 30; if I count 6 numbers it will be half. . .because each number is 5 minutes" (14-year-old). "Half an hour is the same as half turn: the hand must stop in the middle of the whole turn . . . the middle depends on the starting point" (13-year-old). "Half hour means a straight line from the initial position" (11-year-old).

In summary, it appears that the first step in acquiring the watch metric seems to be characterised by children's understanding that there is a connection between the position of the hand and the reading of the watch. In our task, the number 6 and "half hour" were easily connected to each other by 7–8-year-old children. However, in doing so, the young children ignored the rotational aspect of the watch metric and consequently also ignored the difference between reading the watch and determining a time interval. They therefore simply changed the minute hand to 6 in response to the request to "turn the hand a half hour". These children seemed to be concerned with the picture of "x-and-a-half", instead of considering the metric of the space as analogue to the metric of time.

The next step in the process seems to involve the beginning of the analogy between the movement of the hand on the watch and the interval of time elapsed. However, children still seem to be limited in their use of this analogy because they try to reconcile the reading of "x-and-a-half" with the movement representing a half-hour or to be uncertain of how many moves over the numbers to make. Although these children tended to miscount when determining the interval of a half-hour, they seemed to be trying to establish a theorem-in-action to justify the relationship between 6 and half an hour.

It is only when they are older that they coordinate the reading of the watch, where half is fixed, with time intervals, where the half-hour can end at any point on the watch-face. They realise that 6 indicates a half-hour because it is 30 minutes after the new hour started. In this way they can also determine where the minute hand will be after half an hour has elapsed from any starting point.

RESULTS FROM THE TASKS OF COMPARING TIMES

The percentage of errors in activity 6 (48% and 44%, respectively, for the questions "who worked the most?" and "who worked the least?"), which involved the simultaneous comparison of six watches, was slightly lower than that observed in activity 7 (55%), where only two watches were compared. At first glance, this seems surprising because one might conjecture that comparisons among the finishing times of six watches would be more difficult than comparing the finishing times of only two watches.

However, we can identify three major differences between the activities, which lead to a prediction of a higher incidence of errors in activity 7. First, all the starting times were the same in activity 6, namely twelve o'clock, whereas in activity 7 the starting points were different. Second, the watches had no numbers on their faces in activity 6 and this should stress amount of turning as the major input to consider. In contrast, the watches had numbers on their faces in activity 7 and the confusion between time read and interval of time observed in the previous section could therefore be expected once again.

Finally, in activity 6 each watch had moved through different amounts of time and their finishing times were different, whereas in activity 7 the finishing times were different but the time intervals to be considered were actually the same, and this might be counterintuitive.

To explore the differences between activities 6 and 7, we analysed the children's responses and verbal explanations to each of these activities in greater detail.

In activity 6, children's errors seemed to be based mostly on the distance between the hands of the watches at their final position. Of the 26 incorrect responses to the question "which student spent the longest time doing homework?", 23 converged on the watch that displayed 2:45. This supports the interpretation that the figure formed by the hands of the watch influenced the children's response because this watch formed the largest angle. The children's verbal explanations further confirm this idea and can be illustrated by the response of a 9-year-old boy, who, having chosen the watch displaying 2:45, explained his choice: "1 know because of the hands; they are so far from each other in this watch. You see, this hand [pointing to the minute hand] is on the other side". In an analogous way, in response to the question about which student had worked the least doing the homework, 24 students gave wrong answers, 15 of which were either the choice of the watch showing 2:00 or that showing 10:00 (where the angles are of the same size). An illustrative explanation of the reasoning leading to this choice was provided by a 7-year-old boy who chose the watch displaying 10:00: "You see, the hands are very, very close".

Activity 7 involved a comparison between circular and oval watches, each of which had turned through half an hour from different starting points. In 28 of the 30 incorrect responses the pupils indicated that the oval watch, which had started at 1:15, had shown the longest interval. From the children's explanations, two different reasons seem to result in this same choice. Some children simply looked at the finishing time and pointed out that the minute hand on the oval watch was at 9 whereas the minute hand on the circular watch was at 8; so the oval watch had turned more. A second group of children seemed to consider only the figure formed by the hands of the watches in the final position. These children either referred to the distance between the endpoints of the hands or the openness of the angle. Both kinds of response indicate a failure to recognise the impossibility of judging time intervals from the final result only (either by focusing on the figure formed by the hands of the watch or focusing on the finishing time itself).

In activity 8, it was possible to distinguish the choices based on finishing time from those based on the figure formed by the hands on the watch, because the smaller watch ended up with a less open angle and displayed a later time (1:45 in contrast to 1:40). In this activity 22 out of the 26 incorrect responses indicated that the child using the watch that ended at 1:45 had worked the longest doing homework. Thus finishing time was a more important factor influencing children's judgements of time intervals than the figure formed by the hands of the watch in this activity. Once more, children's difficulties observed earlier in coordinating the reading of a watch with the analogue representation of a time interval through movement is confirmed in these activities.

CONCLUSIONS

Our study has allowed us to have a new look at the problem of understanding angles in the context of an everyday cultural practice, namely measuring time with an analogue watch. We will summarise the findings here by first looking at age/schooling effects and then contrasting our results with those from previous work on angles.

Although we cannot distinguish between age and schooling effects in our sample, we can divide the children into three groups according to their performance in our tasks.

Group 1, including children 6 to 7 years of age, had considerable difficulty with all the tasks regardless of whether they were asked to turn the hand "a half-turn" or "a half-hour". When asked to predict where the hand would be after a half-hour, they showed no discernible strategy and were not able to explain why they had moved the hand of the watch as they did. In comparison tasks, the subjects in this group were influenced by the figure formed by the hands of the watch when attempting to evaluate which child had worked the most or the least time doing homework.

Group 2, formed mostly by children 8 to 11 years old, showed a clear difficulty in dealing with comparisons of time intervals, whereas their performance in predicting the position of the minute hand after a half-hour interval was much better. In this prediction, they succeeded when the end of the half-hour interval coincided with the number 6 on the watch-face, but had more difficulty when it did not. They thus seemed to be good watch-readers but could not yet coordinate this reading with measuring an interval of time.

Group 3 was composed of children from 12 to 14 years old. This last group displayed good performance both in the half-hour prediction tasks and the comparison tasks. Children in this group seemed to be able to coordinate fixed spatial positions used in watch-reading with the measurement of time intervals. They understood why the number 6 indicates x-and-a-half in watch-reading and were able to determine a half-hour interval regardless of the size and shape of the watch as well as of starting time.

Interesting similarities can be pointed out between the results of this study on children's understanding of rotation and angle in the context of watch-reading and those obtained when children's concepts of angle are analysed in paper-and-pencil or in LOGO activities. First, in all of these situations it is noteworthy that children identify certain values with particular perceptual figures. Paper-and-pencil tests have shown children's difficulties in recognising, for example, a right-angle when the rays are not horizontal/vertical (see, for example, Close, 1982): they appear to identify 90° with the figure formed by the meeting of a horizontal and a vertical line. Results of children's performance after a relatively small amount of practice with LOGO have also shown that some children do not consider the initial position of the turtle and seem to believe that a 90° turn is needed to obtain a horizontal line; they also do not realise that the angle drawn on the screen is the supplement of the turtle's turns, and they may refer, for example, to a 20° angle as 160° (see Carraher & Meira, 1990). An analogous behaviour in our study was to attribute a fixed position to "half-hour" and ignore starting time. Thus it appears that children start out by considering the figural properties of space as fixed and only later come to view them as related to the transformations from which they result.

We would like to suggest that this approach to the study of children's conceptions of space is a promising one. When a somewhat formal organisation of space is necessary for children to carry out certain widespread cultural practices, such as watch-reading, it becomes possible to investigate their conceptions in new ways. Much more work is needed, however, before one can come to conclusions on whether participation in such activities plays a significant role in promoting children's development of spatial and geometrical concepts.

6

Knowing About Proportions in Different Contexts

Janice A. Singer, Amy S. Kohn, and Lauren B. Resnick
Learning Research and Development Center,
University of Pittsburgh, USA

INTRODUCTION

In this chapter, we develop some specific hypotheses about the origins and development of ratio and proportional reasoning in children. Evidence suggests that very young children have important intuitions about densities and rates. These intuitions, which are exercised and developed in the course of everyday experience with the physical and social world, often allow them to make judgments that would be mathematically described in terms of ratios proportions, and functions. Our developing theory concerns the ways in which these intuitive forms of understanding are transformed into formal mathematical knowledge and also the difficulties children encounter along the way.

Our theory represents an extension of work by Resnick and Greeno (Resnick, 1992; Resnick & Greeno, 1990) on the intuitive origins of basic algebraic concepts such as commutativity, associativity, additive inverse and distributivity. At the heart of Resnick and Greeno's theory is the idea that two separate lines of development merge to create a quantified number concept: one based on *protoquantitative* schemas and one based on counting knowledge of the kind that has been documented by Gelman and Gallistel (1978), among others (e.g. Ginsburg, 1977; Ginsburg & Allardice, 1984; Resnick, 1986).

Protoquantitative schemas allow children to reason about relations among amounts of physical material, including combinations, increases and decreases, and comparisons. These schemas are termed protoquantitative because they enable children to reason without the benefit of, or interference from, numerical quantification. Children know, for example, that combining two separate amounts of a substance produces an amount of the substance that is larger than either part. They also know that taking some objects away from a collection results in a smaller collection. Such decisions do not require counting or numbers. The relations among the physical quantities are, instead, intuitively obvious and self-evident to children. In an apparently separate line of development, preschool children also learn to count and thus to quantify collections of objects. Through practice in everyday contexts of use and the language accompanying such practice, children's early protoquantitative schemas eventually become *quantified*. The quantified schemas maintain the original relationships and allow children to make numerically exact judgements about combinations, changes, and comparisons of physical objects and substances. Still later, numbers and operations on numbers, rather than on physical material, become the direct objects of reasoning, but the relationships specified in the early protoquantitative schemas are still maintained. In this way, it can be said that children's understanding of formal mathematics *inherits* their early intuitive understanding of the physical world.

The issue that we address in this chapter is whether there might be a similar course of development for proportion and ratio: that is, a sequence in which children can first reason protoquantitatively about situations involving proportions or ratios and later carry this knowledge into quantified, mathematically exact forms of representation and reasoning. The story we tell here is more complex than the one for additive algebraic concepts. We present evidence of intuitive schemas for reasoning about densities and rates—both of which count as protoquantitative forms of reasoning about ratios and proportions—but also suggest that quantification of these schemas does not proceed smoothly or directly.

To build our story, we must specify what we mean by ratio and proportional reasoning. We begin, then, with a distinction between *extensive* and *intensive* quantities as defined by Schwartz (1988). Extensives quantify *how much* of a substance or *how many* of a class of objects are present. Extensive quantities behave additively; that is, they can be combined and partitioned in ways that match the combination and partitioning of amounts of physical material in the world. Combining two extensive quantities results in a larger extensive quantity. Partitioning an extensive quantity results in two smaller quantities that, taken together, add back up to the original quantity. The additive algebraic concepts accounted for by Resnick and Greeno's theory concern extensive quantities.

Intensives, by contrast, are relational quantities that describe how two different extensives are related to one another. Rates, such as *5 apples per box,*

$3 per hour, or *30 miles per gallon*, are all intensive quantities. So too are rates that do not specify a base unit of 1, such as 5 *apples for every 3 dollars* or *5 pencils for $2*. Intensives do not behave additively. They describe a feature—such as "thickness" or "density"—that is true of any amount of a substance. For example, the ratio of 5 apples per box holds for the whole shipment of apples, or for one of the boxes in the shipment, or for any five boxes in the shipment. Similarly, 30 miles per gallon describes the relationship between distance travelled and petrol consumed during 1 mile, 10 miles, 30 miles, or 60 miles (assuming a constant speed). Intensives do not behave additively. You cannot add 30 miles per gallon and 10 miles per gallon to get 40 miles per gallon.

To understand ratios and rates, a child must come to understand these intensive quantities: not absolute amounts but the *relations* between two amounts. To understand proportions, a child must also understand how two ratios relate to one another; a proportion is mathematically defined as the equivalence of two ratios. For instance, the following examples all express proportional relationships:

$$(1)\ 5\ \text{apples} : 3\ \text{dollars} :: 10\ \text{apples} : 6\ \text{dollars}$$
$$\text{or}$$
$$(2)\ 5\ \text{apples} : 3\ \text{children} :: 10\ \text{apples} : 6\ \text{children}$$
$$\text{or}$$
$$(3)\ 5{:}3 :: 10{:}6$$
$$\text{or}$$
$$(4)\ 5/3 = 10/6$$

The ratio or rate on the left side of the expression or equation is mathematically equivalent to the ratio or rate on the right side. They express the same, multiplicative functional relationship.

An intensive quantity is a special type of ratio. The two extensive quantities that are combined to form an intensive quantity come from separate measure spaces: for example, miles and gallons, apples and boxes, time and distance. That is, an intensive quantity measures a quality that is derived from combining two different kinds of extensives and, as such, must be based on the relationship of two separate types of things or amounts. Mathematical ratios can relate amounts from the same measure space, amounts from different measure spaces, or simply numbers. They are mathematically defined simply by the fact that they establish a multiplicative relationship between two quantities or numbers.

In this chapter, we first develop evidence for protoquantitative schemas for intensive relations: that is, schemas for density and rate that do not require exact quantification of the two amounts being set in relation to one another. We show that there are, in fact, two different forms of protoquantitative reasoning about intensive relations. First, children are able to make decisions about intensives through direct apprehension of rates and densities. Direct apprehension allows children to respond appropriately to intensives in the physical world *without necessarily computing the relationship between two separate amounts*. Later or in other situations, children show an ability to establish a relationship between two separate amounts explicitly. This is nonetheless a form of protoquantitative reasoning to the extent that children continue to focus on the relationships between physical materials and do not use numbers to quantify those relationships.

In the next section of the chapter, we will look for ways in which the protoquantitative intensive schemas might be quantified, giving rise to true rates and ratios. This requires appreciation of *multiplicative* relations between numbers. What we find however, is an effort by children to apply their well-practised knowledge of the additive properties of numbers to rate and ratio situations.

They do this by thinking out the two quantities that they are trying to relate in terms of *covariation*: as one grows larger (or smaller) by some amount, the other increases or decreases by a corresponding amount. By creating two linked lists, children are able to solve many quantified ratio problems. We call this kind of thing *protoratio* reasoning. It uses numbers for exact quantification, but it does not depend on construction of a true intensive quantity. True ratio and proportional reasoning requires going beyond linked lists, a step that most children apparently find difficult and that some may never take (e.g. Behr, Harel, Post, & Lesh, 1992; Hart, 1988; Inhelder & Piaget, 1958).

PROTOQUANTITATIVE REASONING

A fairly extensive body of literature points to young children's ability to form correct judgements in situations that would be mathematically described as involving ratio or proportional reasoning. Among the judgements that children appear to be able to make are those involving the variables of length and width, which form an area measure (Anderson & Cuneo, 1978; Silverman & Paskewitz, 1988; Wilkening, 1979); time, speed, and distance (Acredolo, Adams, & Schmid, 1984; Wilkening, 1981); ability and effort (Kun, 1977; Kun, Parsons, & Ruble, 1974; Surber, 1980); reward earned and time worked (Anderson & Butzin, 1978); proportion space filled with one class of object versus another (Acredolo, O'Connor, Banks, & Horobin, 1989; Lovett & Singer, 1991; Spinillo & Bryant, 1991); crowdedness, or filled versus empty space (Singer, 1992); food needs and animal size (Singer, Kohn, & Resnick, under review); and density (Kohn, 1993). Each of these studies provides convincing evidence that, if they are *not* required to use numbers or other quantitative measures, children can make judgements that are close to those that would be mathematically correct. This is why we call them *protoquantitative* judgements. The process by which these judgements are made is not entirely clear, however, and there may be two distinct forms of protoquantitative reasoning about ratios and proportions.

Kohn (1993) studied children's understanding of the physical concept of density by asking children to make judgements about buoyancy. The buoyancy of an object is independent of either its weight or its size (volume), considered independently, but depends on the density of the material of which the object is made—that is, on the *relation* between weight and volume. Children and adults were shown a set of objects that varied in density and were asked to decide whether each object would float or sink when placed in a tank of water. The set included small light objects that were dense (and hence would sink) and big heavy objects that were not dense (and hence would float). The subjects were encouraged to handle the objects, and, in fact, most of the subjects hefted the objects and then gave their judgements.

Young children and adults demonstrated striking similarities in their judgements and error patterns. Regression analyses of individual subjects' data showed that 4-year-olds and adults both weighted density more strongly in their buoyancy judgements than either weight or volume. The buoyancy task thus allowed 4-year-olds to demonstrate some correct implicit knowledge of density. They did this without using numbers or any other kind of quantitative measure. Their performance was, therefore, protoquantitative.

Were they, nevertheless, in some sense computing density; that is, separately estimating weight and volume and then combining these estimates to make an informed guess about buoyancy? Not necessarily. It may well be that the young children—and the adults, for that matter—were able to perceive, via tactile and kinesthetic cues, the density of the objects directly. People may have a form of *embodied knowledge* (Johnson, 1987) about physical material that includes information about how "tightly packed" the material is and that does not depend on even a protoquantitative version of first estimating the volume of an object, then estimating its weight, and then combining the two.

Embodied Knowledge of Proportions

More generally, we hypothesize that young children and perhaps even infants and animals have processes available that allow them to perceive certain kinds of rate and density information in the physical environment directly. We mean by this that children can, under certain circumstances, make judgements about proportionality or ratio without first representing and then integrating measures from two or more separate dimensions. Instead they can recognize certain rates and densities in a direct form of perception, as if rates and densities were percepts *afforded* (as in Gibson, 1979) by the environment. In this way, very young children can compare rates and densities and thus reason protoquantitatively about proportions.

An example may help to clarify this point. Consider speed. Speed is an intensive quantity mathematically defined in terms of the multiplicative relationship between two variables: distance and time. But speed is also a physical variable that can be easily judged through a direct form of perception. When looking at two cars going down the street, it is easy to see which one is going faster, without necessarily considering either time or distance. Thus, speed itself (and not an integration of time and distance) can be the object of reasoning.

Evidence for some form of direct apprehension of proportions comes from Singer's dissertation (1992). Singer explored children's directly apprehended understanding of proportionality by comparing their performance on a task in which crowdedness (number of objects per fixed area) could be visually estimated with performance on a task in which children had to imagine the degree of crowding that would result when bunches of objects were put into boxes of different sizes. The subjects were shown computer displays with two "flower boxes filled with flowers" (boxes filled with dots) and were asked to

(a)

(b)

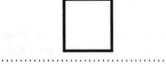

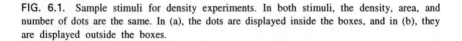

FIG. 6.1. Sample stimuli for density experiments. In both stimuli, the density, area, and number of dots are the same. In (a), the dots are displayed inside the boxes, and in (b), they are displayed outside the boxes.

determine which box was more crowded. In one version of the task, the flowers were displayed inside the boxes. Figure 6.1a shows a sample stimulus. Density (crowdedness), here, could be directly perceived from a visual inspection of the display. In the second version of the task, the flowers were displayed outside the boxes. Figure 6.1b shows a sample stimulus. The densities are the same in the two displays. The children were told that the farmer had not had time to plant the flowers and would do it as soon as he could. They were asked to pick the box that would be more crowded when the flowers were planted inside the box. In this task version, because area and number information were presented separately, an integration of separate extensive quantities was necessary to make density judgements.

Figure 6.2 plots performance as a function of grade-level for the two versions of the task. When the flowers were displayed inside the boxes, all grades performed well. But when the flowers were displayed outside the boxes,

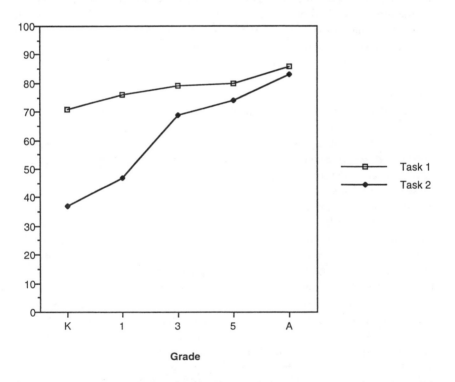

FIG. 6.2. Results from Singer's dissertation experiments. All grades performed well for the first task version in which the dots were displayed inside the boxes. For the second task version, in which the dots were displayed outside the boxes, only the third and fifth graders and the adults used density to make judgements. The younger children chose the box with the greater number of dots.

the kindergartners and first graders performed poorly. They tended to choose the box with the greater number of flowers as the more "crowded" box rather than relating number and area. These results suggest that, before children can integrate two or more dimensions, they can respond to a proportional relationship when a visual estimation of the proportion is possible.

Some of the other studies already cited showing an early appreciation of ratio and proportion may involve this kind of direct apprehension of a perceptually unitary dimension rather than actual computation of relations between two dimensions. A clear example comes from a series of experiments conducted by Wilkening (1981) examining children's understanding of the relation among time, speed, and distance. In Wilkening's (1981) task, children were told a story about some animals on a farm. The animals liked to play by the dog house, but when the dog started barking, the animals got scared and wanted to run away from the dog as quickly as possible. The children were given information about two variables, and their task was to make a judgement for the third variable. For instance, in one task they were told the speed (fast, slow, or medium) of an animal and the time that the animal travelled, and were asked to judge the distance the animal travelled.

Speed was represented by the type of animal. Some animals were fast (e.g. rabbits), whereas other animals were slow (e.g. snails). Time was represented by the length of time a dog barked. Wilkening had different length tape-recordings of a dog's bark. Distance travelled was represented on a storyboard by the placement of a particular animal at a certain distance from the dog house. Children made judgements for all three dimensions; that is, they judged distance given time and speed, judged time given speed and distance, and judged speed given time and distance.

Wilkening found that even 5-year-olds made judgements that reflected the multiplicative relationship between time and speed when making decisions about distance. Wilkening initially concluded that, as early as 5 years of age, children can multiplicatively integrate certain variables. However, by observing their eye movements for the distance judgements (given time and speed), he found that, at all age levels, subjects started moving their eye focus from the initial fixation point (the dog house) when the dog started barking and stopped moving their eyes when the dog stopped barking. Subjects marked the place that the animal would reach according to where their eyes were fixed when the dog stopped barking. Subjects' rate of eye movement was faster or slower depending on what animal was being judged (e.g. eyes moved fast if the rabbit was running), suggesting that they were embodying the concept of speed in a single movement. It appears that children were not integrating the dimensions of home and distance but rather were directly apprehending speed via the use of a kinesthetic strategy.

Most of the studies showing early protoquantitative proportion and ratio do not allow us to distinguish between direct apprehension and computing the relationship between two dimensions. The design of many of the studies concerning physical variables would allow direct apprehension, but there was no effort either to show that it was occurring or to rule it out as a basis for the subjects' judgements. In a few of the studies, it is hard to imagine direct apprehension, at least not on a perceptual, physical basis. For example, in several experiments investigating children's understanding of the relationship between effort and ability (Kun, 1977; Surber, 1980), young children were given information about two of the following variables and asked to make a judgement for the third: ability, effort, and outcome. To illustrate, children were told about a boy who was very good at lifting weights (ability) who found a certain weight to be very light (outcome). The children's task was to judge how hard the person tried to lift the weight (effort). With this task, children as young as 6 years old have shown evidence of integration. Given that effort and ability are conceptual rather than perceptual variables, in this case it appears that children really were integrating information from two different sources.

Protoquantitative Covariation

Studies in children's language learning have shown that, as early as 2 years old, children relate objects according to their sizes. Two-year-olds label objects as big and small (Ebeling & Gelman, 1988; Gelman & Ebeling, 1989; Sera & Smith, 1987), and they use large and small judgements as a basis for pairing objects. But they also show evidence of understanding that the terms express *relations* and not only absolute categories. For example, they say that a normatively small shirt is nevertheless big for a doll. When asked to pick a button that is right for an adult's coat or an adult's shirt, a child's pants, and a baby's sweater, even 2-year-olds modulate the size of their choices according to the relative size of the buttons in the series (Sera, Troyer, & Smith, 1988).

We were interested in whether this early ability to relate two series would allow children to create two covarying series systematically. In a series of studies based on the work of Piaget, Grize, Szeminska, and Bang (1977), Singer et al. (under review) asked children to assign amounts of food to series of fish whose lengths were related in two different ways. In linear series, each successive fish's length was 1 unit (¾ inch) longer than the previous fish. In geometric series, each successive fish's length was double the length of the previous fish. Figure 6.3 shows a sample linear and geometric series. Because we were interested in protoquantitative reasoning, in our first study we did not specify the amounts given to any one fish or mention numbers of any kind in presenting the task. Children were simply asked to feed each fish "just the right amount of food, so that they get neither too much nor too little to eat." Under these conditions, almost every child from first grade on gave food amounts to fish according to the length of the fish: larger fish got more food, and the amount more was roughly proportional to the fish's length. The

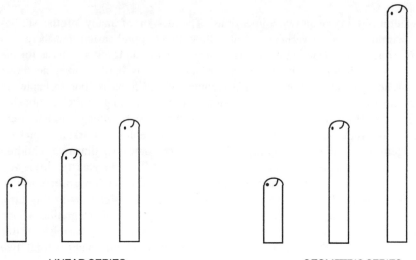

LINEAR SERIES   GEOMETRIC SERIES

FIG. 6.3 Sample stimuli for linear and geometric series for Singer, Kohn, and Resnick (under review) covariation experiments.

children, then, appeared to be distinguishing between linear and geometric series.

But were they really attending to the *series*, that is, to the relationship between successive fish, or were they just globally matching food amounts to perceived size of the fish—which could yield the same results? In the latter case, one would expect that the children's strategy would be disrupted if an amount of food were prescribed by the experimenter for one fish in the series, especially if a surprisingly small amount were assigned to a "big" fish or a surprisingly large amount to a "small" fish.

To test this hypothesis, we ran another version of the fish-feeding study in which a food amount was assigned to one of the fish in the series and children of the same age as the previous study were asked to use that amount to determine how much food to give the other fish. Sometimes, we purposely gave a large anchor amount to a small fish and a small anchor amount to a large fish. Numbers were not mentioned in the instructions. The children were just told, "This fish needs this amount, and you should use this amount to figure out how much to give to the other fish."

Regression analyses tested what dimensions children were responding to in choosing food amounts. Table 6.1 shows the results. Subjects were classified as using a linear strategy if food amounts increased or decreased by a fixed amount in relation to the anchor amount, a correct strategy for a linear series of fish: for example, for an anchor 8 in the second position, feeding 6, 10, and 12 pellets to the fish in the first, third, and fourth positions, respectively. Subjects

TABLE 6.1
Percentage of Subjects at Each Grade Classified According to Different
Strategies

			Strategy		
Grade	Linear	Geometric	Length	Position	Other
Linear Series					
K	37	0	32	19	12
1	44	0	13	31	12
3	62	0	7	31	0
5	75	0	0	25	0
A	81	0	0	19	0
Geometric Series					
K	18	6	52	12	12
1	31	6	44	19	0
3	31	19	31	19	0
5	20	56	12	12	0
A	6	75	0	19	0

were classified as using a geometric strategy if their food amounts increased or decreased by doubling or halving in relation to the anchor: for example, for an anchor 8 in the second position, feeding 4, 16, and 32 pellets to the fish in the first, third, and fourth positions, respectively. This would be correct strategy for a geometric series of fish. Subjects were classified as using a length strategy if they ignored the anchor and assigned food, as in the first study, according to the length of the fish. They were classified as using a position strategy if they always gave the same amount to the first fish in the series, the second fish, and so forth, without reference to either length or the anchor amount. As shown in the table, despite there being no demand for numerical calculation, children's ability to perform in accordance with the mathematical relationship in the series was seriously disrupted by the anchor requirement. Not until fifth grade were 75% of the subjects classified as using the correct linear strategy for linear series. Not until adulthood did 75% of subjects reach this criterion for the geometric series.

This disruption suggests that the strong performance in our initial fish-feeding study was probably not based on reasoning about the relationship between the fish and the food in each *series*, but rather was based on a direct link between fish and food, probably using an absolute or categorical judgement about fish size and food amount. If performance is based on some sort of categorical judgement, then it more closely resembles the direct apprehension solutions to density problems than to computation—even non-numerical—of relations between two variables.

FIRST STEPS TO QUANTIFICATION: PROTORATIOS

The results of our second fish-feeding study should be examined in juxtaposition with the earlier findings of Piaget, Grize, Szeminska, and Bang (1977). With Piaget et al.'s numerically quantified version of the feeding task, children as young as 9 years old succeeded in correctly assigning food amounts to fish. But that finding is at odds with our second fish-feeding study in which even 10-year-olds could not correctly assign food amounts to a geometric series of fish when they were constrained by an anchor and thus could not use categorical size to make judgements of amount.

What might account for this discrepancy? To find an answer, we need to look in detail at how Piaget et al. posed their questions. The children in their study were shown three fish: 5, 10, and 15cm long. They were told explicitly that the second fish eats *twice as much* as the first fish and that the third fish eats *three times as much as the first fish*. The children's attention was thus directed to the multiplicative, scalar relationship relating the fish lengths. When 9- and 10-year-old children then assigned food in the correct relationships, it was assumed that they were using the multiplicative information they were given. But this may not have been the case. The relation between 5, 10, and 15cm long fish is linear. One can describe the relationship as 5, 5 *plus* 5, and 5 *plus* 5 *plus* 5, rather than as 2 *times* or 3 *times* 5 as Piaget et al. did. So children may have ignored the multiplicative relationship and instead worked their way through two additive series, one for the fish and one for the number of food pellets. Figure 6.4 shows how this linked additive strategy might have worked.

From the report in the Piaget et al. study, there is no way to determine whether children were, in fact, using this kind of linked additive reasoning to produce what we call a *protoratio* judgement. However, several other studies on children and adults clearly show this kind of reasoning. A particularly clear example comes from a study by Ricco (1982), who gave French schoolchildren in Grades 2 to 5 (roughly 7 to 11 years of age) problems for which, given the price of a certain number of pens, they had to calculate the price of other multiple-pen purchases. The problems were presented in tabular form, with some lines filled in and others left for the child to complete. For example, one problem was presented as shown in Table 6.2.

Answer	Reasoning
5cm get 3 pellets	
10cm gets 6 pellets	5cm more gets 3 pellets more
15cm gets 9 pellets	5cm more gets 3 pellets more

FIG. 6.4 Possible strategy for solving Piaget et al.'s eel problem.

TABLE 6.2
Type of Table Used by Ricco to Assess Ratio Reasoning

Number of pens bought	Price Paid
1	?
2	?
3	1 2
4	1 6
5	?
6	?
8	?
1 0	?
1 5	?
1 6	?
1 8	?
7 1	?
7 2	?
7 5	?

The second-graders in Ricco's study generally increased the price paid in successive rows of the table, either applying no arithmetic rule or adding some number (not a proper constant) to each successive row. Such a solution reflects protoquantitative reasoning about matching, covarying series. From the third grade on, most children attempted to quantify and used a protoratio strategy. The most common method was to compute a constant difference which was added to successive rows in the Price Paid column, taking into account the "jumps" in the Number of Pens Bought rows: for example, "Five pens cost 20 francs . . . because there is 4 francs difference between 12 and 16. Six pens . . . 24; I add 4. Eight will cost 28 francs. Oh, no! Seven is missing. Seven . . . 28 francs, 8 pens . . . 32 francs."

This type of solution is reminiscent of the numerical reasoning shown by 9 or 10-year-olds selling coconuts on the streets of a northeastern Brazilian city (Carraher, Carraher, & Schliemann, 1985). In one problem-solving episode, a young street vendor apparently did not know how to multiply 35 by 10 to yield 350 as illustrated in the following protocol:

Customer: I'd like 10, how much is that?
M: [Pause] Three will be one hundred and five; with three more, that will be two hundred and ten. [Pause] I need four more. That is . . . [Pause] three hundred and fifteen . . . I think it is three hundred and fifty. (p.23)

The vendor solved the problem, nevertheless, by coordinating increases in two different series of numbers—one standing for the number of coconuts, the other for the amount of money. This means that the child needed additional knowledge—about how two series of composed numbers relate to one another.

Figure 6.5 schematizes the strategy that he used, which is very similar to the one that we hypothesize that Piaget et al.'s subjects may have used in the feed-the-eels problem.

TRUE RATIOS: SCALAR AND FUNCTIONAL REASONING

Full mastery of proportional reasoning requires two important steps beyond the linked additive strategy that we have just described. First, there must be a shift in attention from additive relations to multiplicative relations among numbers. Second, children must learn to reason fluently both within and across measure spaces.

Several studies conducted within the Information Integration Paradigm (e.g. Wilkening, Becker, & Trabasso, 1980) document the relatively late development of children's ability to integrate two quantities multiplicatively. These studies show that multiplicative, as opposed to additive, integration of quantities emerges as dominant only at about age 10 (see Resnick & Singer, 1993, for a further analysis of this body of work as it bears on the development of ratio and proportion). Much the same story seems to hold for sensitivity to multiplicative relations among numbers. Using multidimensional scaling, Miller and Gelman (1983) showed that it is not until Grade 6 that children begin to take into account the multiplicative properties of number when making similarity judgements. Miller and Stigler (1991) reported similar results on a different sample of children. They also found that Chinese and Japanese children show sensitivity to multiplicative properties earlier than do American children, suggesting that differences in the amount of school-based practice in multiplication may be influential. Using a different methodology, Campbell and Graham (1985) confirmed a general insensitivity to factorial properties of numbers among children below Grade 5. These findings taken together suggest that quickly accessed knowledge of the factorial properties of

Answer	*Reasoning*
3 coconuts cost 105 cruzeiros	
6 coconuts cost 210 cruzeiros	3 more cost an extra 105 cruzeiros
need 4 more	6 c-nuts + 4 c-nuts makes 10 c-nuts
9 coconuts cost 315 cruzeiros	3 more cost an extra 105 cruzeiros
	need one additional c-nut to make 10
10 coconuts cost 350 cruzeiros	one c-nut cost 35 cruzeiros more.

FIG. 6.5 Possible strategy used by children to solve the coconut problem.

numbers develops slowly. The importance of such an understanding is highlighted in a study by Glaser and Pellegrino (1982). They found that high scorers on a number-analogy test were much quicker than low scorers to recognize multiplicative relationships between numbers.

Full proportional reasoning requires not only the ability to reason about multiplicative relations but also the ability to reason fluently both within and across measure spaces. The issue of reasoning both within and across measure spaces is often discussed in the literature on proportional reasoning and multiplicative structures as a distinction between *functional* and scalar reasoning (e.g. Karplus, Pulos, & Stage, 1983; Noelting, 1980; Schliemann & Carraher, 1992; Vergnaud, 1983b, 1988). *Scalar* reasoning occurs when a person makes parallel transformations *within* measure spaces. For example, if a person reasons that if 6 pens cost $3, then 12 pens must cost $6, *because the number of pens doubled and therefore the number of dollars must double*, she or he has made transformations *within* measure spaces. No numerical relationship between pens and dollars was directly established. On the other hand, functional reasoning occurs when a person reasons directly about the relationship between two distinct variables, that is, *across* measure spaces. For example, an individual might reason that the *price* of pens in the preceding example is 2 pens for $1 and use that functional relationship to calculate the price of a different number of pens. Price recognizes a functional relationship between pens and dollars. Unlike scalar reasoning, functional reasoning requires the construction of a true intensive quantity, in that extensive quantities from two different measure spaces are related.

Although full competence in proportional and ratio reasoning involves both scalar and functional reasoning, the vast majority of practical proportional reasoning problems can be solved using scalar relationships. There is also some evidence that scalar reasoning is preferred during the developmental and educational process. Vergnaud (1983b, 1988) studied 11- to 15-year-old children's strategies for solving problems in which three values were given: one from one measure space and two from another measure space. The children's task was to find the missing value. An example of a typical problem is the following: "The consumption of my car is 7.5 litres of gas for 100km; how much gas will I use for a vacation trip of 6580km?" Here children are given two values from the distance measure space and one value from the gas measure space, and are asked to find the missing gas value. With a set of such problems, Vergnaud found that scalar solutions to problems were far more prevalent than functional solutions. Even for those problems in which functional solutions would have required simpler arithmetic, scalar solutions dominated. For instance, in the problem "In 7 hours the central heating consumption is 21 litres of oil. What is the consumption in 84 hours?" a functional solution would benefit from the simple division of 21 by 7 to yield 3 litres per hour (an intensive quantity), whereas the scalar solution requires a more difficult division of 84 by 7 and then multiplication of 21 by 12. Nevertheless, most of the children's solutions employed a scalar strategy.

A similar finding has been reported by Schliemann and Nunes (1990). They asked fishermen with varying levels of schooling to solve six proportionality problems about the relationship of unprocessed to processed seafood. Of the six problems, three were designed to be easily solved via scalar solutions, and three were designed to be easily solved via functional solutions. Correct solution rates were 83% for the scalar problems and 70% for the functional problems. A qualitative analysis of the protocols showed, however, that scalar solutions were clearly preferred for both problem types; for the scalar problems, 83.3% were solved via a scalar solution method, whereas only one problem was solved functionally. Even on the functional problems, 72.3% of the solutions involved a scalar strategy and only 12.7% were solved using a functional strategy. For example, when one fisherman was told that a certain type of oyster yields 3 kilos of meat for every 12 kilos caught and was asked how many kilos of oysters they would need to catch for a customer who wanted 10 kilos of meat, he answered:

S: . . . On the average, 40.
E: How did you solve this one?
S: . . . It's because 12 kilos give 3, 36 give 9. Then I add 4 to give 1.

This fisherman, like the others in the Schliemann and Nunes study, used multiplicative relations. But he solved the problem by performing parallel transformations on two different extensive quantities rather than creating an intensive.

The Schliemann and Nunes (1990) results show that even unschooled fishermen can understand and use functional multiplicative relationships. These results also show, however, that there is a clear preference for scalar relationships. This may be because, even before multiplicative relationships are learned and understood, most ratio and proportion problems can be solved by additively linking two lists of extensive quantities. This early use of additive relations may make scalar solutions the preferred solutions to almost all ratio and proportion problems.

CONCLUDING DISCUSSION

The evidence that we have described here makes it clear that intuitive bases for ratio, proportion, and functional reasoning are available to young children. When they are not forced to quantify, children are able to make good judgements about intensives such as rates and densities. We call the knowledge on which these judgements are based *intuitive* to stress that children who use it treat the relationships among amounts of material as self-evident.

There appear to be two different forms of intuition about intensives. One of these, which we have called *direct apprehension*, does not—strictly speaking—require setting two different kinds of material into relation with one another. Rather, it appears that, in certain situations, speed, density of material, crowdedness and the like function as epistemological primitives for children. That is, they are not derived from other features, but are attributes of objects or substances in their own right. Thus, when children recognize that one animal goes faster than another, they are not necessarily making judgements about relations between distance and time. Speediness or slowness is, instead, embodied in the animal and can be matched by speedy or slow embodied motions that the children themselves make (see Johnson, 1987 for a more general discussion of embodied knowledge). Judgements about distance travelled or time taken derive *from* rather than give rise *to* judgements about speed. Only after some time, according to our studies, can children work analytically, deriving a judgement about crowdedness from two separate estimates of size and quantity or about speed from separate estimates of time and distance. These judgements remain protoquantitative, in that they are not based on strict numerical quantification, but perhaps it is important to note that they tend to arise after children are well able to count and measure large amounts.

Another form of intuition comes into play when children reason about covariations between two different quantities. The studies that we have reviewed (see also Resnick & Singer, 1993) suggest that even kindergarten and primary-grade children's capacity to reason about covariation is quite robust as long as they are not pressed to think in numerically quantified terms. There seems to be, in effect, a kind of protoquantitative reasoning about functions: what amount of X *goes with* what amount of Y? But the introduction of anchor amounts requiring not only quantification but also multiplicative numerical relations, apparently disrupts children's ability to use their protoquantitative strategies.

We have, then, a situation in which reasonably robust protoquantitative intuitions exist for intensives and for functional reasoning. Unlike as for protoquantitative intuitions about additive properties and relations, however, quantification does not proceed smoothly. Confronted in everyday situations or in school with the need to solve quantified ratio problems, children seem to prefer solutions that allow them to use their dependable number knowledge, that is, knowledge about additive properties and relations. The protoratio strategy of linked lists of extensives permits this. But this strategy works only, or at least most simply, when problems are solved using scalar rather than functional strategies. The result is, apparently, that initial efforts to quantify ratios drive children's attention away from their protoquantitative intuitions about functional relations.

Our empirically documented story ends here, with children able to solve many of the quantified ratio problems that the world presents to them by using protoratio strategies, but with the mathematical concept of ratio as a multiplicative functional relationship still being elusive. What does it take to cross the threshold into comfort and ease with multiplicative functions? This is a vital question for those concerned with mathematics education, for it is well established that functional reasoning, along with proportions and ratios generally, is a significant challenge for teaching and learning. We do not have a prescription to offer, but our research taken as a whole suggests the need to develop problem situations and mathematical conversation (cf. Bill, Leer, Reams, & Resnick, 1992) that highlight functional relations between quantities and that actively invite children to develop and apply their knowledge about the multiplicative properties of numbers.

ACKNOWLEDGEMENTS

This chapter was supported by James S. McDonnell postdoctoral fellowships to the first and second authors. Additional support came from the Center for the Study of Learning supported by OERI grant #G00869005.

7 Mathematical Concepts at the Secondary School Level: The Learning of Algebra and Functions

Carolyn Kieran
University of Quebec at Montreal, Canada

Algebra and functions—what is the relationship between the two? Are they disjoint; do they intersect; is one a subset of the other? When asked to write a chapter that described student learning of these two subjects of the secondary mathematics curriculum, I began by exploring the question of how various researchers in the mathematics education community distinguish these two domains. This chapter thus opens with an overview of some opinions on the matter. I then offer details of my own view of what is involved in the learning of these two subject areas and present illustrative examples from the research literature that describe features of student mathematical development in algebra and functions. Finally, I attempt to put into perspective these elaborations of what is involved in the learning of algebra and functions and the accompanying examples of student cognition by drawing on a recently developed mathematical learning theory.

DISTINGUISHING BETWEEN ALGEBRA AND FUNCTIONS

Sierpinska (1992, p.36) distinguished between algebra and functions according to the way in which the variables and expressions are viewed:

> Before they start learning functions, the whole experience students have with variables is that in which the fundamental distinction is between the given and the unknown quantities. When it comes to functions they have to make a shift to the distinction between the constant and the variable quantities.

To elucidate her point, she offered the following problem, one that she gave as a test question to a class of 16-year-old students:

Two companies rent photocopiers. The first charges $300 for the rental of the machine per month and $0.04 for each copy. The second charges $250 for the rental and $0.06 per copy.
1. For what number of copies per month would the price be the same?
2. If you are a heavy user of photocopies, which company is preferable?

Sierpinska emphasized that the first question requires thinking in terms of equations and unknowns, whereas the second demands that the number of copies be regarded as a variable upon which depends the other variable, the price. She found that the discrepancy between the two modes of thinking was simply too vast for these students. For the first question, students who were able to answer correctly were generally those who wrote an equation in one unknown, $300 + 0.04x = 250 + 0.06x$. But for the second one, the few successful students were those who interpreted $y = 300 + 0.04x$ and $y = 250 + 0.06x$ as relations between the price and number of copies and used two line graphs in the coordinate system to arrive at the solution (for $x < 2500$, the second company was preferable, and for $x > 2500$ the first company was the one to choose). One could argue that the first question might also have been answered by viewing $y = 300 + 0.04x$ and $y = 250 + 0.06x$ as functional relations and by seeking the point of intersection in a graphical representation. In other words, even questions that have typically been regarded as equation-solving tasks can be interpreted as functions—an issue to be discussed later in the chapter—but the point made by Sierpinska is that there is a fundamental distinction between thinking in terms of equations involving unknowns and in terms of functions involving variables. Sierpinska declared that the difference between those two modes of thinking is so important that in the eighteenth century it was regarded as a demarcation line between two distinct domains of mathematics. She went on to point out (1992, p.37) that:

Even if some objects are common to those domains, the attention focuses on different aspects of them and assigns them different roles. For example, the equation is no more a condition on the unknown which allows one to extract its value. In the context of functions it appears as the principle or the law according to which some variables change as some other variables change.

Sfard and Linchevski (1994, p.191) also referred to this changeability-of-focus aspect in their discussions of the various ways that algebraic expressions can be interpreted:

When you look at an algebraic expression such as, say, $3(x + 5) + 1$, what do you see? It depends. In certain situations you will probably say that this is a concise description of a *computational process*. $3(x + 5) + 1$ will be seen as a sequence of instructions: Add 5 to the number at hand, multiply the result by three and add 1. In another setting you may feel differently: $3(x + 5) + 1$ represents a certain *number*. It is the product of a computation rather than the computation itself. Even if this product cannot be specified at the moment due to the fact that the component number x is unknown, it is still a number and the whole expression should be expected to behave like one. If the context changes, $3(x + 5) + 1$ may become yet another thing: a *function*—a mapping which translates every number x into another. This time, the formula does not represent any fixed (even if unknown) value. Rather, it reflects a change. The things look still more complicated when a letter appears instead of one of the numerical coefficients, like in $a(x + 5) + 1$. The resulting expression may now be treated as an entire *family of functions* from R to R. Alternatively, one may claim that what hides behind the symbols is a function of two variables, from R^2 to R. There is, of course, a much simpler way of looking at $3(x + 5) + 1$: it may be taken at its face value, as a mere *string of symbols* which represents nothing. It is an algebraic object in itself. Although semantically empty, the expression may still be manipulated and combined with other expressions of the same type, according to certain well-defined rules. [Emphasis as in the original version.]

If all of these interpretations can be hooked to what the authors call an "algebraic" expression, then algebra can be viewed as a notational device for representing various ideas and for manipulating the symbols of these representations but the underlying ideas or concepts can include number, computational process, function, and so on. This is indeed a fairly broad perspective on algebra.

Schwartz and Yerushalmy's view (1992) overlaps somewhat with that of Sfard and Linchevski. But Schwartz and Yerushalmy give even more prominence to functional interpretations in that they have proposed that function is the "primitive algebraic object" (1992, p.264). They have elaborated further (pp.265–266):

What kind of object is $x + 3$? It is not a number, as we normally think of number, because we can't tell how big it is. We suggest that it is useful to think of $x + 3$ as a number recipe, i.e., a procedure for doing something with a number in order to produce a new (or not new) number. It is clear that the number recipe object is a different object from any number object that one might supply the recipe with or that the recipe produces when one supplies it with a number. Number recipes are functions (the converse is not universally true) and so far we have used a symbolic representation for them . . . We see that the symbolic representation of function reveals its process nature, while the graphical representation suppresses the process nature of the function and thus helps to make the function more entity-like. A proper understanding of algebra requires that students be comfortable with both of these aspects of function. Indeed, it might be remarked that in the calculus, differentiation and integration are perhaps most readily thought of as operations on functions as entities.

The comments by Schwartz and Yerushalmy imply that a primary distinction between algebra and calculus lies in the nature of the function object itself, as well as in the types of operations that are carried out. (This issue will be revisited in a later section.) The reader will also notice that Schwartz and Yerushalmy use the term "symbolic" representation rather than "algebraic" representation, chiefly because they consider all of the basic functional representations to be part of algebra. Not all mathematics educators agree with the stance that the concepts of algebra profit from being seen through the lens of functions (e.g. Wheeler, 1996); although it is a notion that is beginning to gain more widespread acceptance. An example of the view that there is more to algebra than functions is seen in Bell (1995) who includes functions simply as one of the three main activities of algebra: *generalizing, forming and solving equations,* and *working with functions and formulae.*

An orientation that is similar to Bell's is Usiskin's (1989). He has conceptualized algebra in a manner that includes Bell's three activities, but has added a fourth—the study of structures. He has tied these four conceptions of algebra to various uses of variables: *algebra as generalized arithmetic, algebra as a study of procedures for solving certain kinds of problems, algebra as the study of relationships among quantities,* and *algebra as the study of structures.* Regarding this last conception of algebra, Usiskin has provided examples such as the factoring of $3x^2 + 4ax - 132a^2$. He remarked that, if the factors $(3x + 22a)(x - 6a)$ were checked by substitution of numerical values, there would be some hint that we are generalizing arithmetic. Of course, it is possible to view all four activities as different facets of a functional approach to algebra and, thus, to regard the study of structures as the natural evolution of a computational interpretation of functions (Sfard, 1991). But the usual practice is, according to Usiskin, to treat the variables as arbitrary marks on the paper and to focus on the activity of manipulation. In problems like these, as well as in proving identities such as $2\sin2x - 1 = \sin4x - \cos4x$, "faith is placed in properties of the variables, in relationships between x's and y's and n's, be they addends, factors, bases, or exponents; the variable has become an arbitrary object in a structure related by certain properties" (Usiskin, 1989, p.16).

This latter conceptualization of algebra by Usiskin serves to highlight a general property of algebraic symbols: we can detach a particular meaning from these symbols and manipulate them without concerning ourselves with their referents—but only to a certain extent. As Sfard and Linchevski (1994, p.192) have pointed out, we still need to know what kind of mathematical object the particular expression represents and what we want to do with it:

> When faced with such an equation as $(p + 2q)x^2 + x = 5x^2 + (3p - q)x$, one will not be able to make a move without knowing whether the equality is supposed to be numerical or functional—whether the question is that of the value of x for which the equality holds (this value should be expressed by means of p and q), or that of

the values of the parameters p and q for which the two functions, $(p + 2q)x^2 + x$ and $5x^2 + (3p - q)x$, are equal. The different interpretations will lead to different ways of tackling the problem and to different solutions: in the former case one finds the roots of the equation using the quadratic formula, in the latter the values of parameters p and q are sought for which the coefficients of the same powers of x in both expressions are equal ($p + 2q = 5$ and $3p - q = 1$).

From this first section of the chapter, one might be led to conclude that there could be as many different perspectives on algebra as there are researchers one might choose to listen to. However, underlying all these perspectives—even a functional one—one can find a few common threads. All use algebra at least as a notation, a tool whereby we not only represent numbers and quantities with literal symbols but also calculate with these symbols. One could stretch this definition to the extent of saying that algebra is also a tool for calculus (in fact, historically, algebra led to calculus). However, that would miss the point, which is that the symbols have different interpretations depending on the conceptual domain (i.e. the letters represent different objects in school algebra than they represent in the calculus courses). In addition, some new symbols are generated and the procedures for calculating with the symbols also change in subtle ways as one moves from one mathematical sub-discipline to another. Algebra can thus be viewed as the mathematics course in which students are introduced to the principal *ways in which letters are used* to represent numbers and numerical relationships—in expressions of generality and as unknowns—and to the *corresponding activities* involved with these uses of letters—on the one hand, justifying, proving, and predicting, and, on the other hand, solving. These uses of algebraic letters all require some translation from one representation to another; furthermore, the activities associated with these letter-uses all require some symbol manipulation. Both of these aspects—translation and symbol manipulation—are included in the discussions of the upcoming section. It is to be noted that, as functions can be viewed both numerically as expressions of generality and as objects in their own right that denote change, they are treated both in the next section on algebra and in the following one on functions. In so far as the letters are used to represent the variables of a function rather than its parameters, and individual functions, rather than families of functions, are the subject of study, the material is dealt with in the algebra section.

ALGEBRA

The quintessential element distinguishing algebra from arithmetic is the presence of letters. Every child going through elementary school knows from older sisters and brothers that algebra is all about Xs. "Algebra has been defined, tongue in cheek, as the study of the 24th letter of the alphabet" (Mason, Graham, Pimm, &

Gowar, 1985, p.38). This section examines the conceptual terrain of algebra and describes features of the researched mathematical development of students as they attempt to learn what algebra is all about. The two main parts of this section, which correspond to the principal uses of letters in basic courses in algebra (or in mathematics courses that include algebra), are Expressing Generality and Using Unknowns to Arrive at Problem Solutions.

Expressing Generality

Elementary algebra is sometimes called "generalized arithmetic" because it involves the expression of general statements that represent the numbers and operations of arithmetic. It is worth noting that algebra can, in fact, help students notice properties of numbers that they did not notice in arithmetic. Components of beginning algebra that are intended both to introduce algebraic notation to students and to help them develop their numerical awareness are, first, exploring number facts and relationships, properties, and numerical and geometrical patterns, and, second, expressing the generality of these relations and patterns by algebraic representations. These algebraic representations are subsequently used to justify one's numerical arguments, to prove structural aspects of the number system, and to predict (calculate) the values of non-represented members of a pattern.

Generalizing is a process that all humans engage in. Even before going to school, mathematical generalization occurs, for example, when a child becomes aware that the order in which objects are counted is of no importance and that the numerical result is always the same. Generalization also occurs in elementary arithmetic classes when the algorithms for addition and the other operations are learned and the child realizes that they can be applied to any of the numbers he or she has encountered. Their early work with function machines also provides a context for generalization when they examine the set of inputs and corresponding outputs and generate the rule that produced the pairs. In these three examples, the generalization takes the form of an awareness—perhaps a very subtle one. It is not usually communicated by the child, except perhaps for the rule of the function machine which he or she might be asked to verbalize. But that is usually as far as it goes in arithmetic. In algebra, the student is asked to express that generality in written form using symbolic notation because the symbolic representation will be used to explore the relationship further and as a basis for justifying, proving, or predicting. We now look at a few examples of activities related to expressing generality and at their underlying conceptual demands.

Justifying and Proving

Several excellent examples of the use of letters to express generality and of the subsequent appropriation of these expressions in order to justify one's numerical arguments are provided by Lee and Wheeler (1987) who carried out a study on generalization and justification that involved problems such as:

> *Part 1.* A girl multiplies a number by 5 and then adds 12. She then subtracts the original number and divides the result by 4. She notices that the answer she gets is 3 more than the number she started with. She says, "I think that would happen, whatever number I started with."
>
> *Part 2.* Using algebra, show that she is right.

As there is no constraint to use algebra in Part 1, students believe that a strictly numerical justification is adequate. However, the explicit demand of Part 2 of this task is to verify the generalization suggested in the text by means of algebra. This requires translating the non-specific number and sequence of operations into algebraic notation, and manipulating that notation in order to obtain an expression that can be interpreted in terms of the problem:

$$(5x + 12 - x)/4$$
$$\rightarrow (4x + 12)/4$$
$$\rightarrow 4(x + 3)/4$$
$$\rightarrow x + 3$$

In brief, the major conceptual demands of this problem situation, a situation that involves generalizing and justifying, are the following: (a) translating from a verbal representation to a symbolic one involving the use of a letter as a variable to represent "any number", (b) knowing how to manipulate the algebraic expression into simpler equivalent expressions with the underlying aim of arriving at an expression indicating "3 more than the number she started with", and (c) being aware that the algebraic result—the expression $x + 3$—constitutes a proof or justification of the result that one obtains empirically by trying several particular numbers. Note that the only conceptual demand that is somewhat independent of the context is that of manipulating the algebraic expression into simpler algebraic expressions. But even that activity can allow the student to see at a glance why the result for the above problem is always $x + 3$. The sequence of simplified algebraic expressions can be seen to be quite transparent and can permit a perception of the "$x + 3$-*ness*" in a way that is not so readily available from a linear reading of the text of the problem situation. Such will be seen to be the case, time and again, that the algebraic representation can induce an awareness of structure that is much more difficult, if not impossible, to achieve using everyday language.

Of the 118 Grade 10 algebra students who were given the above problem (students who had already taken algebra for a year), only nine set up the expression $(5x + 12 - x)/4$ and then algebraically worked it down to $x + 3$. Four of these nine students then went on to "demonstrate further" by substituting a couple of numerical values for x. Thirty-four others set up $(5x + 12 - x)/4 = x + 3$

and then proceeded to simplify the left side, yet did not base their conclusions on their algebraic work. Instead, they worked numerical examples and concluded from these examples. Thus, we see that for the majority, this task posed insurmountable problems with respect to using algebra as a tool for both representing a general statement and using it to justify their numerical arguments. According to the researchers, these students seemed completely lost when asked to use algebra. For the few who were able to use algebra in this task, Lee and Wheeler (1987, p.149) pointed out that "formulating the algebraic generalization was not a major problem for the students who chose to do so; using it and appreciating it as a general statement was where these students failed". Thus, for the students who responded to the request to use algebra, their difficulties were related essentially to the third of the conceptual demands outlined earlier. They are not reported as having experienced problems with the technical aspects of expression simplification.

The research literature on simplification of expressions suggests that when students begin to learn these techniques, their performance is quite haphazard, for a while at least (Greeno, 1982). Bell, Malone, and Taylor (1987) have reported that beginning algebra students are often perplexed at being permitted to combine $2a + a + 15$ to $3a + 15$ but not being allowed to simplify $a + a + a \times 2$ to $3a \times 2$, suggesting their lack of underlying knowledge of the structure of arithmetic operations and showing their tendency to simplify in a left-to-right order (Kieran, 1979). Carry, Lewis, and Bernard (1980) have observed that students tend to overgeneralize certain mathematically valid operations, arriving at a single generic deletion operation that often produces incorrect results. Wenger (1987) has described some of the poor strategic decisions made by students with extensive algebra experience—decisions that result in their "going round in circles" while carrying out simplification transformations because they cannot seem to "see" the right things in these algebraic expressions and have no clear sense of where they are going. Thus, students may have the basics of manipulation techniques, but are often thwarted because they lack a global view of how to read an expression and of what should be done with it. Wagner, Rachlin, and Jensen (1984) have reported the incorrect tendency of pupils to convert all algebraic expressions into equations, which they in turn try to solve. This finding, as well as the related results of some other studies (e.g. Chalouh & Herscovics, 1988), has been used to suggest that looking for the value of an unknown in an equation may be more psychologically primitive for our algebra students than dealing with generalized expressions and their transformations. However, the research is not conclusive.

A second example of the use of letters to express generality and to justify one's numerical arguments is provided by the work of Chevallard and Conne (1984), whose research has involved problems such as the following:

Take three consecutive numbers. Now calculate the square of the middle one, subtract from it the product of the other two. Now do it with another three consecutive numbers. Can you explain it with numbers? Can you use algebra to explain it?

By means of such tasks, these researchers have drawn our attention to a rather subtle conceptual demand in the process of translating a numerical pattern into algebraic notation: knowing whether to use three different letters for the three consecutive numbers or just one $(x - 1, x, x + 1)$. The eighth-grade student (approximately 14 years of age), whose work is described by Chevallard and Conne, began with the three consecutive numbers 3, 4, and 5, and then 10, 11, and 12. When asked to explain what was happening, using algebra, he at first wrote $x^2 - yz = 1$, simply replacing all of his trial numbers by letters. He then realized that the use of only one letter would be better and went on to prove the rule governing this numerical relation with the expression, $x^2 - (x + 1)(x - 1)$, which he simplified to 1. Chevallard and Conne emphasized that this student, although only in the eighth grade, was one who had unusual facility with the use of algebraic representations as tools for proving mathematical relations.

A related example comes from the work of Mulligan (1989). In her algebra classes, she introduces Fibonacci-like sequences (each term is the sum of the two preceding terms, except for the first two terms which are chosen arbitrarily) as a means of showing that much of mathematics consists of making observations, looking for patterns, generalizing, and proving. She writes on the board a sequence such as 4, 7, 11, 18, 29, 47, 76, 123, 199, 322, 521, 843, 1364. She then asks her students to prove, for example, that "Given fifteen consecutive terms of a Fibonacci-like sequence, the sum of the first thirteen of them is equal to the fifteenth term minus the second term." Without the tool of algebra, the most that students could be expected to do is illustrate by means of several numerical examples. Mulligan, however, shows her beginning algebra classes how to represent the fifteen consecutive terms of the above Fibonacci-like sequence as the monomials and binomials: a, b, $a + b$, $a + 2b$, $2a + 3b$, $3a + 5b$, $5a + 8b$, $8a + 13b$, $13a + 21b$, $21a + 34b$, $34a + 55b$, $55a + 89b$, $89a + 144b$, $144a + 233b$, $233a + 377b$. They then add the first thirteen terms and compare the sum, $233a + 376b$, to the difference of the fifteenth and second terms, $(233a + 377b) - b$. The major conceptual demand of this task involves deciding what kind of algebraic representation would be most appropriate for a Fibonacci-like sequence. This requires at least being aware that the first two members of the sequence are arbitrary, in contrast to the preceding example of Chevallard and Conne, and that, from then on, successive members are the sum of the two preceding members. As was pointed out by Chevallard and Conne (1984), knowing how to represent this awareness in algebraic notation is not a trivial matter. Once the generalized notation is produced, simplification of the sum of the terms is required, followed by the relating of the algebraic result back to the goal of the problem. In other words, students must realize that as the result of both calculations is the same—$233a + 376b$, for this problem—they have proved what they set out to do.

In algebra, not only are letters used to express properties of numbers such as commutativity of addition, $a + b = b + a$, and distributivity of multiplication over addition, $a(b + c) = ab + ac$, but also to prove aspects of the structure of the number system, for example, that $\sqrt{2}$ is irrational. This usage of letters is generally reserved for more advanced mathematics rather than for introductory algebra courses. The scarce amount of research (e.g. Hanna & Winchester, 1990) that has been carried out documenting students' ability to perform algebraic proofs has, for the most part, been conducted with older, more mathematically sophisticated, students. Thus, this facet of "using algebra for proofs" is not discussed any further in this chapter.

Predicting

Working with geometric patterns is another vehicle for introducing the use of algebraic letters to express generality. In fact, many of these patterns can be recast as numerical ones. Such pattern-finding activity can serve as a basis for later discussions of functions and formulas. A typical example is the following one involving triangular numbers in the form of dots.

As an aid to finding a pattern in this arrangement of dots, students might be asked to make use of a table of values in which the first column points to a position in the sequence and the second column, the number of dots found in that position.

Triangular number (x)	Number of dots (y)
1	1
2	3
3	6
4	10

They are then requested to produce a rule—a general expression—describing this pattern in order to be able to predict, say, the number of dots in the 20th triangle. Of course, the objective could be achieved by brute force—drawing all the triangles, or including every entry in the table after having noticed that each successive entry in the right-hand column is obtained by adding the corresponding number in the left-hand column with the previous entry of the right-hand column (a recursive solution—using the previous output to generate the following output). An expert might express this recursive solution with the notation, $T_n = T_{n-1} + n$. But a non-recursive solution for such patterns, which involves finding the rule linking a left-column member with its corresponding right-column member, has been observed to be difficult for students to derive.

At this point, computer technology can be a useful supplementary tool for either obtaining the rule or generating other pairs of the same pattern—for example, a curve-fitting computer program which could be fed the input–output values of the table and which would then generate the formula corresponding to the data, or a programming language such as Logo that could be run with a recursive form of the rule and which would output the sought-for number of dots that corresponds to an input signifying the nth triangular number.

This issue begs the following question: If technology can be used to generate a formula and/or provide the solutions to questions regarding various output values, why go to the trouble of seeking the algebraic formulation? Why not let the computer do it? It is true that technology can be used as a tool to do some of the things for which we have traditionally relied upon algebra. But in order to make sense of, for example, the formula that is output by the curve-fitting program, one needs to be able to read and interpret algebraic expressions. In addition, not all schools in all countries have access to a full range of computer resources. International participants at the 1992 ICME-7 Algebra Working Group emphasized this point and stressed that non-technological algebraic methods must continue to be taught in our schools (Kieran, 1995). Of course, one could always put forward the argument that neither the computer nor algebra is necessary for the kind of activity of which the triangular numbers example is a prototype; for, once the non-recursive pattern is discovered, though not necessarily expressed in symbolic form [$T_n = n(n + 1) / 2$ or $y = x(x + 1)/2$], one can easily calculate the values of other members of this infinite pattern. In this regard, it might be sufficient to remark that, "there is a stage in the curriculum when the introduction of algebra may make simple things hard, but not teaching algebra will soon render it impossible to make hard things simple" (Tall & Thomas, 1991, p.128, cited in Mason, 1996).

In using algebra as a tool for generalizing and predicting, the following conceptual aspects are touched upon: (a) knowing that a generalization can be expressed using algebraic notation involving two letters (or variable names) signifying the rule of the relation, (b) knowing how to translate the pattern into algebraic notation, and (c) being aware that further pairs of values can be calculated by substituting numerical values for the input variable. Some of these notions are meta-algebraic in that they deal with the knowledge that algebra can be used to represent certain situations and to calculate the values of non-represented members of a pattern. Others have to do with the actual ways in which the letters of the algebraic notation are used to represent facets of the situation in question, as well as with the ways that these letters can be substituted into or manipulated.

Students find such algebraic activities difficult. Arzarello (1992) has reported on a study carried out with 10- to 16-year-olds who were presented with both the recursive and non-recursive formulas for a sequence of square numbers and were asked to generate the same for triangular numbers. The students encountered many problems with notation, for example, not knowing whether $P_{n+1} = P_n + n + 1$ and $P_n = P_{n-1} + n$ said the same thing, and, even when the pupils already knew the relation for the sum of the first n integers, not being able to "see" it in the foregoing formulas.

The functional notation itself has also proved to be an obstacle, even in simpler tasks that do not include translating a pattern into an expression of generality. One of the tasks of the second mathematics assessment of the National Assessment of Educational Progress (NAEP) (Carpenter, Corbitt, Kepner, Lindquist, & Reys, 1981) asked students to evaluate $a + 7$ when $a = 5$ and then $f(5)$ when $f(a) = a + 7$. Although nearly all students (98%) could correctly answer the first question, only 65% were successful with the second one. Such findings have also been reported by others (e.g. Markovits, Eylon, & Bruckheimer, 1986; Thomas, 1969; Vinner, 1983).

Clearly, all of this section on Expressing Generality could have been expounded in terms of functions; for all patterns can be viewed as functions. For example, the Lee and Wheeler problem, described earlier, might have been interpreted as the search for a function equivalent to $(5x + 12 - x)/4$. If students had, say, set up a table of values for the integers from 1 to 10 and calculated the values of y according to the rule presented in the task, they would have seen that all y values of the table were 3 more than the corresponding x values. But, unless the teacher had taken the time to include some work with algebraic transformations, the students would have missed the special structural insights available when carrying out the simplification of $(5x + 12 - x)/4$ to $(4x + 12)/4$ to $4(x + 3)/4$ to $x + 3$. Similarly the dot formations of triangular numbers task could have been recast as the search for a particular function, one involving the number of dots as a function of position in the sequence. However, up to now in most algebra curricula, generalization tasks have not been offered to students in a functional context. Tasks have tended to be presented as the generalization of numerical relationships rather than as the search for and use of functions (whether function be viewed as process or as object). Even though functions are ubiquitous in mathematics, the functional underpinnings of expressions of generality have usually not, up to now, been made explicit in classroom instruction. It could be argued that students are working with functions and are developing functional conceptions even if functional terminology is not being employed; however, such claims are difficult to test one way or the other. The bulk of the available research literature on expressing generality, and there is not that much, has not dealt with functional perspectives on generalization, but rather with the pattern-finding, numerical aspects discussed in this section of the chapter. Whether the next wave of research on the topic will include students' ability to cope with the added conceptual abstractions associated with the notion of function is difficult to predict.

Using Unknowns to Arrive at Problem Solutions

In addition to becoming aware of how to use letters in expressions of generality, algebra students learn how to use letters to represent unknowns. Most of the problems seen above were of the open-ended variety that involved the use of letters to represent variables that stood for a class of numbers. The focus was not on arriving at a specific numerical solution, but rather was on justifying, proving, and predicting. We now look at the use of algebraic letters as unknowns and at the corresponding activity of solving. The two major conceptual aspects involved in this perspective of algebra are translation from a usually verbal representation into an equation and solving the equation.

Translating into an Equation.

Children spend a good deal of their elementary mathematics careers in solving problems. However, they often arrive at answers spontaneously without being aware of the processes they have used to generate these answers (Booth, 1984). They almost never write an equation that represents the structural operations of the problem (Briars & Larkin, 1984). If they do write an equation, it usually represents the operations they carried out in arriving at the final answer to the problem. Usiskin (1989, p.13) has characterized the equation-generation dilemma of beginning algebra students as follows:

> Consider the following problem: "When 3 is added to 5 times a certain number the sum is 40. Find the number." . . . In solving these kinds of problems, many students have difficulty moving from arithmetic to algebra. Whereas the arithmetic solution ("in your head") involves subtracting 3 and dividing by 5 [i.e., the solving operations], the algebraic form $5x + 3$ involves multiplication by 5 and addition of 3 [i.e., using forward operations]. . . . That is, to set up the equation, you must think precisely the opposite of the way you would set it up using arithmetic.

The algebra student must then go on to find the solution by manipulating the equation with another set of simplifying operations. Lesh, Post, and Behr (1987) have pointed out that the essential difference between solving problems arithmetically and solving them algebraically is the need in algebra first to *describe* and then to *solve*. We must add that an important aspect of this conceptual demand is to describe with "forward operations" rather than with the solving operations.

Thus, one of the major obstacles in using algebra to solve problems is the translation of the verbal representation of the problem into an algebraic one. In addition to the use of forward operations, this activity also requires becoming aware of how to use a letter to represent an unknown quantity in the form of an equation that contains the unknown and other data of the problem situation. Bell, Malone, and Taylor (1987) have described some of the difficulties students encounter in this kind of activity. In their study involving three classes of 14-year-olds, they asked students to construct equations for problems such as the following (1987, p.108):

> Students were given the problem of 3 piles of rocks: *A, B, C* where *B* has 2 more than *A* and *C* has 4 times as many rocks as *A*. The total number of rocks is 14. Their task was to find the number of rocks in each pile using *x* and to do the problem in 3 "different ways"—i.e., using the *x* in three different positions.

The researchers reported that all students started with pile *A* as *x*, giving $x + 2$ and $4x$ for the other two piles. With pile *B* as *x*, students wrote $x - 2$ and $4x - 2$ for the remaining two, none using brackets for $4(x - 2)$. The resulting equation, $x - 2 + x + 4x - 2 = 14$, did not provide the same solution as before and consequently led to a discussion on the need for brackets. The researchers noted that the initial conceptual obstacle of how to express word-problem statements (e.g. "15 more than *x*") was overcome; however, the second-order difficulties, that is, treating an algebraic expression as an object (e.g. coping with "15 more than $[x - 30]$"), were less fully resolved.

Chaiklin (1989) has discussed two kinds of processes that students use in translating word problems into equations. The direct-translation approach involves a phrase-by-phrase translation of the word problem into an equation containing numbers, letters, and operations. Real-world knowledge is sometimes required to formulate these equations (e.g. knowing that the term, dimensions, refers to lengths of the sides of the problem figure); but solvers can often get by without having to use such additional knowledge. The principle-driven approach uses a mathematical principle to organize the unknown and numbers of a problem. These mathematical principles are often referred to in the literature as schemata (Mayer, 1980) (e.g. the "rowboat problem" schema includes slots for features such as rowing with or against the current, accompanied by templates for expressing these features mathematically). In general, it has been found that students have difficulty noticing structural similarities among problems with different cover stories (Reed, 1987). Often they resort to direct translation approaches and sometimes substitute various numerical values in order to verify the adequacy of their equations (Reed, Dempster, & Ettinger, 1985). They also attempt to use tables of values as an intermediate step in generating equations for problems such as the distance-rate-time variety; however they are generally unable to represent the underlying relations correctly in these tables (Hoz & Harel, 1989).

Solving the Equation

After setting up an equation to represent a problem situation, the next step is solving it. The techniques of equation solving are considered by many to be the core of algebra. Thus, considerably more research has been carried out in this area than in, say, learning to use the letters of algebra to express generality. (For a fuller treatment of the research literature on equation solving, see the algebra review by Kieran, 1992, as well as Wagner & Kieran, 1989.)

There are two main classes of conceptual demands associated with solving equations: simplifying expressions and dealing with equality-equivalence. The former demand has already been discussed in the section on Expressing Generality and will not be repeated here. When students learn to solve equations, they must cope with two significantly different kinds of equality-equivalence: (a) one is the equality of left and right sides of each equation, which is signified by the equal sign and which means that for some value(s) of x the resulting values of both sides are the same (e.g. in the equation $1 + 5x + 3 = 2x + 7$, the expression $1 + 5x + 3$ is equal to the expression $2x + 7$, when x has the value 1); and (b) the other is the equivalence of successive equations in the equation-solving chain which is implicitly conveyed by the conventional, vertical, sequential layout of the equations. This equivalence is obtained in two ways: (a) by the replacement of an *expression* by an equivalent expression (e.g. in $1 + 5x + 3 = 2x + 7$ where the left-hand expression, $1 + 5x + 3$, is replaced by the equivalent expression $5x + 4$ in order to yield $5x + 4 = 2x + 7$) or (b) by the replacement of an *equation* by an equivalent equation (i.e. one having the same solution) but not necessarily involving the replacement of an expression by an equivalent expression (e.g. $5x + 4 = 2x + 7$ being replaced by $5x + 4 - 4 = 2x + 7 - 4$). Greeno (1982) has pointed out that many algebra students are not aware of these distinctions. He also showed that they do not realize that it is only the correct solution that will yield equal values for the two sides of an equation in any equation of the equation-solving chain. Mevarech and Yitschak (1983) have reported that students have a poor understanding of the equal sign, despite their ability to solve different types of single-variable equations.

Kieran (1981, 1989) has also documented several of the misconceptions associated with learning the meaning of the equal sign in algebraic equations. In a teaching experiment carried out with 12-year-old beginning algebra students (Kieran, 1984), one particular error was detected which suggested an underlying conceptual difficulty associated with the equivalence of equations. Students who committed this error, which was called the Redistribution Error, considered that, for example, $x + 37 = 150$ had the same solution as $x + 37 - 10 = 150 + 10$, that is, that the subtraction of 10 on the left side was balanced by the addition of 10 on the right side. Interestingly, the students who committed this error were precisely those whose preferred method of equation solving at the beginning of the study was the Change Side–Change Sign method (i.e. solving $3x + 5 = 23$ by first transposing 5 to the other side and subtracting, etc.). In contrast, the students who did not commit this error were those whose preferred method of solution at the beginning of the study was trial-and-error substitution. That is, those novices who preferred to use substitution to find the value of the unknown had a better sense of "keeping an equation in balance" than those whose prealgebraic experience had led them to rely on the Change Side–Change Sign solving method. For additional research illustrating students' lack of understanding of the equivalence of equations, see Matz (1979), Lewis (1981), Kieran (1982), Sleeman (1984), Linchevski and Sfard (1991), and Steinberg, Sleeman, and Ktorza (1991).

A "Functional" Approach to Arriving at Problem Solutions

The traditional approach for handling algebra problems by first translating the question into a single-variable equation and then solving for the unknown has recently been receiving calls for replacement, or at least a new method for introducing the topic, by what is known as a "functional" approach. It is a multi-representational approach that permits arriving at problem solutions by several possible routes. One route involves setting up a functional relation involving two (or more) variables, rather than an equation containing an unknown. Solving is often carried out by substituting numerical values for the input variable until the output matches the goal value provided in the problem statement. An alternate form of this route involves setting up two functional expressions and substituting values for the input variable of both functions— often recording these in a table of values—until the output values are the same. With this route, the emphasis is on the computational process aspects of the function; the expression is viewed as a recipe for generating y values from the given x values. Another route, one that can downplay to a certain extent the computational nature of functions and emphasize their nature as objects, is that of setting up two functions and graphing them in order to find the point of intersection. Functional approaches are not new; several decades ago during the New Math movement, an attempt was made to have functions serve as one of the unifying threads of the school mathematics curriculum. What is new now is the presence of computer technology and its use in conjunction with this approach. The integration of multiple representations in the past was simply much less feasible with paper-and-pencil technology. A couple of examples of recent versions of a "functional" approach to problem solving follow.

Fey (1989) and Heid (Heid, 1988; Heid, Sheets, Matras, & Menasian, 1988) have developed a computer-intensive, functional-approach-to-problem-solving, algebra curriculum that has been tested with entire classes of first-year algebra students. It includes many different kinds of software and centres on the use of these computer tools to "develop students' understanding of algebra concepts and their ability to solve problems requiring algebra, before they master symbol manipulation techniques" (Heid et al., 1988, p.2). An adaptation of a sample problem from their curriculum and the functional approach used in presenting it to the students is the following:

> Carla is planning a one-week vacation in the Poconos with her cousin, Kate. She borrows $195 from her mother to purchase a lawn mower so that she can earn money for the trip by cutting lawns. Let's say that she decides to charge $10 per lawn.
>
> 1. Make a table charting her profit for 0, 5, 10, 15, 20, 25, and 30 lawns.
> 2. Now how many lawns must Carla mow in order to "break even"?
> 3. Write the calculations needed to compute Carla's net worth after having mowed 35 lawns.
> 4. Write a rule that explains how to calculate Carla's profit as a function of the number of lawns mowed. Profit = _____.
> 5. How many lawns does Carla have to mow in order to make a profit of $500 for her trip to the Poconos?

In the end-of-year evaluations of the project pupils, Heid (1988) found that they outperformed their counterparts from conventional classes in improvement of problem-solving abilities. It is to be noted that, in Fey and Heid's approach, the computer is not used exclusively, to the possible detriment of learning how to use algebra as a problem-solving tool. Students sometimes use curve-fitting programs to generate functional equations based on a set of data pairs, and at other times generate their own equations. The solving of these equations is, however, generally handled by symbol manipulation programs that have a Solve function. This is in contrast to the functional approach developed by Rubio (1990), which involves sequences such as the five questions above pulled from the Fey-Heid curriculum, but which does not rely on the auxiliary power of computers. After having generated a functional representation such as *Profit* = 10 × *Number of lawns mowed* − 195, students can use trial-and-error substitution methods for the variable, *Number of lawns mowed*, in order to determine the appropriate value that will yield the goal of 500 for the variable, *Profit*.

Another example of a computer-aided, functional approach to problem solving is provided by the research of Boileau, Garançon, and Kieran (Garançon, Kieran, & Boileau, 1990; Kieran, Garançon, Boileau, & Pellietier, 1988). The computer environment, *CARAPACE*, which has been developed by these researchers, requires that the student translate a problem situation into a set of functional relations involving significantly named input and output variables, operations, and constants that are entered into the computer in the form of a multi-line procedural representation. The computer then requests values for the input variable and calculates the corresponding values of the output variable(s), according to the procedural representation previously entered by the student. The initial difficulty that students appear to have with such functional approaches to problem solving is the tendency to put aside their forward-operations-based procedural representation as soon as the actual question is posed (e.g. #5 above of the Fey-Heid example) and to resort to using the kind of arithmetic "solving operations" that were pointed to by Usiskin in an earlier section of this chapter (Kieran, Boileau, & Garançon, 1989). One of the aims of this research was to use these multi-line procedural representations and significant variable names as a device for building a meaningful bridge to algebraic expressions and equations. However, it was found that once students became skilful in using this problem-solving computer environment, they felt no compulsion to shorten their procedural representations or to simplify them so that they resembled more canonical forms of algebraic expressions and equations (Wahl-Luckow, 1993). In effect, the computer tool, *CARAPACE*, replaced algebra as a problem-solving tool. This comment is not to be construed as a rebuke of the use of computer tools in problem solving, but rather as a reminder that not all technology-supported roads lead to developing meaning for traditional algebraic representations and transformations. Some of these roads lead to the creation of alternate problem-solving tools.

FUNCTIONS

By the time students traditionally begin the study of functions, after they have done the equivalent of a course in algebra, they may have already had some experience with two-variable algebraic equations, such as $y = 3x + 4$. But these equations are generally not yet interpreted as formulas that reflect change or as mappings that translate every number x into another. They are still viewed as numbers or as computational processes. The study of functions encourages students to enlarge their perspective on the expressions in these equations.

In a few instances in the preceding sections, we witnessed how beginning algebra could be recast in terms of the learning of functions, for example, how the act of producing a generalized algebraic expression could be viewed as the search for a function and also how the solving of equations could be interpreted in terms of substituting numerical values into a functional expression. In all of these instances, except perhaps for the graphing of functions in order to find a problem solution, functions were considered to be conceptualized as computational processes. To better describe what this means and how it is distinguished from conceptualizing functions as objects, we look briefly at Sfard's model of mathematical learning.

Sfard's Model

Sfard (1991) has suggested that abstract mathematical notions can be conceived in two fundamentally different ways: structurally (as objects) or operationally (as processes). She has claimed that the operational conception is, for most people, the first step in the acquisition of new mathematical notions. The transition from a "process" conception to an "object" conception is accomplished neither quickly nor without great difficulty. After they are fully developed, both conceptions are said to play important roles in mathematical activity. Sfard (1991, p.4) has contrasted the two conceptions in the following way:

> There is a deep ontological gap between operational and structural conceptions. . . Seeing a mathematical entity as an object means being capable of referring to it as if it was a real thing—a static structure, existing somewhere in space and time. It also means being able to recognize the idea "at a glance" and to manipulate it as a whole, without going into details . . . In contrast, interpreting a notion as a process implies regarding it as a potential rather than actual entity, which comes into existence upon request in a sequence of actions. Thus, whereas the structural conception is static, instantaneous, and integrative, the operational is dynamic, sequential, and detailed.

The existence of historical stages during which various mathematical concepts such as number and function evolved from operational to structural has led Sfard to create a parallel three-phase model of conceptual development. During the first phase, called interiorization, some process is performed on already familiar mathematical objects. For the concept of function, a variety of numbers can be used as input for a function machine that performs an arithmetical calculation. The idea of variable and formula can enter into play. The second phase, called condensation, is one in which the operation or process is squeezed into more manageable units. For example, the learner might refer to the process in terms of an input–output relation, rather than indicate any operations. The condensation phase lasts as long as a new entity is conceived only operationally. The third phase, reification, involves the ability to see something familiar in a new light. Whereas interiorization and condensation are lengthy sequences of gradual, quantitative rather than qualitative changes, reification seems to be a leap: a process solidifies into an object, into a static structure. The new entity is detached from the process that produced it.

Sfard has suggested (1991, p.20) that an operational conception of function might include viewing a function as a computational process, and that a structural conception might be evidenced by "proficiency in solving equations in which 'unknowns' are functions (differential and functional equations, equations with parameters), by ability to talk about general properties of different processes performed on functions (such as composition and inversion), and by ultimate recognition that computability is not a necessary characteristic of the sets of ordered pairs which are to be regarded as functions". She has also discussed various representations for functions from a structural/operational perspective (1991, p.6):

The computer program seems to correspond to an operational conception rather than to a structural, since it presents the function as a computational process, not as a unified entity. In the graphic representation, on the other hand, the infinitely many components of the function are combined into a smooth line, so they can be grasped simultaneously as an integrated whole; the graph, therefore, encourages a structural approach. The algebraic representation can easily be interpreted both ways: it may be explained operationally, as a concise description of some computation, or structurally, as a static relation between two magnitudes.

Functions as Processes versus Functions as Objects

Empirical support for the Sfard model with respect to the concept of function is derived from several studies, including her own. Sfard (1987) attempted to find out whether 16- and 18-year-olds, who were well-acquainted with the notion of function and with its formal structural definition, conceived of functions operationally or structurally. Most of the 60 students in the study were found to view functions as a process for computing one magnitude by means of another, rather than as a correspondence between two sets. In a second phase of the study involving ninety-six 14- to 17-year-olds, students were asked to translate four simple word problems into equations and also to provide verbal prescriptions for calculating the solutions to similar problems. They succeeded much better with the verbal prescriptions than with the construction of equations. This evidence suggests a predominance of operational conceptions among Sfard's algebra students. These findings also support the results of an earlier study carried out by Soloway, Lochhead, and Clement (1982) which showed that students can cope with translating a word problem into an equation when that equation is in the form of a short computer program specifying how to compute the value of one variable based on another.

When Freudenthal (1973, 1982) characterized functions, he emphasized the notion of dependency: "Our world is not a calcified relational system but a realm of change, a realm of variable objects depending on each other; functions is a special kind of dependences, that is, between variables which are distinguished as dependent and independent" (Freudenthal, 1982, p.12). Unfortunately, as Shuard and Neill (1977) have pointed out, the idea of functional dependence has been totally eliminated from the current definition of function. In almost all algebra textbooks a function is now defined as a relation between members of two sets (not necessarily numerical) or members of the same set, such that each member of the domain has only one image. Some modern definitions do include mention of a rule; however, the notion of dependency is gone. Thus, the current teaching of functions tends to emphasize more structural interpretations than those that are advocated by Freudenthal; this, however, is not the case with the computer-supported, "functional" approaches to problem solving (Kieran, 1993), which were illustrated in the previous section of this chapter.

Verstappen (1982) distinguished three categories for recording functional relations using mathematical language: (a) geometric: schemes, diagrams, histograms, graphs, drawings; (b) arithmetical: numbers, tables, ordered pairs; and (c) algebraic: letter symbols, formulas, mappings. Because functions are often introduced by means of a formal set-theoretic definition, that is, as a many-to-one correspondence between elements of a domain and range, the representations that are generally invoked are mapping diagrams, equations, and ordered pairs. These representations are then usually extended to include tables of values and Cartesian graphs.

Schwartz and Yerushalmy (1992, p.263) have recently criticized this traditional approach to introducing the various representations of functions:

1. The symbolic representation of the function is relatively more effective in making salient the nature of the function as a *process*;

2. The graphical representation of the function is relatively more effective in making salient the nature of the function as an *entity*;

3. Some operations on functions are more readily understood in the symbolic representation insofar as they appear to operate on the symbolic representation of the function (e.g., composition);

4. Some operations on functions are more readily understood in the graphical representation insofar as they appear to operate on the graphical representation of the function (e.g., translation). [Emphasis added.]

This means that, according to Schwartz and Yerushalmy, the symbolic representation of a function allows students to evaluate and substitute, and thereby focus on the process nature of function; the graphical representation, subject to certain graphing constraints, projects a certain characteristic of an object, its shape. They add that operating on a function can involve the manipulation of certain characteristics of its symbolic representation, such as coefficients or exponents, or certain characteristics of its graphical representation, such as translation, dilation and contraction, and reflection. Schwartz and Yerushalmy (1992, p.288) have emphasized that, "rather than starting, as we normally do, with particular functions expressed symbolically, and then, almost as an afterthought, turning to the graphs of those functions, we turn from the outset to particular functions expressed both symbolically and graphically."

In discussing the operations one can carry out on the graphical representations of functions, Schwartz and Yerushalmy have pointed to translation, dilation, and so on. In this context, I believe that it is important to mention that the transformations one carries out on graphical representations can also involve working with the parametric representations of families of functions. But these letters are different in kind from the letters already discussed in this chapter. They are, in fact, a second level of usage, as compared with the first-level usage involved in expressing generality and in representing unknowns. Sfard's model (1991) suggests that students can benefit from experience with the letters of algebra that represent the first-level variables of a situation prior to being introduced to the second-level usage of letters as parameters. This prior experience with the process aspects of functions (such as are found in activities focusing on the exploration of numerical/geometrical patterns and the representation of these general patterns by expressions such as $y = 3x + 4$ or $f(x) = 3x + 4$, as well as the use of input–output approaches for solving problems) is also important for reification which involves working with these aspects, but from above. In all of these early functional activities, the emphasis is usually placed on numerical interpretations rather than on the relationship itself and on the aspect of change.

But, when students begin to explore the effects on the graph of the function $f(x) = ax^2 + bx + c$ by varying the values of a, b, and c, they are no longer working with variables of the functions $f(x)$, but, as Goldenberg (1988) has pointed out, are studying some function-valued function $f_i(a, b, c)$ whose variables are a, b, and c, and whose value is the function represented in a graphical way. Thus, a not-so-subtle shift occurs when algebra is used as a tool for studying the overall behaviour of functions and of families of functions. The object of study is no longer number but relationships. At this point, certain features of the symbolic functional representation take on new significance. The new objects of attention are the parameters—now represented by letters. Before they were numbers that were held constant while the xs and ys varied. In addition, the form of the expression becomes a carrier of new information concerning the type of function or relation—linear, quadratic, and so on. Translation from verbal or display representations to symbolic ones moves to the background while translations between graphical and symbolic representations move to the foreground.

Past research has shown that the learning of Cartesian graphs and the integration of symbolic and graphical representations of functions can present many difficulties to students (e.g. Bell & Janvier, 1981; Clement, 1985; Herscovics, 1989; Kerslake, 1977, 1981; Leinhardt, Zaslavsky, & Stein, 1990; Ponte, 1984; Swan 1982). It must be noted, however, that many of these studies were conducted with students who had been taught mathematics without the support of computer technology and involved research tasks that did not include such technology. For example, Kerslake gave the 13-, 14-, and 15-year-olds of the Concepts in School Mathematics and Science (CSMS) assessment a task that required describing which of a set of given graphs represented journeys. Only 14% of the 13-year-olds and 25% of the 15-year-olds succeeded—despite extensive classroom experience with travel graphs. Many confused the graph with a "picture" of the situation. (See also the classic race-track example of Janvier, 1978.) Kerslake found evidence to suggest that graphs related to real-world situations are no easier for students to interpret than graphs that are related merely to symbolic decontextualized equations. In addition, many students seemed unable to relate numerical data to the coordinate points and axes of a Cartesian plane. Further indication of students' difficulties with graphs is provided by another British study, the Assessment of Performance Unit (1980), which tested a random sample of 14,000 sixteen-year-olds. This study reported that only 22% of its sample responded correctly to the question, "Which one of the following could be the graph of $y = (x - 1)(x + 4)$?" and only 9%, to the question, "The graph shown is a representation of the function $f(x)$ where $f(x) = x(a - x)$, what is the numerical value of a?".

It has been claimed that the computer and graphing calculator have great potential to help develop student understanding in this area by providing experience in drawing families of curves on the same set of axes, as well as the opportunity to discover not only what parameters are but also the effects of changing them (e.g. Dreyfus & Halevi, 1988; Kaput, 1989; Waits & Demana, 1988). However, computer graphing programs and the graphing calculator are not to be viewed simply as instructional panaceas. As shown by the research of Schoenfeld, Smith, and Arcavi (1993), who described in detail the learning of their case-study subject in the computer-graphing environment *GRAPHER*, and by the related research of Moschkovich (1990), who observed two classes of ninth and tenth graders using not only graphing calculators but also *Superplot* and *Green Globs*, technology-enhanced learning environments do not of themselves help students decide which features of lines or equations are the relevant ones to focus on nor how to describe their observations or conclusions. In addition, Goldenberg (1988) has drawn our attention to some of the perceptual illusions experienced by students and to the potential for misinterpretation of computer-generated Cartesian graphs. It has also been reported by, for example, Mundy (1984), Dreyfus and Eisenberg (1987), Dick (1988), and Vinner (1989) that students have a strong tendency to think of functions symbolically rather than visually; moreover, this is so even if they are explicitly pushed towards visual processing. Sfard's model provides historical and epistemological explanations for the seeming preference of students for process-oriented, symbolic representations rather than the object-oriented, visual, structural representations.

One final example of a study dealing with some of the issues associated with process–object distinctions is that of Moschkovich, Schoenfeld, and Arcavi (1993). These researchers worked with a group of eighth graders who had already had an introduction to the use of algebraic letters and methods. Their aim was to uncover aspects of understanding of linear relations that correspond to the ability to move flexibly between the process and object perspectives in a variety of computer-aided representations (symbolic, tabular, and graphical). The first part of their study focused on a sequence of activities designed to have students become familiar with the object perspective; the second part, on flexibility in moving between representations. Their data (1993, p.25) showed that:

> Coming to grips with the object perspective takes time. Being able to think of functions of the form $y = mx + b$ as members of a two-parameter family in which the parameters m and b: (a) are independent, (b) determine the position of a line graphically, and (c) each "move" the graph of a line in particular ways as they are varied, requires making a lot of connections.

And they repeat in their conclusions (*ibid.*, p.37) that "coming to grips with parametrization is not easy regardless of the visual assistance that computer-based technology can offer."

Sfard (1992, p.77) has emphasized that a lengthy period of experience is required before operational conceptions can be transformed into structural ones. When students are pushed too quickly to understand an object perspective, pseudostructural knowledge can result:

> Pseudostructural conceptions can hardly be avoided within the structural way of teaching. The data suggest that the idea of function as a "thing," when introduced too early, is doomed to remain beyond the comprehension of many students. In such cases, the object-oriented language used by the teacher forces the pupil to look for a more tangible entity which may serve as a reasonable substitute. Being the most natural choice, the signs on a paper turn into the thing they were only meant to symbolize. The signifier becomes the signified.

CONCLUSIONS

In this chapter, we have seen how the traditional approach to teaching secondary school mathematics has been one involving the separation of the study of algebra from the study of functions. This separation has been based chiefly on the distinctions between the ways that letters are viewed in the two subject areas and on the emphasis on equality in one and on change in the other.

The first use of letters that was elaborated in this chapter was that of *expressing generality* and then using these general expressions to justify, prove, or predict. An example that illustrates students' ability to handle such algebraic activity was taken from Lee and Wheeler (1987), who reported that students experienced difficulty in translating a generalizable numerical relation into algebraic symbolism and in using that algebraic expression to justify their numerical arguments. Another example, one that emphasized the problems associated with translating a pattern into symbolic notation, was the study carried out by Arzarello (1992) on generalizing and predicting. The findings of these and other studies have shown that students do not use algebra as a mathematical tool. Nevertheless, students can be fairly competent, technically speaking; that is, they can juggle the algebraic symbols fairly well. This finding of technical ability with respect to simplifying expressions, which has also been noted in several other studies of students who have already gone through the processes of initial learning, must be tempered, however, with the oft-cited observation that students lack a global view of how the letters might be interpreted in these algebraic expressions.

The second use of letters that was discussed was that of using *unknowns* to arrive at problem solutions. This use involved, first, the activity of translating a situation into an equation and, then, solving the equation. The research examples that were presented were highly suggestive of the typical difficulties experienced by students in translating problem situations into equations. Because students have generally had considerably more experience with solving equations than with translating problems into equations and because there is a kind of routine to follow in solving equations, as opposed to the activity of translating situations into equations, they have been found to be relatively more skilled in this area. However, despite their seeming technical expertise, they are unable to provide mathematical justifications of their technical moves in terms of, say, equivalence constraints or properties of equality.

The discussion of Sfard's model sensitized us to a distinction in the study of functions that is even finer than the differentiations one might make between algebra and functions—that of distinguishing between process and object aspects. According to her mathematical learning model, process-oriented, operational conceptions develop before object-oriented, structural conceptions. For the case of functions process-oriented approaches involve working with computational rules; object-oriented approaches for introductory courses tend to involve working with graphical representations, accompanied at a certain point by the corresponding symbolic representations containing parameters. It was noted that there are some research projects now in progress that are attempting, with the help of computer technology, to orient the teaching of algebra around the concept of function. Some of these new endeavours are integrating both process and object interpretations of functions and their various representations right from the outset of the high-school algebra course. It is not yet clear how successful such functional approaches will be not only at including all of the aspects that are usually associated with algebra, in addition to the full complement of functional perspectives, but also in tying both together. Nevertheless, it is hoped that the results of these current projects may help us to better understand whether there are indeed cognitive advantages to be gained from meshing the learning of functions with the learning of algebra.

What is clear from past research is that the traditional curricular separation of algebra and functions has not provided the majority of our students with a strong conceptual base for the various possible interpretations of algebraic notation. As we have seen from the introductory remarks in this chapter, an algebraic expression can be conceived in many possible ways; however, the promotion of flexibility in moving back and forth between these various perspectives has never appeared to be a hallmark of algebra teaching. With the advent of technology, the question is often heard these days about the amount of time that should be devoted to practising by-hand symbol-manipulation techniques. There are those who advocate maintaining technical practice at the level that is currently found in many traditional algebra programs because they believe that practice with symbol manipulation leads to conceptual understanding of these symbols. But what kind of conceptual understanding? Past instruction has been rather remiss in providing conceptual underpinnings for the symbols of algebra. Very often, the only emphasis has been on equations and equation solving; even the use of letters for expressing generality in order to justify, prove, or predict has been sorely neglected. Those who would attempt to give more meaning to the symbols of algebra by using the concept of function as a unifying thread have the potential in their instruction to endow these symbols with a sense that has heretofore been absent.

ACKNOWLEDGEMENTS

The author acknowledges the support of the Social Sciences and Humanities Research Council of Canada, Grant #410-90-1041, and of the Quebec Ministry of Education, FCAR Grant #92-ER-1207. Any opinions, findings, conclusions, or recommendations expressed herein are those of the author and do not necessarily reflect the views of the Social Sciences and Humanities Research Council of Canada or the Quebec Ministry of Education.

III SOCIAL AND CULTURAL INFLUENCES ON MATHEMATICS LEARNING

For a long time in psychological and educational studies there has been a separation between the study of cognition and intelligence, on the one hand, and social psychology and sociology, on the other. This separation has provoked uneasiness but nevertheless has been quite entrenched in the academic disciplines. However, in the last two decades, greater integration has been progressively observed both in theory and in research. The study of mathematical knowledge has proven to be a most fertile ground for these developments. But why should that be so, if mathematics was in the past taken as an exact science expressing universal and undeniable truths?

There are at least three strands of events which can be seen as making mathematics a good domain for the study of "culture and cognition". The first concerned the efforts of international agencies to improve mathematics teaching in a variety of poor countries under the expectation that improving mathematics education and literacy would promote economic development. Many failures in the implementations of the educational programmes designed by the richer for the poorer nations inevitably led to the search for explanations for the difficulties encountered. Diverse explanations emerged in this context, and one of them, the idea of cultural conflict, became an important precursor to the studies of cultural influences on mathematics learning. In the course of the debates about the causes of these failures, Gay and Cole (1967) produced a book which has become a landmark for the studies of cultural influences on mathematics learning, *The new mathematics and an old culture*. In their introduction to the book, the series editors (p.xi) say:

> This remarkable study does what is so often recommended but so rarely accomplished. It demonstrates specifically how a traditional culture affects the learning readiness, indeed the very thinking, of children . . . Children are decisively influenced by the culture of their home and nonschool community. The teacher must identify this culture and understand how it has moulded the child's thinking and affected his (or her) ability to learn, then devise effective strategies of instruction in the light of this understanding. Although the problem is most dramatic in situations like that of the Kpelle, the same conditions influence learning and teaching in every place where the culture of the teacher and the school is different from the culture of the student.

Gay and Cole did in fact accomplish a remarkable shift in the way that the question was analysed: instead of simply asking the question "Why don't the Kpelle learn our mathematics?" they asked the question "What is mathematics among the Kpelle like?". This shift opened the way for studies that consider mathematics as a cultural practice and analyse the activities encompassed in these practices, the resources used, and the assumptions made about what the role of mathematics is in the activities.

A second set of educational issues that led to socio-cultural analyses of mathematics learning relates to the problem of selective school failure observed in a large number of countries. Studies of success in school and staying on after compulsory education suggested that, instead of realising the ideal of equality which was at the basis of the fight for education for all, schools were in fact reproducing the class divisions in society: the working-class pupils were on the whole less successful and stayed on after compulsory education much less often than their peers from the middle and upper class. Just as when the issue was differential success in learning across nations, the relationship between school success and socio-economic status became the focus of much investigation and debate. Among other sorts of explanation, the hypothesis of cultural conflict was viewed as a plausible one. Researchers became aware that cultural practices are not defined in terms of national boundaries but rather in terms of groups or communities with particular identities. Different mathematical practices may coexist even within the same community for different groups. Thus a plausible explanation for the relationship between socio-economic status and school failure was that the culture of the teacher and that of the pupil were mismatched, even though they were part of the same nation.

The convergence of questions and approaches to the study of social and cultural effects on the learning of mathematics has been a healthy influence: the cultural nature of mathematics is much more clearly recognised, the role of cultural inventions in structuring and enabling reasoning is analysed, and differences across groups seem to be better understood. The four chapters in this section examine these issues from different standpoints.

Hatano investigates the cognitive mechanisms associated with the over-learning of a particular way of doing arithmetic. The studies that he reports offer many surprising findings about abacus grand masters: an unbelievable memory for digits and the ability to calculate at speeds that are quite incomprehensible to those of us who rely on oral or written algorithms. The results that he reviews about interference with calculation are also significant: whereas we, who don't use the abacus, suffer tremendous interference with our calculation process if someone speaks to us and we are requested to respond, abacus grand masters can answer simple questions and be completely undisturbed. These results demonstrate the power of the cultural tool, the abacus, in shaping the mental processes used during calculation.

Ginsburg also approaches the question of cultural practices and their influences on children but from a different standpoint: what do the informal, everyday experiences of children contribute to their later knowledge of mathematics and how much might they vary across countries? His work increases our awareness of the simple fact that children have learned quite a lot about mathematics before they enter school, and that this learning should be taken into account when we design teaching approaches.

Schubauer-Leoni and Perret-Clermont raise yet another aspect of the socio-cultural aspects of mathematics learning: any learning or testing event that takes place in school is a social event. For this reason, social factors cannot be ignored in our analysis of the way, how much, and why children react as they do in the course of testing or learning activities. Their historical approach to their own thinking and the sorts of questions that have occupied researchers interested in social influences on learning offer the reader a broad view of issues, methods, and findings.

Finally, the work by de Abreu and her colleagues brings a rather important idea about learning in general to bear on the idea of learning mathematics in particular: schools don't just impart knowledge to pupils; they validate specific forms of knowledge, give them a higher level of prestige, and give a new identity to those who come to master school knowledge. Those who succeed can become teachers, doctors, managers, dentists etc. Learning, therefore, is not a mere cognitive activity; it is an identity-giving activity. Pupils seem to recognise these social implications of learning more and more as they advance in their school career. And those who are exposed to different forms of knowledge owned by different sorts of people are faced with difficult choices, even if these choices are made implicitly. On the one hand, there is school arithmetic, which is not very practical for everyday life and is taught slowly so that what one learns in school might not catch up quickly enough with what one needs to know in life. On the other hand, there is a form of mathematics, learned outside school, which remains invisible to teachers. It leads to correct answers but does not receive validation in the classroom. What can the pupils do to use their unofficial knowledge of mathematics? And what can teachers do to build and develop this knowledge so that pupils' skills are not wasted but rather brought to fruition through their school experiences?

The chapters in this section illustrate the importance of recognising the role of social and cultural influences for mathematics learning. They also make it clear that, although we have clear evidence for these influences, much more is still needed both in terms of research and policies for the school system.

8

Happy Birthday to You: Early Mathematical Thinking of Asian, South American, and U.S. Children

Herbert P. Ginsburg, Y. Elsie Choi, Luz Stella Lopez, Rebecca Netley, and Chi Chao-Yuan
Teachers College, Columbia University, USA

INTRODUCTION

In this chapter we begin with the fact that key groups—nations, social classes, "races"—differ dramatically in school mathematics achievement. But the origins of these differences are unclear. Mere membership in a group does not in itself cause individuals' behaviour. Intervening processes or activities must mediate between group membership and the resulting performance. To explain group differences in school mathematics achievement, previous research has highlighted motivation, education, and "intelligence". We explore a different possible mediator, namely informal mathematical thinking.

National, Ethnic, and Class Differences in Mathematical Achievement

According to recent international comparisons, children from various Asian countries exhibit superior mathematics performance. For example, within the first few grades of elementary school, Chinese and Japanese children outperform Americans on standard tests of mathematics achievement (McKnight, et al., 1987; Stevenson, Lummis, Lee, & Stigler, 1990). Indeed, Stevenson, Lee, and Stigler (1986) claim that Japanese children outperform Americans even at the kindergarten level, although Chinese (from Taiwan) and American kindergarten performance is about the same.

Group differences other than those involving nationality are equally dramatic. School achievement varies by "race" within the U.S. In general,

163

African-American and Hispanic children eventually do poorly in school mathematics and science (Natriello, McDill, & Pallas, 1990; Oakes, 1990); Asian-American children do extremely well (Arbeiter, 1984); and White children fall in between the two extremes (National Center for Education Statistics, 1990).

Another pervasive achievement difference in many countries involves social class. For example, in the U.S., poor children, as a group, generally perform less adequately in school than do more affluent children (Natriello, McDill, & Pallas, 1990; Oakes, 1990). In this regard, Asian-Americans are something of an anomaly: their relative lack of income does not seem to detract from their school performance (e.g. Bempechat, Nakkula, Wu, & Ginsburg, 1993).

One must employ caution in describing group differences in terms of race and class. For one thing, the concept of "race" is misleading. In the U.S., for example, many of those previously called "Black" (and now called "African-American") are in fact racially mixed in various proportions. Because race is more cultural phenomenon than biological fact, we substitute "ethnicity" for "race".

Similarly ambiguous is the concept of social class: this has been variously defined in terms of criteria as disparate as education, income level, and disadvantage. The lower class of one study is not necessarily the same as that in another. Furthermore, it is difficult to equate class in different countries. Is the lower class in Korea equivalent to the lower class in the U.S?

To complicate matters further, race is often confounded with social class. In many countries, persons of "colour" tend also to be poorer than the dominant population. In the U.S., African-Americans and Hispanics are poorer and less well educated than Whites and hence are at especially high risk for school failure (McLloyd, 1990), although there are of course exceptions, as in the case of Cuban-Americans, who are relatively affluent. This situation is not limited to the U.S. In a country like Colombia, the indigenous Indian groups are poorer than the dominant Hispanic population. Therefore, it is often hard to know whether an observed group difference is related to race or class.

Explanations of Group Achievement Differences

Even if it is clear that a group difference is clearly associated with nationality, ethnicity, or class, the explanation must involve more than group membership. To say that Japanese calculate well because they are Japanese is not informative. Theorists have therefore proposed that several types of intervening processes might account for the observed group differences.

To explain Asians' superior mathematics achievement, one body of research has focused on motivational explanations, including parents' high expectations for their children, and parents' beliefs in the importance of effort rather than inherent ability in producing academic success (Stevenson, Lummis, Lee, & Stigler, 1990).

Others have focused on the role of schools. Kozol (1991) observes that the "savage inequalities" of American education serve to place poor children and particularly African-Americans and Hispanics, at considerable disadvantage in the pursuit of educational success. Stigler and Perry (1988) and Stigler (1988) demonstrate that Asian teachers tend to explain mathematics subject matter in more depth and place a greater stress on thinking and understanding than do American teachers. And McKnight et al. (1987) stress the negative contribution of the "unfocused mathematics curriculum" characteristic of the U.S.

Little attention has been devoted to key intellectual factors that might contribute both to the success of some groups and to the failure of others. Among the few available studies are those of Lynn (1982) and Lynn and Hampson (1987), who have claimed that achievement differences between Asians and Americans can be attributed to inherited general "intelligence", as measured by IQ tests. But Stevenson and Azuma (1983) have argued that severe methodological flaws (e.g. non-equivalent tests and non-comparable samples of children) render these data difficult to interpret. (Indeed, we would add that it is virtually impossible to construct equivalent IQ tests across cultures, and in any event IQ measures fail to yield information useful for understanding the processes underlying performance in particular academic subject matter areas.) Furthermore, Stevenson, Stigler, Lee, and Lucker (1985) have provided data showing that at the first and fifth grade levels (mean ages 6.8 and 10.9 years) there are no overall, systematic differences in such specific aspects of cognitive functioning as verbal memory, spatial relations, perceptual speed, general information, and the like, in Japanese, Chinese, and American children. (One exception to this is in the area of rote memory, where Chinese children show superior digit span for numbers, but do not have superior serial memory for words. Stigler, Lee, and Stevenson, 1986, report a similar result.) Sue and Okazaki (1990, p.915) conclude that ". . . the hypothesis that Asians are genetically superior in intelligence would appear to be refuted by empirical data."

Informal Mathematical Knowledge

But could not other intellectual factors be involved? This chapter examines the possibility that groups may differ on what we consider to be a basic aspect of intellectual functioning, namely "informal mathematical knowledge". In recent years, considerable research has been conducted on the development of mathematical thinking from infancy (e.g. Starkey, Spelke, & Gelman, 1990) through the college years (e.g. Schoenfeld, 1985). One striking theme that has emerged is that "informal" mathematical thinking develops in robust fashion before the onset of schooling (Klein & Starkey, 1988; Gelman & Gailistel, 1978; Ginsburg, 1989). For example, by the age of 5 years, children develop basic concepts of addition (Carpenter, Moser, & Romberg, 1982); more and less (Binet, 1969); and counting (Fuson, 1988). Much of this informal mathematics can develop in the absence of adult instruction; indeed, many adults are quite surprised to learn how much their young children or students know in this area.

Current theories stress the central role of informal knowledge in development of mathematical understanding. These theories conceptualize understanding in terms of the linkages among various areas of knowledge, especially between informal or intuitive ideas and the formal symbolism introduced in school (Ginsburg et al., 1992b). Another way of putting it is that the child's informal mathematics represents a kind of intellectual potential, a solid structure on which to build formal, school learning (Baroody, 1987; Ginsburg, 1989; Hughes, 1986). In this volume, de Abreu, Bishop, and Pompeu show how teachers can fruitfully employ the informal mathematical culture of the home to enrich the school curriculum. Conversely, if informal mathematics is deficient, then the foundation for school learning may be shaky and unreliable and may inhibit achievement.

Consider a hypothetical example. In school, it is common for children to produce absurd statements like $42-9 = 47$, on the basis of the following reasoning: "You can't subtract 9 from 2 because 2 is smaller than 9; you have to do 9–2, which gives you the 7 in 47." At the same time, most children know very well that when one subtracts *things*, the result is smaller than what one started with. If only the children were to draw on their informal knowledge, they might have a sensible basis for checking the calculations and understanding the meaning of subtraction. And conversely, if the children did not possess the informal knowledge, then it would be hard for them to understand that a mistake had been made.

We see then that informal mathematics *can* be a useful foundation for mathematics learning in school and that deficiencies in informal knowledge may interfere with schooling. At the same time, one must recognize that the possession of adequate informal mathematical knowledge does not necessarily guarantee school success, because formal education often fails to exploit the potential of informal knowledge. Many schools train children in little more than mechanical mastery of algorithmic procedures necessary for success on achievement tests and do not help them to understand the material in any depth. Because it is presented in isolation from informal knowledge, the mathematics becomes for many children an abstract game with little meaning. In view of the potential importance of informal knowledge for later education, this chapter focuses on its emergence in key groups of preschool children.

National Differences in Informal Mathematics

One hypothesis is that Asians enter school with superior informal mathematical abilities in such areas as counting, concrete and mental addition, concepts of more and less, and the like. This informal mathematics might then provide Asian children with a superior foundation for learning what is later taught (perhaps more effectively) in school.

One line of research supporting this hypothesis relates to Asian counting systems. Miller and Stigler (1987) have found that the counting numbers are easier to learn in Chinese than in English, at least partly because of the more regular and systematic nature of the Chinese system. This system, learned of course before entrance to school, encodes all numbers in a regular fashion, using the base ten system. Thus, the number 13 is said as "ten-three," the number 21 as "two-ten-one," and the like. Facility in counting should be useful in learning arithmetic generally, particularly because many children rely on counting as the basis for addition and other arithmetic operations (Ginsburg, 1989). It is interesting to note that Spanish counting too has several irregular features, particularly the numbers from 11 to 15.

Miura and her colleagues elaborate on this view, suggesting that not only Chinese, but also speakers of several Asian languages, including Japanese and Korean, benefit from the transparent base-ten structure of their counting systems (Miura, 1987; Miura, Kim, Chang & Okamoto, 1988; Miura & Okamoto, 1989). According to Miura, the Chinese and related systems allow Asian school children to appreciate more easily than do English-speaking Americans the base-ten structure underlying the written numbers and the algorithms used for calculation. In brief, Asians' systematic and organized counting language permits an advanced understanding of the base-ten system, which in turn might contribute in important ways to mastery of school mathematics. In indirect support of this notion, Miura (1987) notes that Asian-American high school students who report that "English is not my best language" received higher SAT scores than those reporting proficiency in English. (See also Fuson & Kwon, 1992.)

Other research argues against the hypothesis of Asian superiority in informal mathematics. The general finding of cross-cultural research (Klein & Starkey, 1988) is that children from various cultures, literate and pre-literate, rich and poor, of various racial backgrounds, all display evidence of relatively powerful informal mathematical abilities, although these are expressed in culturally specific and appropriate ways (Stigler & Baranes, 1988). For example, unschooled African children display strategies of addition similar to those of American children (Ginsburg, Posner, & Russell, 1981). In selling goods on the street, largely unschooled children in Brazil develop sophisticated and effective means for mental calculation (Carraher, Schliemann, & Carraher, 1988b).

In what is apparently the only study of Asian preschoolers' mathematical abilities, Song and Ginsburg (1987) demonstrated that Korean preschoolers score slightly more poorly than do Americans on a test of early mathematical knowledge. Yet by the first or second grade, the Korean disadvantage disappears and their performance surpasses Americans'. The writers interpret the result as showing that Koreans do not begin with an intellectual "head start"; their later school success must be attributed to other factors including schooling, academic socialization, and motivation.

Although this may be a reasonable hypothesis, the Song and Ginsburg results are not conclusive. Their method involved a standard test developed for American children (Ginsburg & Baroody, 1983), and may not have been fully appropriate for Koreans. Hence, the present study uses a more sensitive methodology to investigate Chinese, Japanese, and Korean preschool children's early mathematics abilities.

Several researchers have conducted important investigations of the mathematical abilities of school-age children in South America. For example, Carraher, Schliemann, and Carraher (1988b) and Saxe (1988) have shown that Brazilian children of school age exhibit some remarkable mathematical competencies in the context of everyday activities like candy selling. But little information seems to be available concerning the mathematical abilities of other South American children, particularly at the preschool level. Consequently, the present study compares Asian (China, Japan, and Korea), U.S., and South American (Colombia) preschool children on key aspects of basic mathematical thinking.

Ethnic and Social Class Differences in Informal Mathematics

Several studies have examined the relations between ethnicity and social class, and early mathematical abilities. For many years, the dominant theory held that poor children, and particularly inner city African-Americans, suffered from an environmental deprivation causing a cognitive deficit that in turn produced a lack of ability to profit from schooling. Recently, the "cognitive deficit" theory has been challenged by the view that children from different social class, racial, and ethnic groups share basic cognitive competencies but express them in diverse ways depending on local environmental and cultural conditions. According to this view, motivational factors and belief systems play a greater role in determining children's academic performance than do basic intellectual factors (Neisser, 1986).

Several studies have been conducted to examine informal mathematical thinking in lower-class, African-American, and Hispanic preschool children. Kirk, Hunt, and Volkmar (1975) examined several aspects of enumeration (e.g. producing sets of a given number; counting a set of blocks) in African-American and White children, some lower socio-economic status (SES) and others middle-class nursery school children, probably all White, in a small town. The results showed that lower-SES children, both African-American and White, performed at a significantly lower level than middle-class children. One problem with this study, however, is that the testing procedures appear to have been somewhat rigid and therefore may not have been maximally effective in eliciting children's competence.

Ginsburg and Russell (1981) studied several aspects of mathematical thinking in 4- and 5-year-old children, African-American and White, middle- and lower-class, in two urban areas. Tasks included perception of more, conservation of number, counting words, addition, enumeration, and adding and writing of numbers. The findings showed very few differences associated with race (holding SES constant). There were a few statistically significant social class differences, generally favouring the middle-class, but they were generally not large. Ginsburg and Russell state (1981, pp.51–52): "In the vast majority of cases, children of both social classes demonstrated basic competence on the various tasks and similar strategies for solving them. . . At the age levels studied, it is lower class competence that needs explaining, not lower-class deficiency."

Hughes (1986) reported differences in concrete addition between middle- and lower-class British children at 4 and 5 years of age. Although the differences were relatively large, with lower-class children performing about a year behind their middle-class peers, Hughes takes pains (p.34) to point out that lower-class children ". . . still possessed important abilities. . ."

Saxe, Guberman, and Gearhart (1987) investigated early mathematical thinking in 4-year-old white children, both working- and middle-class. Using some tasks deriving from the Ginsburg and Russell research, the study found no differences between middle- and working-class children's ability to recite the counting words, their ability to read numerals, their comparison of number words (e.g. which number is bigger, x or y?), or their counting accuracy. The researchers did find that middle-class children achieved superior scores on tasks involving cardinality (knowledge that the last number counted signifies the set's value) and addition and subtraction.

Entwisle and Alexander (1990) found that African-American and White 6-year-olds did not differ significantly on computational skills as measured by the California Achievement Test (CAT) at the time of beginning first grade. On a "math concepts" subtest of the CAT (1990, p.455) , ". . . white children's scores exceeded those of blacks by a small but significant margin. . .". More important than racial differences, however, are effects of social class. According to Entwisle and Alexander (1990, p.465), "although minority–majority differences in children's math skills are small or absent . . . we find parents' economic resources to be a potent influence on children's premath skills and these resources strongly favour whites."

Starkey and Klein (1991, p.440) studied the early mathematical abilities of African-American, Caucasian, and Hispanic 4-year-olds from ". . . lower SES (impoverished-working poor and underclass. . .) and higher SES (middle and upper class) families. . ." The results showed no significant ethnic differences, but strong SES differences favouring the higher-SES children. The tasks included counting objects, conservation, concrete addition and subtraction, and comparison of spoken numbers (e.g. "Which is bigger, three or four?"). The differences found by Starkey and Klein were larger in magnitude (quite apart from statistical significance) than those noted by other investigators. The authors' explanation is that their lower SES subjects were more severely impoverished, some even being members of the "underclass," than those of other investigators. At the same time, Starkey and Klein propose (p.446) that ". . . the mathematical abilities of low SES preschoolers are quantitatively but not qualitatively different than those of middle SES children . . ."

Jordan, Huttenlocher, and Levine (1992) studied low- and middle-income kindergarten children's performance on various addition and subtraction tasks. Most of the low-income children were African-American and most of the middle-income children were White. The general finding was that both groups performed at equivalent levels on non-verbal tasks but did differ on verbal tasks, with middle-income children exhibiting superior performance. The results also showed that both groups performed well on enumeration and cardinality tasks (although there was a statistically significant but small [4.5 vs. 4.9 out of a possible 5] difference favouring the middle-income children).

In sum, the bulk of the evidence indicates that proficiency in early mathematical thinking may be associated to some degree with income level but not ethnicity. All of the authors cited concur that differences between African-Americans and Whites in this area appear to be of little significance. One exception may be Entwisle and Alexander's (1990) finding that African-Americans and Whites receive similar scores on calculational tasks, but Whites perform better than African-Americans on a test of "concepts". The only available study concerning Hispanics (Starkey & Klein, 1991) suggests that with class held constant they do not differ significantly from African-Americans and Whites.

Although ethnicity does not appear to be an important factor in this area, there is some disagreement about the nature and extent of class differences. For example, Jordan et al. find no social class difference on a concrete addition task, while Starkey and Klein do. Jordan et al. find that middle-class children do better than lower-class children on a verbal addition task. And in general, Saxe et al., Hughes, and Kirk et al. tend to find more SES differences than do Ginsburg and Russell.

To some extent, disagreements among the studies may result from differences in the poverty levels of the samples, as Starkey and Klein suggest. The studies use different operational definitions of social class. To some extent, disagreements among the studies may result from differences in methodology, with some tasks being more sensitive to the capabilities of lower-class children, as Ginsburg and Russell suggest. And to some extent, disagreements among the studies may result from differences in theoretical focus and therefore in the nature of the particular tasks involved. Our conjecture is that although middle- and lower-class children may differ in some aspects of mathematical thinking, it is unlikely that lower-class children lack completely the relevant concepts and procedures fundamental to informal mathematics. Clearly more data are required to examine the nature and extent of possible social class differences in informal arithmetic.

Within the U.S., there is one group of children, often poor, who nevertheless seem to perform exceptionally well in school, namely Asian-Americans. How do these children surmount their poverty and exposure to poor schooling? Many explanations focus on motivational factors (like the tendency to attribute school success more to effort than to ability), general beliefs or world view, academic socialization, and the like (Ginsburg, Bempechat, & Chung, 1992a; Mordkowitz & Ginsburg, 1987). These explanations do not raise the possibility that Asian-American children succeed in school because of an advantage in basic cognitive ability. Yet again, we have little empirical information on this matter, particularly as regards the mathematical abilities of young children.

In view of the paucity of evidence concerning some ethnic groups, particularly Hispanics and Asian-Americans, and the disagreement about the nature and extent of social class differences, the present study investigates early mathematical ability in African-American, Asian-American, Hispanic, and White children, from both middle and lower social class groups. To provide a wider perspective, the study also examines social class differences in children from Korea, and from Colombia, where such differences are extreme.

The Role of Instruction

The study also investigated the role of school instruction in early mathematical ability. We know that informal mathematical thinking can develop without instruction. But what happens with it? To what extent can informal mathematics be accelerated by instruction? Because we were not aware of any research on this topic, we compared Chinese preschool children receiving intensive mathematics instruction in their daycare settings with Chinese peers receiving none.

THE PRESENT STUDY

For all of the reasons given in the introduction, we designed a study focusing on 4-year-olds from several social class groups within the U.S., schooled and unschooled Chinese children from families of factory workers and government officials, middle-class Japanese children, and several social class groups from Colombia and Korea. The study attempts to conduct a sensitive assessment of children's mathematical knowledge. One important lesson of cross-cultural research and of the Piagetian tradition is that sensitive research methods must be employed to uncover intellectual competence. Poor performance may result more from the researcher's lack of knowledge concerning the children and the abilities in question than from the subject's lack of ability (Gelman, 1979). Hence we have developed and employed a method called the "Birthday Party" for accomplishing sensitive testing of mathematical thinking in young children. This technique uses an extended game—a pretend birthday party—to motivate preschool children to engage in mathematical activities. With minor modifications, the game is appropriate for children in various cultures.

METHOD

Overview

The Birthday Party game was employed, with minor variations designed to accommodate local cultural conditions, to collect data over a two-year period in the U.S., China, Japan, Korea, and Colombia. The data are presented as a series of studies designed to investigate the different issues with which this chapter is concerned. Our report is organized in several sections: cross-national comparisons; instructional differences within China; ethnic group differences within the U.S.; and social class differences in various countries.

Subjects

Subjects were selected in a somewhat different manner in each of the locations. In all cases, the groups were approximately equally split between boys and girls. There were 476 4-year-old children in total.

China. Over a two-year period, data from two samples of Chinese children in Beijing were collected. The first sample involved 30 Chinese children whose parents either worked as bureaucrats in the government or as labourers in factories. All of these children attended a preschool with formal instruction. Preliminary analyses showed that the first sample of Chinese children performed at an exceptionally high level on the various dependent measures. We therefore desired to examine the effects of formal instruction on the children's performance. Consequently, during the second year, we obtained a second sample, also in Beijing, comprising 30 randomly selected children from two types of preschools: 15 attended preschools with instruction, and 15 attended preschools without instruction. The parents of these children worked as factory labourers. For purposes of statistical analyses to be reported in this paper, we combined the 30 Chinese children in the first sample, all of whom received formal instruction, with the 15 children from the second sample who also received instruction. Thus, the final sample comprised 45 children who attended preschools with instruction and 15 children who attended preschools without instruction. Of the 60, 30 were boys and 30 girls. The instruction and non-instruction groups were approximately equally divided among boys and girls.

In the Chinese preschools offering formal instruction, there were two periods, each 30 minutes in length, every day, involving lessons in a variety of subjects based on daily teaching outlines established by the Education Bureau. Mathematics was taught twice a week, and about once a week children were assigned homework, some involving worksheets. Chinese preschools without instruction did not have formal lessons or homework, and instead employed games similar to those found in preschools in Japan, Korea, and the U.S. The nature of teacher training also differed in the two types of Chinese preschools. Teachers in the preschools with instruction graduated from college or a teacher training school, whereas teachers in the preschools without instruction were graduates of high school only.

Colombia. Children from three social classes comprised this group of 120 children. There were 68 boys and 52 girls divided approximately equally among the SES groups. SES was determined by parental income and occupation according to Colombian standards. Parents of upper SES generally occupy executive, white-collar professional positions and pay a fee for their children to attend a private preschool which runs an English immersion programme in preparation for later bilingual education. Thus, the children were "taught" in English but tested in Spanish because they were not fluent enough to be tested in the language of instruction. In the preschool, the mathematics "curriculum" consisted entirely in learning the spoken numbers from one to ten. The curriculum used in later grades of this school is described as North American. Middle-SES children are characterized by their attendance at a Spanish-speaking, traditional preschool that is quite structured. Parents generally hold non-executive professional positions. Low-SES children attend a tuition-free school that is Spanish-speaking and traditional. Parents of these children generally hold blue-collar positions at best. In general, the higher the SES, the more likely were children to have participated in earlier daycare experiences of high quality.

Japan. A total of 35 Japanese children, 19 boys and 16 girls, attending a private preschool were selected. This preschool was located in the suburbs of Tokyo and its population reflects the relatively homogeneous and predominantly middle-class society of Japan. Parents of these children were generally college educated.

Korea. In Korea a total of 56 children were selected from four preschools in the Busan area. Half of the children were from two private preschools charging relatively high tuition fees. Their families were affluent and could be considered upper middle-class. The fathers, all college graduates, served in occupations like doctor, government official, professor, and engineer. The other half were from two public preschools serving lower-class families. Fathers of these children were blue-collar workers and graduated from junior high or high school. Children were divided approximately equally by gender among the SES groups.

U.S. A total of 205 American children were studied. The majority of the children were chosen from publicly supported daycare/nursery school centres in New York City. This group consisted of 56 White, 44 African-American, and 56 Hispanic children. Children were divided approximately equally by gender among the ethnic groups. In an attempt to gather data concerning children's SES position, a rough judgement concerning income level was made on the basis of the size of the daycare fee parents paid on a sliding scale. Parents at the lower end may be considered seriously impoverished; many were on welfare. We call children from this group Lower Lower Class (LLC). They seem comparable to the lower-class families studied by Starkey and Klein (1991). Parents in the middle of the distribution were somewhat better off, generally holding blue-collar jobs, and may be considered Working Class (WC). Parents at the upper end resided in a more affluent area of the city and may be considered Middle Class (MC). Our procedure resulted in the following samples: 12 LLC and 28 WC African-Americans; 14 LLC and 42 WC Hispanics; and 5 WC and 51 MC Whites. Unfortunately, this uneven distribution—with Whites wealthier than the other groups—accurately reflects the realities of New York City and many other urban centres. (Note however that the distribution does not reflect the fact that in the U.S. at large there are greater absolute numbers—despite a lower percentage—of White poor than African-American or Hispanic poor.)

A total of 49 Korean-American children, 26 boys and 23 girls, were selected from five sites in New York City and one in Virginia. None of the New York Korean-American children attended the same preschools as the White, African-American, or Hispanic children. Although most families were considered middle-income level, there were some parents who qualified for reduced tuition under a voucher payment system. All of these parents declined to enrol in the voucher programme and chose to pay their children's tuition in full. The educational level of the Korean-American parents was in general higher than that of the other U.S. groups. Most Korean-American parents were college-educated and in some cases had graduate degrees. However, most parent occupations (e.g. greengrocers) did not match their educational training.

How can we characterize the SES status of these children in terms of the larger U.S. population? All things considered, it is probably fair to say that our White and Korean-American subjects were predominantly middle SES and the African-Americans and Hispanics predominantly lower SES.

Training in the Preschools.   To the best of our knowledge, the preschools in the various countries, with the exception of one preschool in China, did not have formal mathematics programmes, although some attention was given to counting and similar tasks in the context of everyday activities and games. For example, as mentioned earlier, in the upper SES Colombian group, the "curriculum" involved teaching the children, who had been attending the school for two months prior to our testing, to count from one to ten.

Procedure

We engaged individual children in a pretend Birthday Party game, involving various attractive activities with toys and puppets. The Birthday Party took approximately 20 minutes to administer, although there were of course variations among individual children. Subjects were tested by a member of the same ethnic background in the child's dominant language.

The Birthday Party theme was chosen because it is a familiar event and enjoyable for 4-year-olds from the various American and Asian cultures. Children were shown a table of Birthday Party toys—including balloons, cups, whistles, yo-yos, and the like—and were asked to make believe that it was their birthday. An animal puppet was used as a friend with whom the children identified. Then the children were asked to engage in such activities as counting out a certain number of toys for the guests. From the child's point of view, the Birthday Party was a series of pretend games offering some amusement.

From our point of view, the Birthday Party was a series of 10 tasks for assessing informal mathematical knowledge (see Appendix). The tasks were selected to cover basic informal mathematical knowledge, as well as digit span memory (recall that Stigler, Lee, and Stevenson, 1986, report a higher capacity for digit span memory in Chinese children than in Japanese and Americans). Tasks were in most cases based on procedures used in the research of Ginsburg and Russell (1981) and the test developed by Ginsburg and Baroody (1990). Each Birthday Party task began with an example to ensure that the child understood the problem. Native speakers translated the tasks into the languages used by the various groups, and minor modifications in language and procedure were made in order to conform to local conditions. For instance, in Korea, dolls were used instead of animal puppets, which are unfamiliar to children in that country. Another example involves language: balloons have multiple names in Spanish depending on the country of origin. Consequently, in New York, to which Hispanic children may immigrate from several different countries (Puerto Rico, Dominican Republic, etc.), the name for balloon appropriate to the child's country of origin was used if the interview was conducted in Spanish. During the second year of data collection, a minor procedural change was made (it is described in the Appendix, which presents details of administration). Because preliminary analyses showed that the procedural change did not affect the results, data from the two different years of data collection were combined in all subsequent analyses.

The 10 Tasks

1. *Finger Displays of Number* investigated the child's ability to make a simple representation of numbers, through the medium of the fingers. The child was asked to hold up the number of fingers corresponding to a friend's age. Four such tasks were given.

2. *Perception of More* investigated the ability to identify, without counting, which of two randomly arranged sets of objects is greater in number. Four cards divided in half, each side containing a different number of dots, were presented quickly to the child, one at a time. The child was asked to point to the side that had more.

3. *Production from 10* investigated enumeration. The child was asked to give a puppet a particular number of Birthday Party toys from a larger set of 10 objects. Three such tasks were given.

4. *Counting by Ones* investigated basic verbal counting activity and focused on the use of generative rules for producing the numbers. After a puppet counted to 3, the child was asked to count as high as possible (and was stopped at 40 if he or she got that far).

5. *Comparison of Number* investigated the ability to recognize which of two

written numbers was greater. Pairs of cards contained in a "magic box" were pulled out and shown to the child. The child was asked to point to the bigger number. There were four problems.

6. *Concrete Addition* investigated accuracy and strategy in addition when concrete objects are present and available for manipulation. After a puppet took out two different sets of objects from a pile, the child was asked to tell the interviewer how many toys were gathered in total. There were three problems.

7. *Digit Span Memory* investigated memory for strings of digits, a capacity that is possibly related to early counting ability and other aspects of informal mathematics. The child was instructed to repeat the sequence of numbers said by the puppet. The questions began with two digits and increased up to five digit lengths. There were seven questions in total. Accurate retention of four digits was required for a passing score.

8. *Concrete Subtraction* investigated accuracy and strategy in subtraction when concrete objects are present and available for manipulation. The child was asked to say how many objects were left after a puppet had given away a number of objects to the child. There were three problems.

9. *Informal Subtraction* investigated accuracy and strategy in subtraction when concrete objects are initially visible but then hidden and not available for manipulation. A number of toys were dropped one at a time into a bag. The interviewer then pulled out a number of objects and the child was asked to say how many toys were left inside. There were three problems.

10. *Informal Addition* investigated accuracy and strategy in addition when concrete objects are initially visible but then hidden and not available for manipulation. The interviewer dropped two sets of the same toy into the bag. The child was asked how many toys were in the bag. There were three problems.

Almost all items require the child to produce a response, e.g. to hold up a certain number of fingers or to remember specific numbers. Only two items—Perception of More and Comparison of Numbers—involve a choice between two alternatives and hence the possibility of success by guessing. Thus, on most items successful response cannot be produced by chance alone.

Subjects' responses were scored for accuracy and, in the cases of Concrete and Informal Addition and Subtraction, were coded for strategy. Because coded strategies were so obvious—e.g. touches objects, verbally counts all—perfect inter-rater reliability was achieved.

RESULTS

National Comparisons

Comparisons among countries reveal the relative superiority of Asian children's understanding of informal mathematics. Total scores representing the number of items passed (out of a possible 10) show that the Chinese, Japanese, and Korean children scored significantly higher than the U.S. and Colombian children (See Table 8.1 and Fig. 8.1). Differences among the Asian countries were relatively small, with success on only about one item separating the highest and lowest scores: the Chinese performed better than the Koreans but not significantly better than the Japanese children. U.S. children performed at a slightly, but significantly, lower level than the Asians, but significantly better than the Colombians, who ranked at the bottom. In all cases, the variation in scores was similar.

Consideration of individual items (See Table 8.2 and Fig. 8.2) reveals a comparable pattern. On most items, the Chinese especially, and also the Japanese and Koreans, performed at a higher level than the Americans, who in turn performed better than the Colombians.

Several items are worth examining in detail. Table 8.2 shows that Chinese children scored significantly higher on Counting than all other groups; the Chinese counted up to about 29 on the average, more than twice as high as the Colombians. The U.S. and other Asian children ranked in between the Chinese and Colombians. Furthermore, U.S. children, despite the relative difficulty of the English number system, performed at a slightly higher level in Counting than did Koreans and Japanese, who performed at about the same level. Especially notable is the outstanding performance of the Chinese on Digit Span Memory. On average, Chinese children retained about five digits whereas the average for the other groups was slightly less than four digits. We note however that digit span is not correlated with success on any other items, for the Chinese or any other groups.

The general superiority of the Asians should not obscure the fact that on two items the countries did not differ a great deal, if at all. On Perception of More, scores were generally high and the range from highest (the Chinese 3.97) to lowest (the Colombian 3.34) was only about 0.6. Virtually all children did well on this task and the variation on it was small, except perhaps in the case of the Colombians. Similarly, on Comparison of Number, all groups were moderately successful, with the range from highest (the Korean 2.98) to the lowest (the Colombian 2.18) being 0.8.

TABLE 8.1
Means and Standard Deviations of Total Scores for All Countries

Country	Mean Total Score (Maximum score = 10)	Standard Deviation
China	7.98	2.20
Colombia	4.08	2.86
Japan	7.23	2.00
Korea	6.96	2.36
U.S.	6.27	2.53

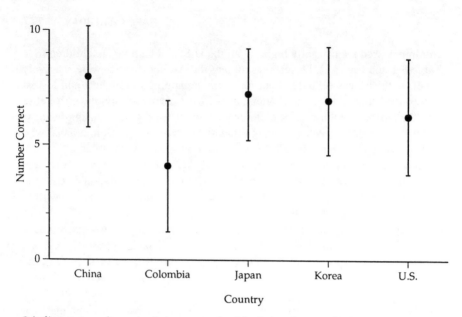

indicates mean; line extends to one standard deviation above and below the mean

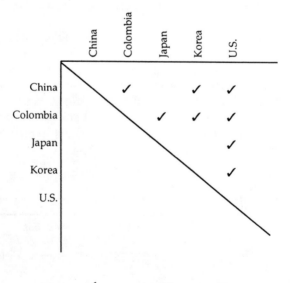

Significance Levels

✓ means significant at $p < .05$

FIG. 8.1. Means (with one standard deviation above and below the mean) of total scores for all countries.

TABLE 8.2
Means and Standard Deviations (in Parentheses) of Individual Items
for all Countries

	China	Colombia	Japan	Korea	U.S.
1. Finger displays of number					
b	3.38	1.59	2.94	3.05	2.25
	(1.17)	(1.30)	(1.19)	(1.31)	(1.36)
2. Perception of more					
b	3.97	3.34	3.89	3.95	3.51
	(0.26)	(1.09)	(0.32)	(0.23)	(0.80)
3. Production from 10					
a	2.65	1.34	2.37	1.79	1.91
	(0.71)	(1.10)	(0.91)	(1.02)	(1.06)
4. Counting by ones					
d	29.58	12.62	17.34	17.55	20.25
	(10.59)	(8.91)	(10.30)	(10.44)	(10.94)
5. Comparison of number					
a	2.65	2.18	2.77	2.98	2.79
	(1.15)	(1.17)	(1.29)	(1.29)	(1.18)
6. Concrete addition					
a	2.55	1.68	2.86	2.41	2.25
	(0.83)	(1.25)	(0.36)	(0.89)	(0.99)
7. Digit span memory					
c	5.03	3.24	3.60	3.70	3.86
	(0.71)	(1.18)	(0.81)	(0.89)	(0.86)
8. Concrete subtraction					
a	2.48	1.38	2.60	2.30	2.17
	(0.91)	(1.16)	(0.74)	(0.87)	(1.02)
9. Informal subtraction					
a	1.95	1.33	2.31	2.02	1.72
	(0.89)	(1.01)	(0.96)	(0.90)	(1.07)
10. Informal addition					
a	2.00	0.69	1.80	1.54	1.47
	(0.97)	(0.91)	(1.02)	(0.95)	(0.96)

a = Maximum score for this item is 3.00.
b = Maximum score for this item is 4.00.
c = Maximum score for this item is 6.00.
d = Maximum score for this item is 40.00.

Consider next the strategies children employed in solving Concrete Addition and Subtraction tasks—the only tasks on which strategies were clearly observable. Table 8.3 shows that Asian children in particular were consistent in use of strategies across all three trials of the concrete calculation tasks, particularly in the case of concrete subtraction. In general, the Asian children were both more consistent than Americans, and more accurate. The data also reveal distinct country differences in the use of strategies. (See Table 8.4, which shows strategy data from the first trial of the concrete addition and subtraction

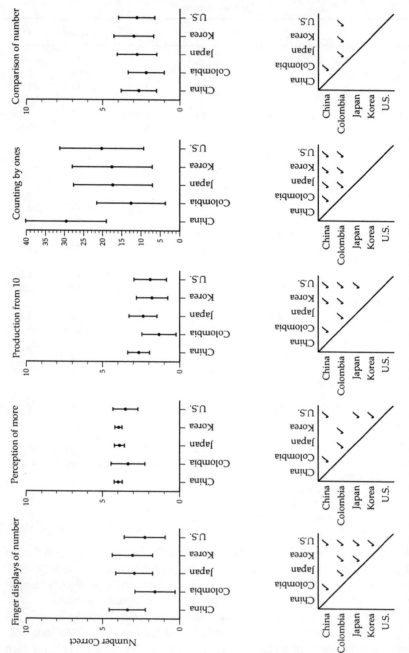

FIG. 8.2a. Means (with one standard deviation above and below the mean) of individual items for all countries.

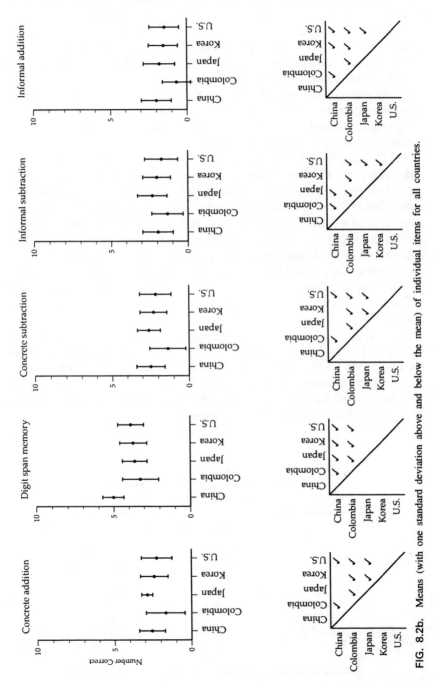

FIG. 8.2b. Means (with one standard deviation above and below the mean) of individual items for all countries.

tasks. This trial was typical of the others.) In the case of Concrete Addition, the dominant Chinese strategy was touching objects while counting all; the Colombian and Korean strategy was verbally counting on from the smaller number; the Japanese strategy was producing the sum instantly without overt counting; the U.S. strategies were quite diverse, with about equal incidence of verbally counting on from the smaller, touching objects while counting all, touching objects while counting on from the smaller number, and knowing the sum instantly without overt counting. Note that use of a particular strategy does not guarantee a specific level of success: Colombians and Koreans used the same strategy with drastically different levels of success.

For Concrete Subtraction, the pattern was similar. Chinese children tended to touch and count all of the remainder; Japanese children tended to produce the answer instantly without overt counting; Korean children verbally counted the remainder; U.S. children used a very wide range of strategies. The only group using a different strategy for subtraction than for addition was the Colombian, who tended to produce the answer instantly without overt counting. These quick answers, which were often wrong, were probably unprincipled guesses. Note that the Japanese also produced quick responses, but theirs tended to be accurate.

The data concerning country cannot be fully understood without further analyses. For example, Chinese children perform at an especially high level, but some of the Chinese children receive formal instruction and some do not. U.S. children rank slightly below the Asians, but the Americans are a diverse group, including African-Americans, Hispanics, Koreans, and Whites. The Colombians do very badly, but that group too is diverse, containing a wide range of social classes. Consequently, we now attempt to tease apart the data concerning national differences, investigating the roles of instruction, ethnicity, and class. The clearest of these results concerns instruction.

TABLE 8.3
Consistency in Strategy Use for Concrete
Addition and Subtraction

Country	Percent of children using one strategy across all three trials	
	Concrete Addition	Concrete Subtraction
China	70.0	83.3
Colombia	41.7	66.7
Japan	77.1	74.3
Korea	67.9	80.4
U.S.	62.4	52.2

TABLE 8.4
Predominant Strategy Use for Concrete Addition and Subtraction

	Predominant Strategy Used for First Trial in:	
Country	Concrete Addition	Concrete Subtraction
China	Touches Items as Verbally Counts All	Touches Items as Verbally Counts All
Colombia	Verbally Counts All	Knows Answer
Japan	Knows Answer	Knows Answer
Korea	Verbally Counts All	Verbally Counts All
U. S.	Verbally Counts All	Verbally Counts All
	Touches Items as Verbally Counts All	Touches Items as Verbally Counts All
	Touching Items as Verbally Counts on From Smallest Number	Knows Answer

Instruction

To what extent does instruction promote early mathematical thinking? Table 8.5 and Fig. 8.3 show that Chinese children who attend preschools with formal instruction significantly outscore, on total number correct, their Chinese counterparts who attend daycare centres without such instruction. The scores of children receiving instruction approach ceiling and their variance is half that of the uninstructed group. A significant difference between means was also revealed in the case of most individual items—namely, Finger Display, Production, Counting, Comparison of Number, Concrete Addition and Subtraction, and Informal Addition. Indeed, it is particularly interesting that Chinese children without instruction performed at about the same level on counting as did Japanese and several U.S. groups (African-Americans and Whites). There were three exceptions to the trend favouring instruction. The most interesting is that both groups of Chinese children performed at very high levels on Digit Span, indeed better than all other groups; schooling is not required for superior Chinese performance in this area. The other exceptions are that both schooled and unschooled Chinese children did very well on Perception of More, on which almost all groups do well, approaching ceiling; and both groups did relatively poorly on Informal Subtraction, a topic with which most groups had trouble.

TABLE 8.5
Means and Standard Deviations of Total Scores for
Chinese Children With Instruction and Without
Instruction

Group	Mean Total Score (Maximum score = 10)	Standard Deviation
With Instruction	8.71	1.38
Without Instruction	5.80	2.76

If the Chinese with instruction are removed from the country comparisons, the Chinese superiority virtually disappears. Table 8.6 and Fig. 8.4 give total scores for all countries, with China being represented only by children without instruction. Table 8.7 and Fig. 8.5 show individual item scores for the same groups. In general, these results show that the Chinese without instruction perform at about the same level as the U.S. children. This was true in the case of counting, as well as in most other areas of informal mathematics. One major exception is that Chinese are still superior to all the others on Digit Span. As already noted, correlation analyses showed, however, that Chinese performance on digit span is not significantly related to performance on other test items. The same lack of correlation holds for other groups as well.

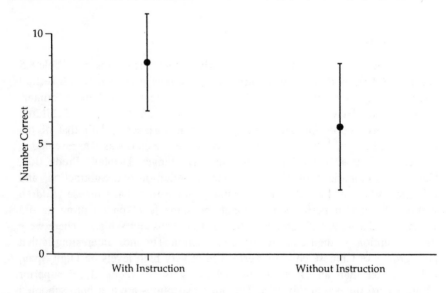

FIG. 8.3. Means (with one standard deviation above and below the mean) of total scores for Chinese with and without instruction.

TABLE 8.6
Means and Standard Deviations of Total Scores for Chinese
Without Instruction and Other Countries

Country	Mean Total Score (Maximum score = 10)	Standard Deviation
China (Without Instruction)	5.80	2.76
Colombia	4.08*	2.86
Japan	7.23*	2.00
Korea	6.96*	2.36
U.S.	6.27	2.53

*Indicates a significant difference ($P < .05$) between China (without) and the other group.

These findings shed a new light on the country comparisons. The apparent Chinese superiority in our national comparison can be attributed to instruction, which clearly can have a major effect on children's mathematical performance, even at the preschool level.

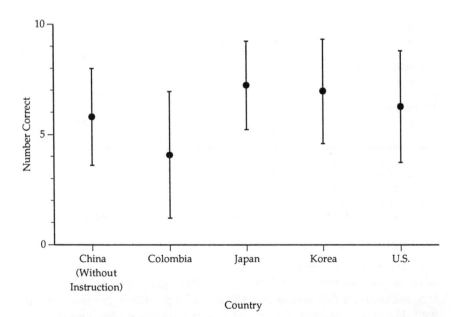

FIG. 8.4. Means (with one standard deviation above and below the mean) of total scores for Chinese without instruction and all other countries.

TABLE 8.7
Means and Standard Deviations (Parentheses) of Individual Items for Chinese
Without Instruction and Other Countries

	China	Colombia	Japan	Korea	U. S.
1. Finger displays of number					
b	1.73	1.59	2.94*	3.05*	2.25
	(1.22)	(1.30)	(1.19)	(1.31)	(1.36)
2. Perception of more					
b	3.87	3.34*	3.89	3.95	3.51
	(0.52)	(1.09)	(0.32)	(0.23)	(0.80)
3. Production from 10					
a	2.00	1.34*	2.37	1.79	1.91
	(1.00)	(1.10)	(0.91)	(1.02)	(1.06)
4. Counting by ones					
d	20.13	12.62*	17.34*	17.55	0.25
	(8.78)	(8.91)	(10.30)	(10.44)	(10.94)
5. Comparison of number					
a	2.00	2.18	2.77*	2.98*	2.79*
	(1.25)	(1.17)	(1.29)	(1.29)	(1.18)
6. Concrete addition					
a	1.93	1.68	2.86*	2.41*	2.25
	(1.16)	(1.25)	(0.36)	(0.89)	(0.99)
7. Digit span memory					
c	4.93	3.24*	3.60*	3.70*	3.86*
	(1.10)	(1.18)	(0.81)	(0.89)	(0.86)
8. Concrete subtraction					
a	1.80	1.38	2.60*	2.30*	2.17
	(1.26)	(1.16)	(0.74)	(0.87)	(1.02)
9. Informal subtraction					
a	1.60	1.33	2.31*	2.02	1.72
	(0.91)	(1.01)	(0.96)	(0.90)	(1.07)
10. Informal addition					
a	1.20	0.69*	1.80*	1.54	1.47
	(1.01)	(0.91)	(1.02)	(0.95)	(0.96)

a = Maximum score for this item is 3.00.
b = Maximum score for this item is 4.00.
c = Maximum score for this item is 6.00.
d = Maximum score for this item is 40.00.
*Indicates a significant difference ($P < .05$) between China (without) and the other group.

Ethnicity

U.S. society is more heterogeneous than the others represented in this study. One of our major questions referred to possible ethnic group differences within the U.S. In examining this question, we did not find it possible to examine ethnicity with class held constant or factored out. Our data confound ethnicity with social class; as pointed out earlier, our African-American and Hispanic groups tended to be lower-class, and the Koreans and Whites middle-class.

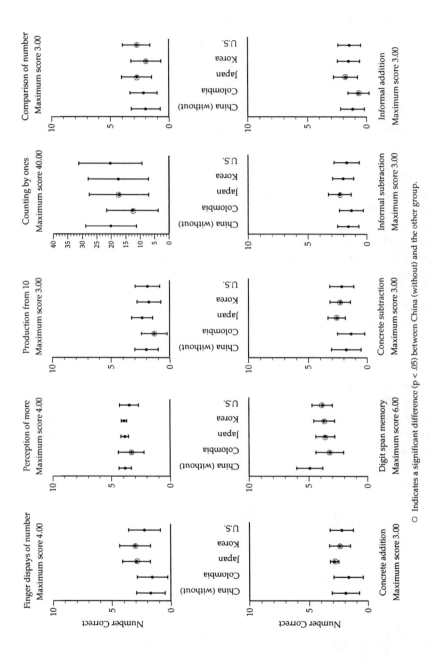

FIG. 8.5.   Performance by Chinese without instruction and all other countries on individual items.

187

Given this caveat, we first examine ethnicity within the U.S. and then present results comparing the various U.S. groups with groups in other countries. Table 8.8 and Fig. 8.6 show these Total scores. The results indicate that Whites score significantly higher than Korean-Americans, who in turn do not differ statistically from African-Americans, with both groups scoring significantly higher than Hispanics. Variances were similar, although that of the Hispanics was somewhat larger than the others, which may be expected from the fact that more children in the other groups approached ceiling than did Hispanic children. In general, the top three groups performed well, with only about one point separating the Whites and African-Americans.

Table 8.9 and Fig. 8.7 show performance on individual items. Within the U.S., item difficulty was not clearly related to ethnic group membership. For example, on Perception of More the ranking from highest to lowest was Korean-Americans, Whites, Hispanics, and African-Americans. For Counting, the ranking was Whites, African-Americans, Korean-Americans, and Hispanics. For Concrete Addition, Korean-Americans were first, with Whites and African-Americans tied for second position.

The data fail to reveal clear patterns in U.S. ethnic groups' use of strategies. In contrast to the results reported for the other countries, U.S. children used many different strategies. Each ethnic group used several strategies and none seemed to predominate as was the case in the other countries. For example, in the case of Concrete Addition, African-Americans used several strategies in about equal proportions: Verbal counting all, Touching items as verbally counts all (either all of the objects or from the larger number), and Knows answer. Hispanic children used either the Knows answer or Touching items as verbally counts all strategy. Korean-Americans tended to use the Verbally counts on from the smaller number strategy. Whites tended to use the Knows answer or Verbally counts or touches items as verbally counts all strategy.

TABLE 8.8
Means and Standard Deviations of Total Scores for
U.S. Ethnic Groups and All Other Countries

Country	Mean Total Score (Maximum score = 10)	Standard Deviation
China	7.98	2.20
Colombia	4.08	2.86
Japan	7.23	2.00
Korea	6.96	2.36
U.S. African-Americans	6.14	2.23
U.S. Hispanics	5.11	2.71
U.S. Korean-Americans	6.45	2.06
U.S. Whites	7.39	2.48

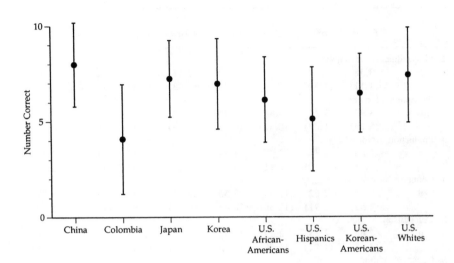

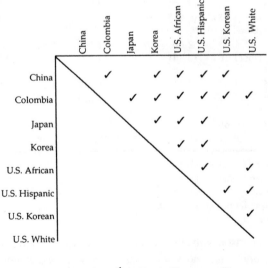

Significance Levels

✓ means significant at $p < .05$

FIG. 8.6. Means (with one standard deviation above and below the mean) on total scores for U.S. ethnic groups and all other countries.

TABLE 8.9
Means and Standard Deviations (Parentheses) of Individual Items
for U.S. Ethnic Groups and Other Countries

	China	Colombia	Japan	Korea	U. S. African	U. S. Hispanic	U. S. Korean	U. S. White
1. Finger displays of number								
b	3.38	1.59	2.94	3.05	2.11	1.88	2.04	2.93
	(1.17)	(1.30)	(1.19)	(1.31)	(1.33)	(1.38)	(1.43)	(1.04)
2. Perception of more								
b	3.97	3.34	3.89	3.95	3.14	3.25	3.90	3.71
	(0.26)	(1.09)	(0.32)	(0.23)	(1.03)	(0.84)	(0.42)	(0.56)
3. Production from 10								
a	2.65	1.34	2.37	1.79	2.05	1.54	1.80	2.27
	(0.71)	(1.10)	(0.91)	(1.02)	(1.14)	(1.08)	(1.02)	(0.90)
4. Counting by ones								
d	29.58	12.62	17.34	17.55	22.73	16.36	18.37	23.89
	(10.59)	(8.91)	(10.30)	(10.44)	(8.48)	(8.90)	(12.59)	(11.58)
5. Comparison of number								
a	2.65	2.18	2.77	2.98	2.64	2.61	2.55	3.29
	(1.15)	(1.17)	(1.29)	(1.29)	(1.04)	(1.25)	(1.17)	(1.09)
6. Concrete addition								
a	2.55	1.68	2.86	2.41	2.32	1.96	2.45	2.32
	(0.83)	(1.25)	(0.36)	(0.89)	(1.01)	(1.14)	(0.74)	(0.96)
7. Digit span memory								
c	5.03	3.24	3.60	3.70	3.75	3.71	3.78	4.16
	(0.71)	(1.18)	(0.81)	(0.89)	(0.81)	(0.82)	(0.82)	(0.92)
8. Concrete subtraction								
a	2.48	1.38	2.60	2.30	1.98	1.91	2.35	2.41
	(0.91)	(1.16)	(0.74)	(0.87)	(1.19)	(1.10)	(0.81)	(0.89)
9. Informal subtraction								
a	1.95	1.33	2.31	2.02	1.50	1.29	1.92	2.14
	(0.89)	(1.01)	(0.96)	(0.90)	(1.05)	(1.07)	(1.00)	(0.98)
10. Informal addition								
a	2.00	0.69	1.80	1.54	1.41	1.21	1.63	1.63
	(0.97)	(0.91)	(1.02)	(0.95)	(0.97)	(0.99)	(0.88)	(0.95)

a = Maximum score for this item is 3.00.
b = Maximum score for this item is 4.00.
c = Maximum score for this item is 6.00.
d = Maximum score for this item is 40.00.

To facilitate comparison with other studies, most of which examined differences between African-Americans and Whites within the U.S., we examined possible differences between these two groups. Whites performed significantly better on six of the items (Finger Display, Perception of More, Comparison of Number, Digit Span, Concrete Subtraction, and Informal Subtraction) and did not differ significantly on four (Production, Counting, Concrete Addition, Informal

Addition). It should be noted that many of the significant differences were small (for example on Concrete Subtraction the White score was 2.41 of a possible 3, and the African-American score was 1.98, a difference of about half a point) and that both groups performed relatively well on most of the items. Despite the confounding of race and class, the results are in agreement with the general finding that differences between African-Americans and Whites in this area are relatively small.

It is interesting to note that African-Americans and Korean-Americans performed at similar levels, differing significantly on only four of the items (Perception of More, Counting, Concrete Subtraction, Informal Subtraction). On one of these items, African-Americans scored higher (Counting,) and on three Korean-Americans scored higher (Perception of more, Concrete Subtraction, Informal Subtraction). Despite the class difference between them, both groups seem to begin with similar informal mathematical abilities, although in later years Korean-Americans as a group enjoy more academic success than do African-Americans.

The results showed that Hispanics performed relatively poorly, a finding that does not seem to agree in part with Starkey and Klein's (1991) results of a lack of ethnic group difference among African-Americans, Hispanics, and Whites, when social class is held constant. In our sample, Whites and African-Americans performed at roughly the same level, despite a confounding of ethnicity and SES, but African-Americans performed at a higher level than Hispanics, despite their similarity in SES.

Comparing the Total scores of the U.S. ethnic groups with those of other countries, we see in Table 8.8 that the Chinese (including those receiving instruction) score highest of all, followed by Japanese, Koreans, U.S. Whites, Korean-Americans, and African-Americans. U.S. Hispanics score at a significantly lower level than the African-Americans, and the Colombians score significantly lower than all the other groups. The general impression is that most groups score reasonably well, except for the Colombians and perhaps the U.S. Hispanics. Examination of Table 8.9 shows a similar pattern with respect to differences in Individual Items among the various groups.

Taken as a whole, these results show that U.S. preschoolers, with the possible exception of Hispanics, possess reasonable competence in informal mathematical thinking, and differ little in this area from their Asian peers.

Social Class

Although social class appears to exert major influences on at least some areas of psychological functioning, it is hard to compare social class across cultures. Can the middle class in the U.S. be considered similar to the middle class in Japan or in Colombia? How can one compare income levels in various cultures? Because we believe that these questions are unanswerable with any precision, we examined

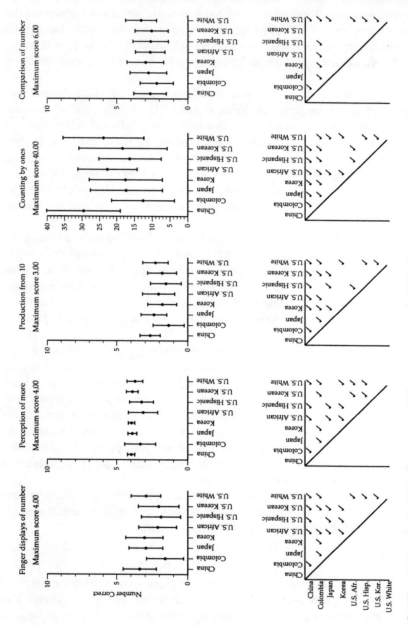

FIG. 8.7a. Performance by U.S. ethnic groups and all other countries on individual items.

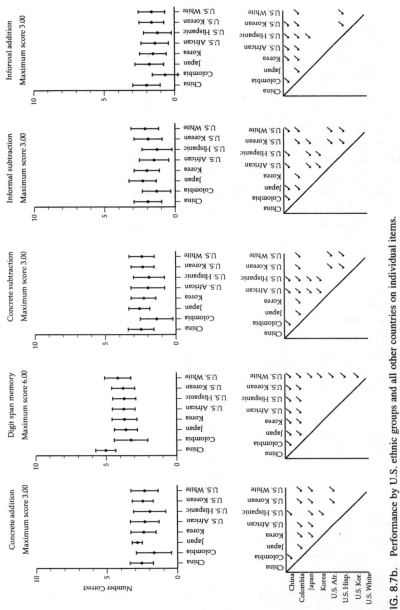

FIG. 8.7b. Performance by U.S. ethnic groups and all other countries on individual items.

the effects of SES separately in the various countries for which social class data were available to us. Because the most extreme differences in social status were found in our Colombian and Korean samples, we present these data first.

Colombia.   In this country, where social status distinctions are large, ranging from affluent parents who send their children to an English immersion school to poor parents whose children attend a state-supported school, performance differences related to social class were pronounced (see Table 8.10 and Fig. 8.8). Total scores and individual items reveal significant differences among the three social classes, reflecting a clear advantage of high income and level of parental education. High-income children performed substantially better (two points higher) than middle-income children. Middle-income children also performed substantially better (two points higher) than lower-class children. This spread among the scores is the most dramatic and extensive of any of our results. Almost all individual items show the same pattern. Only in the case of Perception of More were social class differences statistically insignificant. Clearly SES makes a very large difference in Colombia. Further, it is interesting to note that the most privileged Colombian children do rather well: their Total Scores do not differ from those of U.S. Koreans and African-Americans, lower-class Koreans, and Chinese without instruction.

Korea.   Recall that Korean social class distinctions are relatively large. Our middle-class sample were children of affluent college graduates; the lower-class sample were children of junior high school or high school graduates who held blue-collar positions. The results showed significant differences between the SES groups in Total Scores, with children from middle SES backgrounds performing significantly better than children from lower SES families. The difference was about

TABLE 8.10
Means and Standard Deviations of Total Scores of
Social Class Groups in China, Colombia, and Korea

Country	Mean Total Score (Maximum score = 10)	Standard Deviation
China		
Middle SES	8.23	2.14
Lower SES	7.73	2.26
Colombia		
Upper SES	5.95	2.56
Middle SES	4.08	2.55
Lower SES	2.20	2.16
Korea		
Middle SES	7.64	2.20
Lower SES	6.29	2.35

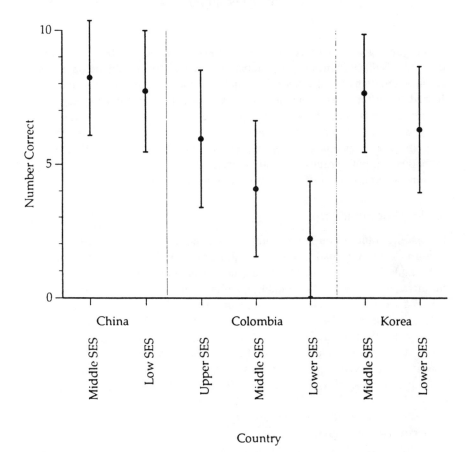

FIG. 8.8.   Means and standard deviations of total scores of social class groups in China, Colombia, and Korea.

about 1.3 points, less than in Colombia. Middle-class children also scored significantly higher on three individual items: Production, Comparison of Number, and Informal Addition. On almost all other items, middle-class children scored higher than lower-class children, but the differences failed to reach statistical significance. In Korea too, SES makes a difference, but not as large a difference as in Colombia.

China.   Examining Total Scores, we found no significant differences between children whose parents held government (middle-class) and factory (lower-class) jobs. This is not surprising, because in China, at least until recently, social class distinctions in a large city like Beijing have been relatively small compared to those

DISCUSSION

Overview

In interpreting group differences, we must keep in mind two basic facts about them. One is that within any group individuals often differ in dramatic ways. Some Japanese children do better than others, and the same is true of African-Americans. Indeed, the differences among individuals within a group are typically larger than the average difference between groups. A second fact is that although group averages often differ, the distributions of scores almost always exhibit considerable overlap. Thus, even though one group scores higher than another on the average, individuals in both groups generally receive scores roughly in the same range. To some extent, group differences appear more dramatic than they really are.

National Comparisons

Comparing countries on Total Scores, we see that Asians exhibit a better overall performance in informal mathematical thinking than do U.S. children, and that U.S. children perform at a higher level than do Colombian children. Nevertheless, the differences between Asian and U.S. children are not large. For example, there is only a one point difference between Japanese and U.S. children, and a difference of less than one point between Korean and U.S. children. This latter finding seems to contradict the results of Song and Ginsburg (1987) who found U.S. children to score slightly better than Koreans. Perhaps the more sensitive methodology contributed to Korean children's improved performance in this study. In any event, at the preschool level, U.S. children differ little from their Korean and Japanese peers.

Examination of individual items shows that the Chinese counted significantly higher than the other groups. As our other results showed, however, this finding is the result of instruction: Chinese children without instruction performed at about the same level as Japanese and several U.S. groups. This finding then fails to agree with the research of Miller and Stigler (1987). Another interesting and similar result is that the U.S. children counted at about the same level as the Japanese and Koreans, who did not differ from one another. Perhaps in the long run the Asian counting system may provide an advantage, as Miura and Okamoto (1989) suggest, by clarifying the structure of the base ten system. But the present data— particularly the lack of a U.S.–Japanese difference—show that early superiority in counting cannot account for Asians' later success in schooling. These data also suggest that U.S. children are adequately equipped with the counting skills that several writers (e.g. Baroody, 1987) have proposed are necessary to learn the fundamentals of early arithmetic.

The results also showed that Chinese digit span is superior to that of both Westerners and other Asians as well. The result agrees with Stigler, Lee, and Stevenson (1986) and with Stevenson, Stigler, Lee, and Lucker (1985), who found a

Chinese (Taiwanese) superiority in digit span, but not serial memory for words, over U.S. and Japanese children. Like the other authors, we cannot explain the finding. But regardless of its source, digit span does not seem to be of great significance for other aspects of mathematics performance. For one thing, the present data show that digit span is not correlated with other informal mathematical tasks. Also digit span does not predict later mathematics learning: Japanese and Korean children perform very well on elementary and high school level mathematics achievement tests, despite their lower digit span scores at the preschool level. This should come as no surprise: doing and understanding mathematics involve much more than the memorization of meaningless material. We should be upset if digit span *were* positively associated with mathematics achievement.

It is interesting but puzzling to note the tremendous variation in the strategies exhibited by the various groups. For example, in the Concrete Addition task, Chinese children touch objects whereas Japanese children produce the answer quickly, without overt counting. U.S. ethnic groups use a variety of approaches. In general, more consistent use of strategies seems tied to success, as was observed in the Asian groups. Perhaps consistency implies that strategies are well learned and therefore can be used efficiently and correctly. (Of course, uniformity of approach may prove stifling in the long term.) Although consistency seems important, the particular strategy employed is less crucial: Colombians and Koreans tend to use the same strategy with very different rates of success, and successful Asian groups used different strategies. We welcome attempts at replication of these results and explanations of them.

All in all, the national comparisons seem to confirm the view that the Asians are superior in informal mathematics, that U.S. children lag slightly behind, and that Hispanic children, namely Colombians, perform worst of all. But national comparisons like the above can be misleading because they ignore a number of specific factors that may vary among the countries, like education, social class, and ethnicity. Consider first education.

Education

Clearly education makes a difference: Chinese children receiving instruction score at a higher level than all the rest, approaching ceiling. No doubt many other children may have benefited from informal instruction at home, but the Chinese training was intense and appeared to stress the kinds of tasks sampled by our Birthday Party procedures. The results may be interpreted as indicating only that focused instruction improves performance on the type of material taught at the time it is taught. The results do not show that instruction of this type is *necessary* for later academic success. We know that Japanese children, who often receive little or no preschool instruction in mathematics (Tobin, Wu, & Davidson, 1989), nevertheless do very well in mathematics from the earliest years of school (Stevenson, Lee, & Stigler, 1986). Nor do the results show that instruction must fail to have long-term usefulness for other groups. For example, research suggests that the Head Start Experience, usually involving some simple instruction in counting and the like, may increase the later school achievement of some U.S. groups in mathematics and other subjects (Lazar, 1983), although we suspect that the reasons for its success might be less the mathematical content *per se* than the motivational training. In brief, one possibility is that preschool instruction may help at least some American children but not be necessary for Asians' later school success. In any event, when the Chinese children receiving focused instruction are removed from the comparisons, Chinese children perform at about the same level as the U.S. group, even in the case of counting, a result that does not seem to agree with Miller and Stigler's (1987) findings. We cannot explain the discrepancy, except to note that their subjects were Taiwanese children and our subjects were from Beijing, and that it is not clear whether their subjects received special instruction in counting.

Ethnicity

Although important, education cannot explain all of the group differences. Why do the Japanese or Koreans perform better than U.S. children or Colombians? Consideration of ethnicity within the U.S. group helps to unravel this issue. As pointed out above, our samples mirror the situation in many U.S. urban areas in which African-Americans and Hispanics tend to be poorer or less well educated than Asians and Whites. Our data show that Whites score significantly higher than Koreans, who do not differ statistically from African-Americans, and that both of these groups score higher than the Hispanics. In general, despite the confounding of race and class, the differences among the Whites, African-Americans, and Koreans were not large.

This overall similarity is an interesting result because many of the African-Americans in this study were severely disadvantaged economically and because in the later years of school, African-Americans generally perform at a lower level than do middle-class Whites and Koreans. Apparently, in the U.S., poor African-Americans at the preschool level do not differ significantly in informal mathematical knowledge from Koreans, and only a little from Whites. This result agrees with previous studies like those of Ginsburg and Russell (1981) and with many research findings indicating significant intellectual strengths in young African-American children and few differences between African-Americans and Whites. It would be interesting to obtain comparable data on poor White children in the U.S.

Our data did reveal some differences between African-Americans and Whites: Whites performed significantly better than African-Americans on six of the items (Finger Display, Perception of More, Comparison of Number, Digit Span, Concrete

Subtraction, and Informal Subtraction), although the differences were small, and the groups did not differ significantly on four (Production, Counting, Concrete Addition, Informal Addition). These differences do not seem to suggest any clear deficit in the African-American children (although our study did not examine the kind of verbal and conceptual problems employed respectively by Jordan, Huttenlocher, & Levine, 1992, and Entwisle & Alexander, 1990). In particular, the African-American children's counting and basic addition skills are as strong as Whites' and should serve as a good foundation for later school learning.

What do these results say about African-American children's subsequent low achievement in school and about the need for Head Start? First, later failure in school cannot be explained by significant intellectual deficits at the preschool level. Initial differences between African-Americans and Whites are relatively small and increase in school (Entwisle & Alexander, 1990), perhaps amplified in some way by the processes of schooling, the expectancies of teachers, and the "savage inequalities" (Kozol, 1991) of the educational system. A similar situation may obtain in the case of reading: thus, Raz and Bryant (1990, p.209) report that in Great Britain ". . . socially disadvantaged children did not fall behind the middle-class children in phonological awareness until they went to school." Second, for African-Americans, Head Start does not seem needed to compensate for initial cognitive deficits in informal mathematics. Its value must be found in other areas, like socialization for schooling, not to speak of the provision of basic healthcare and nutrition.

The data shed new light on the international comparisons. U.S. Whites and Korean-Americans do not differ significantly from Japanese and Koreans, and perform better than Chinese without schooling; African-Americans score at about the same level as Chinese without schooling. At the preschool level, selected U.S. groups perform at about the same level as their Asian peers. Although this result is different from Song and Ginsburg's (1987) finding that U.S. preschool children scored better than Koreans, both studies concur in showing a *lack* of Korean superiority at the preschool level. Whatever academic differences emerge later on, they cannot be explained by U.S. deficiencies at the preschool level (except perhaps in the Hispanic case, which we will explore shortly). African-Americans, Korean-Americans, and Whites all seem to possess key informal mathematical skills. Thus, at the age of 4, before entrance into elementary school, these groups of children possess basic counting and understand the rudiments of addition, at least in its concrete form. The children are intellectually "ready" to learn basic arithmetic as it is usually taught in school. Asians do not begin with an intellectual "Head Start," despite their superior counting system. Most likely, subsequent Asian superiority in mathematics performance results from schooling and motivation.

Why did the U.S. Hispanics do so poorly? Their performance does not appear to be the result of language difficulties (they were tested in their preferred language) or their being engaged in learning two languages (the same was true of the U.S. Koreans). Similarly, we cannot attribute their poor performance to what Ogbu (1986) calls their "caste status": our African-American subjects would be categorized in the same way and yet performed better than the Hispanics.

We offer several conjectures to explain the Hispanic performance. One possibility is that Hispanic children (in our sample, predominantly Puerto Rican and Dominican) are socialized in a "person-oriented" rather than a "problem-oriented" culture (Hertzig, Birch, Thomas, & Mendez, 1968) and hence are not greatly encouraged to develop informal mathematical ideas and skills. A second possibility is that these children do develop an adequate informal mathematics, on their own and without the help of parents, but are not encouraged by their culture to display such knowledge in social situations, and hence test poorly. Because there has been very little research on the U.S. Hispanic group, who are now nearly as numerous as African-Americans, it is important to attempt to replicate these results and to explore possible interpretations.

Social Class

Clearly SES can make a difference. The Colombian results are clearest but the data for Korea are convincing too: for both groups, ethnicity itself is not the sole operative variable; the differences associated with SES are relatively large. (Actually, we speculate that the Colombian effect might have been even larger had the higher SES children not been engaged in the beginning stages of English immersion at the time of testing.) The SES effect is small in a "socialist" country like China which at the time of the study officially minimized even the existence of class distinctions. We must be cautious, however, in generalizing these findings to other countries—for example, to the performance of lower SES U.S. Hispanics —because it is so difficult to equate social class across national boundaries.

Because our study did not examine directly the issue of how SES might exert its effects on the development of informal mathematical thinking, we cannot comment on this matter. All we can say is that the results, particularly the large Colombian differences, may be taken to support the Starkey and Klein view that extreme differences in poverty, with the correlated variations in environment and experience (not to speak of health status) that these suggest, exert a significant influence on early cognitive development. Presumably in some cultures higher SES provides an "advantaged" environment in which early mathematical thinking and the means and motivation for its expression flourish, whereas the same is not true for lower SES. The mechanisms by which the putative "advantages" (as well as their presumed absence) operate need to be elucidated.

CONCLUSIONS

We began with the fact that key groups differ dramatically in school mathematics achievement. But our research shows that informal mathematical abilities are widespread at the preschool level. Not only Asians, but children from various racial and ethnic groups, and from various countries exhibit competence in informal mathematics.

Why then do some do well and others poorly? Some children begin well and enjoy advantages that may accelerate mathematics learning: if they receive preschool instruction (like certain Chinese), or are born into a culture favouring quantitative activity (like the Japanese), or are privileged to be a member of a relatively affluent class (in Colombia or Korea), or of a group with positive expectations about schooling (U.S. middle-class White, Korean-American), then their potential is most likely to be realized.

Other preschool children begin with adequate intellectual ability but eventually perform poorly in school. An important example is African-Americans, whose performance at the preschool level is not much different from that of other groups, including the Japanese. Yet the African-Americans do not, as a group, realize their potential in school. The educational system seems to amplify, rather than modulate, differences with which children enter school. Subordinate groups are generally provided with inferior education, including teachers who expect them to fail.

Still other children may begin with difficulties in informal mathematics, which may then hamper their school achievement. Perhaps this is the case for U.S. Hispanics or lower-class Colombians. But so far the evidence is sparse; more research needs to be conducted to determine whether other factors, like motivation or styles of expression, are responsible for the initially low level of performance.

In general, informal mathematical ability does not appear to be a major mediator of differences in school mathematics achievement. Almost all preschool children seem to have the intellectual potential to learn school mathematics. The failure of some groups probably results from motivation and the system of schooling itself.

ACKNOWLEDGEMENTS

The authors gratefully acknowledge the assistance of Adelaida Garcia, Marymount School, Colombia; Kayoko Inagaki and Hiroko Kondo, Chiba University, Japan; Myung-Ja Song, Dong-A University, Korea; and Ira Blake, Maria Cordero, Christine McCarthy, and Kathleen St. Leger, Teachers College, Columbia University, USA.

This research was supported by a grant from the National Science Foundation, MDR-8751665, for which we are grateful. The paper was completed while the first author was a Fellow at the Center for Advanced Study in Behavioral Sciences. The first author is grateful for financial support provided by the Spencer Foundation, Grant B-1074.

APPENDIX:
BIRTHDAY PARTY GAME

1. Finger Displays of Number

Materials Needed: an animal puppet

Procedure: "We're going to have a make-believe birthday party! How old are you? Let's make believe it's your party and that you're becoming 4 years old today." No matter how old the child says he is, pretend that it's his 4th birthday party.

Demonstration: "Let's give your fingers some exercise, show me 4 years old with your fingers!" If correct, say: "Good, you held up 4 fingers very quickly!" If incorrect, say:" No, hold up 4 fingers like this," demonstrate using your 4 non-thumb fingers.

Next give the following 4 problems. Do not correct the children's answers.

"Let's make believe there are other children at your party!"

a. "Tommy's going to come to your party, he's 3 years old. Hold up 3 fingers!"
b. "Lucy's coming too, she's 5 years old. Hold up 5 fingers!"
c. "Patty's coming too, she's 7 years old. Hold up 7 fingers!"
d. "Carlos is also going to be here, he's 6 years old. Hold up 6 fingers!"

Scoring and Recording: On the answer sheet, circle the number of fingers that the child held up. If the child offers several finger displays, ask her to indicate which is her final answer.

2. Perception of More

Materials Needed: 5 cards divided into halves. Each side has a different number of colourful stickers randomly arranged on it. Demonstration card has 10 vs. 2 stickers.

Other cards have :

a. 6 vs. 9 stickers
b. 12 vs. 8 stickers
c. 8 vs. 4 stickers
d. 3 vs. 2 stickers.

Procedure: "Look at the fun things that will be at your party! We're going to play lots of games. We going to play one about which has more! Here's what the game will be like. Here are some stickers. Look carefully and quickly show me which side has more. Make sure you're right but point really quickly!" Then show the child the demonstration card for 2 seconds. If child is correct, say "That's right, that side has more stickers." If incorrect, say "No, that side has more. See it has a lot of stickers."

"Now I'm going to show you some more cards. Each time you should point quickly and show me which side has more." Then give the rest of the cards in order. Each is presented quickly for 2 seconds. Each time say, "Quickly point to the side that has more." Do not correct the child on these cards. The child should be encouraged not to count the stickers but just to "quickly choose which side has more."

Scoring and Recording: On the answer sheet, circle the number of stickers that the child points to for each card. Also note whether the child used any overt strategy to do this task.

3. Production from 10

Materials Needed: Have sets of 10 of the following items laid out on a separate table: balloons, cups, whistles, yo-yos.

Procedure: instruct the child to lay out the following sets. Correct the child only on the practice item. Do not stop the child when he reaches the correct number. Let the child indicate that he is finished. Remove each set of items from the play table after it is used.

"Mr. [name of puppet-Cow, Dog, Elephant etc.] is going to play with us at the party. Let's help him get ready for the party."

Practice Item: "Mr. _____ needs some balloons. Give him 4 balloons!"

a. "Mr. _____ wants to put the cups on the table. Give him 3 cups!"
b. "Mr. _____ wants some whistles. Give him 8 whistles!"
c. "Mr. _____ wants some yo-yos. Give him 5 yo-yos!"

Recording and Scoring: Indicate the number of items in the sets placed out by the child.

4. Counting by Ones

Materials Needed: Animal puppet.

Procedure: "The next game we're going to play at your party will be counting as high as you can." Hold up the animal puppet. "The [name of puppet—Tiger, Elephant etc.] starts and he goes 1–2–3. It's your turn, now let's see how high you can go! Count up as high as you can go." Let the child count until she feels she cannot go on or until she reaches 40 (with or without errors), whichever is sooner.

Recording and Scoring: On the answer sheet, circle all the numbers said by the child. Cross out each number that the child skips. If the child produces an unusual number or an unusual sequence of numbers, record exactly what the child says. The child's score is the highest number in a correct sequence of counting she reaches with the allowance of one number omitted along the way. That is if the child says, 1,2,3,4,6,7,8,10 . . . her score is 8 — that is the highest number she reached with only one skip. If she says 1,2,3,4,7,8,9. . . her score is 4. If she says, 1,3,2,4,5. . . her score is 1.

5. Comparison of Number

Materials Needed: Cards with written numbers that have been placed in a "magic box".

Procedure: Tell the child: "We're going to play another fun game now! We're going to pick numbers from this box and you can tell which is bigger." Use the puppet to pick up each number. "First we pick 2 and then we pick 4. Which number is bigger? Remember the one that is the bigger number is the winner." Correct the child only on the first item. If the child does not understand the term "bigger", tell the child that "With the numbers 1 and 2, the 2 is the bigger number. It is more."

Continue with:

a. "First he picks 3 and then he picks 2. Which number is bigger?"
b. "First he picks 8 and then he picks 4. Which number is bigger?"
c. "First he picks 9 and then he picks 3. Which number is bigger?"
d. "First he picks 4 and then he picks 10. Which number is bigger?"

Recording and Scoring: Record the number that the child chooses for each item. Note also if the child chooses a number other than those mentioned.

Note: The child does not have to read the numbers. They are read for him.

6. Concrete Addition

Materials Needed: The animal puppet should be used by the examiner to speak and to put out the toys: 5 cups, 10 whistles, and 10 yo-yos.

Procedure: The animal puppet should be made to take 3 cups and then take 1 cup. Say: "Look!! Mr. _____ takes 3 cups and then he takes 1 cup, How many did he take altogether? That's right, he took 4." Correct *only* this item, if it is incorrect, by saying: "No, he took 4." Do not count the cups for the child. On all items, the child should be allowed to touch or count the objects to solve the problems but should not be explicitly encouraged to do so. Make sure that the objects are placed directly in front of the child and that the sets of objects are clearly separated by 12 inches. Lay out the objects one by one.

Continue with the puppet saying:

a. "Mr._____ takes 1 whistle and then he takes 2 whistles. How many did he take altogether?"
b. "Mr. _____ takes 2 yo-yos and then he takes 2 more yo-yos. How many did he take altogether?"
c. "Mr. _____ takes 3 cups and then he takes 2 cups. How many did he take altogether?"

Recording and Scoring: Circle the number of objects that the child says for each item. Check off the strategy used by the child on the answer sheet.

7. Digit Span Memory

Materials Needed: The clown puppet is used throughout this sub-test.

Procedure: "We are going to play a 'say the same number' game! "I'm going to say some numbers now and I want you to repeat them, say them just the way I do." Say: "3–7, Say the same numbers!" Each time say the numbers and wait for the child to respond. Tell the child to "Say the same number" after they are said only if the child does not respond. Correct, if necessary, only the first series by saying, "You should say 3–7." Pause for *1 second* in between each digit.

Continue with:

a. 4–2
b. 9–3–7
c. 2–5–1
d. 4–1–7–9
e. 6–8–2–9
f. 2–5–7–3–1
g. 5–9–2–6–3

Stop after 2 consecutive failures.

Recording and Scoring: Item is counted as a failure if it deviates at all from the digit series spoken. If the child responds correctly, check correct. If the child responds incorrectly, record exactly what the child says.

8. Concrete Subtraction

Materials Needed: The animal puppet, 6 whistles, 7 cups and 4 yo-yos.

Procedure: Say: "Mr. _____ has 4 whistles and because he's so nice he gives 2 away to you. How many does the puppet have left now?" (Example) Remove each object one by one. When objects are removed, push them 12 inches away from the set and keep them in sight. Correct only the example by saying, "No, he has 2 left." Continue with:

a. "Mr. _____ takes 5 whistles and he gives 1 away to you. How many does the puppet have left now?"
b. "Mr. _____ takes 7 cups and gives 1 away to you. How many does the puppet have left now?"
c. "Mr. _____ takes 4 yo-yos and gives 1 away to you. How many does the puppet have left now?"

Recording and Scoring: Record the number said by the child. Also record the strategy used by the child to arrive at his answer.

9. Informal Subtraction and 10. Informal addition (Surprise Bag Game)

Materials Needed: A small party bag for the surprises to be put into. 15 whistles and 10 yo-yos.

Procedure: Say: "Look you're going to have a special bag to bring home! Mr. _____ puts 3 whistles into the bag and then takes 1 away. How many surprises are left in the bag now?" If the child gets this first one wrong, let her look inside the bag to see what the correct number should be. Let her look only for this first item.

After each item, remove all the items from the bag. Be sure to drop each item in one by one in full view of the child.

a. "Mr. _____ puts 2 whistles in the bag and takes 1 away. How many are in the bag now?"
b. "Mr. _____ puts 4 yo-yos in the bag and takes 1 away. How many are in the bag now?"

c. "Mr. _____ puts 5 whistles in the bag and takes 1 away. How many are in the bag now?"

d. "Now Mr. _____ puts 2 yo-yos in the bag and then he puts in 2 more. How many are in the bag now?"

e. "Mr. _____ puts 3 whistles in the bag and then he puts in 2 more. How many are in the bag now?"

f. "Now we're going to make the bag ready for you to take home! Mr. _____ puts 2 stickers in the bag and then he puts in 1 more. How many are in the bag now?"

(A sticker prize should be given to each child to take away with her.)

Recording and Scoring: Record the exact number the child gives as her answer. Note also the type of strategy used by the child to arrive at her answer.

Note

In the second year of data collection, an effort was made to separate the Information Subtraction and Addition tasks by inserting an example of addition before the actual addition problems. This was intended to alert the child to changes in mathematical operations. No significant differences in children's performances were found to result from this procedural change.

9 Learning Arithmetic With an Abacus

Giyoo Hatano
Keio University, Tokyo, Japan

This chapter discusses what kind of mathematics students learn by practising abacus operation intensively. This topic may sound peculiar and almost irrelevant to learning mathematics in Western countries. However, research findings on this topic not only illuminate how the abacus skill is a good example of how over-learned cognitive skills develop, but also have a few general and important implications for the learning and teaching of mathematics.

First, the findings should serve to clarify when calculation devices and aids can enhance the understanding of written calculation algorithms. Calculations with an abacus are at an intermediate level of abstraction between calculations with Dienes blocks or TILEs on the one hand, and written calculations on the other. For example, unlike Dienes blocks or TILEs, abacus beads are all of the same size, and a unit bead may represent one, ten, or a hundred depending on its position (VanLehn & Brown, 1980). Thus learning how to operate an abacus may help students acquire the notion of the place value. Do abacus learners have a better understanding of written calculation procedures? Does the students' experience of using an abacus for calculation help them repair their "buggy" algorithms for written calculation? If not, why not?

Second, research in abacus learning reveals what consequences enhanced calculation abilities have for mathematical problem solving. As will be seen below, expertise in abacus operation is oriented towards increasing its speed, and experts have in fact achieved a high degree of speed, accuracy, and automaticity, although usually not deep mathematical understanding. Even at lower levels of mastery, abacus learners tend to have a highly developed ability for the four calculations. Thus we can examine the effects of this enhanced calculation ability on their performance in a variety of mathematical problem solving areas.

Third, studies on abacus learning and its effect on school mathematics enable us to conceptualize better how non-school mathematics can be used to teach school mathematics. They are expected to specify how much the characterization of street mathematics as consisting of effective and meaningful procedures (Carraher, Carraher, & Schliemann, 1985) can be applied to non-school mathematics in general, because, unlike the street mathematics in Brazil, abacus operation may not be semantically transparent.

After briefly describing how an abacus is used and learned in present-day Japanese society, I will review research findings on the process of gaining expertise in abacus in two sections: first on the process of becoming a master in mental abacus operation and its cognitive consequences, and second on the process from beginner to intermediate, more specifically the development of calculation ability by practice in abacus operation and its effects on mathematical problem solving. In the final section, I will try to derive implications from these findings for mathematics instruction.

HOW AN ABACUS IS USED AND LEARNED

Four Calculations on an Abacus

An abacus is an external memory and computational device. It can register a number as a configuration of beads, and one can produce the answer to a given addition or subtraction by manipulating them, unless carrying or borrowing is involved. In other words, it enables operators to "offload" computation, at least in part.

Abacus operation and paper-and-pencil calculation share the goal (finding the answer) and component subskills (e.g. use of basic number facts, borrowing from the next left). They are different primarily in three ways. (1) Whereas in the paper-and-pencil version every step of calculation has to be done by the human mind, because paper and pencil constitute only a memory device, in abacus operation many steps of calculation are performed by physically moving the beads, as mentioned above. (2) Whereas in paper-and-pencil calculation a figure written in the answer row is not modifiable, a resultant number on an abacus can easily be changed. This allows abacus operation to proceed from the largest to the smallest units (e.g. hundreds to tens to ones) whereas paper-and-pencil calculation proceeds in the opposite direction. (3) Since the Japanese abacus has a bead worth 5 in the upper section and four beads worth 1 each in the lower section (instead of nine 1-beads) in each column, carrying and borrowing procedures on the abacus are more complicated than those with paper and pencil.

Figure 9.1 presents an example of subtraction by abacus. As you can see, what you have to do mentally is to find the complementary number-to-ten of seven and the complementary number-to-five of three. Other steps are just to enter or remove a number as prescribed.

Multiplication and division on an abacus are a little more complicated. For them, abacus operation proceeds from the smaller to larger units. See Fig. 9.2 for an example of multiplication. Here, in addition to finding complementary numbers-to-ten or five, single-digit multiplications have to be done mentally by using *kuku* (multiplication number facts of single digits; this word literally means nine-nines). However, after some practice, it is usually easier to run calculation with an abacus than with paper and pencil, because part of the calculation can be offloaded.

How an Abacus is Used

The abacus was very often used in day-to-day commercial activity in Japan. Until a cash-register, and then a low-price handy calculator, became available, it was an indispensable tool for merchants. Skilled abacus operators could get a good job in institutions where a lot of calculation was needed, for example, a bank. It is still used daily in small shops, or by people who believe that an abacus is more reliable than a calculator when its operator is skilful—an answer obtained by a calculator may be entirely wrong, if there is an input error that is not recognized. However, the abacus is being used less and less often, and its importance has been decreasing.

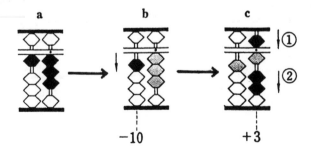

a. Set 13.

b. You cannot subtract 7 from the 3 on the ones rod. So take 1 from the tens rod with the idea of subtracting 7 from 10.

c. Subtract 7 from the 10 that you have got, and add the remainder 3 to the 3 on the ones rod. There is only one counter left to be added. So add 5 with the forefinger, and subtract the 2 which you have added in excess.

FIG. 9.1. Subtraction by abacus, 13–7 = 6. Reprinted with permission from *The League of Japan Abacus Association* (1989).

(1) Set the problem as
    in the figure at the right.

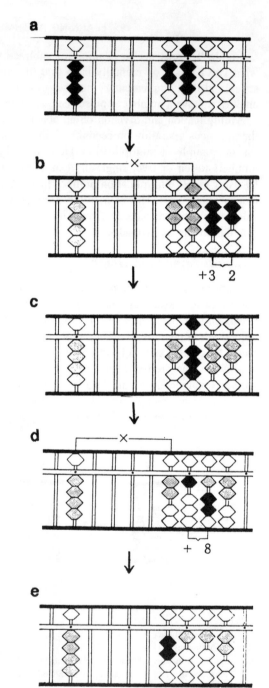

(2) First calculate 8 × 4.
    8 × 4 = 32. So set the
    product 32, with the
    first rod to the right
    of that of the multi-
    plicand digit 8 as its
    tens place.

(3) Clear the multipli-
    cand digit 8.

(4) Next calculate the
    multiplication of the
    20 of 28 by 4. 2 × 4
    = 8. So set the product
    8, with the first rod to
    the multiplicand digit
    2 as its tens rod.

(5) Clear the multipli-
    cand digit 2. As the
    ones place of the product
    of the problem is formed
    on the second rod to the
    right of the problem, the
    answer is 112.

FIG. 9.2. Multiplication by abacus, 28 × 4 = 112. Reproduced with permission from *The League of Japan Abacus Association* (1989).

However, the abacus is still alive in Japanese society. It survives primarily in two forms: as an instructional tool in general education, and as a special tool, skills for which are valued in circles of enthusiasts (like sports, music or other recreational activities). Although opportunities to use it are now minimal, abacus operation is taught at school; all Japanese children learn how to operate an abacus even now, because it is considered a valuable cultural property. About one-sixth of children go to a private school-after-school (*juku*) specialized for abacus two to four days a week for a year or longer. Going to an abacus school necessarily means practising calculation at least 100 hours per year. It usually costs 5,000–6,000 Yen (about $45–55) per month, and if the child takes a qualifying exam (most learners actually do), additional fees are needed. Despite the fact that abacus skills have been losing their utility value, the number of abacus schools has not decreased—a somewhat puzzling phenomenon. Perhaps parents send their children to abacus schools in the belief that the exercise there will foster diligence and punctiliousness, which are important Japanese values, as well as enhance calculation and estimation ability.

Many high schools and some junior highs have an abacus club, whose members compete in matches and tournaments. Usually these players practise at least a few hours every day for several years. This undoubtedly produces over-learned skills. Here we can see an instance of the change in the nature of skills—what used to be instrumental for other goals becomes an autonomous domain of expertise.

These players are not particularly interested nor talented in mathematics. They are probably not superior to their age-mates in mathematics except for their unusual competence in calculation. Some of them become school teachers, but usually not in mathematics but in bookkeeping.

How it is Learned

Basic abacus operation is acquired in elementary school, as mentioned above. At grades 3 and 4 (9–11 years of age), students learn how to use this instrument for adding and subtracting numbers, as well as how to represent a number on an abacus. Advanced skills for abacus operation, however, are usually acquired by studying at a specialized private *juku*, though sometimes through informal observation and teaching. At the abacus school students are given many problems in the four arithmetical operations without the meaning of each step of calculation being explained to them in detail. Each operation can be described by a very limited number of general "productions"—that is, condition–action pairs constituting a production system such as "If an addend needs more beads than available, add 1 to one column left and subtract the complementary number-to-10 of the addend from the target column". This makes it possible for people to learn how to operate the instrument in a few hours. Therefore, training afterwards is geared almost entirely to accelerating the speed of the operation.

Like expertise in many other out-of school domains in Japan, abacus learning is motivated by an elaborated qualification system and frequent exams for qualification. About two million people take some qualifying examination for abacus skills every year. There are a few different qualification systems that have slightly different criteria for qualification. However, they share the basic characteristics: there are degrees for students and degrees for masters; the former are ranked from the 6th- or 10th-*kyu*, (the lowest class) to the 1st-*kyu* (the highest class), and the latter from 1st-*dan* (level 1 master, the lowest) to 10th-*dan* (level 10 master, the highest). A few special divisions are also provided—such as a division for mental instead of physical operation of the abacus.

In this chapter, I call players qualified as 5th- or 6th-*kyu* novices, 3rd- or 4th-*kyu* lower intermediates, 1st- or 2nd-*kyu* intermediates, 1st- to 3rd-*dan* junior experts, and 4th-*dan* or more advanced experts. There are no higher qualifications than 10th-*dan*. However, national champions are referred to as grand experts, because they are considerably different from ordinary 10th-*dan* operators. Using this terminology, what is reviewed in the next section focuses on the shift from intermediate to expert, and the following section concerns the process from beginner to lower intermediate.

BECOMING A MASTER IN MENTAL ABACUS OPERATION: A CASE OF ROUTINE EXPERTISE

In daily observation, three things about abacus calculation as an over-learned skill are especially intriguing. First, skilled abacus operators calculate very fast, often faster than necessary for any practical purpose, but they are motivated to make the operation even faster. Their calculation is accurate, especially when they use the instrument, but is not perfect. They often check their calculation by repeating it once. In other words, their expertise seems to be oriented primarily towards increasing speed.

Second, abacus operation tends to be gradually interiorized. This interiorization can be accomplished to such a degree that most abacus masters can calculate accurately and even faster without an abacus than with the instrument itself. Intermediates move their fingers during calculation without an abacus as if they were actually fingering one, although experts do not do so. Such fingering movements are analogous to mouthing words while reading.

Third, while experienced practitioners are using an abacus they can carry on a conversation. Like experienced drivers, they can do two things at one time—in their case, calculating and asking and/or answering questions. This suggests that after their over-learning, abacus operators need only a limited amount of attention for calculation, and little linguistic processing is involved in it. Experts can converse even when they are operating on a mental abacus.

My associates and I have studied these three phenomena systematically. Let me summarize our findings for each of them below. Because of space limitation, I refer to studies conducted in other laboratories only when they are highly relevant to the phenomenon in question.

Speed of Calculation

Some abacus learners are extraordinarily quick in calculation. How fast can they calculate? Criteria for passing exams for different qualifications give some concrete ideas. When mixed addition and subtraction problems are given aurally, the maximal speed of presentation in matches and tournaments is around 2.5 digits per sec., because the recitation includes units, tens, hundreds, etc., special expressions separating the numbers, and the change of the operation (from addition to subtraction or vice versa). To be qualified as an "expert" (level 4 masters and above) one can make few errors, if any, at this speed, whether with or without using a physical abacus.

When similar problems are presented in print, junior experts (level 1–3 masters) are supposed to be able to process, i.e. to add or subtract, 3 digits per sec., which may include carrying or borrowing. Experts should be able to handle 5–10 digits per second. Remarkable speed is required also for multiplication and division, which are usually presented in print. Experts are expected to find answers for 3×3 or 4×2 digit multiplication within 5 sec. at the slowest. They often rely on a mental abacus even when they are allowed to use a real one, because, as will be shown below, mental operation is quicker than physical manipulation.

How accurate are masters' calculations at this speed? When they use a real abacus, calculation is basically error-free. Their mental calculation is not entirely free from errors, but the accuracy is at a respectable level. In order to be qualified as a level 10 master, no more errors than 2 out of 30 mixed addition and subtraction problems are allowed. Since each item includes 60 digits, the permitted error rate is 0.0011. For the multiplication of 3 by 3 digits, 2 errors are also allowed out of the 30. Since each item typically involves 9 single-digit multiplications and 11 additions, this means that an error rate of 0.0033 is permitted.

Grand experts show greater speed with even lower error rates. A 4th-grade girl, whom Keiko Osowa (Shimisu) and I observed after she became the junior national champion, is a good example. She could solve 30 printed multiplication problems, 3 digits by 3 digits (e.g. 148×395) or 4 by 2 (3519×42), in 58 sec. This was surprising, but her net calculation time was even shorter—she needed this amount of time for writing the answers down. Thus she could solve the same number of problems requiring the inverse operation ($277836 \div 78$, $171850 \div 982$) in 31 sec., because the number of digits in the answers was nearly half. She made just one error on these 60 problems. For printed addition and subtraction problems she could process about 10 digits per sec., also very accurately.

In other words, grand experts can process digits more quickly than they (or we university people) can recite, and can find calculation answers for printed problems and write them down faster than they can copy given numerals. Experts' performance is less dramatic, but is still impressive, particularly because it is generally believed that almost any person can reach the level of expert, if they spend a sufficient amount of time in practice.

Several mechanisms are offered to explain this speed of calculation (Hatano, 1988b). First, *compilation and tuning* (Anderson, 1982): A set of specific productions (e.g. "If addend 6 cannot enter, add 1 to one column left and subtract 4 from the target column") replaces the general production which requires interpretation, and then a few such specific productions are merged into a single production to get the final state directly (e.g. "If 7 is to be added to 6, add 1 to one column left and leave 3 at the target column"). Second, *sensori-motor operation on physical representation of abacus beads comes to be interiorized as mental operation on mental imagery of a configuration of abacus beads.* Through this, the speed of the operation is no longer limited by the speed of muscle movement. Third, *a module-like system is established to represent mentally a number or series of digits in a form of the configuration of abacus beads*, which is activated without any conscious effort or decision-making. Fourth, *the mental imagery of the abacus becomes simplified, disregarding properties unnecessary for calculation* (e.g. colour of beads), so that it can be manipulated even more quickly. Finally, *monitoring of the operation is removed in favour of using one's processing capacity to speed up the operation itself,* since an expert's calculation is so fast that calculating twice is simpler than monitoring. Let me present experimental evidence for the first three mechanisms and explain why other mechanisms like the last two have to be assumed.

(1) First, compilation and tuning of productions. The abacus operation consists of a fixed and very limited number of productions (condition–action pairs), as mentioned in the last section. For addition and subtraction, one only needs to know general productions and number facts concerning complementary numbers of X to 5 and to 10. (Multiplication number facts, *kuku*, have to be known for multiplication and division.) For example, when X is to be added to column K, the following three-term general production is applied:

(1) If there are enough unused unit beads in K, enter X to K; if not, go to (2).
(2) If X is smaller than 5 and the 5-unit bead is unused, enter the 5-unit bead and remove the complementary number of X to 5; if not, go to (3).
(3) Enter one to (K + 1) and remove the complementary number-to-10 of X from K.

However, with these general productions only, one cannot operate an abacus very quickly. A set of specific productions replace the general production which requires interpretation, and then a few such specific productions are merged into a single production to get the final state directly.

Most students are first taught these general productions at abacus school, and sometimes verbalize them as they manipulate abacus beads. At this stage, their calculation is very slow, even slower than their paper-and-pencil calculation. It soon begins to speed up, however, and becomes pretty fast after just a few hours of practice. When asked to explain their operations, they often refer to specific or merged productions, which are not explicitly taught.

More quantitative, though indirect, evidence for the compilation and tuning is that those who go to an abacus school are faster than their age-mates who do not, in single-digit addition and finding a complementary number to ten. For example, as will be discussed in greater detail, Amaiwa and Hatano (1989) showed that 3rd-grade abacus learners outperformed the non-learners on simple addition and on finding a complementary number to ten.

(2) Second, interiorization, i.e. real abacus operation comes to be interiorized into mental abacus operation. This enables abacus operators to calculate faster and faster, going beyond the speed of muscle movement. Hatano, Miyake, and Binks (1977) found that experts' mental abacus operation was faster than their operation with a physical abacus. The amount of time needed for the former was 72% of the latter on the average. In contrast, intermediates in the same experiment took a longer time for mental than physical abacus operation. Mixed results were obtained for junior experts. Two reasons can be proposed for this interaction effect between the extent of expertise and the use of the physical instrument on the time for calculation. First, since the intermediates moved their fingers during mental calculation, they were still constrained by the speed of muscle movement, and thus their mental calculation could not be faster. Second, because mentally holding and changing a pattern of beads required a considerable attentional resource for them, they may not have been able to concentrate on calculation.

Anyway, interiorization seems to be an important mechanism for increasing the speed of calculation. How this process proceeds as operators accumulate practice will be discussed in the next subsection.

It might be added that the 4th-grade girl referred to above used the physical abacus only when she dealt with very large numbers which could not be represented on her mental abacus. She knew she could calculate much faster with the mental abacus than the real abacus. This is true for most experts and grand experts.

(3) Third, a module-like system to represent a number in mental imagery of abacus beads is established. In other words, for experienced abacus operators a

number or a series of digits is always represented on the mental abacus. This is in sharp contrast to our representations of numbers. We have several modes of representations, and use one or a few of them that will best fit a given problem.

Having multiple representations is advantageous for memorizing and solving a variety of problems, but is disadvantageous in a sense, because building and choosing from among them takes time and effort. Since the speed of calculation is most highly valued and no novel problems are posed in the domain of abacus operation, saving as much time and effort as possible by making a module-like system to represent a number may be considered a good strategy. Cognitive consequences of this strategy include increased speed of calculation, enhanced automaticity of the operation, and also a more expanded size of the mental abacus. In fact, the size of the mental abacus is highly correlated with the speed of calculation among experienced operators.

Evidence for the use of a mental abacus to represent numbers, not as a computation device, was obtained by Hatano, Amaiwa, and Shimizu, (1987) who found that junior experts and experts used their mental abacus for memorizing a series of digits, whereas lower intermediates never did so, although they could register a few digits on it. More specifically, junior experts and experts could reproduce a memorized series of digits either forward or backward in nearly equal amounts of time, whereas lower intermediates took a much longer time for backward than for forward reproduction. Intermediates seemed to be in a transitional phase. Moreover abacus masters' memory for digits was more vulnerable to interpolated visuo-spatial tasks than aural-verbal ones, whereas the reverse was true for the less skilled abacus operators.

The formation of a modularized mental abacus is not sufficient to account for the differences between junior experts, who clearly rely on a mental abacus, and experts. Some other mechanisms must be at work, because the speed of calculation becomes even greater after operators move from junior experts to experts. Compared with junior experts, experts' speed of processing numbers for addition and subtraction is supposed to be almost doubled, and grand experts' addition and subtraction are four times as fast as junior experts'. Similar marked differences were observed for multiplication and division (Amaiwa, 1987b).

(4) One additional mechanism may be the simplification of the mental abacus, by disregarding properties irrelevant to calculation (e.g. the colour of the beads), so that it can be manipulated even more quickly. Experts often indicate that their mental imagery of abacus beads are semi-concrete—not very realistic but "symbolic", although still spatial in nature. This indirectly supports the above mechanism.

(5) The final mechanism at work in achieving even greater speeds may be the removal of monitoring. By removing monitoring of the operation, processing capacity is used maximally to speed up the operation itself. Since experts calculate so fast, calculating twice is simpler than monitoring during calculation. Experts often claim that they check the answer by repeating the preceding calculation while writing the answer. A surprising gap in their amazing calculating ability can be interpreted as support for this notion of dropping monitoring during calculation: they often fail to recognize that they have solved the same problem twice when the order of numbers is changed minimally. For example, when the last number is presented first and the other numbers are kept in the same order.

Formation of a Mental Abacus

As mentioned above, experienced abacus operators, almost without exception, can calculate fast and accurately without the physical instrument. It is assumed that they can represent an intermediate, resultant number on their "mental abacus", in the form of a mental image of the configuration of beads, to which they enter or from which they remove the next input number. Since they can use this mental abacus in their head, they do not have to carry the instrument with them, nor do they have to rely on special heuristics as, say, ordinary people do in a supermarket (Lave, 1988). Too much reliance on a cultural tool often makes it difficult to solve problems without it, but this seldom happens for experienced abacus operators.

Although interiorization of abacus operation takes place within a few years after students start practice, this does not mean that a promptly usable mental abacus is readily formed. It must be a long process like the acquisition of other runnable mental models. According to Ezaki (1980), around the time that operators had qualified as intermediates (after 35 months of practice on the average), they became able to add and subtract numbers quickly without the instrument, but the size of their mental abacus was just two or three columns. Therefore, when the numbers had more than two or three digits, they had to calculate by dividing them into manageable numbers of columns.

The size of the mental abacus increases gradually. Practice results in steady progress up to the size of five columns or so. Extension of the mental abacus beyond five columns requires intensive, often painful training. It is claimed that in order to increase the size of the mental abacus by one column, a year of practice is usually needed. The practice should not be within the size of one's mental abacus, because extension is not required nor induced by such practice. However, problems requiring more columns than the operator's mental abacus has cannot be solved in principle. Thus attempts to solve them must fail continuously, for almost a year. If one is solved correctly, out of many problems, this is taken as a sign that the operator will soon become able to solve problems of the extended size. Thus only real experts, after many years of extensive practice, can handle numbers of many digits.

Grand experts in this abacus-derived mental calculation can do mental arithmetic with large numbers without any observable or electrically recordable finger movement, although all but a few intermediates move their fingers during mental calculation, as if they were operating on a real abacus. It is assumed that for these intermediates the simulated finger movement makes the image of abacus beads more vivid and controllable. In fact, prohibition of this movement or compulsory tapping reduced their performance (Hatano, Miyake, & Binks, 1977). In other words, the physical manipulation of material beads is interiorized first into the physico-mental operation on mental beads, and then into the purely mental operation on the mental abacus. As mentioned above, this system for mental representation evolves further.

Skills executed repeatedly in abacus operation are probably used in mental abacus operation without any (major) modifications. When asked to verbalize their calculation procedure, experts claim they are still following the same production rules. Stigler (1984) showed that skilled abacus operators can judge whether a given "intermediate state", i.e. a resultant number in an abacus bead configuration, is obtained in the process of mental calculation, suggesting that they are in fact manipulating the image of the beads in mental calculation. However, close examination of their fingering may reveal some omissions of parts of the procedure.

As suggested by a number of investigators of everyday cognition, if people solve the same kinds of problems thousands of times, they tend to develop skills for aptly representing elements involved in the problems as well as efficient solution strategies to handle the represented problems. In complex knowledge domains like physics and mathematics, where novel problems are continually posed, experts generate an appropriate representation of each specific problem, using their rich and well-organized body of knowledge (e.g. Chi, Glaser, & Rees, 1982). However, in domains of speeded routine problem solving commonly observed in everyday cognition, experts have probably acquired a system of representation readily applicable to the whole set of problems that they expect to come across. The mental abacus seems to illustrate most clearly the formation of a powerful and specific system of representation. Three grand experts studied by Hatano and Osawa (1983) had a large-sized mental abacus. By using it they could reproduce 15, 16, and 16 digits, respectively. They nevertheless did not have exceptional memory in general. Their spans for alphabet letters were 5, 8, and 5, and those for fruit names were 5, 9, and 5. Although the size of numbers that can be handled in mental calculation is a little smaller than the digit span, these grand experts' mental abacus constituted a very powerful system of representing numbers.

Automaticity and Compatibility With Other Activities

As mentioned above, experienced abacus operators can converse during calculation, even when calculating without the physical instrument. Needless to say, the conversation cannot be very serious—usually just a short and simple factual or preferential question–answer exchange. Nevertheless, this is remarkable, considering that we generally ask people around us to keep silent when we calculate, especially when we do so without paper-and-pencil. Their ability to hold a conversation and to calculate at the same time implies that the execution of their skills becomes more and more automatic as they gain expertise. Furthermore, this ability also suggests that their mental abacus operation does not involve much of a linguistic component. We usually hold original numbers and/or intermediate results in a verbal form in mental calculation. Thus our process of mental calculation is vulnerable to verbal interference. Even when the answer to a question asked in the midst of calculation is just simple, uttering it destroys the intermediate result held in the rehearsal buffer. In contrast, abacus experts' mental calculation must be more visuo-spatial in nature.

Hatano, Miyake, and Binks (1977) have found that abacus experts' skills become automatic and compatible with a variety of secondary tasks, in so far as the latter do not require much mental effort, nor share the representational device with the former. They showed a moderately complex figure (e.g. a double-lined triangle with an inscribed circle) or a newspaper headline (e.g. "Don't send weapons to the Near East") to several intermediates, junior experts and experts while they were solving an addition problem aurally presented at a fixed speed of one digit per second. The intermediates could seldom find the right answer for the calculation problem because of the distraction, but the experts could manage to do so, and often correctly recalled the figure later. However, even for them, remembering the headline accurately was hard. Often they recalled only a few characters, without comprehending the meaning of the headline as a whole. Sometimes they reproduced headlines incorrectly in terms of the meaning, such as "Send weapons to the Near East", although they correctly held many local pieces of information. It is true that abacus operation does not require much mental resource of experienced operators, but it does require some.

Hatano, Miyake, and Binks (1977) also posed a factual-preferential question (e.g. "What is the highest mountain in Japan?", "Which do you like better, dogs or cats?") while the operators were trying to solve a visually presented addition problem as quickly as possible. Operators could answer these questions without difficulty, and with a physical abacus, this did not reduce either the speed or accuracy of their calculation. However, without the instrument, answering such a question reduced their calculation accuracy generally, and decreased the speed of computation for the experts and junior experts.

Generally speaking, when a calculation problem is presented at a fixed, below-maximum speed, or when the speed of calculation is constrained by that of muscle movement, experts tend to have a fairly large amount of remaining mental resources, because the calculation does not require much effort from them, and thus they can satisfactorily process the secondary tasks without sacrificing accuracy. However, when problems are processed at their preferred (maximal) speed, their resources are engaged in accelerating the calculation. Thus, even secondary tasks requiring minimum effort will retard their calculation speed; those requiring considerable effort cannot be executed simultaneously with the calculation.

Hatano and Osawa (1983) observed interesting patterns of interaction between the materials for the primary memory tasks and the kinds of secondary tasks, revealing the mental cost to masters of activating an extended mental abacus. They asked two grand experts in mental abacus operation to memorize series of digits or alphabet letters as the primary task. After the presentation of the series but before its reproduction, the grand experts were asked a simple verbal question (the aural-verbal task) or to choose a target drawing from six similar drawings (the visual-spatial task). For both kinds of materials the length of the series was one item shorter than their span as measured earlier in that session—that is, 14 digits and 6 alphabet letters for one subject, and 16 and 5 for the other. Their memory for digits was affected by both of the concurrent tasks, but was disrupted more by the visual-spatial task than by the aural-verbal task, whereas the reverse was true for the memory of letters, which was also disrupted by both of the concurrent tasks. Because we can reasonably assume that the grand experts used their mental abacus for digit memory, it seems that, although their (physical or mental) abacus operation was automatic, the use of the mental abacus fully extended required mental resources and prevented them from responding to the secondary tasks without difficulty.

It also seems that the mental abacus operation is not fully compatible with visuo-spatial concurrent tasks even among the grand experts (probably because the mental abacus resided not in Articulatory Loop but in Visuospatial Sketchpad, to use Baddeley's, 1986, terminology). In other words, when abacus experts calculate mentally, they rely on visuo-spatial imagery of an abacus bead configuration. In agreement with this hypothesis, Hatta and Ikeda (1988) suggest that the right hemisphere, which is assumed to be mainly in charge of the processing of imagery, is more involved in the abacus experts' mental calculation than the left hemisphere. They observed that whereas for ordinary people mental calculation reduced the speed of sequential key pressing by the right hand more than by the left hand, a reversed pattern was observed for abacus experts. These results are consistent with their prediction.

Lack of Flexibility

It should be noted that the process of acceleration of calculation speed, formation of a mental abacus, and gaining automaticity proceeds at the sacrifice of understanding or the construction of conceptual knowledge. For example, it is very hard to unpack a merged specific production to find the meaning of each step. For an abacus expert a number is represented only in terms of a simplified image of beads which does not have rich meaning. No mental resources can be used to reflect on why the procedure works.

As mentioned above, abacus masters are not interested in mathematics in general. Their mental calculation is very, very fast, and respectably accurate. However, it is rigidly proceduralized and not flexible—unlike Professor A.C. Aitken, studied by Hunter (1968/1977, p.37), who had "a large variety of calculative plans at his disposal" and could "solve the same problem in several different ways." In contrast, abacus masters do not adapt their skills to the task demand: nor do they invent new strategies using their mathematical knowledge.

In a study of experts and junior experts, Amaiwa and I (Amaiwa, 1987b) observed that they were not flexible in the use of their skills. They were given multiplication and division problems, some of which could be solved by using simplifying strategies. For example, a multiplication problem such as 99×38 could be solved as $38 \times 100 - 38$; a division problem such as $9250 \div 25$ could be solved as $9250 \times 4 \div 100$ or $925 \times 4 \div 10$. The experts and junior experts did not recognize this possibility and solved all the problems mechanically in the same way, although their calculation was still much faster than that of ordinary college students.

Another study revealed that the experts could not transfer their skills to non-conventional abacuses which were for a 6- or 12-base system (Amaiwa, 1987c). An old version of the Japanese abacus that had five unit beads below the bar was used with an indication that the bead above the bar represented six (for the 12 base system) or without using the bead above the bar (for the 6-base system). The experts performed no better with these abacuses than college students who had had negligible experience with the standard abacus. They could not modify their general productions, say, by replacing 12 for 10 and 6 for 5 and using them in addition and subtraction. Abacus operators apply the calculation procedures thousands of times without comprehending why the procedures work in terms of general principles. It seems that they do not construct conceptual knowledge of the n-base system of numbers.

It is often claimed (e.g. Anderson, 1980) that some degree of automatization of lower-order skills is a necessary condition for higher-order processes to work, because the latter processes need more mental resources. I would like to emphasize that, although this is a necessary condition, it is not a sufficient condition. Abacus experts certainly possess highly automated skills for computation, but they do not use the skills for mathematical or any other analytic thinking, nor do they develop deep understanding of the rationale underlying these skills.

I do not claim that, when they calculate, abacus masters manipulate beads just mechanically without recognizing what is represented by a specific configuration of beads. Certainly the meanings of configurations are readily understood by them, as revealed by Miller and Stigler (1991b). However, this understanding is not very different from that of H_2O as a symbol for water without grasping its constituents or basic properties.

In this sense, experts in abacus operation are distinctly different from experts in knowledge-rich domains like physics, and might be called "routine experts" as against "adaptive experts". Whereas the latter are characterized by their conceptual understanding, the adaptive and flexible use of their skills, and their capability of inventing new procedural knowledge, the routine experts represented by abacus experts "are outstanding in speed, accuracy and automaticity of performance but lack flexibility and adaptability to new problems" (Hatano & Inagaki, 1986, p.266).

THE ABACUS MAKES A DIFFERENCE IN ARITHMETIC

In this section I will discuss abacus skills from an instructional perspective. It is generally agreed that highly automated procedural skills are often efficient but only for limited types of problems. The skills of abacus masters are such skills, and in contemporary society, they may be valued as an extreme point in an autonomous domain of expertise rather than as practically useful tools, for instance, in commercial activity.

Are abacus skills learned in the context of school mathematics much like the skills of experts? As alluded to in the introduction of this chapter, I will discuss this issue in terms of two empirical questions, namely, whether abacus learning would enhance understanding of written calculation procedures, and whether it would facilitate performance in a variety of mathematical problem solving areas. Even if abacus skills in the educational context are efficient but useful only for limited types of problems, their mastery may produce some generalized consequences through sharing components with other skills of the same level and/or by facilitating the development of more complex skills involving the abacus or general calculation skills. Based on the answers to these two questions I will clarify the nature of abacus operation as a form of non-school mathematics or a barely legitimatized component in the current curriculum of mathematics education.

Mapping Instruction Does Not Work

First let me examine whether knowledge of how to do calculation on an abacus can be transferred to the paper-and-pencil mode and, more specifically, whether it can help to remove bugs in the written calculation algorithm. Amaiwa (1987a) tried to apply a simplified version of the "mapping instruction" (Resnick, 1982) between abacus operation and written calculation and found that it did not work well. Her subjects were 26 3rd-graders who solved three-digit subtraction problems almost always correctly with an abacus, but often incorrectly with paper and pencil. In the instruction session, they were individually asked to solve each of those problems on which they had made errors at the pretest for written calculation, alternately by the two computation procedures, i.e. with paper and pencil in steps 1, 3, and 5, and with an abacus in steps 2 and 4. In step 4, to make the mapping of the two procedures easier, the subjects were required to subtract units first, then tens, and finally hundreds, i.e. in inverse order to the standard abacus operation.

Two major patterns of responses were observed. Out of the 38 problems altogether, 24 were − + − + −, i.e., continuously making incorrect responses in written calculation yet correct responses with an abacus; 11 were − + +, i.e. solving the problem correctly on an abacus enabled the subjects to answer correctly with paper and pencil and thus terminated the steps. In the latter type, there seemed to be positive transfer, but results of the post-test suggested that at least some subjects had just copied the answer obtained in step 2 which they believed to be correct. When they were given a new set of problems for written calculation, they tended to make the same types of errors as before. In sum, the subjects generally failed to repair their written calculation procedure by transferring knowledge about the abacus procedure. Another set of similar mapping instructions attempted a few weeks later did not work either.

According to protocols obtained by interviews, subjects who continued to rely on a "buggy" paper-and-pencil procedure while always giving the correct answer with an abacus believed that there was perhaps one correct answer for both procedures. However, they were not confident as to whether getting two different answers necessarily meant that an error was involved in at least one procedure.

Considering that Amaiwa's subjects had learned abacus skills fairly well, it may be surprising that they failed to repair their paper-and-pencil procedure by relying on the isomorphism between the procedures. Her mapping instruction may have failed because the students did not understand the meaning of each step of the "base" abacus operation and thus could not derive specific pieces of information to repair the "target" writing procedure. In abacus operation, as pointed out above, a set of specific "productions" replaces a general production. A few of these specific productions are then merged into a single production to get the final state directly. Therefore, it becomes harder and harder to unpack the operation and find the meaning of each step. In other words, abacus operation as executed by experienced users is semantically opaque, that is, what they do with the instrument is not clearly connected to operations on numbers as conceptual entities.

This semantic opacity was revealed more directly in interviews about the meaning of specific steps with children learning abacus skills (Amaiwa & Hatano, 1983). Those who had had a year of practice at an abacus *juku* could explain the multi-digit subtraction procedure (e.g. 662–363) no better than their age-mates who had just started the practice. For example, only a few of the experienced learners could answer correctly what number is actually borrowed from the next column left or how the number borrowed from the hundred column is distributed to the column of units and tens.

Effects of Abacus Learning on Written Calculation

Despite difficulties in mapping the two sets of knowledge, practice in abacus operation has considerable effects on written calculation, as revealed by Amaiwa and Hatano (1989). The study was concerned not only with the extent of transfer but also with how it was produced—more specifically, whether through enhanced conceptual understanding or due to shared sub-skills. Fifty-three 3rd-graders who had been learning abacus operation at an abacus *juku* and their 57 classmates who were not going to an abacus *juku* were compared in their performances on two speeded tests of basic calculation, and paper-and-pencil tests under a lenient time-limit of multi-digit addition, subtraction, open sentence problems and word problems involving addition or subtraction, and comprehension of the exchange principle between columns. Examples of items from these tests will be given when I discuss the results below.

The abacus learners were much faster than the non-learners in basic calculation both on simple addition (means of 35.2 vs. 26.5 for two minutes, a significant difference at .01) and on finding a complementary number to ten (44.5 vs. 36.2 for one minute, significant at .01). These two measures were correlated .60 among the learners and .44 among the non-learners. The abacus learners were also much better in performance on multidigit subtraction problems. Furthermore, abacus learners solved open-sentence problems—such as "___ plus 8 is equal to 41", "___ – 7 = 27") significantly more often than pupils who were not going to an abacus *juku* and were also better at writing-an-expression for word problems (e.g. "There are 21 boys and 18 girls in Takashi's class. How many pupils are there?"). To control for unknown differences between the learners and non-learners, school grade in language was entered as a covariate in these statistical comparisons. Since there were no differences between the abacus learners and non-learners in grade in science or social studies when the grade in language was entered as a covariate, it is reasonable to claim that this quasi-experimental design worked pretty well and that the above differences were due to transfer from abacus learning. The effects of abacus learning upon paper-and-pencil calculation were thus fairly far-reaching and substantial.

How did such transfer occur? I infer that it was produced not through facilitated conceptual understanding, but through proficiency in shared subskills of simple computation. Proficiency in simple computation is a plausible candidate, because (a) a number of other studies as well as the present one revealed that abacus learning greatly enhances simple computation skills, and (b) eliminating its effect in statistical analyses makes other differences negligible. Convincing results as for (a) are obtained in an unpublished recent study by Amaiwa. For twelve months she followed up 30 3rd-graders who began to go to an abacus school from the start of the school year. The number of single-digit additions made in two minutes increased from 30.8 to 40.2 (three months later) to 46.2 (seven months later) and to 56.9 (a year later).

Because abacus operation often requires finding complementary numbers-to-10 (as in the third term of the general production on p.216), abacus learners must be quicker than non-learners for single-digit additions involving carrying and the corresponding subtractions. Moreover, although the operation does not require the use of single-digit addition number facts consciously when neither carrying nor borrowing is involved, because the answer can be obtained just by manipulating beads (as in the first term of the general production), it is conceivable that such number facts also become readily retrievable by repeatedly observing these additions and the corresponding subtractions. Abacus learners are expected to be quicker, say, at finding sums of two single digits, because they are so accustomed to encoding numbers, either given aurally or in digits, into configurations of abacus beads, and vice versa.

I believe that the component skills trained in abacus learning are used in written calculation. Written calculation skills consist of sets of productions, and each production is "fired" more or less automatically—whenever its condition is satisfied, the corresponding action is executed. Since abacus-learning students are very good at these skills, they can concentrate on higher-order processes including the monitoring of the steps of executive strategies and checking answers (as suggested by Case, 1982). It may also be possible for them to constrain their problem solving by quickly estimating the answer at sight. Another possibility is that their confidence in their ability to solve multi-digit subtraction makes them less "biased" towards addition than non-learners, when subtraction is in fact required. This possibility cannot be ignored, because in this study most of the errors that the non-learners made in open-sentence and writing-an-expression problems resulted from using addition when subtraction was required, and the reverse was rare.

However, despite their improved written calculation skill, abacus learners did not show an enhanced comprehension of the place value principle or trade between columns, which is the conceptual basis of the borrow-and-decrement procedure in both abacus and written calculation. When required to judge whether paired sets of numbers, expressed in terms of units, tens and hundreds, were equal or not—for example, comparing [9 tens and 9 units] with [8 tens and 10 units]; [8 hundreds, 2 tens and 6 units] with [7 hundreds, 11 tens and 16 units])—abacus learners and non-learners performed equally poorly. Even when used as an additional covariate, the comprehension assessed by this measure did not affect at all the differences between the learners and non-learners observed in other tests.

Why did practice in abacus operation have no effect upon this conceptual understanding? I interpret this to be also due to the semantic opacity of abacus operation. In addition, practice on an abacus neither requires nor encourages conceptual understanding, because the same instrument is used throughout without changing constraints, and speed is emphasized (see Hatano & Inagaki, 1986). As a result, abacus operators apply the trade principle thousands of times without consciously recognizing it.

Abacus Operation as a Form of Non-school Mathematics

Abacus operation in Japan seems to have much in common with street mathematics in Brazil (Carraher, Carraher, & Schliemann, 1985): (a) both are used for commercial activities; (b) both can be acquired without systematic instruction; (c) both are outside the mainstream or the "official" arithmetic knowledge taught in school. In short, both are essentially forms of non-school mathematics.

However, the two are radically different in semantic transparency, i.e. how clear the meaning of each step of calculation is. The steps of street mathematics are clear in meaning, because the representations manipulated in it are information-rich, and the ways of manipulation are analogous to actual activity dealing with goods or coins and notes. For example, in order to find the price for twelve lemons of Cr$ 5.00 each, a 9-year-old child who was an expert street mathematician counted up by 10 (10, 20, 30, 40, 50, 60) while separating out two lemons at a time (Carraher, Carraher, & Schliemann, 1985). On the contrary, representations of numbers on an abacus, though visibly concrete, are impoverished in meaning, and the method of manipulation is just mechanical.

Where these differences come from is an interesting question that merits close examination but I can discuss it only briefly here (see Hatano, 1988a, for more detailed analyses). I think the differences in semantic transparency can primarily be attributed to their functions in and the nature of the activities they serve. Street mathematics is a means by which a vendor and a customer reach an agreement that calculation is performed correctly. It is an inter-personal enterprise that requires semantic transparency—otherwise the customer may be suspicious. This semantic transparency also serves to make calculation accurate. It cannot be very quick, because it manipulates rich representations. However, the economy in which young Brazilian vendors live does not usually give priority to high efficiency in calculation. In contrast, abacus operation is basically a solitary activity, handling large numbers quickly and accurately. Operators are not interested in the semantic transparency of the calculation process, because they believe that their skills ensure the correctness of the answer. Even when abacus operation is used in interpersonal situations of buying/selling, both the vendor and the customer are willing to accept the answer in most cases, as they trust the skills. In fact, not a few Japanese customers seem to think that abacus operation is more dependable than calculation with a calculator. Experienced abacus operators must be able to handle impoverished representations, because the economy in which abacus operation developed has always required efficiency.

IMPLICATIONS FOR MATHEMATICS INSTRUCTION

Studies on expertise in abacus operation are reviewed in the preceding two sections separately, because I strongly believe that solving problems with an abacus has very different meanings for intermediate to expert operators on the one hand and novice to intermediate operators on the other. Although both groups use the same instrument, and run basically the same operation (even when the former uses a mental abacus), goals and contexts of expertise in the operation radically differ. Whereas the former are players involved in matches and tournaments and aim at improving their skills in an autonomous domain for pleasure, the latter are elementary school children learning it in the context of arithmetic. The contrast is like that between competitive marathon racers and joggers for health. Only the latter are only concerned with whether the practice is good for their health. For the former, whether it effectively improves their competence as athletes is the primary interest. Likewise, the effects of practice in abacus operation on mathematical thinking are irrelevant for abacus experts. What we can learn from research about such practitioners, although generally applicable to the acquisition of highly speeded and automatized cognitive skills, cannot be regarded as pertaining specifically to mathematical cognition.

Further interesting suggestions for mathematics instruction can be drawn from the review of research on abacus-learning school children since they learn arithmetic with an abacus. I believe that we can derive two instructional implications from the above analyses. First, we should not underestimate the significance of practice in basic computation for the development of mathematical cognition. Abacus learning is seen as having very limited instructional value, once we accept the premise that comprehension is much more important than proficiency. However, the present data indicate that enhanced proficiency in basic skills has wider effects than usually expected. It seems that "practice for proficiency in skills has its place" (Brownell, 1956, p.129) in mathematics education, although too much emphasis on proficiency may be detrimental to conceptual understanding. Toyama, the founder of Association of Mathematics Instruction in Japan, also claimed that computational ability is instrumental to problem solving ability, although he stated at the same time that practice in computation should not be mechanical but be based upon full understanding of the meaning of the operations (in Toyama & Gimbayasbi, 1971).

Considering the semantic opacity of abacus operation, it is highly unlikely that its practice induces mathematical intuition (Resnick, 1986). However, abacus learners tend to do well in elementary school mathematics, and this "success" may give them confidence in their mathematical ability. They tend to be free from "maths anxiety".

Second, educators should try hard to find ways to use students' non-school mathematics effectively in mathematics instruction. There can be a variety of non-school mathematics, each relating to school mathematics in its own way. Assuming that students are competent in non-school mathematics, the challenge for educators is to find how it can be connected to school mathematics. Although I very much like the basic idea of Carraher, Carraher, and Schliemann (1985), that is, mathematics learning in daily life produces effective and meaningful procedures which can complement potentially richer and more powerful mathematical tools acquired in school at the expense of meaning, how to achieve this integration is yet to be investigated.

As Bryant (1989) pointed out, students probably have difficulty in "seeing that there is a connection to make". This would be the main reason why Amaiwa's mapping instruction did not work, and why able street vendors could not solve school maths problems correctly. It is an educator's responsibility to help students recognize the connection.

Moreover, not every maths routine that emerges in non-school settings can simply serve as a basis for understanding how and why the corresponding "school maths" routine works, because, though it is trusted, its meaning is not apparent. "Our lives are filled with procedures that we carry out simply to get things done" (Hatano & Inagaki, 1986, p.266). Both adults and children perform at least some everyday problem-solving procedures only because they "work", without bothering with the meaning of each step. Subtraction using an abacus, like pressing a key of a calculator for finding the square root of a given number, can be considered as one such procedure. After repeating the procedures hundreds of times, we can be quite skilful, i.e. we can become "routine experts". Such procedures can be used as the source for meaningful analogical learning of a school maths procedure only if they are unpacked and the meaning of each constituent step is clarified through students' reflection on them.

Despite this routine character, component skills involved in the procedures can be transferred to school procedures, since the actions of the specific condition–action pairs constituting a component skill are triggered automatically whenever the conditions are met (Anderson, 1982). Thus practice in one out-of-school set of mathematical skills may facilitate the acquisition and performance of school maths procedures sharing some component skills. We should examine the significance of such transfer from educational perspectives.

The development of mathematical cognition can be conceptualized as a process of interaction of non-school and school maths procedures. The nature of this interaction varies according to the characteristics of the non-school procedures. Thus selecting proper versions of non-school mathematics and placing them appropriately in the curriculum is one of the major responsibilities of educators.

ACKNOWLEDGEMENTS

The author would like to thank Professors Shizuko Amaiwa and Keiko Shimizu, and Mr. Shinnichi Ezaki for providing their latest available information concerning research and practice in abacus, and Professors Kayoko Inagaki and Shizuko Amaiwa for commenting on an earlier draft of this chapter.

10 What Children and Teachers Count as Mathematics

Guida de Abreu
Department of Psychology, University of Luton, UK
Alan J. Bishop
Faculty of Education, Monash University, Australia
Geraldo Pompeu Jr.
Catholic University of Campinas, Brazil

INTRODUCTION

The studies on 'everyday mathematical cognition' developed in the last decade (see Lave, 1988; Nunes, 1992b), have contributed to the view of mathematics as a cultural phenomenon, which was initially elaborated in connection with the mathematics of indigenous groups (Gay & Cole, 1967). Mathematics knowledge has been and continues to be developed in the course of the history of particular cultural groups (D'Ambrosio, 1985b; Bishop, 1988) and can have different expressions in different cultures and also in different contexts within the same culture (Ascher, 1991). As a cultural product, mathematics involves both specific systems of representation, such as counting and measuring systems, as well as values about the uses of that knowledge (Bishop, 1988, 1991). From the educational point of view, societies transmit to new generations not only ways of coping with mathematics embedded in particular cultural practices, but also values which are attached to that mathematics. In modern societies, where multiple mathematics coexist, such as the traditional oral mathematics and the school written mathematics, mastery of one mathematics or of another can put a person in a particular social position. In fact, in some cases the traditional oral forms of knowledge are denied or viewed as 'no knowledge' (see Freire, 1972).

The contrast between mathematical cognition associated with different practices, in particular between school mathematics and out-of-school mathematics, has been documented in recent years in several studies (Carraher,

Carraher, & Schliemann, 1988a; Lave, 1988; Saxe, 1990; Nunes, 1992a). These authors have focused, in particular, on the way in which specific systems of mathematical representation embedded in a context of practice mediate cognition. Yet, someone living in a specific group is exposed both to the mathematics and to the "valorisations"[1] attached to it by the group. These valorisations are expressed through beliefs and attitudes towards mathematics and thus are part of the affective domain. However they have not yet been integrated into studies of culture and mathematical cognition (McLeod, 1992).

Now that differences in methods and strategies associated with specific mathematical practices are becoming better known there are some questions concerning the 'situatedness' of mathematical thinking and learning that need further understanding. Why does a child choose different strategies to solve similar problems when they are related to different practices? Why does a child who performs better in oral methods choose written methods at school? What kinds of constraints make children take those decisions? We would like to suggest that focusing on the valorisation of the practices, in particular the beliefs and attitudes of children exposed to different sorts of mathematics practices is a way of pursuing that understanding.

Research on the development of understanding in the classroom, in particular the work of Edwards and Mercer (1987), supports our idea that specific uses of mathematics might not be 'natural' but are rather the product of a developmental process of cognitive socialisation, where certain forms are sanctioned as appropriate and others excluded. Edwards and Mercer stressed the asymmetry of power in the relationship between teacher and pupils. Although they used empirical evidence from English classrooms, where teaching is based on a child-centred approach which assumes that the child should construct their own understanding, they observed that it is the teacher who decides whether children's contributions are appropriate or not. In the case of children growing up in societies where they are exposed to different mathematics, such as when the classroom practice excludes outside school mathematics, the children might be given the message that the school way is more 'proper' than the other forms. At the same time the same children could experience outside school situations where the ways of coping with mathematics excluded from the classroom might be legitimate. What are the beliefs and attitudes of these children in relation to these different practices? How might these beliefs and attitudes interfere in their school learning? The answers to these kinds of questions will help devise routes to bring children's outside school knowledge into the classroom—a bridge that we do not yet know how to build (Carraher, 1988; McLeod, 1992).

---

[1]Valorisation here refers to the social representation of mathematics, its conception, value and the affect attached to it (Eds).

Our aim for this chapter is to initiate a discussion on how beliefs are associated with specific mathematical practices, that is how they are linked with mathematical actions, and how they determine children's and teachers' attitudes to mathematics. We have provided some empirical evidence (Bishop & Abreu, 1991; Abreu, Bishop, & Pompeu, 1992) which showed that the split between a school mathematics culture and an out-of-school mathematics culture is manifested both in children's mathematics and in their beliefs about the mathematics.

COGNITION, BELIEFS, AND ATTITUDES

When individuals are confronted with situations outside school that potentially involve mathematical problems they do not just follow a rigid sequence of cognitive strategies to solve these problems. Since the individuals are more in control, they first decide if they will cope mathematically with the problems or follow other routes. Some may like mathematics and feel comfortable in choosing a mathematical strategy. Others may hate mathematics and try to avoid it. These individuals are experiencing the situation they were confronted with both cognitively and affectively. Besides, those who decide to mathematize the situation can follow a variety of strategies. Although certain strategies are more used in certain contexts of practices, in general in outside school contexts individuals are more free to choose the strategies that they feel comfortable with. For example, Saxe (1990) shows that Brazilian children working as candy sellers solved mathematical problems (a) relying on other people, (b) using practice-linked strategies, and (c) using school-linked strategies. All these strategies were accepted as legitimate in the candy-selling practice.

At school, learners also experience mathematics and the learning situation as both cognitive and affective (Evans, 1991). Nevertheless, the only valid form of 'official' display at school is cognitive. Affective factors are neglected and relegated to a position of less importance. In addition, at school learners are not free to choose between several strategies but have to base their strategies on uses of systems of mathematical representation that are legitimised by the teacher.

In parallel with current school pedagogic practices, research on attitudes and beliefs about mathematics has been conducted separately from research on how people learn mathematics. Factors linked to affect have been mainly treated as individual factors and studied under the influence of the theoretical framework of social psychology. Research on attitudes has a long history in the field of the mathematics education (McLeod, 1992). On the other hand, research on beliefs is relatively recent, with very few studies before 1980 (Thompson, 1992). Beliefs have been included in studies on attitudes, and it is difficult to separate them. In the field of mathematics education, there appears to be a confusion between the theoretical model about attitudes that influenced the research before the 1980s, and the research since 1980 on beliefs. Whereas research on attitudes was mainly guided by a behaviourist framework, with attitudes linked to *what the person does*, the research that spread during the 1980s about beliefs in mathematics education has been informed by the cognitivist model, linking beliefs to *what the person thinks*. This shift from observable behaviour to what the person thinks was not substantially accompanied by either theoretical or methodological changes. McLeod (1992, p.576) remarks that research on affect follows "a very practical approach, using questionnaires to gather common sense data on beliefs and attitudes towards mathematics. This kind of evaluation usually does not attempt to present a theoretical framework for the assessment of affect, nor does it include data from small scale, qualitative studies that could provide a more detailed picture of students' affective responses to mathematics."

The way in which research on attitudes and beliefs continues to be treated in the field of mathematics education takes traditional conceptualisations as unproblematic. However recent developments in cognitive and social psychology question the very nature of beliefs and attitudes as being located in an autonomous individual (Moscovici, 1988). Beliefs and attitudes are the product of social life. They also reflect the way in which social groups valorise their practices. Walkerdine (1988) argues that the transmission of school mathematics as a 'neutral' way of knowing, which is disembedded and can be applied in any context, is part of the maintenance of the modern social and political order. She used the framework of 'discursive practice' analysing the relation between signifier and signified in the home and school mathematical practices of young children. Her focus was on how the child's construction of mathematical knowledge is regulated in the discourse of school and home practices. Her analysis showed how the school 'empties' and 'represses' the multiple and embedded mathematical understandings which the child has constructed at home and replaces this with a unique and presumably disembedded and therefore 'superior' form, school mathematics. Similar arguments were made by Wertsch (1990) in relation to Western forms of knowledge in general. He refers to different forms of knowledge as 'voices' and stresses that school knowledge emerged from a specific mode of discourse which had assumed the status of a 'voice of decontextualized rationality'. Wertsch also stressed the need for investigations into how children make judgements on what 'voice' to invoke in particular contexts. In spite of this growing concern that valorisation should be taken into account in studies of human cognition, it is still unclear how to achieve this integration.

Harris (1989), in discussing children's psychological understanding of emotions, referred to two aspects which could be central in the integration of beliefs and attitudes in a theory of cognition. First (p.2) he stressed the role of beliefs in psychological understanding "even when two people are confronted by the same objective situation, they may appraise it differently depending on what they want or believe". Second (p.12) he stressed that ". . . cultural practices encourage the suppression of certain emotions and the display of others; which particular emotional themes are amplified or stifled will vary from culture to culture". The idea of restrictions on what a person will display to others in a social situation was previously pointed out by Harré (1986; p.294). He states that "developing human beings change not only in respect to what they know they can do, but also and most importantly to what their society permits them to do, that is what they may do".

The interaction of cognition, beliefs, and attitudes, as suggested by Harris and Harré, has not yet been researched in the field of mathematics education. Variation in mathematical performance across contexts has been explained solely as a cognitive phenomenon in the approach known as *situated cognition*. The literature reviewed above supports an alternative explanation for 'situatedness' in mathematical cognition: beliefs and attitudes towards mathematics may constrain the adoption of particular forms of mathematics in specific contexts. Children who can perform better with out-of-school mathematics might not use this mathematics in school because they believe it to be inadequate. Moreover children's beliefs might reflect the constraints imposed by the teacher who is the mediator of the school culture.

WHAT CHILDREN COUNT AS MATHEMATICS

In this section we report some empirical data from a research project, which was based on a theoretical approach intergrating mathematical cognition and beliefs, and in a methodological approach which uses qualitative case studies. Several studies by Carraher, Carraher, and Schliemann (1988) (see also T. Carraher, 1988; D. Carraher, 1991) undertaken in the north east of Brazil with children who belong to working-class backgrounds and who usually engaged in different mathematical practices, showed that they use mathematics in situated ways. Children who were quite competent problem solvers in mathematics embedded in outside-school practices had difficulties with school mathematics. The performance of the same children varied according to their uses of oral mathematics and written mathematics. The authors observed that children's choice of oral or written mathematics depended on the situation. This situation could be 'real' as was the case with the study of child street vendors (Carraher, Carraher, & Schliemann 1985) or 'simulated' as in the study with school-children (Carraher, Carraher, & Schliemann 1987). The same children who used between 80 and 89% of oral calculations in a 'simulated store' situation, used between 10 and 29% of oral calculations when presented with computing exercises (Carraher, Carraher, & Schliemann 1987). The children were much more accurate when using oral mathematics. Why then did they choose written mathematics? A close look at these children's school practices shows that in their schools they were assessed by their performance on written tests. Their performance in those tests determined whether they succeeded and were promoted to the next grade or whether they failed and had to repeat the same grade. Outside school, the children worked as street vendors, and in this practice as long as the child gets a correct answer, and is quick, customers are not concerned about the way the children calculate. However, the differences do not stop here. Success in school is the prerequisite for the children to get a better job in their future, whereas success in the out-of-school mathematics will just assure the children of continuity in the low-status jobs that they are already engaged in. In these circumstances we expect that children acquire beliefs and attitudes towards the mathematics of different cultural practices which lead them to use some forms and exclude others in specific situations.

The Context of the Study and Subjects

The subjects of this study were school-children at two primary schools in rural areas of the island of Madeira. Madeira is a Portuguese Autonomous Region located in the Atlantic Ocean off the West African Coast. The population is about 280,000 inhabitants and the language is Portuguese. The island economy is centred on tourism, which is supported by the traditional activities of agriculture, fishing, and local crafts. Formal schooling on the island is subordinated to the national system of education, which in Portugal is strongly centralised. Compulsory schooling until 1964 was restricted to the four years of primary education, and until the 1960s school was not compulsory for girls. A law from 1986 extended compulsory schooling to a nine-year period for children aged between 6 and 15 (Lei 46/86, 1986). However, failure is still very high in the four grades of primary school (*Primeiro ciclo do ensino básico*). The rate of repetition in these grades (children who fail the tests are not promoted to the next grade) is about 37% in Madeira (Diário, 1990).

As the system is highly centralised, children in Madeira are exposed to a school mathematics curriculum mainly prescribed from outside and based on a culture-free view of learning. Their failure is interpreted as due to their own lack of intellectual abilities to master the skills that school intends to transmit. Nevertheless, a close look at their life outside school reveals a similarity with the Brazilian children studied by Carraher, Carraher, and Schliemann (1985). They fail in school but they usually engage in economic activities outside school. These children are used to shopping for their families in local markets, bakeries, and groceries; some of the boys work in agriculture in the non-school period of the day, and some of the girls do simple work on embroidery. Apparently these children should be competent problem solvers when coping with mathematics problems embedded in their out-of-school practices. We found this context suitable to search for an understanding of the issues raised above, in the sense that children appeared to be exposed to distinct mathematical practices in school and out-of-school. To make the contrasts clearer, we decided to focus on children from two rural schools located in the area of Camara de Lobos, where the island plantations of grapes and bananas are concentrated. One of these schools was located in a village where part of the population also engages in fishing.

The participants of the study were the pupils of three third grade and one sixth grade class. We chose these pupils in order to be sure that they had been exposed to school mathematics practices for a relatively long period. The sixth grade was the most advanced level in the two rural schools and was chosen in order to investigate if the relationship between the two mathematics changes with the advance of schooling. From these classes 20 children (16 third graders and 4 sixth graders), aged between 7 and 13, were selected as case studies, balancing boys with girls, and also children less successful in mathematics at school with children who were more successful. To select the children, the researcher asked the teacher of each classroom to give some names of boys and girls that she judged as the best pupils (more successful) and others as the worst pupils (less successful) in school mathematics. We also used gender as a criterion in order to take into consideration the fact that boys and girls might be involved in different cultural practices outside school. The child's school performance was considered in order to try to explore whether there are differences between children who are 'more successful' and those who are 'less successful' in school mathematics in the way that they establish the relationship between out-of school and school mathematics.

Method

A four-stage research approach was adopted involving qualitative research methods. The first stage involved classroom observation. The second stage was an individual interview about the child's life outside school and his or her beliefs about mathematics. The third stage involved group activities where the children were presented with two kinds of tasks involving measurement: (a) tasks where they were asked to imagine they were farmers; (b) typical school tasks, taken from their textbooks. The fourth stage was a final individual interview and again they were asked to solve tasks about measurement. All the stages were carried out by the first author, who grew up on the island, and her knowledge of the local culture and language clearly helped in facilitating the interviews. Children were interviewed in their schools, but outside the classroom. The interviews were conducted based on a combination of ethnographic and clinical Piagetian method, as described by Carraher, Carraher, and Schliemann (1988a: pp.15 and 41). Children's interviews were audio-tape recorded, written notes were taken during the interviews, and the children's written calculations were also kept.

Results

Classroom Observations.   The main question we had in mind when doing the classroom observation was whether the teaching practices allowed the children to bring their out-of-school mathematics into school. For the four classrooms, the observations showed that school mathematics is taught as 'the only way to solve problems'. Teachers based their programme on textbooks not connected to children's local culture. All the lessons observed during one month of stay in the schools used a whole class approach and consisted of: (a) exposition of a specific mathematical content by the teacher; (b) some practice of the content with exercises on the blackboard for all the classroom; (c) individual exercises to be done by each child; (d) correction of the exercises on the blackboard. When correcting the exercises, teachers used to call children by their names, thus providing opportunity for all of them to participate. However, when a child's answer did not coincide with the 'correct expected answer' the teacher passed the question on to another child without asking the first child to explain the reasoning that led to the wrong answer. The most obvious evidence that teachers wanted children to follow school ways to cope with mathematics was related to reprimanding the children for counting on their fingers. It was obvious that all these teachers were doing their best to help the children. They were acting as mediators of a traditional school culture where there is no acknowledgment of mathematics as a form of cultural knowledge. Nevertheless, these observations did not provide particular information about how the children were coping with the two mathematics. This is the aspect that we explore in the rest of this section.

Mathematical Activities Outside School.   The first point that we tried to clarify in the individual interview was the actual involvement of each child in the home culture. Although all the children belonged to a similar home background we found it necessary to have a clear description of this point, because they may appear to be equal participants in the same out-of-school practices, but they may not be involved in the same way. Obviously, from a perspective that views mathematics as embedded in the context of practice, the type of involvement makes a difference to the child's knowledge. We asked the children to report on the activities in which they normally engaged concerned with helping their families. We found that the majority of the children helped their mothers in housework, which for some included buying food in the nearby groceries. All the boys engaged in farming activities, some of them helping their parents and others working in the neighbourhood to earn money. Some of the girls also helped in farming, but in different tasks from the boys. We also asked them to describe some of the routine activities they did in order to verify their uses of mathematics in those situations. We have chosen to analyse here how two girls explain the activity of buying bread for the family. The structure of the activity can be described in three phases: preparing to buy bread; buying bread; checking the result at home. Now let us see how the two girls describe the activity.

Example 1: Rita, a fisherman's daughter, 10 years old, third grader, described by the teacher as having difficulties at school:

Rita: Saturday morning is my day, I go and fetch bread early in the morning.

Interviewer: And how many loaves of bread do you fetch?

Rita: Fifteen.

Interviewer: Who gives you the money?

Rita: My mother, my father and when they don't have any money I do not go.

Interviewer: And how much does each loaf cost?

Rita: 30 (escudos).

Interviewer: And how do you know, for example, how much seven loaves cost? Who does the sums?

Rita: The seller. But, if I arrive home and the sum is wrong I need to go back.

Interviewer: But, when you arrive home who checks if the sum is wrong?

Rita: Me (she demonstrates writing an addition where for each loaf she writes 30 escudos).

Example 2: Ana, a farmer's daughter, 8 years old, third grader, described by the teacher as a successful pupil:

Interviewer: (she said that she used to buy bread for the family, she used to buy 3 loaves for 90 escudos). And if you bought five how much would they cost?

Ana: I do not know, we never buy five.

Interviewer: And if your mother asks you to buy only one, how much will you pay?

Ana: One I do not know. My mother gives me the money and if it is short he (the seller) tells me and the next day I bring the money that was missing. If it is not short he gives me the change.

Looking at the two examples we note that the structure of the activity is the same for the two children, although the kinds of social constraint imposed by the interactions in the family seem to be rather different. Rita copes with a situation where she needs to use mathematics. When buying she needs to make sure she gives the right amount to the seller or receives the correct change, by checking at home if the change is correct. In contrast, Ana does not need to solve any mathematical problems during the three phases because her family solves them for her. The point that we want to stress here is that the emergence of a mathematical problem in the out-of-school world, seems to be linked to the social constraints that the children experience, although they may be involved in similar practices. Moreover, Ana has the best performance in mathematics among the girls in school, but she does not seem to link mathematics to the everyday shopping situation. In contrast, Rita the pupil described as 'having difficulties', can cope mathematically with the shopping situation; she uses very simple strategies, and probably the ones she feels more confident with.

The emergence of mathematics is linked to the social constraints applied to the activity of the particular child. Whether these differences in the children's out-of-school mathematics might be related to differences in their school performance is still not clear. Will the children who are more used to out-of-school mathematics bring this knowledge to help solve the research tasks? How do these differences of being more or less used to out-of-school mathematics affect their performances?

Solving Simulated Everyday Problems in School. Taking into consideration the fact that the children lived in agricultural areas we presented them with 'imagine being a farmer' tasks, which aimed to provide a research context suitable for the evocation of their out-of-school mathematics. One of the tasks consisted of finding how much wire would be necessary to fence a farm. It was presented as (a) a group activity, where each target child worked with one or two partners of the same classroom, gender and level of school performance as judged by the teacher, and as (b) an individual task in the second individual interview. As materials, children were given cards symbolising farms. Both the group and the individual tasks were structured to make it likely that the child would need to cope with the addition of halves. This is the aspect that we analyse below.

Group task.   Each child in the group was given a card with a particular format (see Fig. 10.1) and received the instruction:

Imagine that you are farmers. These cards here represent fields of bananas or grapes. This is your farm, and this is yours. Now imagine that each of you wants to build a fence of wire around the property. Working together decide how you can find out the amount of wire each of you needs.

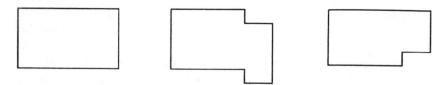

FIG. 10.1.   Formats of the cards symbolising farms, which were presented in group task.

After letting the children talk a bit about what they would do, the interviewer gave them a stick 6cm long, which did not fit neatly into the lengths of the sides (for example the rectangle is 3.5 sticks of length and 2 sticks width) and asked them to measure all the way around to find how many of the sticks they would need.

Although this was a group task each child in the group had his or her turn. The different strategies used by the target children to cope with the task are described below.

1. Iteration around the perimeter of the farm, measuring the halves, but counting only in integers.
2. Iteration around the perimeter of the farm, considering the halves, but counting only in integers until they found another half and then compensating.
3. Iteration around the perimeter of the farm, considering the halves, and incorporating them into the counting.
4. Iteration on each side, considering the halves, and subsequently adding the sides, without the need to measure the parallel sides in the rectangle.
5. Iteration around the figure, turning the stick at the corners, counting on the integers with no need to refer to the halves.

All the strategies listed above, excluding the first one, gave a correct measurement. Fourteen out of the sixteen third grade children, independently of their actual school performance, showed an understanding about adding two halves to complete one unit, although the majority of them had not yet been introduced to fractions or decimals at school. The four sixth grade children also did the task very well when using oral methods. However, unlike the third grade children all of the sixth grade children had frequently to cope with decimals in their school mathematics. One sixth grade group after correctly finding the perimeter of one of the farms using exclusively oral methods decided to use the school algorithm to find the perimeter of the other farm. In this circumstance we were able to observe first that they had difficulties coping with the halves in the written school methods and second that they did not connect answers from the oral with the written method, as in the example below (see Fig. 10.2):

3.5

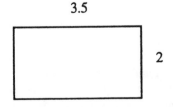

FIG. 10.2. Format of the "farm" measured by the sixth-grade group.

Ermelinda: one, two, three and a half
Ma Jose: This should be the same (opposite side).
              Three, three, six, seven.
Ermelinda: One, two (width)
Interviewer: How much wire is necessary to fence all the way around?

(the children produced the following written algorithm:)

$$
\begin{array}{r}
3.5 \\
3.5 \\
2 \\
\underline{2} \\
7.4
\end{array}
$$

Ermelinda: It is seven point four.
Interviewer: Let's do it in our heads. Three and a half plus three and a half?
Pupils: Seven
Interviewer: Plus these two sides?
Pupils: Eleven.

In this example, according to the system of representation they used, they obtained a different result, and made no attempt to connect the two. The girls, before using the written representation, performed the additions of the two lengths orally, a move that would encourage them to doubt the written result if they had made the connection.

Individual Task.   Each child in the second individual interview was again given a card symbolising a farm and asked to find how much wire they needed to fence all the way around using a ruler graded in centimetres. The card had the format of a rectangle and measured 17cm length and 10.5cm width. Only 7 out of 19 target children (at this stage we lost one of the Third Grade target pupils because he was away from school on consecutive days) obtained the correct measurements. All of them in fact gave measurements to a very close interval of approximation, between 16 and 18cm for the side of 17cm, and between 10 and 11.5cm for side of 10.5cm. Here we want to comment on the strategies of the seven children who obtained the correct measurements because it was among them that we observed a contamination of children's oral reasoning by the school written representation. From the seven children who obtained correct measures, two solved the problem in writing, and got wrong answers which indicated the same difficulty related to place value, observed in the earlier example. The remaining five provided oral solutions, one of which was correct and four were wrong. All these four wrong answers resulted from the addition of 10.5 plus 10.5 as being 30. The interviewer was puzzled and asked them to explain where this 30 came from. She observed that although they correctly read their measurement as a ten and a half, the half was added as being five. This appears to be a contamination of children's oral reasoning by the written representation of half as (0.5) as exemplified in the following interview, with a sixth grade boy considered successful in school:

> Interviewer: Now, please measure your farm to see how much wire you need to fence it.
>
> Adriano: This is length 17, and this 10, . . . it's more, 10, it's 10 and a half (width).
>
> Interviewer: So, how much all the way around?
>
> Adriano: 10 and a half, plus 10 and a half, . . . 5 and 5, 10. Here is these two sides (width), and these and these I need 30 centimetres. 17 plus 17 is 34. . . 30 from here, 64.
>
> Interviewer: Now explain to me how from adding 10 and a half to 10 and a half you came to 30?
>
> Adriano: Firstly I added 5 and 5 to get 10 (the two halves). And after that I added the tens without the halves. 10 and 10 is 20, and plus the halves is 30.

The other three children who used the same strategy as Adriano were all third graders, but with a history of repetition in school that makes it likely that they had been introduced to school ways for adding halves. In conclusion, children can successfully cope with mathematical situations, such as adding halves, before being taught them at school. However, after being introduced to formal school representations children manifest difficulties. School representations are not connected with the previous out-of-school representations.

Solving School-like Problems. Outside school the children are free to choose the strategies about which they feel more confident but in school they have to conform to different rules. The correct solution of a mathematical problem in school generally involves the use of a particular school method to find the solution. The same groups of children were presented with school-like problems taken from their own textbooks to see whether they would follow school procedures to solve school tasks although some of the children could perform better using an out-of school procedure. For example, they were asked to solve the following problem in the same way they would do if asked by their teacher:

> The ribbon measures 21 metres. If we use 12 metres of ribbon, how much will be left?

Looking at the solutions of the third grade groups we note that *all but one* adopted the following procedure: reading the problem; discussing what operation is required; concluding that it is a subtraction or what they call a 'minus sum'; and performing the written calculation. All of them obtained a wrong result! At this point they were asked to do the same calculation without writing, and were explicitly allowed to count on their fingers. Without exception, all the groups succeeded in finding the correct answer. Now we will quote a passage from the interview with the pupils who first solved the problem orally:

Joel:	(after reading twice) Nine is left.
Interviewer:	Your partner is saying that nine is left, how would you say that answer to your teacher?
Nuno:	The ribbon has nine metres.
Mario:	It cannot be like that.
Interviewer:	Have a go.
Mario:	The ribbon has nine metres left.
Interviewer:	Now that sum that you did in your mind, do it in writing.
Joel:	Do it this way, put 21 minus 12 (numerical expression). Now put 21 and below it 12, after the minus sign, now do the sum, the result is nine.
Mario:	I know how to do this. 'Two minus one is one, and two minus one is one. Oh! No. Eleven! (he checks the answer again)
Joel:	(does the calculation again with his fingers) It is nine. Count (demands to the partner) from 12 to 21.
Nuno & Mario:	(both count) It is nine.

The spontaneous discussion and checking of the answer only emerged in this group, who began with the oral calculation. The other groups accepted the wrong result without any doubt, although in some cases they obtained a number bigger than the minuend, as in the following example:

Interviewer:	How would you solve it?
Paulo:	Less (subtract)
Joao:	$\begin{array}{r} 21 \\ -12 \\ \hline 109 \end{array}$
	Twelve to eleven is 9, one left, two to twelve is ten.
Interviewer:	How many metres were left then?
Pupils:	One hundred and nine.
Interviewer:	Paulo, please, take a look at what they did and give your opinion.
Paulo:	For me it is correct.
Interviewer:	And for you?
Joao:	I did it.

The sixth grade pupils solved the above problem providing a written answer without any difficulty. However, when they were asked to solve a perimeter problem involving decimals, we found that, similarly to the third graders, they did not use their out-of-school knowledge to check the school written solutions. The problem was taken from their textbook, and consisted of *'Using the ruler, find the perimeter of the figure below* (see Fig. 10.3)':

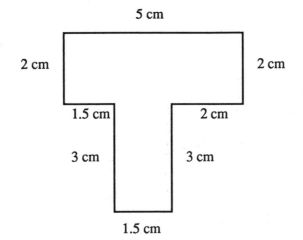

FIG. 10.3.   Perimeter problem presented to the sixth grade pupils involving decimals.

All the four groups provided a written solution, three with incorrect answers, respectively 5.4cm, 4.8cm, and 3.7cm. It can be observed that two of the results are measurements that are smaller than the biggest side of the figure. Yet they did not realise by themselves that the result was incorrect. The group that succeeded used a mixed strategy; they added orally 1.5 plus 1.5 and replaced it by a 3 in the written addition.

In summary, we observed that (a) children who have difficulties in school mathematics could succeed in solving many mathematical problems by using their out-of-school practices; (b) that the success of the children is particularly linked to the use of oral mathematics; (c) that children had more difficulties in solving mathematical problems when using the school mathematics, but only rarely attempted to connect the out-of-school with the school mathematics. These findings agree with those of Carraher, Carraher, and Schliemann (1985, 1987), showing that children use mathematics in situated ways. In addition, the fact that the children did not connect out-of-school mathematics with school mathematics replicates Cobb's (1990) observations among American children.

Children's Beliefs About Mathematics

Some of the questions emerging from the above findings are: Why were the children so reluctant to use their out-of-school mathematics to solve their school problems? Why did they not recognize their superior performance in the out-of-school mathematics? We can search for explanations in terms of the particular school culture to which they are exposed. For example, we observed that teachers reprimanded them for counting on fingers. A real teacher was not present in the research situation, but they still persevered in using one method rather than the other. Our hypothesis is that external constraints about the appropriate way for solving a task in a specific context are internalised by the children as beliefs and attitudes about mathematics. In other words, situated uses of mathematics are influenced by an affective component, which comprises the beliefs and attitudes the child has acquired in relation to particular uses of mathematics. To examine this hypothesis we investigated (a) children's beliefs about the use of mathematics in different social practices, and (b) children's beliefs about the 'appropriateness' of out-of-school mathematics to which they eventually referred during the research. Below we discuss our findings concerning these two aspects.

Children's Beliefs About Mathematics Used Outside School.   Do children recognise the use of mathematics outside school? In what situations? The children's beliefs about situations where people use mathematics were investigated in the first individual interview. In this interview the researcher used a set of pictures with people engaged in activities which were part of the life in the community. In the first instance we gave the child a set of 12 pictures involving people in offices, children at school, people in local markets and shops, and people making baskets (a widespread local craft), and asked them to sort the pictures into two groups by placing on one side of the table those pictures where people had to use mathematics and on the other side those where people did not use mathematics. We observed that more than 50% of the children identified all the pictures as situations where people use mathematics, except for the picture with people making baskets, (only 37% of the children believed that they need to use mathematics). It was apparent that children believed mathematics is used in some practices more than others.

In a second task each child was shown five pictures (see Table 10.2) one at a time and asked (a) to describe what people were doing, (b) if they needed to use mathematics, and (c) if yes, what they would need the mathematics for; and if not, the interviewer presented a counter-argument to the child. Table 10.1 summarizes children's answers and the respective justifications.

We confirmed our initial observation that children believed that mathematics is used in some practices more than in others. It can be observed in Table 10.1 that all the children believed that people use mathematics in a supermarket. They justifed this by referring to the trade involved between someone who is a seller and a buyer. With respect to people in charge of selling they referred to marking prices, operating the cash register and checking change. With respect to the buyers they referred to the need for checking the payments to prevent the seller from taking advantage of them.

TABLE 10.1
Children's Beliefs About the Need to Use Mathematics in
Out-of-school Situations and Their Justifications.

Pictures	Frequency	Justifications
1. Public fish market	17 (89%)	to count money; to do sums; to cope with change.
2. Carpenters making furniture	16 (84%)	to measure; to communicate to the customer, to do sums to earn money; to sell but not to make furniture.
3. Children measuring and drawing a circle	12 (63%)	to measure; to draw a circle and angles; to count; to work to earn money.
4. People working in farming	12 (63%)	to sell their products; to distribute the seeds; for the worker to receive the money; to count money.
5. People in a supermarket	19 (100%)	to buy and sell.

One of the target children was not considered in this tabulation because his answers were not clear.

The justifications that children gave for the use of mathematics in the fish market, carpentry, and farming confirmed that they associate the use of mathematics in practical situations with trading transactions. This aspect comes up more clearly in the carpentry situation. The picture was about people involved in making furniture. The children were able to give that description. Yet, when we looked at children's justifications about why carpenters use mathematics, we found that nine children referred to the trade aspects (such as selling the furniture) and only five referred to the use of measurement (two children gave no justifications).

At first glance these justifications may appear to be related to an ability of some children to conceive of arithmetic (manipulation of numbers) as part of mathematics, but not of geometry (measurement, shapes, drawing lines, etc.) In fact, this is the impression we got when only the sixth grade children could identify circles and angles as part of mathematics in relation to picture three. However, when we examined the sixth grade children's answers to the use of mathematics in the picture of carpentry we observed that: (a) two children said that it was necessary to use mathematics, (in order to communicate with the customer about the number of shelves in a cupboard; to measure); (b) the other two said that it was not necessary to use mathematics, (one of them did not see any mathematics in that situation because the people were involved in manual work); when the interviewer counter-argued by asking what they would do if someone asked for a table of specific size, the answer was 'to sell they would need (maths), but not to make the furniture'. A former student, talking about farming, produced a similar justification that 'mathematics is necessary to sell the products'. Since he used to work in farming, in Madeira where the land is dug in specific shapes to allow for irrigation, the interviewer asked him about that activity. He answered that he never thought about keeping to a specific shape or about measuring it, but that he always got a very good result. These observations suggest that a child may identify measurement and drawing circles as part of mathematics in one practice, but not in other practices.

Besides these differences about what is mathematics in a specific practice, the other relevant aspect of the data is the fact that only 63% of the children conceived of farming as a situation that involves the use of mathematics. Why did 37% of the children dismiss the use of mathematics in a situation so close to their everyday lives? Why did they have no doubts that the work of a cashier in a supermarket involves mathematics, and yet doubted that the work of a rural worker might involve mathematics as well? If, instead of looking at the mathematics involved in each situation, we look at the people involved, we can observe that people who work as cashiers in the supermarket are those who had successfully completed the basic school education. In contrast, farming involves low-status jobs which can be occupied by people who fail or drop out from school. To acknowledge mathematics in farming would mean recognising forms of mathematics that are excluded by their schools as proper knowledge.

Is Outside-School Mathematics a Proper Mathematics?   When children referred to their parents' ways of doing sums or when they demonstrated how they would solve a problem outside school, the researcher used this information to explore their beliefs about the existence of differences between the two mathematics. In particular, we tried to explore their beliefs about (a) whether the out-of-school ways of solving a problem are the same as or different from the school ways, and (b) what is the easiest or the best way to do it. Ten of the children believed that they and their parents solve problems outside differently from the way they do it in school. It was very difficult for the children to explain what these differences were. Six of them referred to the strategies used to solve calculations, and the other four did not know how to explain the differences. Only two children clearly demonstrated how they calculated their earnings in a part-time job in agriculture outside school and how they would have to do the same calculation at school. The others vaguely referred to a mixture of oral and written strategies but without any demonstration. However, none of them showed any difficulties in judging what they believed to be the best mathematics. Seven out of these ten children

(11 years old) who worked in agriculture earning 800 escudos a day calculated how much he earned in a week in the following way:

Interviewer: What will you do, work on the paper or work in your head?
Marcio: On the paper.
Interviewer: Alright. do it for me.
Marcio: 1 8
               1 8
               1 8   16
               1 8   24
               1 8   32
               1 8
               ‾‾‾‾
               48

Interviewer: Then how much have you earned?
Marcio: Four thousand and eight hundred.
Interviewer: Could you please explain to me what you have done?
Marcio: 8 plus 8 is 16, plus 8 (. . .) 48.
Interviewer: And this side what you mean by these ones?
Marcio: Those are the days.
Interviewer: Who taught you to do these sums?
Marcio: My brother
Interviewer: How would you work out that sum in school?
Marcio: I will do six times eight, is. . . is. . .
Interviewer: How much is it?
Marcio: Thirty six.
Interviewer: No!
Marcio: Forty eight.
Interviewer: Which way do you prefer to do?
Marcio: This here is quicker (school multiplication).
Interviewer: And what way do you do your sums at home?
Marcio: This one here (the demonstration above).
Interviewer: Why?
Marcio: I do this one here and use this (school) to check if it is correct.

Marcio's belief that the school methods are quicker carries no prejudice against his home mathematics, and he seems to be able to gain benefit outside from what he is learning in school. But his school learning does not benefit from his out-of-school knowledge because his school does not accept the out-of-school strategies to check the answers. However, there are children who develop beliefs that could be barriers in the development of their mathematical understanding. Rita, the third grade girl mentioned in the case of buying bread for example, believes that the outside strategy is not adequate:

Interviewer: And do you do the sums at home in the way you have learned at
               school?

Rita: Some.
Interviewer: And the others, how do you do them?
Rita: Wrongly (i.e. not the proper way).
Interviewer: Is it 'wrongly' or you do it in a different way?
Rita: In a different way.

On another occasion she expressed the belief that:

If there were no schools here, one would not know how to go shopping, we would not know how to buy things.

In contrast with Marcio, Rita's beliefs do not seem to be beneficial in any way. Instead of leading to a connection between the two forms of knowledge, we can expect that the belief in the inadequacy of the out-of-school methods could lead to their suppression. To some extent, this suppression is displayed by some children who perform oral additions using the formal 'written algorithm'. For example, Marisa, a successful sixth grade girl, was asked 'If you buy two kilos of oranges at 75 escudos each, how much are you going to pay?' She did, orally, the following sum: '75 plus 75, trace (a reference to the drawing of the line) 5 and 5 is 10, and seven and seven 14, 150'. The interviewer asked her to do another, to add 17 with 17, she answered 34 and explained: '7 and 7, 14, carry one, plus the 2, 3'.

In conclusion, what children count as mathematics involves both knowledge and beliefs about mathematics. The situated character of mathematical cognition in relation to different practices is associated with different strategies as well as with beliefs concerning the practices. The belief in the superiority of the school mathematics generates an asymmetry in the relationship between in-school and out-of-school mathematics. Therefore, children's beliefs do not support the connection between the two practices. Representations linked to school practices compete for superiority with the out-of-school practices. Although children generally attain correct answers with their out-of-school representations, the majority do not make any connection between the two forms of knowledge.

Considering that both the school and the out-of-school mathematics practices are linked to specific socio-cultural contexts, children's lack of connection between the different mathematics practices reveals the conflict existing between the two practices. Conflict is used here in the sense that the school culture does not acknowledge the out-of-school practices as proper mathematics, which is reflected in contradictions in children's performance. The next section will consider some educational aspects of attempting to cope with that culture-conflict situation, in order to consider what teachers might be able to do to help the learners resolve the conflict.

EDUCATIONAL APPROACHES TO CULTURAL CONFLICT

As discussed in the previous section, there are several important elements in the school learning situation which contribute to the potential conflicts experienced by the child. First, the form of representation used for the mathematics can differ—out-of-school mathematics is essentially oral whereas school mathematics is predominantly written. This relates strongly to the language and terminology used for mathematical activity, both in thought and in operation, and has implications for the kind of teaching used.

Second, we have seen that the teachers and their teaching apparently made little reference to mathematics outside school, or even recognised that outside-school mathematics might be a legitimate form of knowledge for schools to consider. There is also little evidence that the school mathematics curriculum referred to any out-of-school mathematical knowledge.

Although it would be simple to blame teachers for causing this cultural conflict for the learners, it must be remembered that *the teacher is only one person in a system which also may do little to recognise the learners' cultural conflict.* The teacher must teach in relation to an agreed curriculum, and the text materials may not refer to anything other than the official school mathematics. Assessments and examination will almost certainly be in strict agreement with the standard curriculum. There can be little opportunity for the teacher to take into account the out-of-school mathematical knowledge of the pupils.

However, we can certainly imagine teaching situations and systems where it is possible to recognise children's out-of-school knowledge. Several countries now allow schools and teachers considerable freedom in adapting their teaching and the curriculum to the particular socio-cultural context of the learners. Much depends on the attitude of governments towards teachers and on the teachers' own attitudes, beliefs and skills.

Robitaille and Dirks (1982) have made an important contribution to our thinking on this topic. According to their analysis (p.17), a mathematics curriculum exists at three different levels: 'We may distinguish among the curriculum as intended, the curriculum as implemented, and the curriculum as attained.' At the *intended* level the focus is on the formal prescribed curriculum often laid down by the state or the national government. The level of the *implemented* curriculum is in schools and classrooms where the mathematics 'knowledge environment' is created by the teachers and their materials. The *attained* level of the mathematics curriculum is what the learners actually learn as a result of teaching.

This analysis makes it clear that there is not *one* mathematics curriculum which is planned by the government, taught by the teachers and learned by the pupils. Whatever is planned will inevitably be shaped in schools and classrooms by individual teachers with their personal store of beliefs, knowledge, and experiences. Further, in interaction with the implemented curriculum, learners (as we have already seen) construct their own understanding of what mathematics is, which includes the possible conflict between school and out-of school mathematics. This analysis not only rejects more realistically the situation regarding teaching and learning mathematics, but also recognises the power and potential given to schools and teachers to modify their teaching and their curricula (except perhaps in the most regimented educational systems).

In fact, where there is official recognition in the intended curriculum of the importance of learners' out-of-school cultural contexts, it is possible to describe different levels of school and teacher response that can be adopted. These are summarised in Table 10.2, using the headings of teachers' beliefs, curriculum, teaching, and representation, which are of course of crucial importance.

There appear to be three significant levels of response. At the first level the belief is that the learner's out-of-school mathematical culture can be useful for supplying examples for the school mathematical activities. The school curriculum allows for some adaptability of context so that the teacher can refer to relevant contexts and examples. There would need to be some modification of teaching style in order to allow the learners to demonstrate their knowledge of other contexts and this will mean some modification of the representation systems experienced in class. At this level the child's out-of-school context is becoming accepted and assimilated into the official curriculum and

TABLE 10.2
School and Teacher Responses to Cultural Conflict

Levels of response	Teachers' beliefs	School and classroom curriculum	Teaching approach	Representation of knowledge
Level 3	Adults in the community should share in determining education	Curricula jointly organised by teachers and community	Shared teaching by teachers and community's adults	Local languages incorporated. Bi-lingual, bicultural teaching
Level 2	Learner's out-of-school culture should influence school education	Curricula restructured due to learner's culture	Teaching modified throughout year	Community languages and representations encouraged
Level 1	Learner's out-of-school culture useful as examples	Some learners contexts included	Some modification for some learners	Some variations of representation accepted

procedures. This is the level at which "realistic mathematics education" (see for example Gravemeijer's chapter in this book) becomes important.

At the second level however, the school and the teacher believe that the learner's out-of-school culture should significantly influence the formal education in the classroom. This will mean that the curriculum and the teaching should be restructured in some way to take account of the learners' culture. Perhaps certain orders and sequences of knowledge will vary from school to school, depending on the kinds of representations and language used in the local community. Indeed in cases where the learners' mother-tongue language differs from that used in school, this would be the level where that mother-tongue language could be formally recognised and accepted for school and classroom use. At this second level we find certain changes in school practices in order to take into account learners' out-of-school knowledge. It may, for example, be sensible to incorporate some small-group collaborative learning into the classroom teaching situation where there is considerable experience of small-group procedures outside the school. Saxe (1990) refers frequently to the use of group processes amongst the street vendors whom he studied in Brazil and that knowledge could certainly help to shape classroom procedures.

Up to this level the teachers and the school are responsible for making decisions about curricular and teaching practices. At the third level of response to the children's socio-cultural environment, we would expect the adults in the local community to play a significant role in determining the quality of education in schools. They share the decision-making, help organise the curriculum, and participate in the teaching. It may be necessary for local languages to be incorporated into the school teaching and for classrooms to be bilingual and bicultural learning contexts. At this level, we can see a true amalgamation of school and community knowledge, which should in theory remove any sense of culture conflict for the learners.

However, although much responsibility for recognising and responding to the *idea* of cultural conflict rests with the system and with the official educational hierarchies, a great deal will still depend on the teacher and the school. Developing teachers' attitudes, beliefs, and knowledge is a most important area of work if there is to be any real chance of learners' cultural conflicts being resolved. It is to this aspect that we turn in the next section.

THE TEACHERS' PERSPECTIVE

In this section we report on such a study, by the third author, (Pompeu, 1992) which considered changes in teachers' attitudes and beliefs about various aspects of mathematics teaching. In order to tackle cultural conflict he developed what he called an 'ethnomathematical approach' to the curriculum and investigated how teachers changed their attitudes, beliefs, and knowledge as a result of their increasing involvement with this approach to the curriculum.

Ethnomathematics is an emerging field of research defined by d'Ambrosio (1985b, p.45):

> We will call ethnomathematics the mathematics which is practised among identifiable cultural groups, such as national-tribal societies, labour groups, children of a certain age bracket, professional classes, and so on. Its identity depends largely on focuses of interest, on motivation, and on certain codes and jargons which do not belong to the realm of academic mathematics. We may go even further in this concept of ethnomathematics to include much of the mathematics which is currently practised by engineers, mainly calculus, which does not respond to the concept of rigour and formalism developed in academic courses of calculus.

While there are other views on ethnomathematics (see Ascher 1991 for example), d'Ambrosio's broad definition allows educators to develop curricular approaches which differ markedly from more formalist ones. In the study to be reported here, an ethnomathematical approach (Pompeu, 1992) to the mathematics curriculum was developed which could allow schools and teachers to respond at levels 2 and 3 (see Table 10.2) to their pupils' out-of-school cultural contexts. In this particular study a level 2 approach was investigated.

Describing the Mathematical Approach to the Curriculum

In order to characterise the approach and to contrast it systematically with the officially proposed curriculum for São Paulo, Brazil, a distinction between the intended, the implemented and the attained curriculum were used (Robitaille & Dirks, 1982). The officially sanctioned curriculum and the ethnomath-

TABLE 10.3
Two Approaches to Teaching Mathematics

Canonical-Structuralist Approach	*Ethnomathematical Approach*
A GENERAL PERSPECTIVE Mathematics should be seen as:	
(a) A THEORETICAL subject (it concerns abstractions and generalisations);	(b) a PRACTICAL subject (it is applicable and useful);
(c) a LOGICAL subject (it develops internally consistent structures);	(d) an EXPLORATORY AND EXPLANATORY subject (it investigates environmental situations)
(e) A UNIVERSAL subject (it is based on universal truths);	(f) a PARTICULAR subject (it is based on truths derived by a person or group of persons).

AT THE INTENDED CURRICULUM LEVEL
The mathematics curriculum should:

(a) be CULTURE FREE (its truths are absolute, and independent of any kind of cultural or social factors);

(b) be SOCIALLY/CULTURALLY BASED (its truths are relative, and dependent on social or cultural factors);

(c) be INFORMATIVE (it emphasises procedures, methods, skills, rules, facts, algorithms and results);

(d) be FORMATIVE (it emphasises analysis, synthesis, thinking, a critical stance, understanding and usefulness);

(e) be CONSERVATIVE (it promotes control over the environment and the stability of the society);

(f) be PROGRESSIVE (it promotes the growth of knowledge about the environment and progress/change of the society).

AT THE IMPLEMENTED CURRICULUM LEVEL
Teachers should teach mathematics as:

(a) a ONE-WAY SUBJECT (Mathematical knowledge is transmitted from the teacher to the pupils);

(b) a DEBATABLE SUBJECT (mathematical knowledge is discussed among pupils and teachers);

(c) a SEPARATED SUBJECT (Mathematical lessons do not rely on knowledge which pupils bring from outside school);

(d) a COMPLEMENTARY SUBJECT (mathematics lessons are based on knowledge which pupils bring from outside school);

(e) a REPRODUCTIVE SUBJECT (mathematical knowledge is taught from standard mathematical texts);

(f) a PRODUCTIVE SUBJECT (mathematical knowledge is developed from pupils' own situations).

AT THE ATTAINED CURRICULUM LEVEL
Pupils should be able to

(a) FIND CORRECT ANSWERS to problems (it is the pupils' final answers to problems which are important);

(b) ANALYSE PROBLEMS (it is the pupils' understanding of the structure of a problem which is important);

(c) USE THE FORMAL MATHEMATICAL METHOD to solve problems (these methods are the ones which will produce the right solutions);

(d) USE APPROPRIATE PROCEDURES to solve problems (it is the pupils' ability to determine the appropriate solution procedure which is important);

(e) REASON MATHEMATICALLY about problems (it is HOW to solve problems mathematically that is important for pupils to know);

(f) MAKE MATHEMATICAL CRITICISM about problems (it is WHY to solve problems mathematically that is important for pupils to know).

ematical approach developed by Pompeu differ in their basic conception. The official curriculum is an instance of a canonical-structuralist approach (see Howson, Keitel, & Kilpatrick, 1981) and emphasises the sequential teaching of increasingly more complex mathematical structures, whereas the ethnomathematical approach stems from the conception of mathematics as a cultural activity. The two approaches are summarised in Table 10.3.

Research Procedure

In the practical phase of the research study, the teachers and the researcher planned and developed together six different teaching projects based on the characterisation of 'ethnomathematics' and on the human activities identified in the first phase. Each project was designed by the teachers as a micro-curriculum sequence of activities based on their pupils' knowledge of a particular aspect of their reality. The teaching projects developed were the following ones:

(a) "The Skipping Rope" project – a *counting* project based on activities involving skipping games with ropes, by pupils of between 6–10 years;
(b) "The Hop Scotch" project – a *locating* project exploring the layout and organisation of different 'hop scotch' patterns with pupils of 9–13 years;
(c) "The Windmill" project – a *measuring* project where different geometrical figures are used to make windmills with pupils of 9–15 years;
(d) "The Queimada Game" project – a *playing* project based on a popular children's team game, where pupils of 10–15 years experiment with the shape of the playing area and the rules of the game;
(e) "The Hot Air Balloon" project – a *designing* project where pupils of 11–16 years designed and built different paper balloons having been given certain dimensions;
(f) "The Brazilian Economic Plan" project – an *explaining* project where pupils of 13–16 years studied and explored the meanings and implications of different aspects of the economic plan.

The 19 teachers then applied the teaching projects in their own classes in 12 ordinary council/state Brazilian schools. These projects were applied to about 450 pupils, and each project was used for between 3 and 5 weeks (i.e. between 15 and 25 hours of mathematics class time). In order to analyse the effects of the teaching projects, from the point of view of the teachers' attitudes, a questionnaire was given to the teachers, with interviews, on three separate occasions during the research: (1) at the beginning of the study, (2) after the projects were developed, and (3) after they were used in class. Although data were also collected from the learners, the main aim of this study was to explore teachers' changing attitudes.

This questionnaire was generated from the descriptions given in Table 10.3. It contained four questions, (regarding each of the main sections of Table 10.3), each one with six alternatives (as in Table 10.3). The teachers were asked to rank these alternatives according to their own attitudes towards the question being asked. In addition, for each question, teachers' comments and personal definitions were requested.

Analysis of the Questionnaire

As a preliminary analysis, the 'Kendall Coefficient of Concordance (W)' (Siegel, 1956) was applied to the answers given by the teachers to those questions, and it revealed that the value of 'W' (i.e. the extent of teachers' agreement) was significant at the .01 level for all the questions and for all the applications. Therefore, it was possible to define a 'Standard Teachers' Answer' for each of the four questions and for each of the three occasions when the questionnaire was answered. Siegel's advice (p.238) is that "the best estimate of the 'true' ranking of the N objects, is provided, when W is significant, by the order of various sums of ranks". This then is what will be reported below. The results for the four parts of the questionnaire are as follows:

Question 1.   For me, mathematics is:
  (a) a theoretical subject
  (b) a practical subject
  (c) a logical subject
  (d) an exploratory and explanatory subject
  (e) a universal subject
  (f) a particular subject
(In the actual questionnaire these terms were defined and described.)

On the three occasions when the questionnaire was applied, the standard answers were as follows:

		Occasion		
		Initial	*Pre-teaching*	*Post-teaching*
	1st	b	b	d
	2nd	c	d	b
Rank	3rd	d	e*	c
	4th	e	f*	f
	5th	a	e	e
	6th	f	a	a

* = equal ranking

Looking at the standard answers to question 1, an important finding was the fact that alternatives 'b', 'c', and 'd' were ranked in the first three positions on each occasion. It means that mathematics, for those teachers, was basically seen as a 'practical', 'logical', and 'exploratory and explanatory' subject. In addition, alternatives 'd' and 'f' from the ethnomathematical approach, were the only ones that increased in importance throughout the study.

A teacher's written statement which reinforces the quantitative findings is: "In this research study, I acted in two different, but possible and complementary ways: as a teacher and as a learner. As a teacher, I tried to show my pupils a new face of mathematics. A face which is hidden by the school. A mathematics which can be seen as practical, pleasurable, formative and necessary. As a learner, I changed my own view about this subject with the aim of reaching a 'reconciliation' which I judged to be impossible before."

Question 2. For me, mathematics occupies an important place in the school curriculum because it is:
   (a) culture-free
   (b) socially/culturally based
   (c) informative
   (d) formative
   (e) conservative
   (f) progressive
(In the actual questionnaire these terms were defined and described.)

On the three occasions the results were:

		Occasion		
		Initial	*Pre-teaching*	*Post-teaching*
	1st	d	d	d
	2nd	f	f	f
Rank	3rd	c	b	b
	4th	a	a	c
	5th	b	c	a
	6th	e	e	e

* = equal ranking

Analysing these standard answers to question 2 about the intended level, there are three important findings. First, alternatives 'd', 'e', and 'f' (mathematics is a 'formative', a 'conservative', and a 'progressive' subject) did not change their rank on the three occasions that the question was answered (the 1st, the 6th, and the 2nd positions respectively). Second, alternative 'b' (mathematics is a socially/culturally based subject) showed the biggest increase in importance in rank throughout the research study. Finally, alternatives 'a' and 'c' (mathematics is a 'culture-free' and an 'informative' subject) decreased in importance in rank during the development of the research study. Concerning the increase of importance of the alternative 'b', a teacher wrote: "What a big mistake it was to think initially that the 'cultural and social' basis of mathematics has so little importance. Mathematics is basically a product of the culture of each race. It grows from the need of each society, and the experience of each one. These are the bases of its truths."

Question 3. For me mathematics should be taught as:
  (a) a one-way subject
  (b) a debatable subject
  (c) a separated subject
  (d) a complementary subject
  (e) a reproductive subject
  (f) a productive subject
(In the actual questionnaire these terms were defined and described.)

On the three occasions the results were:

| | | *Occasion* | | |
		Initial	*Pre-teaching*	*Post-teaching*
	lst	f	b	b
	2nd	b	d	f
Rank	3rd	d	f	d
	4th	e	e	e
	5th	a	c	c
	6th	c	a	a

Analysing these standard answers to question 3 about the implemented level, we find that the alternatives 'b', 'd', and 'f' (a 'debatable', a 'complementary' and a 'productive' subject) occupied the first three rank positions on each of the three applications.

A teacher made the following remark about this question: "I believe that the way in which mathematics is normally taught today, only contributes to minimising the number of people who like it. The way of teaching should be clearly linked to the teachers' attitude towards his/her pupils. The majority of teachers think that it is easier, and more convenient, to 'repeat' mathematical concepts, assuming that they are absolute truths. In such a way there can be no discussion, and there is no space for pupils to question, to find out, to analyse."

Question 4. For me, pupils who have learnt mathematics should be able to:
   (a) find correct answers to problems
   (b) analyse problems
   (c) use the formal mathematical methods to solve problems
   (d) use appropriate procedures to solve problems
   (e) reason mathematically
   (f) make mathematical criticism
(In the actual questionnaire these terms were defined and described.)

On the three occasions the results were:

		Occasion		
		Initial	*Pre-teaching*	*Post-teaching*
	1st	b	b	b
	2nd	f	f	d
Rank	3rd	e	d	f
	4th	d	e	e
	5th	c	a	c
	6th	a	c	a

Analysing these standard answers to question 4 about the attained level, alternative 'b' ('analyse problems') was ranked in the first position on all the three occasions. In addition, alternative 'd' (use 'appropriate procedures' to solve problems) showed the biggest increase in importance during the research study, while alternatives 'e' and 'f' ('reason mathematically' and 'make mathematical criticism' about problems) decreased in importance. Also alternatives 'a' and 'c' ('find correct answers to problems' and 'use the formal mathematical methods to solve problems') were those that were ranked in the two lowest rank positions throughout the research study.

Overall, at the end of the whole research experience, the teachers' preferred views were that:

1. Mathematics should be seen as an *exploratory* and *explanatory* subject, investigating environmental situations.
2. The mathematics curriculum should be *formative*, emphasising analysis, synthesis, thinking, a critical stance, understanding, and usefulness.
3. Teachers should teach mathematics as a *debatable* subject where mathematical knowledge is discussed among pupils and teachers.
4. Pupils should be able to *analyse problems* and understand the structure of problems.

Although the Standard Teachers' Answers reported here cannot characterise completely the extent of the changes that took place in teachers' attitudes and beliefs regarding the mathematics curriculum, it is interesting to note that after the study these teachers became much more concerned with many of the aspects emphasised by the ethnomathematical approach at its four levels of analysis. As well as changing some of the teachers' attitudes, the approach also reinforced and supported some of the pre-existing attitudes of the teachers who also felt dissatisfied with the curriculum normally being used.

CONCLUDING REMARKS

In this chapter we have explored two related aspects of mathematics education, taking the socio-cultural context into account. In the first, the focus of study was the learner, who ultimately is the person who must make sense of the whole educational experience. From the reported research we can see how the differences between the learners' perceived out-of-school and in-school mathematical cultures result in certain kinds of cultural conflicts. This is clearly *not* a simple matter for learners of merely recognising the differences and reflecting on their relative importance. The classroom situation is one where there is an asymmetry of power between teacher and learners (Bishop, 1991), resulting in certain values being developed rather than others, and certain forms of knowledge being accepted as more important than others. The learners, from their relatively powerless position, have their mathematical knowledge, attitudes, and beliefs shaped by the actions of their teachers.

Thus it is of paramount importance to learn more from research about teachers' knowledge, attitudes, and beliefs, and particularly how these might be changed to enable the learners to resolve the conflict situation. The second study focused on this aspect. Although certain attitudes seemed to remain prominent throughout the study, there were attitudes that changed as a result of the teachers' engagement with a specifically culturally focused project.

From this study, Pompeu (1992, p.287) concluded that in order to implement successfully an ethnomathematical approach in schools, teachers have to learn to:

- accept and understand, as far as possible, their pupils' social and cultural backgrounds,
- act as micro-curriculum developers, and skilled problem-solvers,
- encourage their pupils to assess and be critical of their own work.

If this can be done, then the prospects of changing teaching situations and processes in such a way that contrasts between school and out-of-school mathematics can become the basis of positive rather than negative learning experiences, are much more promising in the future.

ACKNOWLEDGEMENTS

Guida de Abreu's research was sponsored by CNPq/Brazil. Geraldo Pompeu's research was sponsored by Capes/Brazil.

11 Social Interactions and Mathematics Learning

M.L. Schubauer-Leoni,
University of Geneva, Switzerland
A.-N. Perret-Clermont,
University of Neuchâtel, Switzerland

In this contribution we describe the evolution of a field of research in which we have been involved for some 15 years, investigating cognitive and social aspects of mathematics learning. Our aim is not to present a succession of research results but rather the progressive modification of the issue under study. The visible outcome was sometimes answers to the questions raised, but often also of the *modification of the research questions*, and as a consequence the search for changes in *methods appropriate* for their investigation. We will also refer to other work, which is not directly centred on the learning and teaching of mathematics, to which we have contributed and which has played a part in the progress of our studies of children and school mathematics.

A FIRST STUDY: PIAGETIAN VS. SCHOOL TASKS

In the late 1970s we were immersed in the study of the role of social factors in development, bringing to the fore the role of interpersonal interactions as providing the driving force behind cognitive development (Perret-Clermont, 1976, 1980; Mugny, Perret-Clermont, & Doise 1981; Perret-Clermont, 1982; Perret-Clermont & Schubauer-Leoni, 1981). At that time our institutional involvement in a department of educational sciences and our pedagogical concerns induced us to deal more precisely with learning tasks that were meaningful in the school context and hence different from those usually implemented in the studies of the mechanisms of thought in general. We were profoundly interested in the considerations given by psychopedagogists to the connection (and disconnection) between developmental psychology and the teaching of mathematics (Brun & Conne, 1979), and we tried to extend the research paradigm that we were using in the work on the social construction of intelligence to include the testing of the possible benefits of peer interaction on children's learning of elementary school mathematics.

We started this line of research with primary school children solving and representing additive problems of the type $a + b - c = x$. The task that we used in these studies was as follows. On the table there is a handful of sweets and a non-transparent empty bag. The experimenter (E) invites the child (C) to pay attention to what will happen. E picks up two sweets, shows them to C and then puts them into the bag. Then E repeats the action this time picking up four sweets, shows them to C and puts them into the bag as well. Finally, E takes one sweet back from the bag and asks C : "Is it possible to know how many sweets are now in the bag?" Once the child has answered "five" and made explicit the complete additive/subtractive composition of elements involved, E gives him/her paper and pencil with the following instruction: "You have to explain to a child who has not seen what we have done with the sweets everything that happened with these sweets and how many are left at the end. Try to make him/her understand what we have done with the sweets in order to end up with five in the bag".

The first study (Schubauer-Leoni & Perret-Clermont, 1980), set out to investigate:

1. Whether there is a link between three types of observations: the operative competences of a 7–8-year-old child in a Piagetian task involving the additive properties of number; the ability to respond correctly in school tests of the type "a + ... = b" or "a + b = ..."; and the child's capacity to draw on the "arithmetic code" learned at school when asked to report additive actions on paper.
2. The effects of the interpersonal context in which the written formulation of an addition problem is carried out.

With respect to the first question, we observed that the expected connections were much more complex than we had anticipated, thereby replicating earlier observations by researchers such as Brun (1979) and Vergnaud (1981). Being at the most advanced level in the Piagetian operational tasks appeared to be neither a necessary nor a sufficient condition to solve the gap-filling equations proposed. In none of our problems was operatory competence a sufficient condition for the pupils' use of arithmetic writing at the time of encoding an addition problem. This was for us, at the time, an initial threat to our then rather rigid structuralist understanding of the functioning of the mind, and a disappointment because the implementation of the new mathematics curriculum in Swiss schools relied on the assumption that giving the child adequate opportunities to develop the basic operatory notions would allow for a general grasping of the meaning of numbers and of numerical systems. We were then unaware of Reed and Lave's (1981) pioneering work distinguishing between two classes of arithmetical strategies: those that deal with quantities as such and those that deal with number names and that are reinforced by school socialization. This discussion of the communalities and differences of the arithmetic behaviour in oral or written forms, in everyday life or in school-promoted practice, has been enlarged since then by ethnographic studies (for a review see Nunes, 1992, and Nunes, in press) which produce very interesting evidence to distinguish the uses of (different) symbolic systems from the understanding of cognitive invariants.

Carraher, Carraher, and Schlieman (1985, 1987) as well as Nunes (1992) were concerned with refuting hypotheses about differences in psychological processes between users of different systems of signs, or with observing effects of symbolic mediations in the organisation of human activity as the systems are used. In contrast, our own concern, arising from our earlier studies of the role of socio-cognitive conflicts in cognitive development, was with those characteristics of the social contexts that elicit the use of one or another system of signs to represent quantities and operations and which bring about more or less explicit formulations of these.

In order to test the effects of interpersonal contexts on these encodings by the pupils, we designed an experiment with four experimental conditions: (a) two children interact to formulate their message about the problem for a decoding peer who will then decode their message; (b) two children interact to formulate their message about the problem for a decoding peer without the benefit of feedback from the latter; (c) a child formulates his or her own message for a decoding peer who will then decode the message; (d) a child formulates the message for a decoding peer without the benefit of feedback. Hence two of these conditions involved collective resolutions and two did not. The children's productions varied a lot: some wrote the "orthodox" formal arithmetic formulas but others responded to the experimental demand with drawings or texts, in ways very similar to those reported later by Hughes (1986).

The scenario of the task, the type of problem and the instructions are similar to those described earlier on with only a difference of *content*. This time the experimenter is not presenting sweets to put in a bag but flowers to make a bunch : "you pick two flowers, and then you pick six more; and then you meet a schoolmate and you give him/her three of these. With how many are you left for your bunch?". In this case the *additive* composition is: $2 + 6 - 3 = 5$.

During the pretest, the pupils were tested individually outside the classroom and had to produce a first encoding relative to an addition problem of the same type as that later given in the various experimental conditions. The pairs of children who were to work together in the coding task were organized on the basis of the individual productions in the pretest, so as to give rise to cognitive confrontations thought to be beneficial, and also in order to vary the pairs of children as a function of whether or not their members had resorted, in the pretest, to canonical mathematical formulations or to "unorthodox" natural language or drawings. The experimental conditions were followed by individual post-tests in order to measure the effects of these different experimental conditions by comparing the characteristics of formulations produced in the post-test with those of the pre-test.

The results supported our hypothesis in that the pupils who solved the task in pairs and had feedback from a decoding peer (condition *a*) made the most progress: in this group there was a tendency to mention all the quantities and the operations carried out in the situation they had been asked to describe explicitly. When the results of the pre- and post-test were compared, we observed that 93% of the subjects in this experimental condition gave more explicit answers in the post-test than in the pretest. In contrast, this increase in explicitness was observed for 76% of the subjects in the other conditions. Only two children who worked alone and had no feedback from a decoding peer (condition *d*) showed regression on this measure.

It was also observed that pupils who solved the problem in pairs and had feedback from the decoding peer were more likely to use the formal mathematical code (numbers and signs) rather than natural language or drawing in the post-tests: in this experimental condition subjects more often used the formal code (5 times out of 14) than those who worked in pairs but did not receive feedback (2/12), those who worked alone and had feedback (1/6), and those who worked alone and had no feedback from a decoding peer (1/7).

These results are consistent with those obtained previously when the children worked on operative tasks (in the Piagetian sense) either in social settings or alone. However, there are some aspects that are more difficult to explain within the classical experimental research paradigm of the social construction of intelligence. In particular, in this study we observed that the pupils tested individually (experimental condition *d*), who were questioned on three separate occasions (pretest, test, post-test) using the same adult–child face-to-face method, modified their written production more appreciably than expected: either by showing signs of progress, or by producing "regressive" type encodings during the post-test. These results aroused our curiosity. We went back to the audiotapes and listened to all the testing sessions in search not only (as we had done previously) of cues about how the children express their logical thinking, but also in search of the reasons for the unexpected changes in the performance of children who worked alone and without feedback. In our previous research those subjects who worked with a peer showed systematically more cognitive progress than those who worked alone: the latter made very little or no progress. In contrast, in this study we observed two different types of results: working with a peer was better only in condition *a*, where problem solving was followed by interaction with a decoder, and, unexpectedly, subjects performing the task alone also showed progress in the post-tests. Why should the results of this last study differ from the previous ones?

— An analysis of the children's reactions led to the following hypothesis about the differences between the task in this last study, which we will refer to as a "mathematical task", and the previous tasks of conservation of number, of quantities, and of spatial relations, the "Piagetian tasks". Piagetian tasks have often been considered as "purely cognitive" tasks, but we are now convinced that they are no less "socio-cognitive" than other mathematical tasks. Certainly they have some specific characteristics that relate to the central interest of Piagetian theory: they involve judgements and reflective skills.

The mathematical task of the present study differs from the Piagetian tasks because it calls on *symbolic* skills, which have not only a reflective but also a primary *communicative* function. This communication does *not take place in a social and historical vacuum* but as a continuation of previous discussions about operations (addition and substraction) that have been approached previously elsewhere (i.e. in the classroom and perhaps at home). It is important to recognise that *mathematical notions* are not the product of the individual mind of a socially isolated child, whose cognitive activity functions *ex nihilo*, but are socio-cultural constructs that pre-exist the child's activity and are made accessible to the child through more or less formal social transmission. Mathematical notions are socially situated within networks of specific social practices, of which classroom practices are an example. One must take this into account when considering whether it is possible for the developed adult mind or for the growing mind of a child to abstract general concepts independent of the social networks in which they are constructed or learned. Symbols and symbolic mediations (writing, formal mathematical code, and even drawing) have their traditions and these are conveyed to the children outside the testing or experimental situation.

The *cognitive* and *social* experience of being asked to make a judgement on the conservation of quantities is different from that of being asked to solve a mathematical exercise. The difference led us to revisit the role of the decoder. Whereas the presence of the peer for the collective production of a notation helped the subjects keep different elements in mind at the same time and confront their evaluation, when the task involved the use of symbolic knowledge, the presence of the decoder appeared to be essential to give meaning to the coding task itself and did not serve only as a feedback. The presence of the decoder stressed the *communicative* function of the notations. Other cues heard in the tape recording of the sessions led us to reconsider the role played by the characteristics of a *mathematical* task in determining the types of social interactions that can take place around it. Through this analysis, we realized that we had underestimated the role of two parameters in the paradigm of this first study: these were *the major impact of the mathematical object* on which the interaction between peers was focused, and *the role of the adult experimenter in the emergence of responses* produced in interaction. The following studies attempted to explore these parameters.

THE MEANING ATTRIBUTED TO THE OBJECT IN TERMS OF THE QUESTIONING CONTEXT

New studies[1] have then both confirmed the superiority of experimental conditions that involve peer collaboration in the production of written formulations of arithmetic operations (Brun & Schubauer-Leoni, 1981) and have also, owing to the establishing of formulation typologies (Brun & Schubauer-Leoni, 1981; Schubauer-Leoni & Grossen, 1984), enabled the expression of subtle differences when analyzing the written formulations produced by pupils at different stages of the experiment. These studies have provided the opportunity to analyse the impact of communication situations between coders and decoders according to whether the decoder "says" or "does" what he understands from a message (Schubauer-Leoni & Grossen, 1984) or by maintaining the exchanges between the coder and decoder until a consensual response is obtained from the two participants (Saada & Brun, 1984). This last study, moreover, provided an opportunity to underline the importance of the prompts provided by the adult in enhancing the coder–decoder interaction. Subsequent analyses (Schubauer-Leoni & Perret-Clermont, 1985) have taken into account the particular nature of the scholastic mathematical object as an object having a social and cultural history but also a scholastic one, which plays a part in the everyday scholastic practices of the pupil. For this reason, during a lesson or a test the child always tackles and relates to the situation in terms of the customs (simultaneously cognitive, social, and didactic) acquired elsewhere at school and possibly at home in relation to this object.

The nature of the object "written formulation of addition problems" is, at this point of our research programme, changed in two ways: first, the mathematical object is not cognitively superimposable on other Piagetian operatory knowledge, and second, its social existence within the realm of scholastic reality means that the child brings with him/her, to the place where he/she is questioned by the psychologist, inherent customs in relation to the scholastic object encountered elsewhere in class.

Consequently we must ask: What is the role played by the adult who poses questions about the pupil's productions? In other words, our initial research

[1]Carried out in collaboration with J. Brun and psychopedagogists concerned with mathematics (Swiss National Research Foundation, contract No. 1.706.078).

questions have now a wider object: *in what sorts of contexts (cognitive, material, relational) is mathematical knowledge displayed or acquired?* What are the *representations which enable the pupil, faced with question acts, to formulate response acts that* are both cognitively satisfactory and relevant—that is, acceptable—in the given socio-cognitive context (Perret-Clermont et al., 1984; Schubauer-Leoni & Perret-Clermont, 1985). Pupils interpret social situations and tasks simultaneously. What are the representations that they construct of their endeavour?

MOVING FROM A BIPOLAR TO A TRIPOLAR MODEL OF KNOWLEDGE CONSTRUCTION

Our first experiments, as mentioned above, followed the Piagetian tradition in that they considered the questioning carried out by the experimenter as neutral and limited to recording visible indications of the child's thinking that were unfolded under his/her eyes. Hence, the descriptions of the patterns of social interactions that took place in the experimental conditions did not take the experimenter into account; and we wrongly considered the pre- and post-tests as "individual" sessions with no awareness that the experimenter–child relation is the locus of a series of social interactions, just as much as the peer–peer relation.

There was another oversimplification in our first approach. The Piagetian bipolar model of knowledge building (subject – object) had been substituted by a primary tripolar model (subject 1 – subject 2 – object). Because of the new importance that we had given to the impact of the interaction between peers, this model risked underestimating the role of the object by stressing the child 1–child 2 bipolarity. But when we started to take the type of task, and in particular the status of the mathematical object, more explicitly into account as the centre of joint activity it became clear that the object played a central role, not only as a "task" but also as a mediation that specified a social system in which the adult is in a high position when asking the questions. The model, which was formerly bipolar (*subject–object*; or *peer–peer*), now becomes clearly tripolar—*questioner–questionee/s–object*—and integrates the experiment as an integral part of the observation. It is interesting to note that this epistemological shift from the conception of the observer as "neutral and external" to a consideration of the observer as constituent of the object under observation took place long ago in other domains such as nuclear physics (see, among others, for the discussion of this point: Prigogine & Stengers, 1979; d'Espagnat, 1979; Perret, 1981).

The different places in which the experiments were carried out (in and out of the classrooms, in school-like formal settings or not) made us aware of the function attributed to the questioner in terms of his/her institutionalised role. Hence our further experiments started to differentiate between the teacher questioner and the psychologist questioner (that is, the experimenter outside the classroom) in order to understand the status of the replies of those pupils questioned by someone having one or the other social role.

Finally, this first stage of work on mathematical contents made us aware of the temporal dimension at work in the pupils' generation of a response. We categorized the experimental productions according to a pretest, intervention, post-test scheme, focusing our attention primarily on changes from the pre- to the post-test. But the consideration of this three-step intervention as a whole, whereby an experimenter acts on three occasions with repeated similar or dissimilar demands addressed to the subject, led us to introduce the concept of the *experimental history of the subject*. This concept allows for a more dynamical approach of the testee's productions because they are considered in a temporal perspective, and opens the way to new questions on the construction and transmission of knowledge. It also raises the question of the link between the social conditions of the appropriation of an object of knowledge and those of its display or use: a point made also, from another perspective, by Forman (1989), who observes that the traditional pre- and post-test decontextualized approach is inadequate to evaluate the success of peer collaboration.

THE EMERGENCE OF THE NOTION OF A "DIDACTIC CONTRACT"

The tripolar dynamics of the approach described above has merged with one developed elsewhere by other researchers in the domain of the teaching of mathematics (Brousseau, 1988; Chevallard, 1988). Brousseau and Chevallard, have already stressed the triangular nature of the teaching relationship, which is bound by an implicit "didactic contract"—that is, a system of reciprocal and specific expectations with regard to the knowledge taught. From our standpoint as social psychologists, we have thus pursued our work in order to show experimentally the workings of a contractual relationship of this sort between, on the one hand, *the teacher, the pupil, and an object of mathematical knowledge* and, on the other hand, between *the experimenter, a subject, and an object of mathematical knowledge*. The didactic contract functions, through representational systems which it activates, as pre-eminently "practical knowledge" (as Bourdieu calls it), knowledge that is not thought of as such and which serves practical ends.

This new phase in our work was carried out in different directions and through diverse approaches. In particular we wanted to study the dynamics of the interaction between peers and with the adult in order to obtain a more detailed description (than previously allowed for, Semin, 1989) of the *simultaneously interactive and representational* nature of the processes involved.

Instead of defining tasks only by their content (for example, the written formulation of addition problems), we considered more broadly the general situation in which subjects were set in the experiment, and we introduced the concept of "experimental staging" (Perret-Clermont et al., 1984). A research design was organized in such a way as to alternate the questioning contexts: first in class, then in face-to-face situations, then once again in class for the third phase. This was done in order to make possible the identification of the meanings that pupils confer on the situation when they try to make sense simultaneously of the task and of what they consider to be the adult's expectations. Obviously pupils are affected in their views by their implicit knowledge learned in the everyday functioning of the didactic contract in the classroom and by the habits that they have acquired in such context (Schubauer-Leoni, 1988). The analysis of protocols of the second phase, where the child is in face-to-face interaction with the adult, demonstrated how social and cognitive elements are interwoven in the subject's understanding of the situation (Schubauer-Leoni, 1986b).

THE STUDY OF THE DIDACTIC CONTRACT VIA THE TEACHER

The studies described up to this point have as a common feature the consideration of the child as the main focus of study. They centred on the child–task (object of knowledge) interactions and on the child–partner (adult or peer) interaction. The widening of the underlying model from bipolar to tripolar made us aware that we had so far concentrated our attention only on certain elements of these triangular relationships, leaving the others in the background: all the previous analyses gravitated around the person in the "lower social position"—as if the adult experimenter or teacher in the "higher position" was not an essential element in the dynamics of these sociocognitive encounters. This led us to set up studies of the didactic contract from the point of view of the teacher's expectations with regard to the pupil's behaviour in certain tasks.

Our next step was a study carried out with a teacher of a class of primary school children aged 8–9 years. It involved several interlinked experimental phases:

Phase 1: the teacher conceives of and writes up a mathematical task for the pupils (typical task within the current didactic contract) and is invited by the researcher to explain the rationale of the choices that were made.

Phase 2: the teacher makes predictions as to the behaviour and performance of each pupil with regard to the task.

Phase 3: the teacher administers the task to the pupils as usual.

Phase 4: the teacher corrects the answers as usual.

Phase 5: the researcher submits to the teacher a task that is unusual for, and at the

outer boundaries of, the didactic contract in force. The teacher is asked to
determine the interest and feasibility of this task for the class.

Phase 6: the teacher formulates expectations of each pupil's behaviour and
performance with regard to this unusual task.

Phase 7: the teacher administers the task to the pupils.

Phase 8: the teacher corrects the answers to this second task.

The research corpus corresponding to these eight experimental phases gave
us access to two types of contractual behaviour: those produced under the
terms of the usual didactic contract (phases 1 to 4) and those produced in a
situation where the contract is broken (phases 5 to 8). The study (described in
Schubauer-Leoni, 1986a, 1989, 1991) illustrated the indivisibility of the three
terms of the didactic relationship. Indeed we repeatedly observed that the
teacher considers the *task*—and hence the mathematical knowledge that it
conveys—*in terms of how pupils react to it*; the teacher describes his/her
present pupils in regard to *how they are expected to tackle the task* according
to his/her view of possible solutions. In a later study concerning the teaching
of algebra in secondary schools in Switzerland and Italy (Schubauer-Leoni &
Ntamakiliro, 1993), the same type of phenomenon was again observed.

Above all we observed that teachers differentiate between cognitive levels
of responses to the task according to their representation of each pupil; the
didactic contract appears to be the result of differential expectations by the
teacher who, without realizing it, creates expectations in mathematics that are
part of the sociological characteristics of the pupils in the class. The teachers
tended to overestimate the performances of pupils from privileged social
backgrounds and underestimate those of the pupils from underprivileged ones.

Through a classic effect of social categorization, the "weaker" pupils (in
terms of the actual results on the task and the mark obtained) from the
privileged social group were perceived as being more in line with their peers
from the same social group; by the same token, the "stronger" pupils from the
underprivileged social group tended to be "lowered" in favour of a
resemblance between members of their sociological group. It should be noted
that this effect becomes even more marked the further the task departs from the
usual didactic contract (phases 5 to 8). This differentiation was definitely not
intended by the teachers who considered themselves committed to the cause of
equal opportunity and democratisation of access to school and knowledge.

The results of this study, and in particular, the differential function of the
didactic contract, were confirmed when other corpora, including further data
about the same teacher but also other teachers, were taken into account. For
example, we also considered the comments written in the school reports
addressed to the parents.

A further detailed analysis of the modes of administering the tasks to the
pupils was carried out in this as well as in other studies (Schubauer-Leoni,

1989; 1993). It illustrates the complexity of the phase during which the task is transmitted by the teacher to a pupil or a group of pupils. From the very beginning, we find traces of a differential didactic contract in the sense described above. We also observed that pupils look for clues to the meaning of the situation in which they are questioned and try to get confirmation (real or decoded as such) from the teacher or the experimenter in order to define their position as testees. The observation of these adult–child transactions reveals misunderstandings that seem to be due to unshared implicit references about different orders of reality or about supposedly common experiences during the didactic or experimental history. This is indeed the major problem in achieving intersubjectivity between co-actors (Rommetveit, 1974; Grossen, 1988).

THE STUDY OF THE DIDACTIC CONTRACT VIA THE PUPIL

We continued our research into the didactic contract by providing the pupils with the opportunity to play the role of the teacher. The purpose of such an unusual approach is to identify the principal ingredients of the teacher's gestures as decoded by the pupils. Of course this detour requires at first an analysis of the difficulties that pupils will inevitably encounter in trying to occupy a social and cognitive position that is not "normally" their own within the didactic contract.

For this investigation (Schubauer-Leoni, 1986a) we organized role-playing situations during which the pupils (7–8 years old from 2nd primary and 11–12 years old from 6th primary) were first requested to think up mathematical scholastic tasks for another pupil in their class (2nd–2nd) or for younger pupils (6th–2nd). They were then requested to play the role of the teacher giving the task to a pupil.

This study demonstrated three processes: (1) The types of tasks conceived by the "little teachers" are directly based on usual scholastic tasks with a clear emphasis on *calculation activities*: lists of operations to be carried out appear as prototypical representations of what is for them a mathematical task in school. (2) The tasks, provided by the "little teachers" in written form and then directed by them to their "pupils", revealed the difficulty for these children of taking the adult's role and formulating questions. We observed that the young "teachers" systematically constructed their questions on the basis of the replies, hence spontaneously taking their "natural" place of repliers. It was also observed that during the interaction with the "pupil", the "little teacher" is often keen to answer in the place of his/her interlocutor. This strategy is sometimes replaced by the adoption of an attitude of reprobation towards the supposed ignorance of the pupil being questioned! (3) When requested to choose a class mate to give the task to, the "little teacher" tended to choose the pupil whom he/she considered to be the weakest, apparently in order to guarantee a certain distance between the "teacher" and the "pupil", as if there was a prerequisite to be able to consider himself/herself authorised to take on a role that would otherwise have no legitimacy.

All these elements recall the existence of power games in most interpersonal relationships (Goodnow, 1989; Forman, 1992). But above all they underline the function of the knowledge taught as mediating the social relationship in the teaching situation, knowledge that presupposes (or bears on) a system of non-interchangeable social positions.

Thus what seems to matter, and to determine the nature of the games, is the fact that children, when confronted with the task, have to take on a role of expert and a role of novice respectively.

From a methodological point of view, these studies mark the transition from an approach centred on the *effects* of certain interactions to one focusing on the *processes* put into action by those interacting in order to make sense of the task and of the situation into which they are thrown. These two stages of work in the field of mathematics learning, have their parallels in other areas (Schubauer-Leoni et al., 1989; Perret-Clermont et al., 1991; Perret-Clermont, 1992 a, b; Schubauer-Leoni & Grossen, 1993; Grossen, Liengme Bessire, & Perret-Clermont, 1997).

The impact of various social demands on children's drawings (Goodnow, 1989) or on the pupil's cognitive behaviours (Roazzi & Bryant, 1992; Grossen et al., 1996) has been established. In mathematics, in particular, Säljö and Wyndhamn, 1987, and Brossard (1994) deliberately manipulated the interpretational premises of the tasks submitted to the pupils, in order to show the effects of pieces of information about a task on the way in which the pupils handled arithmetical problems.

THE DIDACTIC CONTRACT AND THE
INSTITUTIONAL META-CONTRACT

Human communication systems have often been described as based on communication contracts (Rommetveit, 1974; Ghiglione, 1986, 1987) i.e. operating systems of norms and values that are organized in the form of implicit and explicit roles that guide the acts of those interacting (Goodnow, 1989). The studies that we have described therefore show not only traces of the existence of such contracts in exchanges about mathematics, but also the connection between this cognitive activity and the social situation. They also demonstrate that the cognitive activity is never exclusively related to the knowledge contents or to the thought operations that are needed to deal with these contents.

At the same time this cognitive activity relates to an interpretation of the situation as it evolves during the interaction (Grossen, 1988; Perret-Clermont & Schubauer-Leoni, 1989; Perret-Clermont et al., 1990, 1992; Schubauer-

Leoni et al., 1992). More specifically, each contract (didactic or experimental) not only governs the meanings of reciprocal behaviour but, in turn, is also under the control of *a meta-contract of an institutional nature*—a contract superimposed on the contract which governs the participants' framing of meaning (Rommetveit, 1974; Hundeide, 1981, 1985; Chevallard, 1989, 1992; Schubauer-Leoni & Grossen, 1993). Relating to an object of knowledge implies relating to those who (re)present it and to the institutions that have set them in this role.

We examined the impact of the rapport that pupils have with the institutional settings (Schubauer-Leoni, 1990; Schubauer-Leoni et al., 1992; Iannaccone & Perret-Clermont, 1993). Two comparable groups of pupils (2nd primary 8–9 years old) were required to produce a written formulation of the same calculation problem either *in class* (collectively under the responsibility of the experimenter, but with an *individual* written response from each pupil in keeping with the way that written work is usually carried out in the class) or *outside the class in a face-to-face* situation with the experimenter. We observed that the pupils' written responses varied as a function of these settings: in the classroom in the presence of their own teacher, the pupils had recourse to conventional arithmetic writing more often, whereas outside the class, face-to-face with an unknown adult, natural language and drawing were more often used to deal with these calculation problems.

These results show an effect on the child not just of the problem but also of the institution in which the problem is posed. Säljö (1991) also produced evidence in this direction in his study of children's use of a postage table and of proportionalities in and out of a mathematics class.

THE ORGANIZED BREAKING OF
THE DIDACTIC CONTRACT

Work on didactic (or experimental) interactions in mathematics does not seem adequate to us if it only deals with situations in which the "contract" is functioning "happily". To study only what is taken for granted by the participants in the interaction risks leaving hidden the fundamental basis on which the contract functions. Starting from other work carried out in the field of mathematics didactics and of psychology (IREM de Grenoble, 1980; De Corte & Verschaffel, 1983; Are, 1988; Brissiaud, 1988; Alves Martins & Carvalho Neto, 1990; Carvalho Neto, 1990; Giosuè, 1992) we constructed a study based on the "absurd problem" paradigm (with questions such as: "There are 15 girls and 12 boys in a class. How old is the teacher?"). Our aim was to understand the contractual conditions and the interactional dynamics that make it possible for a pupil to move from trying to solve a problem to rejecting what has been said (Schubauer-Leoni & Perret-Clermont, 1987; Perret-Clermont et al., 1992; Schubauer-Leoni & Ntamakiliro, 1994). The body of work carried out in the field of "absurd problems" agrees in showing the degree of subjugation to the usual didactic contract in that there is a massive production, by the pupils, of replies that are calculations based on the entirely irrelevant information imparted. Only the teacher's explanation of what is "really" expected (i.e. an explicit enlargement of the didactic contract) with regard to problems of this type makes it possible for children to avoid the "taken for granted" arithmetical composition (Giosuè, 1992).

Conversational analysis of the interactions between the experimenter and pupils illustrates the dynamics of the negotiations which allow the experimenter to "extract" responses from a pupil who pays lip service to the adult's demand but does not really change his or her mind about the problem (Perret-Clermont et al., 1992).

This research (Schubauer-Leoni & Ntamakiliro, 1994; Schubauer-Leoni & Grossen, 1993) has provided the opportunity to make progress in understanding the intersubjective, situational, positional, and institutional dimensions of the pupil's reply. This is done through the comparison of two types of "impossible" problems: a manifestly absurd problem (that of the age of the teacher given the number of pupils in the class) and a problem in which the degree of absurdity is more camouflaged ("A farmer has 87 rows of 150 lettuces. What is the surface area of the piece of land?"). The complexity of spatial measurements (Vinh Bang & Lunzer, 1965; Rogalski, 1992; Vergnaud, 1983) and children's relatively late mastery of the notion, is expected to play a leading role in their consideration of an eventual rejection of the problem: given the restrictions imposed by the institutional contract, why not take "a lettuce" as a unit of measurement? Our analyses of the interactive dynamics at the time that the 5th primary pupils (11–12 years old) were handling the two types of absurd problems suggest a conflict of rationalities. The pupils seem torn between their personal rapport (or "private component"; Chevallard, 1992) with the problem which makes them believe that the problem is "absurd", and their institutional rapport ("public component") which makes them write that the teacher is 27 years old and the surface area of the piece of land measures 13050 lettuces!

A PSYCHOSOCIAL THEORY OF SOCIAL INTERACTIONS AND A DIDACTIC THEORY OF DIDACTIC INTERACTIONS

It is useful to differentiate between the objects of study according to the ecological position that they occupy in different scientific debates. In order to make progress in the study of the teaching and learning of mathematics, it is necessary to carve out the object of study: what, of all the complex phenomena that can be observed, is to be studied? Different lines of research make their choice differently depending on their precise ends. Thus it appears to us wise to avoid superimposing fields of research too hastily and to favour a differentiation which, even if it might appear a little formal or arbitrary in the beginning (and it is), should in the long run help us to express the results of these different lines of research in relation to each other. In the area that interests us we observe, in particular, the emergence of two relatively new scientific fields:

- On the one hand, *a "contextual" science of the knowing subject* which is born out of *theories of the subject* that no longer place the subjects in isolation but situate them in relationship with their social and cultural universe. This science endeavours to render an account of the regularities and specificity of the subjects' (in our case, the pupils') socio-cognitive behaviours within structured "community of practice" areas (such as the scholastic institution for example).

- On the other hand, a *theory of situations* aiming to identify *situations which would bring about the emergence of expected knowledge* in the subject. The aim is to understand which situations establish which relations with the object of knowledge, and invite which approaches to the given factors, give rise to which cognitive elaborations, mobilise which know-how, which tools, or which memory. It is a question of contributing to a science of situations which are themselves prone to bringing about the intervention of a rapport with knowledge compatible with the rapport expected in the different institutions (first relative to taught mathematics; but also relative to the mathematicians' community as a whole). Here we find ourselves at the heart of the concerns of didactic theory. Although we are interested in the subject (and more specifically in the *pupil*-subject), the way in which the latter functions becomes an indicator of the possibilities offered by the situation.

These two fields of research differ above all with regard to the direction of their approach: one targets the subject via the situation; the other targets the situation via the subject. These differing focuses of attention are not at all mutually exclusive but have brought with them different methods of approach, observation, and validation on the part of scientists from the two domains. One must take care not to generalize or transpose the "results" from one domain to another without all the necessary precautions. It is, however, particularly interesting to articulate these fields one with the other: the work that we have described was born first from an attempt to understand the subject's cognitive functioning within his or her social interactions, and then focused on the particular, where his or her field of interaction is of a didactic nature. The object of study thus changed to: what understandings do the subjects (be they teacher or pupil) elaborate when they interact "didactically" in a given context?

AN EXAMPLE OF RESEARCH INTO DIDACTIC INTERACTIONS

The methodological transition (described earlier) from an approach centred on the *effects* of certain social interactions to an approach pertaining to *processes* of attribution of meaning to the interactions (and in particular to the participants' question/reply conjunctures) came about in parallel with work carried out elsewhere by mathematics didactitians who wanted to describe precise didactic phenomena (Brousseau, 1990; Chevallard, 1992; Vergnaud, 1983). In particular we were very interested in the emergence, in the didactic field, of a theory of "didactic engineering" of teaching situations (Artigue, 1988). This permitted us to enlarge the study legitimately from "natural" didactic interactions (mainly centred on the understanding of an habitual didactic contract) to "original" situations contrived, by didactic engineering, to provide a more general understanding of "how one induces mathematical cognitive functioning with its points of reference within the general body of mathematics situations, through the setting up of a didactic situation" (Brun & Conne, 1990, p.265). For these authors ". . . it is thus the parameters of this situation, and not individual characteristics, which are our variables" (p.265). But the theoretical goal can be extended to include the study of the interactions between the parameters of the situation and the socio-cognitive functioning elicited from the subjects or brought in with them.

A didactic engineering study in which four pupils interacted in getting to grips with a task pertaining to the notion of distance between two points was the object of two analyses. The first, conducted by Brun and Conne (1990), produced evidence for the function of representation in fostering the contact between the pupils' knowledge and the situation; the other, conducted by Schubauer-Leoni (1994) dealt more specifically with the level of analysis relative to the inter-individual and situational functioning that was permitted by the diverse parameters of the situation.

One of the characteristics of this experiment was the manipulation, during the first stage of the experiment, of the information placed at the disposal of two groups of two pupils in order to promote (during a subsequent stage of the experiment) cognitive confrontation between them. The aim was to demonstrate the notion of distance as being conceptually linked to a certain unit of measurement. The material used consisted of four foam cubes marking out two distances. The teacher placed the cubes on the floor at a distance of four metres for the first couple and at a distance of three metres for the second couple. The first group had at its disposal an unmarked stick measuring 50cm (the pupils are unaware of both the length of the distance and that of the measuring stick); the second group had at its disposal a stick of 25cm. During the first stage of the experiment each couple of pupils attempted to estimate the distance between the two plots placed on the floor with the aid of an unmarked stick; then, during the second stage, these distances were destroyed and the pupils, in a foursome, discussed and decided together which of the two groups had "the longer distance".

This was a difficult task. Indeed, as the measuring sticks were of different length and as the children were not immediately fully aware of what this meant for establishing the relative lengths, they were soon confronted with the puzzling result that the longest distance (4m) measures only "8 sticks" (8 × 50cm = 4m) while the shortest distance (3m) measures "12 sticks" (12 × 25cm = 3m). We observed the meshing of the different socio-cognitive constructions of the four pupils in the course of the argumentative exchange leading them to construct a certain representation of the problem together. We will not report here the detailed analysis of the different sequences (Schubauer-Leoni, 1994), but we can give a broad outline of the results:

- The agreement between the four children was not founded on constructions of the same order: one pupil was able to unravel the conceptual relationships between the variables of the problem and came to a conclusion at this level; but two other pupils could not come round to an acceptance of the difference between the two distances (a difference not in their favour) except by means of a factual procedure aimed at reconstructing the two presumed distances on the floor; the fourth pupil seemed to take a complaisant attitude, only taking part in the physical manipulation of the objects and without taking part in the debate about the relationship between the measurements obtained and the measuring apparatus in use.
- Given the information originally at the disposal of the two pairs of pupils at the time when they were interacting in a foursome, it had been particularly important to grasp the importance of a common construction of the problem and of the need felt by each individual to look for other information to complete that already at their disposal. In terms of intersubjectivity, a first agreement emerged when the pupils discovered a material world taken to be common to all. In this phase the pupils expressed themselves through the following type of formulations: "you had two bits of foam there too . . . and a stick?".
- Once this first level of common reality was constructed, the pupils were then able to engage in communication based on their previous activities and their respective experiences ("we measured with a stick", "what was your result?"), finally allowing for the size of the measuring stick ("was it a big or a little stick?").
- The idea of comparing results: "us twelve, you eight" was then called into play by taking into account the double relationship between the measurements obtained with the help of the two measuring sticks ("eight times of ours [big] that means two times more than with your little

measuring stick"). However, this logical explanation was not taken up by the other partners who preferred: "to do it again with the stick" in order to "see" and to come to a final agreement in this way about "who had the biggest distance".

- A detailed analysis of the protocol shows that it is not possible to give a simple description of the momentum between the respective progress of each child; each pupil ventured his own representation of problems which he tested out as the interaction advanced. This is the same as saying that, at an interactional level, the subjects did not have to put together a complete piece of reasoning in order to be able to introduce possible alternatives to the elaborations of the others, and subjects in the grips of a certain conception of the problem seemed momentarily insensitive to counter-propositions founded on other representational premises. The pupil usually needs to follow an hypothesis through to the end—and to deal with it in terms of his own representation—before being able to take a concurrent representation into account.

This analysis, which took into account certain conversational characteristics of the exchanges (Trognon & Retornaz, 1989; Trognon, 1992), showed that there were different ways of centring on the problem at various stages of working together in groups of four. We concluded that the abilities of the four pupils were important but so also were the didactic possibilities offered by the task itself and by the variables that it calls into play. This recalls the approach of Hoyles and Noss (1992) with which they analyse examples of what they call "a pedagogy built into the structure of the activities themselves" and observe small-group discussion and work processes elicited by this structure.

EPILOGUE

In this contribution we have tried to trace the evolution that our object of study has undergone as we were trying to come to grips with the sociocognitive processes at work when pupils are invited to learn culturally shaped notions such as those taught in mathematics in schools. Starting from the benefits of earlier work in cognitive and social psychology we underwent a shift in the psychological unit of analysis away from the individual thinker more or less affected by social factors of his or her environment (Doise, Mugny, & Perret-Clermont, 1975; Donaldson, 1978; Gilly, 1989; etc.) to an approach of those kinds of transactions that take place between persons socially situated as "novices" or as "experts" (pupils and teachers for instance) in social encounters in which transmission of knowledge or display of competencies is expected and sometimes even part of an institutionalized "contract".

This led us to search for new concepts and paradigms in order to describe the meshing of the cognitive and semantic psychosocial processes at work at the moment in which subjects deal with tasks but also "longitudinally", since previous experience and social roles and routines prestructure the understanding of a given situation and of the possible goals attainable through it.

This shift allows for new research ventures at the cross-roads of other scientific traditions, such as the anthropological approach to cognition and ethnomethodological studies of learning environments. In reviewing them, Cole (1991, p.413) points to the dramatic change that cognitive psychology undergoes "once one adopts the view that cognition refers not only to universal patterns of information transmission that transpire inside individuals but also to transformations, the forms and functions of which are shared among individuals, social institutions, and historically accumulated artifacts (tools and concepts)."

From a didactic perspective new understandings of these socio-cognitive phenomena can inspire the "engineering" of different social settings, which are sometimes disruptive towards the usual institutionalized practices and social routines and which elicit in the learner different types of commitments in the didactic encounters and hence different modalities of socio-cognitive functioning. We can mention the field work of Pontecorvo (1990) and Pontecorvo et al. (1991) on the role of debates in knowledge construction, of Gudmundsdottir (1991) on meaning construction and narrative structures in teaching, and of Lampert (1992) in the specific area of the community of mathematical practice, as very suggestive contributions in this direction. These offer new perspectives which need more exploration.

ACKNOWLEDGEMENT

We are grateful to the Swiss National Research Foundation which rendered this research work possible thanks to the contracts FNRS No. 1.706.078 & 10-1977.86 & 11-28561.90, and to Anne-Marie Rifai for her help with the translation.

IV CONSTRUCTING KNOWLEDGE IN THE CLASSROOM

In the last section, different perspectives on the social and cultural influences on mathematics learning were examined. The four chapters in Part III concentrated on learning that takes place outside school and on how it is related to school learning. This section focuses more specifically on the learning of mathematics *in school*. What are the consequences of the fact that learning takes place in this particular setting, that the learners are *pupils* and that the events during which they learn are *mathematic lessons*? And how do we design more effective lessons?

When an event takes place in a particular setting and the participants have specified roles, the setting and the roles played cannot be considered as accidental to the learning process: they shape the interactions that are supposed to result in learning. A mathematics lesson is a recognizable event: it is about mathematics, and the teacher poses problems, gives explanations, assesses the answers, orchestrates the pupils' behaviour; the pupils try to solve the problems, offer their answers for assessment, listen to the explanations, and implicitly accept the authority of the teacher to teach and to run the lesson. All this might seem irrelevant to the learning of mathematics, but the papers in this section argue that it is not. There are two powerful social consequences of the fact that learning takes place in mathematics lessons, both of which have been analysed most often in the works of French researchers.

The first is called the "didactical transposition" and refers to the fact that the mathematics of mathematicians is not the same as the mathematics that can be carried out in the classroom. Chevallard (1985) describes this process as the transformation of scientific into taught knowledge. In order to make mathematics into an object of teaching, it is necessary to analyse it into conceptual fields, to consider the difficulty of the forms of representation; to try to connect the topics to be taught in a sequence that is likely to make sense to the learner, to find ways of making it interesting to all pupils, not only those who might become mathematicians. Pupils must make sense of mathematics from inside (as mathematicians do) but also from the outside, as users of mathematics for other purposes. Pupils learning in school need to accept that they are seeking answers that the teacher already knows, not for new discoveries in mathematics. They need to recognize that there is a cultural production to be mastered.

This transformation from scientific into taught knowledge is inevitable because the logic of science is often not easily connected with the logic that people construct in their everyday lives. For example, the child has many ways of manipulating quantities to solve problems in everyday life: putting more objects into a container, taking some away, constructing correspondences, counting, separating, joining. However, this variety of actions on quantities can be formally represented by two operations, addition and subtraction. If a teacher were to concentrate in the classroom only on the formal notions of addition and subtraction and their properties, his or her pupils might not be able to connect their learning in the classroom with their knowledge of quantities developed outside. The taught knowledge of additive situations has to consider the knowledge of operations on quantities developed outside school. But it is also important to remember that taught knowledge must not disfigure scientific knowledge: teachers must be attentive to the scientific knowledge as a goal to be achieved. The didactical transposition involves three elements, teachers, pupils, and the object of study, and all three need to be considered.

The process of didactical transposition begins even before teachers prepare to teach their lessons: it is also involved in the making of policies about education that define what the goals of the curriculum are, what is taught at what age level, what pupils are assessed for, how many hours of mathematics teaching and in sessions of what length the pupils will receive. The very length of a class influences the teachers' choice of what a piece of taught mathematics might be but, beyond that, there is also the issue of how long one might need to teach algebra and what knowledge of algebra pupils will be asked to display in examinations. These pressures on teachers often influence their choices of problems—teachers might feel that spending two weeks to solve a problem might be too much, pupils should solve at least three or four problems in each lesson. They therefore choose problems that can be solved in short periods of time and that conveys to the students the idea that, if they have not solved the problem in a certain amount of time, they just don't know how to and might as well give up, because there is no point in trying.

The second concept that captures the influence of the classroom as a setting for learning on pupils' performance and views of mathematics is explored in greater length in this section by Douady: the notion of "didactical contract". The didactical contract, as she explains, encompasses many layers of meanings of how teacher and pupil interact. She deals in greater detail with a specific aspect of this relationship, one that merits much more attention than it has received in the literature so far: whether mathematics is at stake for the pupils and for the teachers. When mathematics is the real reason why both pupils and teachers meet in the classroom, designing instruction is a matter of what is the best way to teach. When mathematics is not at stake for the pupils (for example, when the pupils are in the classroom simply because they must be there), designing instruction requires a plan to change the pupils' views of and commitment to mathematics. If teachers ignore this issue and mathematics is not at stake for the pupils, learning is unlikely to become an accomplishment for all pupils.

One of the important consequences of the use of computers in the classroom, as illustrated in Noss's chapter, is that the didactical contract can be changed in significant ways. Pupils can work longer in solving a problem because that is quite acceptable when working with computers; they need to use a different type of language and the formal characteristics of computer languages can be helpful in the development of some aspects of taught knowledge, such as introducing the notion of variable, which is often difficult to teach without such a support; and pupils develop a different sense about their knowledge by taking more responsibility about what they want to do with it.

The chapters by Streefland and Gravemeijer also take mathematics lessons as their centre of attention and they do so in a specific way: these two chapters illustrate how it is possible to design instruction about complex (even if basic) concepts in mathematics by drawing on pupils' knowledge from outside the classroom. The teaching approach that their work represents, known as realistic mathematics education, involves a commitment on the part of the teacher to pose problems whose sense pupils can perceive: they can imagine why and how they might try to approach these problems. The taught knowledge of mathematics is developed through several resources which are typical of classroom situations:

- the pupils produce their own representations for problems and thereby connect what they know with what they are learning in the classroom;
- the teacher proposes forms of representation which allow the pupils to connect their common knowledge with an aspect of mathematics;
- the pupils compare their solutions for accuracy and efficiency, and thereby simultaneously recognize the validity of their everyday knowledge but also appreciate the value of mastering mathematical techniques not used in informal settings;
- the pupils can hold greater responsibility for their learning because they can see the sense of the problem and they are asked to justify and explain their solutions as well as listen to their peers' explanations: they are not only assessed but also assess different mathematical productions.

It is noteworthy that the authors of chapters in this final part of the book work in three different countries. In spite of the differences that exist between the three countries in the mathematics curriculum and in teaching practices, their approach to the design of mathematics instruction shows that mathematics lessons cannot be viewed as simple intellectual exercises, where thinking takes place without any social reference. The nature of the lessons will implicitly tell pupils what mathematics is, what it is for, what they can do with it, and whether they can control their own learning or whether it needs to be controlled from the outside, by someone else. The nature of the message transmitted in these aspects of the mathematics lesson determines what pupils learn; either mathematics or a series of techniques to be forgotten as soon as the examinations are over.

12 Meaning Mathematically with Computers

Richard Noss
Mathematical Sciences, Institute of Education,
University of London

INTRODUCTION

At the centre of mathematical learning there is a tension. Without formalisation there is no mathematical meaning: yet formalisation is most often seen as an insuperable obstacle in the construction of meaning, even counterposed to meaning itself. And without meaning there is no mathematics.

This poses an acute problem for mathematics educators. For it raises fundamental questions of where meaning comes from, even whether it makes sense to talk of meaning in the abstract, separated from the medium in which it is expressed. From a pedagogical point of view, the construction of environments in which children (and adults) play with mathematical structures—or more precisely, situations onto which mathematical structures might be mapped—is attractive; but the extent to which interaction with such environments results in mathematical learning depends critically on the relationship between the environment and the ways in which objects and relationships within the environment are combined, spoken about and expressed. That the particularities of different practices matter is evident from the work of Nunes et al. (1993) who show how the differences between the symbol systems of oral and written arithmetic structure calculating activity; similarly Hoyles and Noss (1988) illustrate how a computational medium may mediate children's expression of algebraic variables.

There are also epistemological questions concerning the relationship between a knowledge domain and its forms of expression. Do the standard ways in which knowledge is dichotomised—formal/informal, logical/intuitive etc.—really point to two different types of knowledge, or are they more accurately represented as two types of learning? More fundamentally, if there are *two* types of knowledge, are they distinguishable in terms of their structures and meanings, or is the distinction one that rests on learnability? From the point of view of mathematics this question points to a fundamental issue: what is the relationship between a piece of mathematics, and the various ways in which it might be represented? Are we justified in talking about a (unique) mathematical idea represented in various ways? Or should we better acknowledge that there are no mathematical ideas without representation, and that a change in the mode of representation necessarily entails a change (however subtle) in the idea itself?

One clear implication is related to the role of abstraction and formalisation. Does formalisation offer (merely) a way to express 'an idea'? Or is some kind of formalisation an essential ingredient of the mathematical 'essence'? In pedagogical terms, is it possible for mathematics to be learned in a way that seeks to obviate the need for the abstract and formal or would we be better off trying to build formalisation into environments that somehow connect with children's experiences? Should we bypass formalisation, or seek to exploit it?

The most eloquent adoption of the latter position has been offered by Papert (1980) who argues that the failure of so many children (and adults) to learn mathematics is precisely due to the impoverishment of their culture, and the scarcity within it of adults who know how to 'speak mathematics'; and, of course, that programming a computer in Logo provides just the kind of rationale for symbolic/formal expression with which conceptual frameworks for mathematical learning can be built. In the years that followed Papert's assertion, there was considerable debate concerning its truth. (Some of this debate became quite heated: see, for example, Pea & Kurland, 1984, and the rejoinder by Papert, 1987.) Now there has emerged a significant body of literature which seems to support some of Papert's claims (see, for example, Hoyles & Noss, 1992). Even so, the evidence is not universally accepted; fundamentally, the extent to which Papert's assertions are seen as validated presupposes an agreement on what is meant by mathematics, and indeed, on the kinds of meanings that are key to constructing mathematical understandings. To address these questions I must inevitably stray from the domain of psychology into epistemology and beyond. Accordingly, I begin by clarifying what might be meant by the notion of mathematical meaning.

MATHEMATICAL MEANING

According to Kegan (1982, p.19):

> Meaning . . . is the primary human motion, irreducible. It cannot be divorced from the body, from social experience, or from the very survival of the organism.

Meaning depends on someone who recognises you. Not meaning, by definition, is utterly lonely. Well-fed, warm and free of disease, you may still perish if you cannot "mean".

While Kegan argues nicely for the critical importance of meaning in general, it is rather difficult to attribute quite the same urgency to mathematical meaning. Nevertheless, there may be some point in taking seriously his assertion that there are dire consequences for human beings in failing to mean, and that by implication, a failure to mean *mathematically* forms a major stumbling block for learners engaged in mathematical learning.

Focusing on meaning has two consequences. First, it encourages us to look at the ways in which children *express themselves mathematically*, rather than simply on what mathematics they learn. While this latter question continues deservedly to receive plenty of attention in the psychology of mathematics education literature, it sometimes does so at the expense of examining the ways in which children make use of their available conceptual and material tools, and the settings in which such expression takes place. (There are some notable exceptions: see, for example, Carraher *et al.*, 1988; Saxe, 1991; and the 'ethnomathematical' literature exemplified by, for example, Gerdes, 1988.)

Second, it forces us to think more clearly about what mathematics is. If we expect to be able to recognise mathematical expression, we must be clear how we would know it if we saw it. Just what counts as mathematics is, of course, still a subject of debate among philosophers and (to a much lesser extent) among mathematicians. But although it is seldom made explicit, the debate also underpins much of the discussion of the mathematics curriculum. Further, addressing the question of meaning allows the possibility that mathematics has blurred boundaries; that there may be forms of mathematical expression that do not conform to the somewhat arbitrary norms of (Western) mathematics classrooms, and that these might be valuable either in their own right, or as a precursor to future learning.

Kegan's message is that meaning depends on being recognised. My premise in this paper is that mathematical meaning can be derived from being recognised by a computer. I am aware of the dangers of this metaphor: the difficulties arising from anthropomorphising the computers' role are well documented, and it is clear that many workers baulk at the idea that computers can be anything other than a dehumanizing element in the educational setting (see, for example, Sloan, 1984). Nevertheless, at the very least, the novelty of the computational medium sharpens our awareness of children's ways of expressing mathematical ideas, and focuses attention on questions of mathematical meaning that are largely taken for granted with older technologies such as paper and pencil.

It is on these kinds of tools, computational environments, that the rest of this paper will be focused. I will draw on a corpus of data derived from studying children's work in a variety of computer-based mathematical environments which attempt to facilitate mathematical expression and learning. I will concentrate on three kinds of mathematical meaning which seem to be particularly critical in terms of refining what it means to do, as well as to learn, mathematics: these are *formalisation*, *generalisation*, and *abstraction*. Each of these forms of meaning are examined from the starting point of a vignette involving computationally-expressed mathematics. Finally, I attempt to draw together some of these findings and develop a possible theoretical framework within which to interpret them.

FORMALISATION

The following simple Logo[1] procedure produces a parallelogram:

```
TO SHAPE  :SIDE1  :SIDE2  :ANGLE
    REPEAT 2 [FD :SIDE1 RT :ANGLE FD :SIDE2
    RT 180 - :ANGLE]
END
```

This procedure, or ones similar to it, formed the basis of a study some years back (Hoyles & Noss, 1987). It is worth looking in a little detail at the deceptively compact code. First, it gives the procedure a name, SHAPE, which encapsulates the process of drawing a given shape. Second, it specifies precisely three inputs (SIDE1, SIDE2, and ANGLE). Thus what varies is demarcated by the form and structure of the program. Once values of these inputs are chosen, everything else is determined. For this reason, the program indexes the most important facets of SHAPE to discriminate while 'using' it, and it contains pointers as to what is worth bringing into conceptual focus. Third, the structure of the procedure contains a formal representation of the main relationships of the parallelogram: (a) that its opposite sides are equal (have the same name), that its adjacent angles add up to 180 degrees; (b) that its adjacent sides are *not* necessarily equal (they have different names); and (c) that there is a symmetry accruing from the REPEAT 2, which we (but not necessarily the children) might characterise as rotational symmetry of order 2.

Essentially, the procedure contains the structure of a parallelogram: although this does not, of course, imply that decoding its syntax is natural or simple for learners. It turns the process of drawing a parallelogram into an object: this transition between process and object is not only a central characteristic of mathematical activity, but one that is far from trivial for learners (Douady, 1991; see also, Sfard, 1991).

---

[1]For the definitive introduction to Logo programming see Harvey (1985), and for the geometry of the 'turtle', see Abelson and diSessa (1980).

It is worth drawing attention to the oversimplification that resides in the use of the term 'contains the structure of a parallelogram'. In fact, this is a shorthand for a more complex observation which highlights the way in which the structure of the symbolic description of the parallelogram in the program code mirrors the visual representation, and vice versa.

As it turns out, this duality plays a central pedagogical role. A number of the 11-year-old pupils involved in the study began their activities in the belief that a parallelogram was a 'lopsided rectangle': this naturally precluded a rectangle from being a parallelogram. One of the outcomes of the study was that some pupils managed to link the symbolic representation of the procedure with its output on the screen, and used this to infer something new (to them) about the way in which the *mathematical* notion of parallelogram subsumes the special case when the angle is 90°. In fact, we might say that they had formed a theorem-in-action (this is a notion derived from Vergnaud, 1983, to which I shall return below) which runs something like this:

A quadrilateral is a parallelogram if it can be generated by the given program

or more interestingly, a corollary:

A rectangle is a special case of a parallelogram

and a proof:

Let :ANGLE = 90.

There are three key issues here. The first involves noticing that a more rigorous statement of the 'theorem' might require that, say, :ANGLE is not equal to 0: this is nicely caught in the act of running the program with particular instantiations of the variable's inputs—the program is a general description of a parallelogram while any particular 'run' of the program is a special case. So the tension between the general and the particular, between formality and meaning, is exploited rather than denied: there is a sense in which the formal acquires its meanings precisely through this ability to see the general through the particular.

The second issue concerns the necessary formalisation involved in interpreting or constructing the procedure, a formal way of communicating with the computer which is demanded by the programming language. At first sight, it is therefore tempting to equate the style of interaction with the most formal of mathematical activities. The unforgiving nature of the computer seems to demand a rigorous and stylised communication between learner and machine; and this seems to be equated with just the kind of formalism epitomised by traditional (Euclidean) proof—that has been expunged from the curricula of the UK (among other countries).

However, this way of viewing computer activities is inadequate. It runs counter to the ways in which the above 'theorems' were, in fact, developed by pupils, in the course of exploratory and playful interactions which focused as much on the visual output as on the structure of the symbolic code. There was a complementarity between rigorous form and informal structures of activity. In general, the example points to the ways in which the computer allows the development of linkage between formal and intuitive meanings, as a medium to *informalise the formal* (see Noss, 1991).

A third issue arises directly from the meanings attributable to the symbolic and formal. As I hinted earlier, mathematical expression using traditional tools demands a rigour that is highly tuned to the purpose of establishing mathematical truth, but far removed from everyday discourse. It seems likely that this gap between what is expected in mathematical activity and that which characterises normal life is responsible for at least some of the difficulties experienced by children in learning mathematics (see Noss, 1988, for some evidence on this issue).

In the computational setting, the situation is rather different from that involving the older technologies of pencil and paper. In the parallelogram task, for example, there is a basic rationale for interacting with the formal world of symbols: to construct a particular shape. Conversely, the awareness of the properties of that shape can (not *must*) be interpreted symbolically by reference to the textual structure of the code that gives rise to it.

It might be helpful to present some illustrative data on this issue. The episode I have chosen is from recent work with Boxer, which for the purposes of this paper, may be thought of as a development of Logo[2]: its most striking difference being that all text (including procedures) is written in boxes (which may be named or not, and which expand and contract as text—or anything else—is inserted). This simple visual metaphor has some attractive features: for example, subprocedures become boxes within boxes; and values of variables can be simply inserted into suitably-named boxes.

The example in question concerns two 11-year-old children, Nico and Mathew, working with Boxer[3]. They had a fair degree of experience with the medium, for the most part working on their own projects. Mathew and Nico were working with sprites, enhanced turtles whose shape can be programmed and set in motion. We knew that the children were working on the idea of symmetry in their class lessons, and we therefore were not surprised when Nico suddenly announced 'I want one sprite to go one way and the other to go the other way'.

---

[2]The details of Boxer—which is certainly much more than an extension of Logo, indeed much more than a programming language—are not relevant here. See diSessa (1990) for a description of the medium and its design principles.

[3]This episode was reported in Noss & Hoyles (1995).

We[4] helped Nico to put his idea into practice by defining a 'naughty sprite'— called MAT—which, when ordered to turn right, turned left, and vice versa. Quite simply, whatever the well-behaved sprite—NICO—drew, MAT drew a reflection in a line corresponding to the initial sprite-state. In Boxer, this can be done in a very straightforward and mathematically appealing way: but this need not concern us here (see Noss & Hoyles, 1995). Instead, we want to focus on the fact that, in the boxes in Fig. 12.1, MAT and NICO are the programs which define the behaviour of the corresponding sprites. The two sets of symbolic representations, taken together, exhibit an unmistakable symmetry—and this in turn reflects (and is reflected in) the symmetry of any graphical output created by running MAT and NICO together.

We also built for them a box (procedure) GO, which allowed the two sprites to draw (almost) in parallel: and we left the children to their own devices. In the following session, they had tried out GO, and explored a range of possible constructions—and, we conjecture, discriminated a number of properties of such drawings. Mathew and Nico expressed a wish to build a new naughty sprite— named DENISE, after their teacher!—which would switch FORWARD and BACK rather than RIGHT and LEFT. This they did, and proceeded to use their three sprites separately and together (using GO, amended appropriately). But as soon as they started to explore what could be drawn in this way, they noticed 'something missing'—the graphical output was not symmetrical; moreover, it was generally evident 'what was missing' in the picture (see Fig. 12.2).

After some thought, Nico suggested that a way to restore the situation was to create a '*really naughty sprite*' (called SUE), one that did 'everything wrong': that is, switched RIGHT and LEFT, as well as FORWARD and BACK. How did Nico know what SUE should do? It is certain from the speed at which he suggested it, that he did not analyse what was missing from the diagram in a step-by-step form and 'translate' it into symbolic form. On the other hand, it seems that he translated his perceived geometric asymmetry into a symbolic asymmetry—something is missing in the picture; is there something missing in the code, at least in the union of the codes of the three sprite codes? He was looking at the 'shape' of the symbolic representation, certainly not analysing the effect of each command and predicting its geometrical outcome, yet with some appreciation of the consequences of the changes made on the graphical image. SUE was easily constructed and the (visual) symmetries much admired.

At this point, we decided to intervene. We provided them with a challenge to create the following figure (see Fig. 12.3) using the smallest possible number of commands and using (in turn) one, two, three or four of their sprites.

---

[4] The research of which this episode forms a part was undertaken in collaboration with Celia Hoyles.

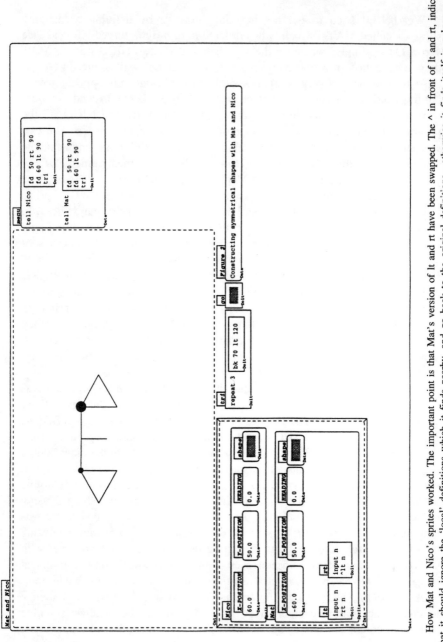

FIG. 12.1. How Mat and Nico's sprites worked. The important point is that Mat's version of lt and rt have been swapped. The ^ in front of lt and rt, indicate to Boxer that it should ignore the 'local' definitions which it finds nearby, and go back to the original definitions—otherwise it finds itself in a loop.

296

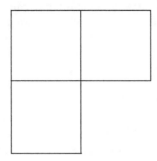

FIG. 12.2.   The graphical output with MAT, NICO and DENISE—'something missing'.

Two points stand out. First, the way the task was 'seen' by Mathew and Nico and the actions required for its solution were clearly mediated by the tools available for its solution. That is, the children's view of what the task involved, as well as its resolution, was structured by the availability of the range of sprites which they had at their disposal (and which they had—for the most part— constructed). So, for example, when there was a single sprite, the task was perceived as 'rotating an object': when there were four, it was seen as locating the piece that needs to be reflected in two perpendicular mirrors. Second, the activity lent itself to the children making generalisations about what could or could not be constructed by different combinations of their sprites. These were articulated with varying degrees of (verbal) fluency, but amounted to statements such as:

> A figure has at least one line of symmetry if and only if it can be drawn by MAT and NICO doing the same things.

and

> A figure has at least two lines of symmetry if and only if it can be drawn by MAT, NICO, DENISE, and SUE doing the same things.

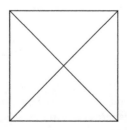

FIG 12.3.   The 'smallest number of commands' task.

Let me sum up. In suitably designed computational settings, there is an interplay between symbols and their effect, between the formalism and the output derived from it. There is, in fact, an extension of meaning: meanings are no longer to be found primarily among the symbols themselves, but in the result of 'running' (testing, executing) them. In the example above, there is a splendid interplay between the children's (intuitive/informal) appreciation of symmetry at a visual level, and their growing awareness of the symmetrical forms of the symbolic representation. The very use of the metaphor 'symmetry' to apply textual/symbolic representations, draws attention to the power of the idea within the discourse of mathematics: and we might note in passing that this 'feeling for symmetry' among symbols is a powerful mathematical tool which is traditionally ignored in mathematics curricula.

I do not want to overestimate the ease with which this passage between textual and visual takes place. Rather than elaborate on this theme here (see Noss & Hoyles, 1992, for a discussion of the difficulties involved) I prefer to focus my attention on facets of computationally-expressed mathematics which are not based on textual/symbolic interaction, but which nevertheless provide considerable information about the ways in which mathematical *generalisations* are constructed.

GENERALISATION

Cabri Géomètre is a program that provides an elaborate computational toolkit for exploring Euclidean Geometry (a useful description can be found in Laborde & Laborde, 1995). It is difficult to convey in text what the program makes possible; in essence, Cabri allows the creation of Euclidean objects (points, lines, line-segments etc.), Euclidean constructions (parallel lines, perpendicular bisectors etc.) together with a range of useful and powerful facilities (the textual definitions of figures etc.). There is one fundamental way in which the computer adds to Euclid, and it turns out to be critical: any *created* point can be moved via the mouse, and as it moves, *all constructions depending on the position of that point move accordingly*. The qualification that the point is created is important: points that rely for their existence on other constructions cannot be similarly moved at will—doing so would destroy the relationships within the constructions.

Consider a simple example. Create a triangle ABC, and construct the perpendicular bisectors of AB (L1) and AC (L2). Now construct a point P which is the intersection of L1 and L2. Figure 12.4 shows the result, together with a textual description of the construction (provided by Cabri). Figure 12.5 shows the result of moving A (note that P, for example, could *not* be moved in this arbitrary way as it depends for its existence on A, B, and C). Question: What is the Locus of P as A is moved arbitrarily around the plane (screen)?

I have asked a number of people this question: for the most part, I receive (initially at least) some puzzlement (especially from mathematicians) who object that "locus questions" usually (always?) demand that the point being

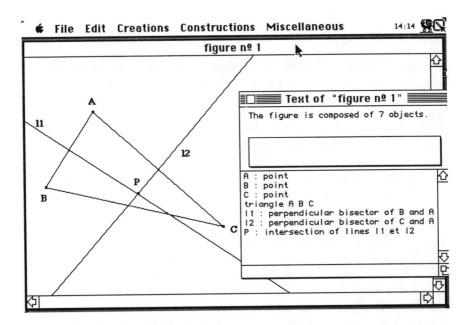

FIG. 12.4. A triangle ABC with perpendicular bisectors of AB and AC meeting at P. The textual description of the triangle is shown.

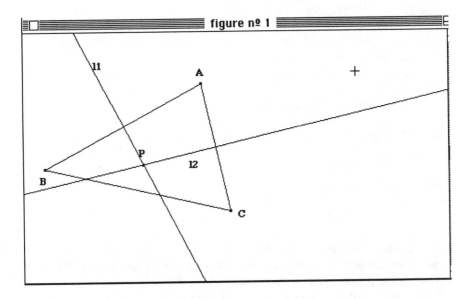

FIG. 12.5. Triangle ABC with A moved to the right.

moved is constrained in some predictable way (along a line or a circle for example). The idea of 'waving' a point around in space simply does not normally occur in school-mathematical problems and certainly not in the theorems of Euclid.

Cabri enables a locus to be drawn automatically (by specifying the point that is varying and the point whose locus is in question). Asking Cabri to do so reveals that the locus is the perpendicular bisector of the remaining side, BC. Of course it is: there is a familiar theorem that the three perpendicular bisectors meet in a point (points like P). And so, given that 'waving' A around does *not* alter the position of B or C, the locus of P will simply be all the possible positions of the intersection of the perpendicular bisectors, and they *must* be on the perpendicular bisector of BC!

What can be gleaned from this example? First, it should be clear that, just as in the paper-and-pencil situation, the activity takes place within the context of a particular example: points are not created 'in general', they are located at a particular position in the plane. Unlike the pencil-and-paper situation however, any created element (point, line-segment etc.), can be moved; as soon as the facility to move such elements with the mouse is recognised, it is hard for the learner *not* to think of them as anything other than *representatives* of a very large set of possibilities. Thus a central characteristic of what it means to think mathematically—the idea of mathematical generality—is altered by virtue of the medium in which the mathematics is expressed. The need to think about a single instance as a representative of a general class is extremely difficult (see Mason & Pimm, 1984, for a discussion of the relationship between the particular and the general). The Cabri example above illustrates a way in which the computer invites the learner to bear in mind the general, while working on the particular.

Second, and much more importantly, it provides insight into *why* the assertion is true: moving A with the mouse evidently does *not* move B and C—the key insight into the theorem. This is hard to establish on paper: it may be that the action of moving the mouse and seeing the screen feedback is crucial in generating insight of this kind. (It may also be that insights derived in this way are not apparent to all: it could be that there is some interaction with styles of computer-use, preference for visual or symbolic reasoning, or other psychological variables which are outside the scope of this paper.)

Third, the fact that the locus *looks* certain to be the perpendicular bisector of BC however the triangle is constructed, is not the same as *proving* it (and, incidentally, the 'waving' theorem is not obviously equivalent to the traditionally stated fact of the collinearity of the three perpendicular bisectors). In fact, it is worth asking what *would* constitute a computer-proof? Cabri will, if asked, check the validity of a given conjecture (say, are these three points collinear?), and will, in the appropriate situation, answer 'Your conjecture is true for this example, but false in general'. How does Cabri know? Does it check for every point on the plane (inconceivable), or have a theorem-prover built in to the system (unlikely, given that it runs on a modest desktop computer)? Or does it check for a small set of points? If so, how many would be needed? What reply would be satisfactory? The fact that this latter is not immediately evident, illustrates nicely the extent to which the computer throws into relief hitherto taken-for-granted questions of truth and falsity, and casts into doubt the very nature of mathematical certainty itself.

Why isn't this theorem obvious from the outset? Clearly it has to do with the 'unusual' way in which the problem was posed, a way that was entirely dependent on the means available for manipulation of the concepts and moreover, a way in which the statement of the question spilled over the traditionally strong boundaries between mathematical and everyday language. The example illustrates just how much mathematics itself relies on the specificities of the signs used to express it, and the technologies with which it is expressed. As Vygotsky has shown, sign forms mediate people's interactions with their environment—and the ability to read and express themselves within a sign-system depends on the extent to which people are enculturated into their use.

Finally, it is clear that in a pencil-and-paper setting, the idea of 'proving' a geometrical relationship by recourse to a single geometric example is at best misleading and at worst, downright wrong. Teachers routinely attempt to overcome this obstacle by asking a class of pupils to each choose an example and compare their answers: but it is a commonplace that children are reluctant to view their example as representative of a more general class of geometrical objects (a similar difficulty in an algebraic/computational setting is discussed by Noss, 1986). On the other hand, the Cabri setting makes such a strategy possible: indeed it is the 'preferred' strategy within the medium. Generating a set of cases from a single example is what Cabri does best. There is, of course, a price for this: dragging the corner of a figure hardly constitutes a rigorous proof. However, it is not unlikely that such experiences could be exploited (by a suitable pedagogy) as a bridge to an appropriate mathematical strategy, rather than constituting the barrier that the pencil-and-paper version seems to constitute. Most importantly from a pedagogical point of view, *seeing* that a property applies in general (almost) at least raises the potential question of *why* it does so, and perhaps, the *sense* of asking what properties apply in general.

It might be useful to give an example which occurred recently, during a 90-minute session with two 13-year-old girls, Carla and Kay[5]. Their task was to construct a reflection of a figure (actually a J) in a line; and then to reflect that reflection in a second line (see Fig. 12.6).

---

[5]The episode reported is part of a research project funded by ESRC, and supported by the National Council for Educational Technology.

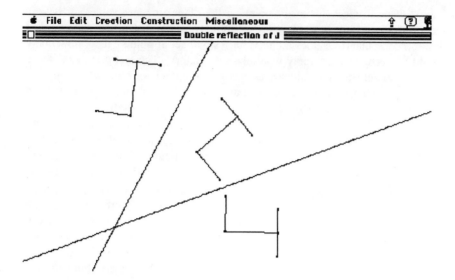

FIG. 12.6. The J reflection task.

Carla and Kay managed this without difficulty (Cabri has a menu item called 'symmetrical point' which drastically simplifies the construction). By dragging points of the initial J (top left) around, the pair could see that the final J (bottom right—the double-reflection) moved accordingly; when I asked them to describe the motion, Carla said 'It's about 70 degrees'. That is, she had no difficulty in recognising that the transformation had become a rotation, but had no way to describe the size of that rotation other than by articulating her guess for the special case that happened to confront her on the screen at the time I made my enquiry. I might also note that despite being extremely cooperative and motivated children, neither were in the least bit surprised or interested by the fact that two reflections somehow made a rotation—despite my desperate attempts to share my mathematical enthusiasm with them[6].

The question was whether they could say how the angle varied—and despite some pretty severe questioning on my part, they could not. So I prompted them to explore the sizes of angles using Cabri, as it is a simple matter to ask for the sizes of specified angles (these change as figures are 'dragged'). They marked and measured the angle between the initial and final Js, which they constructed as being at the point where the two 'vertical' lines of the J's met and noticed that this changed not only when the initial J's position was moved, but when the angle between the mirrors was altered as well.

---

[6]Such, I believe, is the result of a mathematics curriculum that is long on asking 'what happens?' and short on asking 'why?'.

After some prompting they decided to measure the angle between the mirrors, and then, in reply to my questioning, Kay said: 'It changes at twice the speed of this one'. There are two points of interest. First, it is revealing that she focused her attention on the 'speed' with which the values changed: presumably she meant that for a given change in one element (say, the mirror) the change in the other was double the amount. By employing the idea of 'speed', she is clearly thinking about the relationship dynamically—and expressing it in a way that, while nicely summing it up in terms of the specificities of the Cabri environment, is strictly limited to it.

Second, it is worth pointing to the incomprehensibility of Kay's utterance without reference to where she was pointing as she said it. This is a result of the fact that Cabri deliberately side-steps the difficulties of textual/symbolic manipulation (like Logo or Boxer) in favour of 'direct manipulation' of the figures via the mouse. Interaction is through pointing and clicking, not by entering lines of text and pressing <return>—as we have seen, this is a powerful way to 'express' mathematical actions. But there is a price to pay: any language underlying actions is auxiliary to those actions. In Logo or Boxer, the (typed) language is part of the interaction; in Cabri, it may occur in terms of vocal interactions with a teacher or researcher, but it need not. Carla did finally state—with fairly heavy-handed intervention on my part, 'The angle between them [the Js] is twice the angle between the mirrors', thus re-expressing the relationship between the angles independently of the medium. The key point is that Cabri does not offer a convenient linguistic or notational framework in which to express relationships—meanings may be established but they absolutely require human intervention to express them in any forms that we recognise as mathematical[7].

As a final example of the ways in which mathematical meanings are established within computational environments, I now turn to the issue of *abstraction*, which will turn out to be fundamental for the remainder of this chapter.

ABSTRACTION

Mathematics is the systematisation of relationships: it is, in Ada Lovelace's[8] words, 'the language of unseen relations between things'. Whereas, say, physics and chemistry derive their meanings in relation to the material world, mathematics is concerned with relationships *between* objects which might be in the real world, but which might just as easily consist of relationships. Mathematics involves abstractions.

---

[7] I hope it is clear that this is not a criticism of Cabri; on the contrary, I do not regard human intervention in computational settings as a regrettable limitation of the technology—far from it.

[8] Lovelace was a colleague of Charles Babbage, and, incidentally, the daughter of Lord Byron.

It is this layering of meaning that involves mathematicians in a discourse which has quite distinctive rules, and certainly ones that differ substantially from those which operate elsewhere. If meaning is not derived from direct recourse to the real world, it has to be derived from mathematics itself: thus the rules that operate within mathematics have not only to be different from everyday rules, but they must be explicit[9].

Of course, what exactly counts as 'the real world' is problematic, although not an issue that I intend to pursue in this context. We might think of the J shapes being reflected in the previous example as 'real' (although they were, of course, merely pixels on a computer screen); certainly the notion of 'reflection' as an entity necessitates seeing that what happens to one J happens to all possible instances, and that the situation is consistent across all of them: in that sense, reality is at (at least) one remove.

The issue of consistency is closely related to mathematicians' quest for generalisation; as such it is quite special to mathematics. Consider, for example, the situation of mixing liquids, beloved of school mathematics textbooks. In real situations, liquids are mixed (in recipes, for example) by *adding* appropriate quantities. Of course, provided that the right amount is added, the situation is (mathematically) the same as if ratios and proportions had been considered at the outset. But the mathematical situation differs markedly in all but the simplest cases (doubling, trebling etc.). In mathematics, the rules regarding ratio and proportionality have to apply consistently (generally) across all domains, in situations where the quantities are discrete or continuous, positive or negative, real or imaginary.

It is on the issue of ratio and proportionality that I focus in the next example, based on a study (Hoyles, Noss, & Sutherland, 1991) involving 13-year-old children. This study involved the design, teaching, and evaluation of a ratio and proportion *microworld*[10] consisting of on/off computer tasks based on Logo, small-group and class activities; the study aimed to probe children's understandings of ratio in the context of pencil-and-paper as well as their activities on-computer. The methodology we employed was broadly along the lines of a teaching experiment, in the sense of Steffe (1991, p.178): 'The basic and unrelenting goal of a teaching experiment is for the researcher to learn the mathematical knowledge of the involved children and how they construct it'.

The microworld was evaluated summatively on the basis of written pre-post- and delayed post-tests, which aimed at probing the pupils' intuitions and understandings about ratio and proportion with paper and pencil. The items

---

[9]Paul Goldenberg has pointed out (personal communication) that the nearest that everyday discourse comes to that of mathematics is in the playing (and construction) of games.

[10]A *microworld* consists of a computational environment designed for the student to encounter particular mathematical ideas, and appropriate settings and situations in which to explore them.

Jo and Pat are painting the garden shed. They want it to be grey. The shop only has small tins of white paint and small tins of black paint. Jo mixes ten tins of white paint with fifteen tins of black paint. Pat has two tins of white paint. Here is a table showing these amounts:

	Amount of white paint	Amount of black paint
Jo	10	15
Pat	2	?

How many litres of black paint must Pat use to get the same shade of grey?

Pat needs .... tins.

FIG. 12.7. A point question.

did not explicitly involve ratio and proportion but were set as word problems involving two separate contexts, both of which necessitated multiplicative operations for their correct solution. One context was concerned with mixing paint (*paint context*) (Fig. 12.7); the other involved enlarging photographs of rugs (*rug context*) (Fig. 12.8).

The literature has quite a bit to say about the different strategies children employ in problems such as these (see, for example, Tourniaire & Pulos, 1985; Hart 1981; Johnson 1989). There is general agreement that children are reluctant to use generalisable strategies such as those involving the 'rule of three', and even to view such problems as multiplicative rather than additive. In our study, we interviewed a subset of the children in depth before and after their activities with our microworld. Not surprisingly, we found that a number of the children consistently used an (incorrect) additive strategy, which, for example, generated a negative number for the amount of paint (one question asked for the missing quantity of paint in the situation Jo 8:3, Pat 4:?. An additive strategy would result in Pat's quantity being −1). In cases where we pointed out the impossibility of such an answer, children readily agreed to

You collect photographs of rugs. You have just received a new set of photographs to add to your collection. You need to enlarge or shrink them to fit into the spaces in your catalogue. One of the 'new' lengths is unknown. Find the missing length marked "?" on the diagram.

FIG. 12.8. A rug question.

adopt some different strategy even if it was at odds with their original one. Some children adopted different strategies for each distinct question (or category of question). We became fascinated by this, and tried to probe their recognition of the underlying mathematical structure of the questions, their sense that this was invariant across the questions, and their appreciation of the need (actually *our* need) for an overall consistent strategy. We asked questions such as 'If your life depended on it, which question are you certain is right and why?'.

The findings of the study could be grouped in three broad categories. First, it was clear that children who adopted a range of strategies were entirely unconcerned with our need for consistency—they assumed the validity of their everyday strategy of using a range of different strategies for situations that (unknown to them) embody the same underlying structures. Second, they were, for the most part, happy to indulge our whim, and pick (sometimes at random) one strategy out of many as representing their 'best bet' if their lives depended on it. On the other hand, there was some evidence that the experience of working within our microworld encouraged some pupils to reject 'pattern-spotting' (positing *any* pattern—between, say, numbers or figures—as equally valid irrespective of any mathematical structure underlying the pattern), in favour of a greater sensitivity to this structure. There was some shift away from addition (the usual pattern chosen), towards *consistent* attempts (not always successful or explicit) to apply multiplicative operations. It is worth noting that, during the experiment, there was no attempt to 'teach for transfer' of proportional ideas from computational to non-computational work.

What light does this throw on the question of abstraction? Primarily, the example illustrates an important, and perhaps general, outcome of this kind of computer work. Stated baldly, it is that the construction and reconstruction of programs encouraged children to represent strategies explicitly so that they could be discussed and justified away from the computer. In so doing, in *explicitly* articulating relationships, there is, perhaps, some pressure to move beyond the here-and-now of pragmatic solution strategies, towards the peculiarly mathematical practice of generalisation and consistency. The hypothesis is that the computer activity provided a language with which to think about and discuss relationships in the abstract, rather than objects (such as rugs and photographs) in the concrete.

It is almost impossible to point to specific facets of the computer activities that may have generated this change, although considerable details are provided in Hoyles, Noss, and Sutherland (1991). But one anecdote might serve to explain a little more fully. At the outset of the experiment, we attempted to prevent children from using doubling as a strategy to enlarge their screen objects. Our rationale was clear: we expected from the literature that children would 'naturally' double, but that doubling was not seen by them as a multiplicative strategy—instead it is a special case which is at best seen as adding ('add another one'); more usually it is not viewed explicitly at all. So our wish to discourage children from adopting doubling stemmed from an assumption that doing so would do nothing to encourage them to abstract from their strategy, to see the generality of what they were doing, and therefore minimise the likelihood that they might see pencil-and-paper situations as proportional.

In fact, our pilot work convinced us that we were mistaken, and we subsequently came to view computationally expressed doubling as a transitional and intuitive strategy on which to base a generalised multiplicative one. For some children, the fact of adopting a doubling strategy *explicitly*—by, for example, having to write a program fragment such as

$$2 * :SIDE$$

acted *not* as a deterrent to a generalisation, but as a bridge towards it. Substituting different values for 2, including non-integer ones, turned out to be much less of a conceptual leap than it is in pencil-and-paper settings. And although we cannot be sure, we are fairly confident that this kind of activity was partly responsible for the children's tendency to view pencil-and-paper problems we posed more consistently, more abstractly, more *mathematically*.

Before we leave this example, it is worth discussing in a little more detail some aspects of the findings which throw some light on the specificities of the computer's 'effect'. To do so, a little background is necessary. Existing research makes it clear that there are a number of issues of problem design which influence children's performance on ratio and proportion problems. Among these is whether the scale factor is perceived as an integer or as a rational number. For example, Bell, Greer, Grimison, and Mangan, (1989) found that in questions concerned with isomorphism of measures, the two quantities to be multiplied played distinct roles and that there were 'sharp increases in difficulty when the multiplier changes from an integer to a decimal number . . .' (*ibid* p.447).

We subjected data gleaned from the children's responses (and responses of children not in the microworld group) to a variety of qualitative and statistical analyses which are reported in full in Hoyles, Noss, and Sutherland (1991). I wish to concentrate on one aspect of the analysis: namely the individual pupil response profiles of the children in the microworld group[11]. A classification was carried out which looked at the response combination of individual pupils *item* by *item*. McNamara's related groups chi-squared test was applied. This indicated that responses to 14 out of 18 items showed a significant change

---

[11]The remainder of this paragraph and the table below are taken from the Final Report (Hoyles et al. 1991).

($P < 0.05$) in favour of a programme effect. The previous analysis, at a group level, had indicated the influence of context and scale factor on pupil responses. We therefore turned to an analysis of individual pupil profiles of responses with respect to these same variables; that is, within the four subcategories paint integer, paint fraction, rugs integer, and rugs fraction. This analysis revealed significant differences in profiles of response as follows:

- It was found that for *paint integer* questions, pupils with all the answers *incorrect* at pre-test produced most response changes at post-test. The majority of these changes represented a move from addition to a correct strategy.
- For *paint fraction* questions, the likelihood of a change from an incorrect to a correct strategy was approximately the same as the likelihood of change between incorrect strategies, whilst the probability of an incorrect response still predominated even at the post-test stage.
- For *rugs integer* questions, the changed pupil responses were no longer so confined to pupils who had all incorrect responses at pre-test. Pupils originally used a variety of strategies, and adding was not the dominant approach. Following the microworld experience there was a strong likelihood of change in the direction from an incorrect to a correct strategy.
- For *rugs fraction* questions there was a relatively high likelihood of change but in the main this was between incorrect strategies rather than from a correct to an incorrect strategy.

A summary of this analysis is given in Table 12.1. It is extremely difficult to sum up these findings succinctly. Nevertheless, irrespective of overall effects of the microworld activity (which were present) the results indicate that there were effects that were differentially distributed across the specificities of both

TABLE 12.1
Pupil Strategy Changes Between Pre and Post-tests

	Integer	Fraction
Paint	Majority of changes from addition to a correct strategy	Likelihood of change from incorrect (both add and other) to correct strategy approximately equal to change between incorrect strategies (from add to other and vice versa)
Rugs	Likelihood of change from incorrect to correct strategy (incorrect strategies not dominant in pre-test)	Significant move away from addition, change equally likely from addition to correct as addition to other.

problem context (rugs/paint) and preferred scale factor (integer/fraction). Why, for example, did paint/integer show the most marked improvement? Why did rugs/fraction show a significant movement away from addition, but not necessarily towards the correct strategy?

Our answers to such questions must remain provisional, pending further investigation of these and similar effects. However, it is not unreasonable to conjecture some linkage between the microworld experiences and the changes in performance. The microworlds did *not* involve explicit teaching of proportional rules: they *did* involve class-discussion, groupwork, and a range of activities which were both on-computer and off-computer whose objective was to generate in the pupils a need for a theoretical (mathematical/formal) strategy rather than an everyday/informal one. And, of course, we placed the pupils in a variety of computational situations in which they had no choice other than to formalise their thinking in some way—with fairly conclusive feedback. So it seems that the crucial effect was one of encouraging the pupils to think about relations rather than objects, to focus their attention on the ratio-as-a-thing (even if the expression of that ratio was not properly formed) rather than on the respective sizes of the lengths or amounts.

Such a hypothesis would go some way towards explaining the results. It is plausible that the paint/integer scenario was, in some ways, a highly intuitive situation, but the intuitions point in the 'wrong' way. When paint is mixed, it is *added*: and there is no visual cue to provide any kind of feedback—in a sense one answer is as good as any other. On the other hand, if the child has begun to build a conceptual framework in which the focus is not so much on amounts, but on the abstraction 'relations-between-amounts', it is possible that this might form the basis of future representations of similar problems. Of course, this does not mean that such representations will be 'correct' (from a mathematical point of view), as the rugs/fraction data indicates: here there *is* a visual cue and there is similarly a range of everyday strategies that will give roughly the right answer.

TOWARDS A THEORETICAL FRAMEWORK

The foregoing examples convey a sense of computational expression sitting somewhere between everyday, informal mathematics (which some might not want to call mathematics at all), and formal, rigorous mathematical expression. The question remains: what is the relationship between the two? What kinds of abstractions can be built with computers, and how do they resemble and differ from mathematical abstractions expressed with mathematical formalisation?

In Noss and Hoyles (1992) we coined the term *situated abstraction* to summarise the ways in which people make and express mathematical sense with mediating tools (such as computational environments) other than the ascetic language of mathematics itself. Situated abstractions are prototypes for mathematical abstractions. A situated abstraction is powerful enough to entirely encapsulate a mathematical relationship, but unlike its expression in mathematical formalisation, it is bound into the setting, it is mediated by the technology[12] and its associated language. Thus, the idea that 'rectangles are parallelograms with inputs of 90' is an abstraction which nicely encapsulates the geometry in symbolic terms, but which is mediated by the situation in which it is produced (where 90 is the input to a procedure—not a general concept of angle). It is an abstraction in the sense that it is a generalisation of a mathematised relationship (quadrilaterals and parallelograms involve a mathematical model of four-sided structures), and it is important to notice that even the particular observation '*This* rectangle is a parallelogram' acts as a paradigm case for a much more general observation provided it is framed in terms of a programming language or something like it.

This example points to the crucial issue. All expression (mathematical and otherwise) is mediated by the available language. But in mathematics, one particular form of expression is privileged: namely that whose purpose is to construct long fragile chains of reasoning to establish truth. It is tempting therefore, to count as abstractions only those expressions that are 'free' of context, cut off from the concrete. By focusing on situations that retain elements of both 'concrete' and 'abstract', we draw attention to *domains of abstraction* in which there is a rationale, *a meaning*, for expression of a mathematical kind *other* than that of the mathematician.

Other workers have drawn attention to similar phenomena. For example, Papert (1992, p.xvi) argues that '. . . what Hoyles and Noss call a "situated abstraction" . . . I call an "object to think with". These phrases refer to the fact that something can be concrete in its form but general enough to be used as a reference marker in other situations'. Perhaps Papert is right, perhaps there is only a difference of terminology. In choosing the term situated abstraction, however, I want to concentrate on the central paradox which the idea of 'object' blurs: namely, how (if at all) does a *situated* abstraction become *desituated*? How, in Papert's terms, does the concrete become abstract?

A second related notion is Vergnaud's (1983) *theorem in action*, a term that nicely captures the idea that people behave in ways which indicate that they *implicitly* understand a more general relationship. The key difference between Vergnaud's construct and the idea of situated abstraction is precisely that the former remains implicit, unarticulated. In the Cabri example above, for instance, geometrical knowledge is constructed and reconstructed through practical interaction with the computer, but at the same time, the relationships

---

[12]The situation does not have to involve the computer: a recent example involved Joe—aged 8—who, immersed at school in the use of pegs and pegboards, stated that 'a prime number is one which you can only make with a line of pegs'.

between the points and lines have to be explicit, they are articulated (note that in this case, the articulation is not 'textual' but achieved through pointing and clicking within the constraints of the program's spatial metaphor). 'Theorems' of this kind may be implicit but they are not unarticulated (Hoyles, 1993, describes it as 'formalising the action by the articulation of situated abstractions'). It is the computational practice that mediates the expression of the 'theorem': they are abstractions which are mediated by the particular formal symbolism and situated within a particular computational context.

How does the notion of situated abstraction help to disentangle setting-specific knowledge, from more general, mathematical knowledge? This problem is an example of a general difficulty: that of finding a way out of the cognitive cul-de-sac presented by the 'situated learning' literature. This poses particular difficulties in the context of mathematics, where there is a sense in which mathematical expression is—by definition—unsituated. The general problem has recently been addressed by Edith Ackermann (1990), whose reanalysis of Piaget's water-level experiments attempts similarly to emphasise the coordination of local knowledge in building abstractions. She argues that '. . . children can be said to move from concrete to abstract—or from situated to decontextualised—only because the materials that their minds differentiate-and-coordinate are broader, and can be removed from here-and-now contingencies' (*ibid* p.403). Ackermann would argue that the induction of general laws flows from the regularities children discover in specific contexts, *and* that they apply general rules in order to make sense of local situations.

Ackermann's analysis is interesting because it offers a way out of the cul-de-sac. She describes Piaget's theory as primarily describing how children become progressively detached from the world of concrete objects and local contingencies, and counterposes this with the perspective of, for example, Papert, Turkle, and others, who focus on the opposite pole: of children's connectedness to their situation, and sensitivity to variations in their environment. Her attempt to synthesise these positions sees 'constructing invariants as the flipside of generating variation' (*ibid* p.383).

It is not obvious how this helps in the case of mathematics. After all, mathematics is about abstractions. It is expressed in a language designed to capture and manipulate relationships—necessarily a refined language with rules and meanings that differ significantly from those of everyday communication. What does it mean to become connected with mathematics? And how might that connection assist in constructing invariants which can be expressed in the language of mathematics?

Let us return to the third example above, the ratio and proportion tasks, and in particular, the way the concept of doubling as expressed in a program became a step towards a more general mathematical understanding. What was particular in these activities? There was a set of computational objects carefully designed to evoke particular mathematical ideas in the minds of the learners. These objects had a number of characteristics: they were designed to allow interesting interactions; they gave learners control over what mattered (to us) mathematically[13]; and they provided a language with which teachers and children could share discussion of mathematical properties and relationships. The objects of the computational environment were *tuned* to maximise the probability (no more than this) that interestingly mathematical properties would be noticed by the children.

Thus the crucial contribution of the computer was that it mediated the child's interactions with the mathematical ideas. By immersing learners in a microculture of this kind, we were (in a limited way) successful in simultaneously connecting children to particular objects (houses, stick-figures etc.), *and* offering them a language with which to express generality and to make abstractions—albeit abstractions that fall short of the scope offered by mathematical formalisation.

The notion of tuning is intended to focus on the idea that the specific forms of mathematical expression offered by an environment play a critical role in establishing the forms of discourse that are appropriate and which thereby indicate to the student the extent to which they are valid mathematically. The Cabri case illustrates the point nicely. Certain things are possible, others are not. The design choices of Cabri are not arbitrary: constructed points cannot be dragged (as they can, say, in *MacPaint*) because to allow users to do so would diminish the likelihood of their focusing attention on the Euclidean system. Similarly, the choice of constructions is limited (there is no angle-trisector, for example); were it more elaborate, the user would gain in the facility with which geometrical objects might be constructed, but lose in the extent to which he or she might be encouraged to reflect on their mathematical structure. In other words, Cabri is tuned to a particular pedagogical purpose.

The rationales that underlay the designers' decisions are firmly based in the mathematical structures they wanted to model, and it would be unrealistic to think that a user of the program would spontaneously build for themselves a model that corresponded in its entirety to these structures, considered as a unified system. On the other hand, we could think of the program as inducing the learner into a specific mathematical discourse or microculture (in this case that of Euclidean geometry), and at least form a basis on which global and generalised mathematical understandings could be built by carefully designed pedagogical input. Papert (1972) makes such a claim for the learning of algebra—a claim given some credence by Noss (1986) and Sutherland (1989); Leron and Zazkis (1992) make such a claim in the context of group theory.

---

[13]For example, we constructed procedures (JUMP and STEP) which obviated the necessity for children to use angle at all in their activities as we wanted them to focus their attention elsewhere.

The particularities of these microcultures are important, especially when we bear in mind that the idea of mathematics as a language is metaphorical rather than real (see Pimm, 1987). Michel Otte (1990) argues convincingly that theoretical thinking (of which mathematical thinking is an example), involves a 'variability of distance' between what is expressed and what is being expressed about—between signifier and signified. I claim that it is this variability which endows mathematical formalisation with its power to express generality, and to bring into relation objects that themselves may be relationships and/or abstractions. Our microcultures, populated more or less densely with computational objects to manipulate and reconstruct, *constrain* this variability.

Viewed in this way, it is possible to reconceptualise the kind of computational worlds outlined in the above examples. The essence of such environments is that this variability between knowledge and expression can be tuned appropriately; and that, as the examples above show, they can be controlled by the learner, used to generate abstractions which consist of more than the parts that are presented. But there is a further, more critical element: namely that these microcultures offer a link into the wider mathematical culture of which they form a part.

This last point is related to Vygotsky's perspective on the relationship between the 'two kinds of knowledge' with which I began this paper. For Vygotsky, one distinction between 'spontaneous' and 'scientific' concepts is that the former are constructed from the bottom-up, while the latter are developed from the top-down. Scientific knowledge flows downwards to coordinate the fragmented and unsystematised knowledge that is a result of spontaneous learning, to systematise the situated understandings developed in practice. As Saxe (1990, p.12) puts it: 'For Vygotsky, it is in the interaction between the top-down movement of scientific concepts and the bottom-up movement of spontaneous concepts that we find intrinsic links between the individual and social history.'

It is perfectly possible to create situations in which 'scientific' or mathematical learning takes place—how else does anybody learn mathematics? But the challenge of designing computational environments is to devise situations, or microcultures, that link to the broader mathematical culture of which they form a part, to afford the reformulation and reconstruction of situated abstractions into mathematical abstractions. The power of the 'doubling' example above is not only that it was based on children's existing, 'spontaneous' concepts, but that it existed within a discourse, a microculture which made it a natural part of broader mathematical culture, where doubling is merely a special case of a more general multiplicative law (or invariant).

A final point. Emergence from situatedness is a far-from trivial process, nothing short of, in Saxe's words (1990, p.12), 'a melding of the individual with the sociohistorical'. It would be asking too much to expect this kind of process to be effected purely by the child–computer interaction, without direct pedagogical intervention, or social interaction between peers. Papert is fond of stating 'Do not ask what Logo does to children; ask what children can do with Logo'. To which it might be appropriate to add: 'Do not ask (only) what children can do with Logo; ask what teachers can do with Logo-enculturated children'.

NOTE

These ideas are discussed in full in Noss and Hoyles (1996).

13 Mediating Between Concrete and Abstract

Koeno Gravemeijer
Freudenthal Institute, The Netherlands

INTRODUCTION

One of the problematic issues in mathematics education is the question of how to teach students abstract mathematical knowledge. In the mainstream information processing approach, one usually presents concrete models to help students acquire this abstract knowledge. However, 'concrete' in the sense of tangible does not necessary mean 'concrete' in the sense of making sense. This observation is in line with research findings (which will be presented later) that the use of manipulatives[1] does not really help students to attain mathematical insight. Moreover, even if a certain mastery is attained, application appears to be problematic. The manipulatives-approach fails probably, because—although the models as such may be concrete—the mathematics *embedded in the models* is not concrete for the students. Or to put it another way, the manipulatives-approach passes over the situated, informal knowledge of the students. Alternative approaches depart from the idea that situated, informal knowledge and strategies should be the starting point for developing abstract mathematical knowledge.

In this chapter we will present such an approach based on what is called '*a domain-specific theory for realistic mathematics education*'. This is an approach for mediating between concrete and abstract based on self-

---

[1]In mathematics education, the term manipulatives is used as a collective noun for tactile material and graphical representations, that function as models.

developed models. We may characterise this approach as 'bottom-up' since the initiative is with the students. As such, it is in contrast with the top-down character of the manipulatives-approach, where models (e.g. manipulatives) are derived from abstract mathematical knowledge. Both approaches will be described and explained from a learning sequence on long division. It will be argued that the realistic approach deals with the problems with 'insight' and 'application', encountered in a top-down approach. The bottom-up character of the realistic approach is expected to guarantee insightful mathematical knowledge and the realistic concept of generalising is presented as a bottom-up alternative for the top-down concept of transfer.

LONG DIVISION WITH MANIPULATIVES

In the mainstream information processing approach, formal crystallised expert mathematical knowledge is taken as a starting point for developing instructional activities. In general, representational models and manipulatives are designed to create a concrete framework of reference in which the intended mathematical concepts are embodied. That is to say, that abstract mathematical knowledge and procedures are introduced, exemplified and learned with manipulatives. This approach is based on the idea that everyday life reality is not pure enough for the learning of mathematics. Everyday situations are thought to be too complex; there is too much distraction from the mathematics embedded therein (see for instance Gagné, 1965). Therefore an artificial environment is created where no frills distract from the mathematical content.

For instance, base ten blocks, often referred to as 'Dienes blocks'[2], constitute such an environment. The blocks exemplify the base ten position system and the students will learn how to deal with this system by working with the blocks in a prescribed manner. The characteristics of the positional system are incorporated with rules such as:

- Exchange groups of ten blocks for a higher-order blocks if there are more than ten of a kind.
- Notate the number of blocks in a strict order, corresponding with an increase in value.

In general, however, the main concern is not with the position system as such, but with the written algorithms. Therefore other rules are added. With addition and subtraction for instance, the students must start with the smallest

---

[2]However, base ten blocks are just one category of the MAB block Dienes invented. In his view one should vary over various number systems (e.g. base three, base six and base eight, next to base ten) to account for mathematical variability.

blocks: first the ones, next move to the tens etc. This is demanded because working from right to left, which implies starting with the smaller units, is the standard procedure for column algorithms. A more natural approach might be to start with the larger units.

In this approach long division is built on the idea of division as fair sharing. One starts with small numbers. A problem like 81÷6, will be thought of as dividing 81 blocks over 6 persons. First 6 of the 8 ten-rods are distributed, then the remaining tens are exchanged for ones, and the resulting 21 ones are divided, each gets 3 and the remainder is 3. Given the size of the numbers, this could be one of the problems presented at the beginning of a manipulatives-based learning sequence. Usually problems with a remainder are avoided in the beginning, however.

Next, to make the shift from dealing with blocks to the paper and pencil algorithm, a procedure like the one outlined above is soon replaced by procedures executed with imaginary blocks, using a standard form that resembles the written algorithm. This shift is also necessary when larger numbers are introduced. Moving to larger numbers, larger dividends come first and larger divisors follow later. When dealing with larger numbers working with real blocks actually becomes undoable. Take for instance 1476÷ 24. Here the students would have to exchange a one thousand block and four squares of one hundred to get 147 rods that will have to be divided over 24 people (Fig. 13.1).

Thinking along the lines of fair sharing, this procedure makes sense. In applications however, long division does not necessarily have to involve fair sharing. Suppose, for instance, that the problem 1476÷24 was about 1476 bottles which are to be packed in crates that can contain 24 bottles. Here it does not make much sense to consider fair sharing or distribution. Moreover the procedure becomes rather confusing.

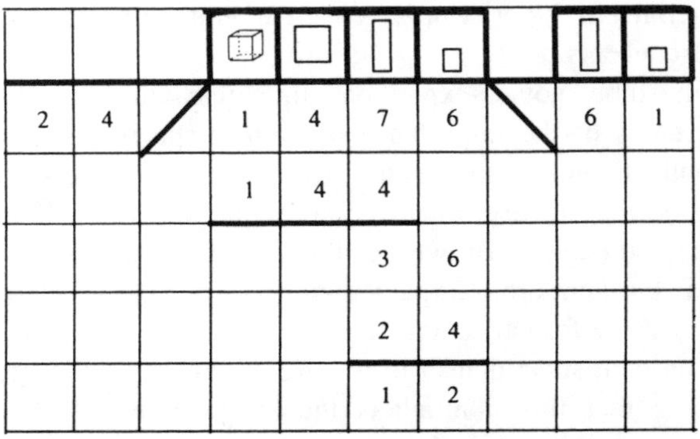

2	4		1	4	7	6	6	1
			1	4	4			
				3	6			
				2	4			
				1	2			

FIG. 13.1.   1476 divided by 24.

1. Executing the procedure sketched above might make one wonder. Why should 1476 be represented with blocks and 24 not? For addition both numbers are represented with blocks, for division apparently only the dividend is represented with blocks.
2. Compared with the other operations there is also a change of strategy; where previously one always worked from small to large, one now starts with distributing the largest blocks.
3. If the blocks are thought of as a representation of the applied situation, other inconsistencies arise. In the bottle-packing problem, the bottles are first represented by blocks: 1476 bottles represented by 1476 ones, organised in one cube of thousand, four squares of a hundred, seven rods of ten, and six ones. After the execution of the division procedure, the answer is represented with six rods and one unit block, now representing 61 crates! So at first the blocks represent *bottles* and in the end they represent *crates*. That is to say if we refrain from the remainder (twelve); these blocks still represent bottles.

Research Findings

One can now say that research has shown that this approach does not work. First, because the students do not gain much insight (Labinowitcz, 1985; Resnick & Omanson, 1987). Second, because even if students learn to master the concepts and procedures that are taught they lack the capability to use them in applications (Schoenfeld, 1987).

Careful analyses from a constructivist point-of-view have resulted in a convincing explanation of what goes on in regular classrooms and what goes wrong with 'conveying knowledge' with the help of manipulatives (Cobb, 1987). In short, the mathematical concepts embodied in the didactical representations are only there for the experts who already have those concepts available to see. For the students there is nothing more to see than the concrete material. In other words, concrete embodiments do not convey mathematical concepts.

At the same time, novice-expert paradigm inspired research generated a growing awareness of the importance of domain-specific, situated, informal knowledge and strategies. Research illustrates that in everyday situations, people are quite able to use whatever holds the situation offers to develop rather efficient strategies (Brown, Collins, & Duguid, 1989; Lesh, 1985; Nunes, 1992). Furthermore, Carpenter and Moser (1983, 1984) found that young childrens' performance on word problems is far superior to their performance on bare sums thanks to the use of informal strategies. (We may note in passing that this contradicts the suppositions of the information processing approach, where applications are postponed.)

In conclusion we may say that shortcomings of a manipulatives-based learning sequence are exposed as 'lack of insight' and 'problems with applications', and we may also conclude that these problems stem from passing over the importance of informal knowledge and strategies.

New Approaches

Educationalists attach different consequences to the recognition of the importance of informal strategies and situated cognition.[3] The CGI-project, for instance, opts for innovating mathematics education by informing teachers about informal strategies (Carpenter et al., 1989). CGI stands for *'Cognitively Guided Instruction'*: the idea is to present research findings on informal strategies to teachers to help them construct a referential framework. With the help of this framework the teacher can then guide the spontaneous learning process of the students.

Brown, Collins, and Duguid (1989) propose a teaching model which they call *cognitive apprenticeship*. They base this model on the assertion of the indexical character of all knowledge; '. . . knowledge is situated, being in part of a product of the activity, the context, and culture in which it is developed and used.' (*ibid*, p.32) All words, they argue, are at least partially indexical. What is meant by indexical is illuminated with pure indexical words like 'this', 'here', and 'now' which can only be interpreted in the context of their use. Since all words are at least partially context-dependent, 'the meaning of a word cannot, in principle, be captured by a definition, even when the definition is supported by a couple of exemplary sentences.' (*ibid*, p.33) They conclude that new knowledge and skills have to be developed in applied situations. Since most applied situations are too complex for novices, they plead for cognitive apprenticeship on the analogy of apprenticeship in vocational training. Keywords in this concept are coaching, scaffolding, and fading.

They point to Schoenfeld (in press) and Lampert (1986) for a concrete elaboration of similar instructional concepts. Taking Lampert (1989) as an example, one sees that she actually thinks in terms of a top-down model. She describes an instructional experiment on decimals in which the system of decimal fractions and its notation system are taken as given and the instructional activities focus on *connecting* the informal, situated, knowledge of the students with this prefabricated system. A clear advantage of this approach is that negotiations about interpretations and meanings are made explicit and placed at the centre of the instructional process. From a constructivist point of view, a drawback however is that prefabricated knowledge is taken as an immediate goal for instruction. This is, for instance, expressed by the use of 'tools' as a metaphor.

---

[3]In the following we will use the terms 'situated' and 'situations' in a restricted sense, referring to the kind of situations where students develop informal strategies, e.g. situations that are personally meaningful for the students.

Socio-constructivists argue that all knowledge is self-constructed and that mathematics education should acknowledge idiosyncratic constructions and foster a classroom atmosphere where mathematical meaning, interpretations, and procedures are explicitly negotiated. A taken-as-shared basis for communication is thus established in the classroom community. According to Cobb, Yackel, and Wood (1992a) the teacher should at the same time stimulate a process of acculturation into the practices and interpretations of the wider community. In this socio-constructivist teaching approach, the self-invented problem solutions of the students are to be framed as topics for discussion, to function as the starting points for the acculturation process of the classroom community. However, socio-constructivism does not as such offer heuristics for developing a teaching approach that is compatible with a constructivist epistemology. Therefore a supporting instruction theory is needed.

For mathematics education a suitable domain-specific instruction theory can be found in the theory for *realistic mathematics education* (Treffers, 1987).[4] This theory will be the focal point of this article. In the following, we will introduce this theory briefly first, then we will present description of a realistic course for developing long division. This example will be used as a concrete base for a more elaborate description of the key principles of the "realistic" theory. Finally we will discuss whether this approach supports applicability.

REALISTIC MATHEMATICS EDUCATION

Realistic mathematics education is rooted in Freudenthal's interpretation of mathematics as an activity (Freudenthal, 1971, 1973). Freudenthal takes his starting point in the activity of mathematicians, whether pure or applied mathematicians. He typecasts their activity as an activity of solving problems, looking for problems and organising subject matter—whether mathematical matter or matter from reality. The main activity, according to Freudenthal, is organising or mathematising. Interestingly, Freudenthal sees this as a general activity which characterises both pure and applied mathematics. Therefore, when setting "mathematising" as a goal for mathematics education, this can involve mathematising mathematics and mathematising reality.

---

[4]Realistic mathematics education will not be compatible with constructivism in every shape or form. However socio-constructivists accept endpoints that fit with the realistic approach (Cobb et al. 1992a). Moreover, they accept a certain amount of guidance by the teacher. In our opinion, realistic mathematics education can be made compatible with socio-constructivism if notions like 'negotiation of meaning' are integrated in the realistic approach. This idea is being worked out by Paul Cobb (Vanderbilt University), Erna Yackel (Purdue University Calumet) and the author.

One could remark that Freudenthal's concept of mathematics as a human activity is mainly concerned with the individual, in what Ernest (1991) calls 'the private realm'. There are other scientists who stress the opposite, 'the social realm' (*ibid*), where mathematics comes to the fore as mathematical discourse (Balacheff, 1990; Schoenfeld, 1987). However, the social interaction is not neglected in realistic mathematics education. It comes to fore in the teaching and learning process, which we will discuss later.

Freudenthal uses the word 'mathematising' in a broader sense than just as an indicator of the process of recasting an everyday problem situation in mathematical terms. It is also employed within mathematics. In Freudenthal's view mathematising relates to 'level-raising'—in a mathematical sense. The idea of level-raising is at the heart of Freudenthal's (1971, p.417) concept for learning mathematics, since: 'the activity on one level is subjected to analysis on the next; the operational matter on one level becomes a subject matter on the next level'. To characterise level-raising, we can consider characteristics of mathematics, such as generality, certainty, exactness, and brevity. So to clarify what is to be understood by mathematising we can look at specific means to improve those characteristics:

- for generality: generalising (looking for analogies, classifying, structuring);
- for certainty: reflecting, justifying, proving (using a systematic approach, elaborating and testing conjectures, etc.);
- for exactness: modelling, symbolising, defining (limiting interpretations and validity);
- for brevity: symbolising and schematising (developing standard procedures and notations).

In realistic mathematics education, mathematising mainly involves generalising and formalising. Here formalising embraces modelling, symbolising, schematising, and defining, and generalising is to be understood in a reflective sense. It refers to *a posteriori* constructions of connections, not to a premeditated application of general knowledge. There is little explicit attention for proving, but reflecting and justifying will be indispensable of course. We may note in passing that, for the students, generalising and formalising will not be the issues, they will be guided mainly by considerations of efficiency.

Freudenthal espouses mathematising as the key process in mathematics education for two reasons. First, mathematising is not only the major activity of mathematicians. It also familiarises the students with a mathematical approach to everyday life situations. Here we can also refer to the mathematical activity of 'looking for problems' which implies a mathematical attitude, which encompasses knowing the possibilities and the limitations of a mathematical approach, knowing when a mathematical approach is appropriate and when it is not. The second reason for espousing mathematising is related to the idea of reinvention. In mathematics, the final stage is formalising by way of axiomatising. And, says Freudenthal, that is fine for mathematicians, but this end point should not be the starting point for the mathematics we teach. Starting with axioms, he argues, is an anti-didactical inversion; the process by which the mathematicians came to their conclusions is turned upside down in education. He advocates mathematics education organised as a process of guided reinvention, where students can experience a (to some extent) similar process to the process by which mathematics was invented. In the following we will illustrate this approach for realistic mathematics education with long division as an example.

Developing Long Division

In the realistic approach contextual problems[5] are used as a starting point, preferably problems that allow for a variety of informal solution procedures; that is to say, applied problems precede instruction on the algorithm. The instructional sequence on long division could start with a problem like the one described by Dolk and Uittenboogaard (1989). Here children of about 8 or 9 years old were asked to solve the following problem:

> Tonight 81 parents will be visiting our school
> Six parents can be seated at each table.
> How many tables do we need?

The teacher gave the students a lead in by drawing a few tables (see Fig. 13.2). The students produced all kinds of solutions:

- some used repetitive addition: $6 + 6 + 6 + \ldots$, or stepwise multiplication, probably based on addition, $1 \times 6, 2 \times 6, 3 \times 6, \ldots$, some only wrote down the resulting sequence 6, 12, 18, . . . ;
- some used 10×6 as a starting point, in order to continue by multiplication or repetitive addition;

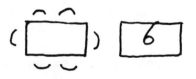

FIG. 13.2.   Setting out tables.

---

[5]Contextual problems describe situations where a problem is posed. More often this will be an everyday life situation, but not necessarily so; for the more advanced students, mathematics itself will become a context.

- one student knew $6 \times 6 = 36$ by heart, which was doubled to get $12 \times 6 = 72$, one 6 was added, and finally one more 6.

The teacher stimulated the students to compare their solutions. Obviously most found the first jump to 10×6 a handy short-cut. When a similar problem (concerning the same night at school) was administered afterwards, it appeared that a substantial number of the students imitated the 'ten times' short-cut spontaneously (see Fig. 13.3). The problem read like this:

> One pot serves seven cups of coffee, each parent gets one cup.
> How many pots of coffee must be brewed for the 81 parents?

Only one child stuck to the single step method. Thirteen used 'ten times', compared to six in the first round. From the work of three children it was not clear how they arrived at their answers.

It should be noted that the teacher made no suggestions whatsoever to use 'ten times' in the coffee task. Rightly, he expected that those who saw its advantage and trusted it, would use it on their own initiative.

The procedure that is employed here to solve what in principle is a division problem, can be labelled as 'compounding'. One tries to approach the dividend as closely as possible by adding up multiples of the divisor. As a matter of fact, we ourselves prefer this strategy for mental divisions. For instance, the easiest way to find the average fuel consumption of one's car is to reset the odometer when the tank is full and to compare the number of kilometres with the amount of fuel needed to refill it next time at a gas station. One can even try a more precise estimate, while driving away from the gas station. In our country gas consumption is measured by kilometres per litre of fuel.

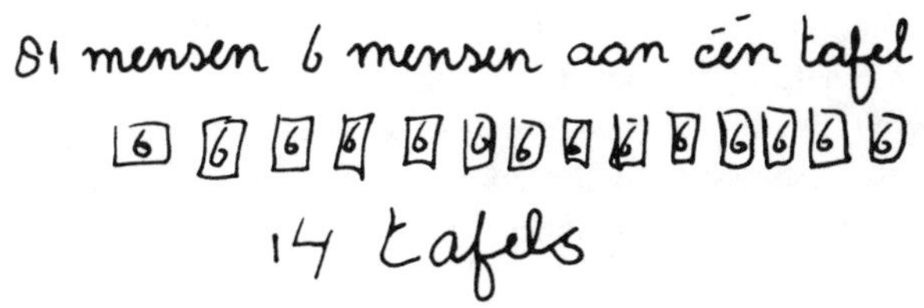

81 people; six at each table (*tafels*)

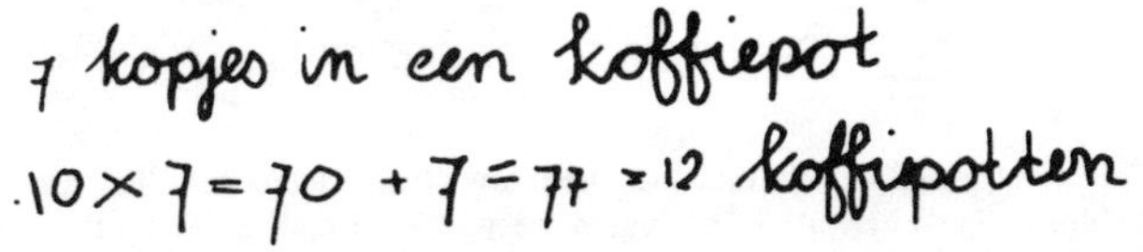

Each pot holds seven cups, how many pots (*koffiepotten*) are needed?

FIG. 13.3.   The solution procedures of one of the students.

(a) 34 / 467 \ 13.7
    34–
   127
   102–
   250
   238–
    12

(b) 34 / 467.0 \ 10+3+0.7=13.7
   340– [10 × 34]
   127
   102– [3 × 34]
   25.0
   23.8– [0.7 × 34]
    1.2

FIG. 13.4. (a) Standard procedure and (b) Interpretation.

Suppose you used 34.09 litres for 466.8 km, which would require the division 466.8 ÷ 34.09. To keep it simple let us do 467÷34. Obviously, 34 goes at least ten times into 467. Ten times 34 gives 340 to start with. Two more times? No, three more times gives 340 + 102 = 442, which means 13 km per litre. Or more precisely, one decimal at least: with 25 left by 467 − 442 do 0.5 × 34 = 17, 0.7 × 34 = 17 + 7 = 24. So our estimate would be 13.7 km per litre.

If we compare this calculation with the column algorithm, it appears that our mental arithmetic resembles the standard procedure (Fig. 13.4a). In fact, the standard procedure can be translated into the mental procedure (see Fig. 13.4b).

However, the algorithm is so condensed that one hardly realises that in the first step 10 × 34 = 340 rather than a mere 34 is subtracted. On the other hand, it is not so difficult to recognise the underlying repetitive subtraction behind this procedure: after any subtraction of a multiple of the divisor, one concentrates on what is left. In fact the column algorithm of long division is nothing but the most abbreviated manner of performing a division by counting how often the divisor can be subtracted from the dividend.

In realistic mathematics instruction it is attempted to teach the standard procedure by letting it evolve from informal ones in a learning process, which starts in a situation where the mathematical model of repetitive subtraction offers itself in a natural manner. From the start onwards, rather large numbers can be allowed for in the assignments. This is the case in the following problem that is presented in the broader context of a story about Dutch sailors whose ship was stranded on the isle of Nova Zembla[6] (Fig. 13.5).

The captain of the stranded ship is told that there are 4000 biscuits left. The crew consists of 64 members. Each man gets 3 biscuits a day, which means 192 biscuits a day for the whole crew. How long will this supply last?

FIG. 13.5.   Overwintering in Nova Zembla.

4000			4000			4000	
<u>192</u>	−1 day		<u>192</u>	−1 day		<u>1920</u>	−10 days
3808			3808			2080	
<u>192</u>	−1 day		<u>384</u>	−2 days		<u>1920</u>	−10 days
3616			3424			160	
<u>192</u>	−1 day		<u>768</u>	−4 days			
3424			2656				
<u>192</u>	−1 day		<u>1536</u>	−8 days			
etc.			etc.				

FIG. 13.6. Repetitive subtraction of smaller or larger quantities.

Identifying with the situation, we can almost see the supply of biscuits diminish day by day, every time a ration is consumed. What makes this problem interesting is the variety of solving procedures on different levels. The students would continue to subtract 192 one at a time. They would use multiples of 192, as well as, say, decuples, or doubling (Fig. 13.6).

With an appropriate contextual problem one can induce children to use decuples. Take for example the problem in Fig. 13.7. The information about the reduction can work as a suggestion to calculate the number of reductions. It will call the students' attention to the opportunities offered by the decimal system. Even then various solutions are possible (Fig. 13.8).

Such steps on the way to the column algorithm are opportunities for students to make discoveries at their own level, to build on their own experiential knowledge and perform short-cuts at their own pace. Working with realistic problems also implies a different approach to the problem of the remainder, i.e. as a real life phenomenon that calls for practical solutions,

1296 supporters want to visit the away soccer game of Feijenoord. The treasurer learns that one bus can carry 38 passengers and that a reduction will be given for every ten buses.

FIG. 13.7. Feijenoord.

---

[6]Examples taken from a Dutch textbook series: Gravemeijer, 1983.

```
38 / 1296   \          36 / 1296   \          36 / 1296   \
   380 –  10x              380 –  10x             1140 –  30x
   916                     916                     156
   380 –  10x              760 –  20x              152 –  4x
   536                     156                       4
   380 –  10x               76 –  2x
   156                      80
    38 –  1x                76 –  2x
   118                       4
    38 –  1x
    80
    38 –  1x
    42
    38 –  1x
     4
```

FIG. 13. 8. Various levels of curtailment.

rather than as a peculiarity of non-terminating divisions which must be justified by formal arrangements. If the context is taken seriously, then '34 rem.4' is not an acceptable answer. What can we do with these 4 supporters? Well, there are several possibilities: distribute them over the other buses, order an extra bus (or a car), or speculate on the withdrawal of at least 4 supporters at the last moment.

The continuation of this instructional sequence will include fractions and decimals. The fuel consumption problem shows how the solution procedure can be extended to incorporate decimals (or fractions) in the quotient. The same situation suggests how to deal with decimals in divisor and dividend: we are dealing with a ratio. A rate of fuel consumption of 34.09 litres for 466.8 km is the same as that of 3409 litres for 46680 km. In other words the division can be freed from decimals by multiplying divisor and dividend with the same factor; the ratio stays the same.

Teaching–Learning Process

Up to now contextual problems and individual solution procedures have dominated our discussion of realistic mathematics education, although we have already mentioned the whole class discussion of solution procedures for the table setting at the PTA.

This kind of interaction is one of the core activities in realistic mathematics instruction: the discussion of solution procedures and problem situations. These discussions centre around the correctness, adequacy and efficiency of the solution procedures and the interpretation of the problem situation. In this context the socio-constructivist assertion must be taken into account, that there is no such thing as *the task*. A so-called 'taken-as-shared' interpretation of a task is interactively constituted in the classroom community. This incorporates (implicit) negotiation of notions such as 'what counts as a problem' and 'what counts as a solution' (Cobb et al., 1992a; see also Yackel, 1992). Specifically for realistic mathematics instruction this interpretation of a task must be directed at the real life character of contextual problems, since there is always a tension between practical solutions and a mathematical interpretation of the task. One must acknowledge that one cannot bring the reality into the classroom. Although students will be able to identify with well chosen contextual problems, these will never become real life problems. The extent to which practical considerations are valued is part of what will be established as the classroom culture.

Note that those notions of what counts as a problem and what counts as a solution are not self-evident. This was clearly illustrated when we presented 12-year-old low-attainers with a problem about a school party. There are 18 bottles of cola for 24 students and the bottles must be distributed over the tables fairly, taking into account the different numbers of students at each table (tables with, 12, 4, . . . students). What was intended as 'the task' was the production of equivalent ratios (bottles over students). Some students, however, did not want to interpret the task this way, they thought equivalent ratios of the bottles over students misplaced, since: 'Some students don't drink cola' and: 'They don't drink the same amount.'

A whole class discussion in realistic mathematics education differs to some extent from what is seen as mathematical discourse. Mathematical discourse is identified with conjecturing, justifying and challenging, and although there is a resemblance with the activities in realistic mathematics education, there is a difference in focus. Part of the discussion is about the interpretation of the situation sketched in the contextual problem. Another part of the discussion focuses on the adequacy and the efficiency of various solution procedures. This can implicate a shift of attention towards a reflection on the solution procedure from a mathematical point of view. The latter discussion will have the closest resemblance with what is seen as a mathematical discourse.

To elucidate mathematical discourse, one can think of Lakatos's (1976) famous reconstruction of the coming about of the Euler formula as a paradigm. However, this may lead to an overestimation of the importance of the discourse as a mathematical activity, since this was a process of a different magnitude—the elaboration of the Euler formula was enacted over many decades. Moreover, the idea of a mathematical discourse models practices of the mathematical research community, it does not cover applied mathematics. In realistic mathematics education, practices of applied mathematicians are thought to be more relevant for primary school mathematics.

Realistic mathematics education places the student in quite a different position from traditional educational approaches. Students have to be more self-reliant; they cannot turn to the teacher for validation of their answers or for the directions for a standard solution procedure. Research by Desforges and Cockburn (1987) shows that it is difficult to implement a problem solving approach. Students seem to feel insecure and keep asking for directions and approval, while teachers experience that it is much easier to deal with a class that is executing routine tasks, than it is with students who are left to their own devices to solve problems. These problems could in part be due to a change in the so-called 'classroom social norms' (Cobb, Perlwitz, & Underwood, 1992b). Cobb et al. (1992b) argue that classroom social norms are to be explicitly renegotiated. The students have to become aware of the change in what is expected from them in mathematics lessons; they are no longer expected to produce 'correct' answers quickly, following prescribed procedures. In realistic maths, as in inquiry maths[7], they have other obligations, such as explaining and justifying their solutions, trying to understand the solutions of others and asking for explanation or justifications if necessary. This change in social norms corresponds to another role of the teacher. The authority of the teacher as validator is exchanged for an authority as a guide. He or she exercises this authority by way of selecting instructional activities. initiating and guiding discussions, and by reformulating selected aspects of students' mathematical contributions.

KEY PRINCIPLES OF REALISTIC MATHEMATICS EDUCATION

The aforementioned teaching strategy is only possible when the learning sequence consists of contextual problems that give rise to a variety of solution procedures which allow for discussions about adequacy and efficiency, and that can lead to a reflection on these procedures from a mathematical point of view. This brings us back to the learning sequence and its underlying theory. In the following we will elucidate the realistic approach by elaborating three key principles which can also be seen as heuristics for instructional design.

'*Guided reinvention*' and '*progressive mathematising*' shape the first principle. According to the reinvention principle, the students should be given the opportunity to experience a process similar to the process by which the mathematics was invented. To design such a course, the history of mathematics can be employed as a source of inspiration. The reinvention principle can also be inspired by informal solution procedures. Informal strategies of students can more often be interpreted as anticipating more

---

[7]A term used by Cobb and his colleagues after Richards.

formal procedures in such a case, mathematising similar solution procedures can constitute the reinvention process. In general we will be looking for contextual problems that allow for a wide variety of solution procedures, preferably solution procedures that together already reflect a possible learning route through a process of progressive mathematisation.

The second principle we want to discuss, is in the idea of a *didactical phenomenology* (Freudenthal, 1983). According to the didactical phenomenology, situations where a given mathematical topic is applied, are to be investigated for two reasons. First, to reveal the kind of applications that have to be anticipated in instruction, and second, to consider their suitability as points of impact for a process of progressive mathematisation. If we see mathematics as historically evolved from solving practical problems, it is reasonable to expect to find the problems that gave rise to this process in present day applications. Next we can imagine that formal mathematics came into being in a process of generalising and formalising situation-specific problem solving procedures and concepts about a variety of situations. That will therefore be the goal of our phenomenological investigation, to find problem situations for which situation-specific approaches can be generalised, and to find situations that can evoke paradigmatic solution procedures which can be taken as the basis for vertical mathematisation.

The third principle is found in the role that *self-developed models* play in bridging the gap between informal knowledge and formal mathematics. Whereas models (embodiments) are presented as prefabricated models in a customary information processing approach, models are developed by the students themselves in realistic mathematics education; i.e. models evolve in solving problems. They come to the fore in modelling problem situations and solution procedures. At first therefore a model is a model *of* a situation that is familiar to the student. By a process of generalising and formalising, the model then becomes an entity of its own, which makes it possible to use this model as a model *for* mathematical reasoning (Streefland, 1985; Treffers, 1991; Gravemeijer, 1994). This transition from 'model-of' to model-for' is similar to the theoretical reconstruction of the genesis of subjective mathematical knowledge by Ernest (1991, p.78):

> What is proposed is that by a vertical process of abstraction or concept formation a collection of objects or constructions at lower, preexisting levels of a personal concept hierarchy become 'reified' into a object-like concept, or noun-like term.

In what follows we will illuminate these key principles of realistic mathematics education with the sequence on long division as an example.

Reinvention/Mathematising

The difference between mathematics instruction from the realistic approach and from the information processing approach is most apparent in how the applications are dealt with. The usual view on mathematics is that of the ready-made system with general applicability, and on mathematics instruction as breaking down into learning formal mathematical knowledge and learning to apply it. For the realistic approach the emphasis is on mathematising; mathematics viewed as an activity, a way of working. Then learning mathematics means doing mathematics, of which solving real life problems is an essential part. Manifold contextual problems are integrated in the curriculum from the start onwards.

The two fundamentally different views on mathematics and mathematics education imply essentially different mathematical learning processes. With mathematics as a formal system, its applicability is provided by the general character of its concepts and procedures, and thus, first of all, one must adapt this abstract knowledge to solving problems set in reality. One has to translate real life problems into mathematical problems. This can be visualised as shown in Fig. 13.9.

The model describes the process of solving a contextual problem with the help of formal mathematical knowledge. First the problem is translated; it has to be formulated in mathematical terms, as a mathematical problem. Next, this mathematical problem is solved with the help of the available mathematical means. And finally the mathematical solution is translated back into the original context. Transformation of a contextual problem into a mathematical problem implies a reduction of information; many aspects of the original problem will have been obliterated. The translation from the mathematics back into the original problem, therefore asks for an interpretation of the mathematical solution in the context of the original problem. The aspects that were obliterated have to be taken into account again. It can also be the case that the original problem does not allow for the exactitude that is suggested by the mathematical solution.

On the whole the 'translation' described above boils down to recognising problem types and establishing standard routines. As soon as we choose to teach 'mathematics as an activity', problem-solving takes on a different

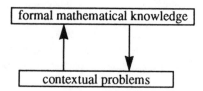

FIG. 13. 9.   Application of formal mathematics.

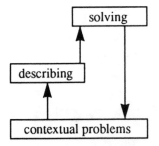

FIG. 13.10.   A student's description of the number of tables needed for 81 parents.

meaning. It becomes problem-centred, i.e. rather than using a mathematical tool, the problem is the proper aim. However, even if interpreted as an exploration, problem-solving passes through the same three stages of:

- describing the contextual problem more formally;
- solving the problem on this (more or less) formal level;
- translating the solution back;

the character of these activities is now fundamentally different. Rather than aiming to fit the problem into a pre-designed system, one tries to describe it in a way to come to grips with it and this occurs in particular through schematising and by identifying the central relations in the problem situation. Rather than using commonly accepted mathematical language, this description can be sketchy and use self-invented symbols (see Fig. 13.10).

The description does not automatically answer the question; rather it simplifies the problem by describing relations and distinguishing matters of major and minor importance. Solving the problem as it is stated at this more or less formal level differs greatly from applying a standard procedure. It is a matter of problem solving as well. Translating the final solution does not differ that much from translating a solution that is produced by a standard procedure. But translation and interpretation are now easier because the symbols are meaningful for the problem-solver, who is the one who gave them their meaning (Fig. 13.11).

An instructional programme that consists of problems of this kind, creates the opportunity for students to learn mathematising contextual problems. Numbers of similar problems in a row will evoke another process. Problem

FIG. 13.11.   Realistic problem solving.

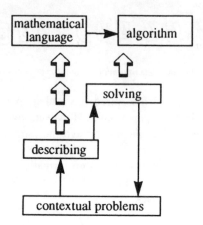

FIG. 13.12. Vertical mathematising.

descriptions can develop into an informal language, which in turn can evolve into a more formal standard-like language, due to a process of simplifying and formalising. Again this is a process of mathematising, albeit stretched over a longer period of time. Something similar happens to the solving procedure. In the long run-solving some kind of problems may become routine, i.e. the procedure is condensed and formalised in the course of time. Genuine algorithms can thus take shape (Fig. 13.12).

This then is a learning process by which formal mathematical knowledge itself can be (re-)constructed (Fig. 13.13). Following Treffers (1987), the latter process, focusing on the mathematisation of mathematical matter, is

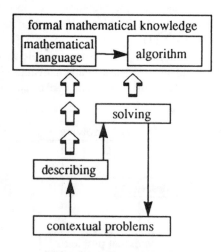

FIG. 13.13. Reinvention.

called vertical mathematisation. This is distinguished from horizontal mathematisation, which is mathematising contextual problems. Freudenthal (1991, pp.41–42) characterises this distinction as follows:

> Horizontal mathematisation leads from the world of *life* to the world of *symbols*. In the world of life one lives, acts (and suffers); in the other one symbols are shaped, reshaped, and manipulated, mechanically, comprehendingly, reflectingly: this is vertical mathematisation. The world of life is what is experienced as reality (in the sense I used the word before), as is symbol world with regard to abstraction. To be sure the frontiers of these worlds are vaguely marked. The worlds can expand and shrink—also at one another's expense.

As Freudenthal indicates, the boundaries between what is to be denoted as horizontal mathematisation, and what as vertical mathematisation, are vague. The crux is in what is to be understood as reality. Freudenthal (1991, p.17) elucidates: 'I prefer to apply the term "reality" to that which [one] at a certain stage of common sense experiences as real.' Reality is understood as a mixture of interpretation and of sensual experience; this implies that mathematics too can become part of one's reality. Reality and what one counts as common sense is not static but grows under the influence of the learning process of the person in question. This is also how Freudenthal's statement about 'Mathematics starting at, and staying within reality' (Freudenthal, 1991, p.18) must be understood. One might argue that this idea is better expressed by 'common sense mathematics' than by 'realistic mathematics'.

Summarising, in realistic mathematics education, mathematics is primarily seen as a process, a human activity. However at the same time the reinvention principle ensures that this activity results in mathematics as a product. Vertical mathematising is in the core of this process. Vertical progress is reflected in a sequence of gradually more and more formal symbolisations and solution procedures. This is shown in the long division sequence that starts with informal notations which lead to more formal schemas resembling the standard written algorithm. At the same time elaborate solution procedures like repetitive subtraction are shortened with the help of decuples and centuples, ending in the maximal curtailed standard algorithm.

This progress is supported by suitable contextual problems. That is where horizontal mathematising comes in; the contextual problems can facilitate certain interpretations and strategies. Distributing rations in the Nova Zembla story, for instance, is easily interpreted as a situation for repetitive subtraction. The reduction given for ten buses, in the supporters problem, can function as a hint for using decuples.

In designing the sequence, the reinvention principle is used as a guidance by asking: 'How could I have invented the standard procedure for long division?' The answer is based on the establishment that the long division is based on repetitive subtraction, and that is related to informal strategies of adults or students (like the one used for calculating fuel consumption). This kind of deliberation helps the designer find contextual problems that can function as anchoring points for a learning sequence.

Didactical Phenomenology

To conceive of division as distribution does not need explanation; even without instruction young children know what to do. This can be illustrated by the solutions of 8- and 9-year-olds for the problem of dividing 36 by 3 (Galen et al., 1985). They had never done multiplications with numbers bigger than 10, let alone performed the inverse division procedure. Of course, rather than using a formal representation like $36 \div 3 = \ldots$, we presented the contextual problem shown in Fig. 13.14. The students invented all kinds of solving procedures:

- Dividing on a geometric basis (Fig. 13.15a). The area of a square with 36 sweets is divided in three equal parts.
- Distributing one by one (Fig. 13.15b). The sweets are distributed one by one. One by one they are crossed out of the total and added to one of the rows. (The students even tried to copy the children's portraits faithfully.)
- Grouping in triads (Fig. 13.15c). Some students drew groups of three. These students probably reasoned: each time one sweet is distributed to each of the children, the supply diminishes by three. So they figured out how many groups of three one could create.
- Using multiplication facts (Fig. 13.15d). Other students came up with a method of grouping that seems to be based on multiplication facts. The students will know that $12 = 3 \times 4$; perhaps 3×4 is recognised in the

Three children divide 36 sweets.
How many sweets will each of them get?

FIG. 13.14. Dividing sweets.

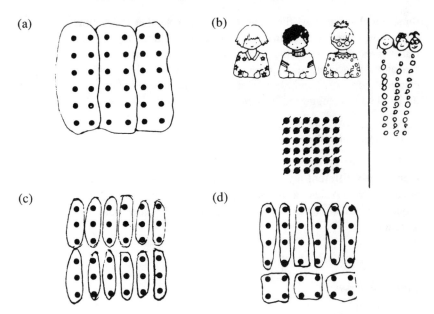

FIG. 13.15. (a) Geometric division (b) Piece-wise distribution (c) Triads (d) Division based on 3 × 4= 12.

pattern. Of each twelve, four can be given to each child; doing this three times gives each child twelve sweets.

All in all, division comes to the fore as 'repetitive subtraction', as 'fair sharing' or 'distribution', and as the 'inverse of multiplication'. Where repetitive, subtraction can be conceived as the counterpart of multiplication as repetitive addition (see also Freudenthal, 1983). Repetitive subtraction and distribution are also referred to as 'ratio division' and 'distribution division' respectively (see Fig. 13.16). The distribution division appears most clearly in the geometric solution and in 'distributing one by one', where the student interprets the problem by creating three equal groups.

Some students ask the different question 'How many groups of three can be made?', which aims at a ratio division. The relation between both has already been indicated above. Distributing one by one focuses on creating

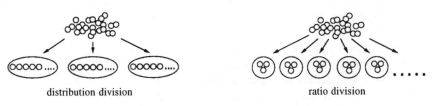

distribution division   ratio division

FIG. 13.16.   Two basic forms of division.

three equal groups. At the same time it appears that every time each child is given one sweet, the original number of sweets decreases by three. Therefore, this approach leads to the question about the number of times this can be repeated. However, it requires a translation of the problem, because the original contextual problem aims at a pure distribution division. A ratio division can be suggested by a problem like the following:

A net can hold three balls.
How many of such nets will be needed for 36 balls?

Taking our point of view on multiplication, the two division types can be seen as two different inverse operations. In a times b equals c, the two factors have different roles; a is taken b times. In applications the difference is especially clear, when b is a magnitude (Freudenthal, 1983). Take for instance:

3×12 sweets = 36 sweets,

with its inverses:

36 sweets $\div 12$ sweets = 3,

and

36 sweets $\div 3 = 12$ sweets.

Besides this there are other applications where both factors are magnitudes, as in:

quantity $\times$ unit price = total price,
time $\times$ speed = distance, etc.

For the educational designer the problem arises of which type of division to choose as the starting point for the development of long division. In fact learning sequences for both division types have been worked out in realistic mathematics education.

Exploiting the matter-of-course character of the distribution division, the distribution division was elaborated in a sequence initially. At the start of such a sequence, the piecewise distribution was supported with drawings of hands or cups or whatever, very similar to the drawings of the children in the sweets division problem. These elaborate descriptions are needed for the step from distributing piecewise to distributing larger portions (Fig. 13.17). This elaboration was abandoned towards the end of the sequence. Eventually the children drew only one column, because all columns were the same.

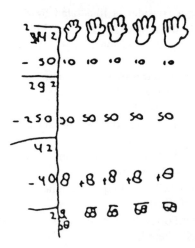

FIG. 13.17. A scheme for distribution division

Although comparative research shows that such a distribution division sequence was far superior to a traditional approach (Rengering, 1983), there are good reasons to switch to ratio division:

1. Ratio division can more easily be connected to the column algorithm. Solving the contextual problem does not have to be reformulated in terms of repetitive subtraction, and no sub-stage is needed where the complete division process is represented with hands or cups.
2. The ratio division has the advantage that many applications correspond with ratio division. Moreover, traditionally instructed children find it difficult to relate the long division algorithm to ratio division type of applications. Research by Hart (1981) shows that, rather than using the column algorithm, students are inclined to solve applied (ratio) division problems by repetitive subtraction.
3. The "busing problem" as such yields an argument for choosing the ratio division; thanks to its dynamic character, the "busing problem" may function as a paradigmatic situation. Thinking of buses will enable the students to "concretise" a division problem that is presented numerically.
4. It is not so difficult to extend the ratio division procedure to distribution problems (as will be shown later). And whatever division type is chosen as a starting point, both have to be integrated in the learning sequence.

In addition to the distinction between ratio division and distribution division, other phenomenological variations must be taken into account.

Which varieties one can consider is illustrated by the diversity of meanings that can be attributed to the remainder. Treffers, Moor, and Feijs (1989) listed the following examples for the division 26 ÷ 4 :

1. 26 passengers have to be transported by cars.
    Each car can carry 4 passengers.
    How many cars will be needed?   [7]
2. A rope of 26 metres is cut into pieces of 4 metres.
    How many pieces does one get?   [6]
3. If 26 bananas are to be fairly divided among 4 people,
    how many bananas will each get?   [6½]
4. A 26 km walk is divided into 4 equal stretches.
    How long is each of them?   [6.5]
5. A rectangular pattern of 26 trees with 4 trees per row,
    how many rows will there be?   [?!!]
6. A rectangular terrace with a size of 26 square metres
    has a width of 4 metres. How long is this terrace?   [6.5]

The interpretation of the remainder largely depends on the situation in which the result of 26 ÷ 4 has to be used. It will be clear that a formal treatment of the remainder detached from applications will not prepare the students for this wide variety of interpretations. The student will have to encounter all kinds of situations, not only to become familiar with different interpretations, but also to learn to attune the interpretation of the remainder to its meaning in the problem situation.

Self-developed Models

At first glance, models are less prominent in realistic mathematics education than in manipulatives-based mathematics education. However the models differ mainly in role and character. This can be elucidated by analysing the position and role of models in relation to formal and informal knowledge, in both approaches.

In the information processing approach, expert mathematical knowledge is embodied in concrete models, more often manipulatives. We may characterise this as a top-down strategy; formal expert knowledge is taken as the source for the didactical models. However, the informal knowledge of the students is neglected. Moreover, the implicit supposition is that formal mathematical knowledge is generally applicable, because no attention is given to applications initially. Later models are developed to support application, however, without abandoning the idea of general applicability.

If situated knowledge is taken into account, we can imagine three levels, i.e. if we envisage informal knowledge at the same level as applications. In this way the models can be regarded as a sort of two-way intermediary:

between situated knowledge and formal knowledge on the one hand and between formal knowledge and applied situations on the other (see Fig. 13.18). An objection to an intermediary model would be that there is still a top-down element in this approach; the formal knowledge is treated as a given and the intermediate model is derived from this formal mathematical knowledge.

In all those cases the label 'model' refers to concrete models such as manipulatives and visual models. However, we can also use a broader concept which includes 'situation models' and 'mathematical models'. In realistic mathematics education paradigmatic situations can develop into situation models. In the learning strand on long division, 'repetitive subtraction' can be seen as a mathematical model.[8]

Following the reinvention principle, a bottom-up approach is pursued. The idea is that the students construct models for themselves and that these models serve as a basis for developing formal mathematical knowledge. To be more precise, at first a model is constituted as a context-specific model *of* a situation, then the model is generalised over situations. Thus the model changes character, it becomes an entity of its own and in this new shape it can function as a basis, a model *for*, mathematical reasoning on a formal level.

The bottom-up character of this approach also comes to the fore in the nature of the models; in realistic mathematics education the models are inspired by informal strategies, whether used by students or in the history of mathematics.

The exposition above indicates that there are four levels in realistic mathematics education: situations[9], 'model of', 'model for' and formal mathematics (see Fig.13.18). Considering long division, the first level can be associated with real-life activities such as sharing sweets among children— not with paper and pencil. Here the students bring in their domain-specific situational knowledge and strategies and apply those in the situation. The

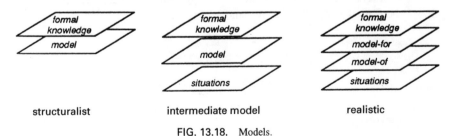

structuralist   intermediate model   realistic

FIG. 13.18.   Models.

---

[8]Realistic mathematics education also operates with tacit and visual models. As is the case with two digit addition and subtraction, where a bead string and the empty number line are used (see Gravemeijer, 1993).

[9]More often situations are presented in contextual problems, where the situations are to be imagined by the students.

second level is entered when the same sweet division is presented in a written task and the division is modelled with paper and pencil. A characteristic problem for this level is the problem 'busing the Feijenoord supporters'. Here the students create a model of the situation: filling buses is modelled by repetitive subtraction. However, the situation still pervades the solution process. The third level contains the next step in the development of long division; the focus is shifted towards strategies from a mathematical point of view. Taking the optimal centuple or decuple is made a topic of discussion with the question, 'What is the biggest neat portion that one can take away at once?'. Now the student is just dealing with the numbers, without thinking of the situation. The fourth level, finally would contain the standard written algorithm for long division.

Note that the term model should not be taken too literally. It can also concern a 'model situation', scheme, a description or a way of noting. In the above example of long division the situations for application of the long division are modelled with repetitive subtraction. And it is this procedure of repetitive subtraction that legitimises the formal long division algorithm.

Instead of referring to models, we can describe the levels in more general terms (see Fig. 13.19):

1. the level of the situations, where domain-specific, situational knowledge and strategies are used within the context of the situation (mainly out-of-school situations);
2. a referential level, where models and strategies refer to the situation that is sketched in the problem (posed in a school setting mostly);
3. a general level, where a mathematical focus on strategies dominates the reference to the context;
4. the level of formal arithmetic, where one works with conventional procedures and notations.

Such a general description has the advantage that not every learning strand has to be forced into a 'model-of'–'model-for' description[10].

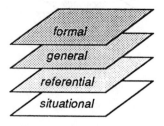

FIG.13.19.   Levels.

---

[10]Sometimes it will be artificial to try to fit a realistic learning strand into the 'model-of'–'model-for' description.

Comparing the role of models in the various approaches, it appears that in realistic mathematics education models are explicitly placed at an intermediate level between situated and formal knowledge. According to the 'model-of'–'model-for' distinction, this intermediate level is then separated into a referential level and a general level. The referential level contains the models, descriptions, concepts, procedures, and strategies that refer to concrete or paradigmatic situations. Thanks to generalisation, exploration, and reflection, this level is developed so that a reflection on the strategies becomes more dominant. The formal level can be seen as a formalisation of the general level, or in other words, the general level functions as the 'concrete' base for the formal level.

Note that the levels mentioned above differ from the Van Hiele levels that Treffers (1987) uses to sketch a domain-specific theory for realistic mathematics education. Treffers integrates the Van Hiele levels with Freudenthal's concept of mathematising as level-raising and with Freudenthal's didactical phenomenology. He envisages a learning process structured by numerous micro-levels in the spirit of Freudenthal, globally structured by the Van Hiele levels. Furthermore, the Van Hiele levels are broadened by incorporating phenomenological aspects. Van Hiele (1973, 1985) discerns three levels of thought, which we can illustrate with number concept:

- at the first level, numbers depend on observable quantities and actions with manipulatives (at this level, the number word 'five' is only understood as adjective: five marbles', 'five dots' etc.);
- at the second level, the relations between numbers or quantities are objects of investigation and a framework of number relations takes shape. Numbers become junctions in this framework (at this level, the number word 'five' takes a noun-like status and will be associated with 2+3, 4+1, 6-1, half of 10 etc.);[11]
- at the third level, the relations themselves are objects of investigation. A coherence is found, which enables one to integrate those relations in a formal and at the same time meaningful system.

The first discrepancy is of course that Van Hiele only discerns three levels. Furthermore, the highest Van Hiele level is not pursued in primary school arithmetic. The highest level would involve a reflection on the systematics of

---

[11]In the realistic interpretation the number relations also include relations with numerical phenomena in reality. Take for instance 52. Mathematically, 52 will be related with 50 + 2, 2 × 26, 2 × 25 + 2 etc. Contextually, 52 is also related to 52 weeks a year which is associated with 4 × 13 (weeks in a season), 52% of the voters (a little bit more than one half), two quarters and two pennies, 52 metres (about the size of our church), 52 years (in relation to the ages of people one knows).

the operations in arithmetic, which leads to arithmetic theory eventually touching on Peano's axioms. The highest level in elementary arithmetic is Van Hiele's second level, the level where numbers serve as junctions in a network of number relations. This level can be connected with both the general level and the formal level in our scheme, since there is no difference between these two in the sense of levels of thought. The difference between these two levels is not fundamental, but in the rate of formalisation. The formal level is characterised by the use of strictly formalised symbols, routine procedures and maximally curtailed standard algorithms.

The level of situations corresponds with Van Hiele's first level, the referential level represents the activities that must facilitate the shift from the first Van Hiele level to the second Van Hiele level—activities that deal with what Van Hiele calls 'exploring relations'.

We should remark that both the levels we discern and the Van Hiele levels are local levels; they are tied to a specific topic, basic facts, two digit addition and subtraction, written algorithms, fractions, and so forth. The levels are not absolute in another sense—the different levels are not segregated. The idea is that the student should be able to revert to a lower level. The lower levels are meant to be incorporated into the higher levels. The general level—with the model-for function—is not detached from the originating contexts: e.g. the formal algorithm for long division is justified as a procedure for repetitive subtraction, and this notion of repetitive subtraction in turn relies on knowing that division can be interpreted as repetitive subtraction in contextual problems.[12]

DISCUSSION

The theme of this chapter is how to help students learn abstract mathematics. The mainstream information processing approach of 'embedding the mathematics in concrete models' leads to insufficient understanding and lack of applicability. A bottom-up approach should deal with the problem of insufficient understanding. Realistic mathematics education fulfils the requirement of a bottom-up approach. That leaves us with the question of whether the realistic approach also helps to improve applicability. The answer to this question lies in the role of *generalising* vs. transfer in realistic mathematics education.

---

[12]We should acknowledge that these models have to meet several specifications in order to fulfil the bridging function between informal mathematical knowledge. They must connect naturally to the informal strategies of children and naturally lead to formalising and generalising. Moreover they should anticipate further elaboration and wider applicability. Finally they should enable the student to think of a contextual problem to concretise a formal numerical task (see also Treffers, 1991).

Generalising vs. Transfer

One could criticise the idea of generalisation suggested above; the situatedness of knowledge might cause barriers that hinder transfer—what is learned in one situation does not seem to be applicable in other situations. However, we must realise that, although it may seem rather obvious to equate generalising with transfer, these are two different things. The key difference between transfer and generalising (as it is meant in realistic mathematics education) lies in the presence or absence of a routine character in what is to be applied. Transfer deals with the applicability of a routine or a strategy in a new situation. When generalisation is at stake in realistic mathematics education, students are solving non-routine problems in a non-routine manner, i.e. the situation is a genuine problem solving situation, in which the students will have to bring to bear all the (informal) knowledge and strategies they have. Here a new situation is not a situation for transfer in the sense of finding out what routine or strategy has to be used. It is about a realistic problem that has to be solved within the context of a situation one has to identify with. The crux is in the phenomenological characteristics of that situation. Consequently contextual problems that could be categorised as ratio division are interpreted as situations for repetitive subtraction.

Generalising does not imply the transfer of a routine procedure, it implies an *a posteriori* construction of connections between various situations. We can use Steffe's distinction between 'being efficient in-action' and 'being efficient prior-to-action' (Steffe, personal communication) to clarify what is going on. A student who is guided by the phenomenological characteristics of a contextual situation when solving a ratio division with repetitive subtraction, is efficient in-action. A student who recognises a contextual situation as a division problem which can be solved by a written algorithm is efficient prior-to-action; the student must anticipate the applicability of this particular solution procedure before deciding to apply it. If the student in the first case realises that his/her solution is similar to the solution to other contextual problems solved earlier, this student is generalising. In the second case one could speak of transfer of the written algorithm.

One may wonder if this interpretation of generalising can be retained when the distribution division is taken into account. Here it will be less self-evident to interpret the situation as a situation for repetitive subtraction—apart of course from the repetitive subtraction of ones. Interestingly already some of the solutions given by the 9-year-olds for '36 sweets divided among three children' reflect repetitive subtraction of threes. The next step of course is using multiples of ten.

Here again the choice of the contextual problem is essential. Dividing money, for instance, brings along an interpretation of the situation in terms of bills, bills of one dollar, two, five, ten, twenty, one hundred dollars (see Fig. 13.20). When dividing $10,000 among 17 people it makes sense to give each participant $500 first. This leaves 1500 dollars (10,000–8500) to be divided etc. The whole story can be notated in a subtraction scheme that is very similar to that of the ratio division $10,000 ÷ $17.

As shown in Fig. 13.20a and b the difference between the two situations is reflected in the notation. In the distributive division 17 × 500 is subtracted in the first step, in the ratio division this is 500 × 17. Knowing that 17 × 500 and 500 x 17 can be seen as two manifestations of the same multiplication—the student can connect the same scheme for repetitive subtraction with two kinds of division.

Again, generalising involves making *a posteriori* connections. Application or transfer would imply an *a priori* restructuring of the task in terms of a repetitive subtraction, based on the following kind of reasoning: giving each person $1 boils down to subtracting $17 from the available amount each time. Therefore finding out how much each gets is similar to finding out how many times $17 can be subtracted from $10,000.

Generalising is fostered by looking for similarities; this enables one to classify problem situations as belonging to the same type. At the same time, the solution process can be structured and thus, generalising takes shape as an organising activity, as a form of mathematising. Whether generalising in turn fosters transfer is another question. First we must notice that the problem solving approach in realistic mathematics education is different in character from the process connected with the idea of transfer. This could be expressed as top-down (transfer) versus bottom-up (mathematising). Transfer in an applied situation suggests something like looking for the ready-made routine that fits the situation at hand. In realistic problem solving, one starts with investigating the situation. Mathematising the situation one may hit upon a similarity with other situations and realise that earlier invented solution procedures could apply here as well. Thus the way in which students approach applied problems is fundamentally different from what goes with the idea of transfer.

Concerning transfer or application, it is worthwhile to look at Barnes' (1982) analysis of the activities of physicists in normal science. According to Kuhn, their work consists of finding new applications for an accepted theory.

(a)	100000			(b)	10000		
	8500	–	500 (dollars)		8500	–	500 x
	1500				1500		
	1360	–	80 (dollars)		1360	–	80 x
	140				140		
	136	–	8 (dollars)		136	–	8 x
	14				14	–	

FIG. 13.20. (a) $10,000 ÷ 17   (b) $10,000 ÷ $17

However, to make a theory applicable to a new situation, Barnes argues, a constructive activity is needed to make the new situation fit for application. He illustrates this argument with an example from mathematics: to be able to apply the formula for the area of a triangle to calculate the area of a parallelogram, one must divide the parallelogram into two triangles (by constructing a diagonal). The original area formula cannot be applied on a parallelogram without this construction.

Following Barnes' line of thought, application presupposes the primacy of the 'theory' that is to be applied. In other words, one decides to try to apply a certain procedure and next one tries to interpret the situation in such a way that this procedure can actually be applied. In simple cases application will demand only recognition, in more complex cases it takes some effort to find cues that might suggest trying a specific procedure. We can conclude by asserting that if a solution procedure is rooted in a generalisation over various situations (as described above), there will be a wide range of situations where application will be relatively easy.

14 Charming Fractions or Fractions Being Charmed?

L. Streefland
Freudenthal Institute, Utrecht, The Netherlands

INTRODUCTION AND OVERVIEW

Mathematics seems to differ from physics in the role that common sense can play in its development. In physics, all great discoveries are related to great names, right from its beginning—Aristotle, Galileo and so on. In contrast, elementary mathematics was created by many unnamed people in many different places in the world and local communities still have their own informal mathematics related to their everyday and professional lives (for example, see Nunes, 1988). Recognising this role of common sense in the development of elementary mathematics, Freudenthal in his final work (1991) argued that, provided common sense is not blocked, attaining mathematical insights a bit more advanced than the most elementary ones is a question of extending one's common sense and using it. H e often stressed the need to keep open the common sense sources of insight for learning. This is the perspective that will be pursued in this chapter with respect to fractions.

Fractions evolve from everyday experience of fair sharing. However, fractions offer a model that does not reflect real life exactly. To use fractions as a model, some conditions need to be satisfied:

- equal or equivalent units;
- the sharing must be exhaustive; that is, nothing remains;
- there is equality or equivalence of shares.

Everyday life shows a much more variegated image of division and sharing than its mathematical representation by fractions. In everyday life, people's

347

feelings, preferences, needs and possibilities play a decisive role. In order not to take parts of the mathematical process and its outcomes for granted it is better to start the learning of fractions with everyday situations that conflict in some sense with mathematical representation. For instance, one can start with units such as apples that are neither equal nor equivalent. In such situation, pupils may meet the conflict provoked by the mathematisation of the situation and its description afterwards. When different units have been divided, for instance, into four equal parts, and then a quarter of a big apple is added to a quarter of a small apple, they obviously do not result in half an apple. To put it briefly, the fraction-provoking *model* of fair sharing must be made explicit to the pupils at the beginning of instruction through its conflicts with everyday situations (Streefland, 1991).

Fractional language can be used to *describe the results* of fair sharing. In this sense, 'fraction' manifests itself in its conception of part–whole relations, describing the parts that fair sharing results in. A shift to another conception of fraction occurs as soon as part–whole descriptions are applied to *the sharing process itself and its results in advance*. For instance, after having shared an apple with two children, *each of them gets one half of one apple*—'half' here represents the description of the results of sharing. If two or more children come to take part in the sharing, the *apples will be halved* 'halving' refers to the process of dividing in half and anticipates the result before the operation is carried out The shift from speaking about one half of an apple to speaking about halving or taking half means shifting from a part–whole relation to an operator.

The conception of fractions as operators has been emphasised by mathematics educators and mathematicians in many respects (see, for example, Braunfeld & Wolfe, 1966; Freudenthal, 1983; Hilton, 1983; Usiskin, 1979). However, the mediating role that quantities and magnitudes can play in the facilitations of operations with fractions has often (but not always; see, for example, Freudenthal, 1973; Sawyer, 1969) been overlooked.

The aim of this chapter is to present an approach to the teaching of fractions that takes the role of magnitudes into account and aims at moving children's conceptions one step further, to the understanding of fractions as operators. I would like to suggest an answer to the question 'How can we guide primary-school children in their attempts to master an operational concept of fractions—that is, a concept that is applicable in all its operational aspects?'.

In order to answer this question I will pass in review:

- A bird's-eye view on fractions
- Some chocolate bars for some children
- How to proceed? A dilemma
- Table arrangements
- Activity of fair sharing and
- On the way to formal operations.

A BIRD'S-EYE VIEW ON FRACTIONS

Traditionally, fraction-generating fair sharing occurs with one unit only—for example, sharing one apple. The resulting parts are labelled as fractions and then calculation with fractions is introduced. Figure 14.1 illustrates this approach. A unit is divided into four parts which are then labelled $1/4 + 1/4 = 2 \times 1/4 = 2/4 = 1/2$ and so on:

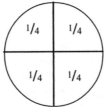

FIG. 14.1. One unit equals four quarters.

This approach does not appear successful. In more recent approaches there has been a switch to, among other changes, the use of situations of fair sharing involving more than one unit. For instance, 'divide 3 chocolate bars among 4 children; how much will each child get?'. The consequences of this simple change were considerable. I will mention them briefly one by one:

- A number-free or qualitative approach in the first instance makes it possible for children to address situations like: some children divide some bars of chocolate; how much will each one get, more or less than a whole bar? What will happen if a few kids join the group of sharers? Will the children then get more or less?
- The comparison of situations and estimation becomes meaningful. For example '3 bars, 4 children', 'does everyone get more or less than $1/2$ of a bar or than a whole?'.
- Because there are several units and the dividers are explicitly participants, the division can be done in various manners. For instance, by first sharing two bars, everyone gets half a bar; then the third bar is shared to all children and everyone gets a quarter bar. The division can also be done by bar; $1/4$ bar for each repeated three times.
- The consequence of using different ways of sharing is that the first notions of the concept of fractions go hand in hand with the (informal) operations. Furthermore, equivalence no longer needs to be exacted from the physical correspondence or parts, as in the traditional approach. It comes naturally from the division; portions like $1/2b + 1/4b$ and $1/4b + 1/4b + 1/4b$ are the same; therefore also $1/2b$ and $1/4b + 1/4b$ are the same. In short: the equivalence becomes more widely operational.
- The different manners of division can occur spontaneously in a year group of pupils, but one can also steer this process by letting it be imagined as

taking place in a coffee shop or a similar place. The speed of the kitchen and service—first two and later one, or one at a time—then determine how things are divided at the table.

- By the presentation of the dividers in the situation, attention can also be drawn—albeit with the necessary limitations—to how they are seated at the table. A separate symbol can be thought up for this purpose (by the pupils).

For example, $\frac{6}{8}$ which stands for 6 bars or something else on the table and 8 children seated around, which leads to $\overset{Q}{4}\ \overset{Q}{4}$, two tables, each with 4 children and therefore 3 bars on each table $\frac{3}{4}\ \frac{3}{4}$, in order to divide fairly. In this manner the fractions are closely related to ratios. Moreover, the seating arrangement can take place in a progressive process of schematisation by applying all sorts of abbreviations to the scheme. Equivalent situations can be brought forward (Fig. 14.2). By the various forms of dividing, each person's portion per table can be determined in the scheme. A close link will be established between the situation $\frac{3}{4}$ and the portion ($^3/_4$b).

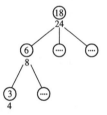

FIG. 14.2.   Scheme for seating arrangement.

The previous point shows that in the suggested approach fractions and ratios are intertwined. Nevertheless we try to follow the course of fractions here.

- Starting from someone's portion—for example, $^1/_4$b, one can look back at the situation of origin, $\frac{1}{4}$, $\frac{2}{8}$, $\frac{3}{12}$, ... to consider equivalences. This can be also done with problems such as: can someone with $^1/_2$b + $^1/_3$b have been sitting at table $\frac{2}{5}$?
- Varied distribution results in a division situation with a number of descriptive relationships, $^1/_2$b + $^1/_4$b or $^1/_4$b + $^1/_4$b + $^1/_4$b or 3 × $^1/_4$b and so on, all standing for each person's portion of $^3/_4$b. This anthology of descriptions for one and the same situation was given the name mini-monograph (Streefland, 1991). By referring back to division situations the pupils can (re)construct mini-monographs. Later on all kinds of other considerations lead to the production of relationships for example, by applying commutativity, '$^1/_2$b + $^1/_4$b' is replaced by '$^1/_4$b + $^1/_2$b', or by considerations of equivalence '6 × $^1/_4$b can be replaced by 3 × $^1/_2$b'.
- In context situations in which division (or measuring) takes place, the objects can be represented by their shapes and by their values (length,

weight, price, and so on). The forms can be represented into visual models, to which the values are then linked and their correspondence can be maintained in the notation, as in the example below.

$^1/_4$b	$^1/_2$b	($^3/_4$b)	1b
(20c)	(40c)	(60c)	(80c)

- $^1/_2$b + $^1/_4$b with a price per bar of 80 cents then becomes $^1/_2$(80c) + $^1/_4$(80c). By way of the result of 60c, one arrives at $^3/_4$b. In this manner these values (of magnitude) become excellent intermediaries for the execution of the operations with fractions in a roundabout manner. In the next section, some of these building blocks will be elaborated further with comments and reflective notes.

SOME CHOCOLATE BARS FOR SOME CHILDREN

In order to start a course on fractions some bars of chocolate are given to some children to share fairly. The ' somes', however, have not been specified any further (Fig. 14.3).

FIG. 14.3. What share?

What will each of the children get when the bars are shared out among them? That depends. . .

What can you tell about the number of bars and children, if each child will get precisely one bar, more than one bar, precisely half a bar . . .
Suppose some more children join the group. What will happen then?

Comments

The previous situation of fair sharing is presented qualitatively. As a consequence the children get access to it as much as possible, not being blocked by numerical constraints and demands. They can ride, so to speak, on their common sense understanding of the situation while at the same time leaning upon their experience and imagination. The children's insight in the situation increases due to the qualitative analysis that is carried out. The teaching and their learning and development are intertwined or integrated.

With respect to fair sharing as a model, I refer to the introduction of this chapter. The importance of fair sharing as an access to fractions is both reflected by the history of mathematics and recognised by many authors from different disciplines, for instance Piaget, Inhelder, and Szeminska (1966), Desforges and Desforges (1980), Frydman and Bryant (1988), Miller (1984), and Streefland (1978), to mention just a few.

The way fraction-provoking fair sharing was interpreted as a model is partly based on Piaget's work. However, fractions defined Piaget's interpretation of fair sharing and not the other way round. Streefland (1991; 1993a) examined how the context of fair sharing can have a long-term role in the teaching–learning process, both through the sharing activities and the (visual) material operated on.

The relationship between fair sharing and fractions is not a question of concretising or illustrating some mathematics but of mathematical activities and mathematics evolving from sharing activities. It concerns the constitution of mental objects (from mathematics), instead of the attainment of concepts (cf. Streefland, 1978).

WHERE DO WE GO FROM HERE? A DILEMMA

The preceding section discussed an introduction to fractions. But what are we aiming at in a course about fractions? This can hardly be said at this stage, but one aspect became very clear. Fractions are about relations: how can they be described and mathematised? By keeping the situation purely qualitative only judgements of the kind . . . 'if there are . . . bars than children then . . .' could occur. And this was exactly the aim: to explore various relations between the numbers of bars and children and their consequences for fair sharing, performed just as a thought experiment. However, when sharing situations get more specified by the numbers of goodies and shareholders, several important questions can be raised. Let me try to illustrate this a little further. Let the situation be, for instance: '24 children share 18 bars of chocolate fairly'.

Now it has already become a mathematised situation. The numbers 24 and 18 reflect the outcomes of the mathematical activity leading to it, which was probably counting in one way or another. This means that a shift has been made from a qualitative to a slightly mathematised situation. Important questions for its further analysis in a mathematical-didactical sense are:

- Does the situation or the context in which it occurs contain meaningful phenomena to shape the teaching–learning process onwards, while moving further into mathematics?
- What are the different accesses to sharing situations as in the preceding example?

The last question provokes the following dilemma, namely:

(a) Either proceeding with sharing the goodies fairly, steered by the number of participants in the situation;

(b) Or proceeding with dividing the participants—that is, spreading them over a varying number of tables, for instance, followed by sharing the goodies corresponding to the share-holders at each table;

(c) Or proceeding with both (a) and (b)?

I will take position (c), while starting with the elaboration of (b).

TABLE ARRANGEMENTS

Let's return to the '24 children share 18 bars' situation. Since the sharing takes place somewhere—and here I hit upon the point of transferring meaning from the context situation to the process of mathematising—one can imagine the sharers as seated around a large table with bars on it. This is what might be represented by a special symbol to be invented by the learners themselves. Let us take a few snapshots from the classroom of what happened in a teaching experiment (cf. Streefland, 1991 pp.75–79).

Snapshot 1. Starting with Table Arrangements

'*De Smickel*' , a pancake-restaurant, on a busy day.

> While the Fractured family and their guests in the birthday party are busy polish–
> ing off their pancakes, an entire school class enters '*De Smickel*'—24 mouths! It is
> very busy! What should the waiter do? Put them all at one table or . . .?

The teacher draws on the blackboard (Fig. 14.4):

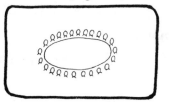

FIG. 14.4.   24 around the table.

The pupils wait, curious but patient.

Or . . . at two tables (Fig. 14.5)?

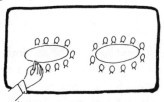

FIG. 14.5. 24 at two tables.

Without any further explanation, the drawing is completed. The class begins to fidget, a sign that a storm of protest, after the initial calm, is not far away. The teacher takes advantage of this change in atmosphere.

Teacher: Boys and girls, this is really a drag, all this drawing.

The group emphatically agrees and a more practical solution is soon found.

Group: You should just write '24' for the class.
T.:   OK, but what should we do with the tables?
G.:   Just make a circle or a square.

On the blackboard appeared: $\underset{24}{\bigcirc}$

T: 24 children at one big table. Now, the food, let's say 18 pancakes.
G.:   In the circle of course!
T: So like this $\underset{24}{\textcircled{18}}$. 24 children at one big table and 18 pancakes on the table.

In this way, with combined effort, the class worked at constructing this symbol which, in turn, became a building block for a diagram that would serve to show the table arrangements: $\underset{24}{\textcircled{18}}$ can be $\underset{12}{\textcircled{9}}$ and $\underset{12}{\textcircled{9}}$ but also $\underset{8}{\textcircled{6}}$ and $\underset{16}{\textcircled{12}}$. Not, in fact, that so much effort was needed; it all went quite naturally and this symbol was an obvious choice.

For the moment, however, we didn't want to make it too complex. *The insight must first be present that each table—regarded as (independent) division situations—produces the same portion for each person.* It was by no means certain that all the children were aware of that or would accept it without question.

Snapshot 2: Schematising

Tree.   Soon, a diagram is drawn on the blackboard (Fig. 14.6).

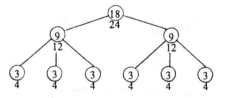

FIG. 14.6. A seating arrangement tree.

'It's just like it was', comment some of the children. And, indeed: dividing 3 whatever it is among 4 people has become a familiar situation.

A more appropriate diagram for *'De Smickel'* would have been as shown in Fig. 14.7. But for clarity's sake it was 'smoothed out'. Too soon, as we would see;

not everyone worked so neatly on paper right away. Just as was the case with the apples with their realistic frills, some of the students would need time here to model the diagram and to do away with the realistic traits, even though everything seemed so obvious at first.

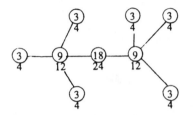

FIG. 14.7. A seating arrangement 'octopus'.

Clara, for instance, who has eaten at *'De Smickel' knows* that the tables there aren't round, so she draws rectangular ones. In Marja's drawing, the branches are at first like octopus's arms, pointing every which way, just as in our example. Alwyn and Kevin just didn't see tables as being connected, so they at first drew separate ones, rather than one connected diagram. They all, however, soon got used to this schematisation and, after a bit of practice, most of them were doing quite well.

When deciding each person's portion, the number-symbols proved too much for Margreet. She drew a distribution—on her own initiative! And she would continue to do this, as would others for some time still.

The potential of this means of schematisation for further progress can be seen directly during each person's construction of seating arrangement trees. Frans, who enjoyed stating his opinion loud and clear, not only demonstrated that he knew that equivalent tables were involved here; he also immediately saw ways of making his diagram more efficient (Fig.14.8). The rest of the diagram (and even more) could be left out. It was all the same anyway!

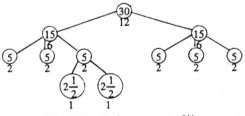

FIG. 14.8. Each person gets $2^1/_2$.

This mathematical equivalence was not immediately as clear to everyone as it was to Frans. After all, there were other ways of looking at it. Michael preferred to sit at $\frac{30}{12}$ because there it would be the most fun with all those children. Margreet viewed the situation more economically and made her decision for $\frac{30}{12}$ rather than

$\overset{\textstyle 13}{6}$ based on the fact that the larger table had 15 more things to eat. She is not alone in this preference, Kevin thinks so too. But Beatrijs says, 'Uh-uh, 'cause there're less children at $\overset{\textstyle 13}{6}$!'

The clashing standpoints are at first furiously defended. General discord! Frans gets involved in the discussion. 'It is all the same,' he says ''cause half of 30 is 15, and half of 12 is 6. So it stays the same!' This sows the seeds of Kevin's change of heart. 'Teacher, teacher,' he calls, demanding attention and pointing (Fig. 14.9.)

FIG. 14.9.   '15 and 15 is 30, and 6 and 6 is 12!'

Kevin explains what he means by his comment. At the same time, the teacher rounds off the lesson saying: ' But I understand why Beatrijs, Margreet and Kevin think like they do. They only paid attention to *one* of the numbers: either to the things to eat or to the number of children sharing them. But what we've *learned*—and that's hard—is to pay attention to *both* numbers *at once.* You have to look at both numbers when comparing— that's what it is about!'

Snapshot 3: Short-cuts

Nevertheless, we still have a long way to go. Frans demonstrated spontaneously that the diagram can be shortened. Others, too, soon constructed diagrams of this nature. A variety of possibilities for shortening would yet appear in the course of the future learning processes; leaving out or erasing branches, filling in only essential parts of the diagram . . . and so on. The access and exit proved to be particularly important.

Access: If you start your diagram with more than two tables, you will reach the end sooner. For instance see Fig. 14.10 and then (if possible) further.

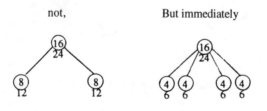

FIG. 14.10. Numerical shortening.

An uneven number of people sharing can help the children to discover this.

Exit: The quicker a familiar division situation is recognised in a table in the diagram, the sooner one can leave the tree to determine each person's portion. And then there are all the different ways of serving up and distributing. Consequently situation and result are not only symbolically distinguished, but at the same time closely connected. $\frac{③}{4}$ will belong inseparably to $^3/_4$ and vice versa. It must become an automatism. On the other hand, from $^3/_4$ via $\frac{③}{4}$ the series $\frac{③}{4}, \frac{⑥}{8}, \frac{⑨}{12}, ...$ can then be called up as a way of thinking. Eventually, the trees will be pruned back to no more than trunks, for example (Fig. 14.11), thereby producing a class of equivalent tables similar to ratio tables. In this way an initiated process of progressive schematisation can be continued for a long time to come.

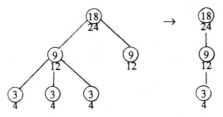

FIG. 14.11. From tree to trunk.

The computer was of assistance here. A computer program for seating arrangements was written in Fort on an IBM. It aimed at a fast repetition of the schematisation process just as has been described previously. Abbreviations of the schemes that had been observed in the individual schematisation processes of the pupils when using pencil and paper were assimilated in the program. The computer program used these moments to enable the children to choose their preferences in making short-cuts in the schemes. The use of the computer was justified in our view because a learning process of several months could now be speeded up in order to reflect on one's own learning.

Comments

The symbol created not only represents the sharing situation but also reflects it. An advantage of constructing such a symbol is that the sharing situation (table-symbol) and its outcome after fair sharing (fraction) become distinct mathematically. Moreover, the table-symbol can be applied as a building block for schematising the different arrangements of tables. Imagining the process of arranging whatever company around the tables supports the process of schematisation. At first children will follow their preferences of halving (and/or doubling). As a consequence many of the constructed schemes turn out to be symmetrical, although different ways of partitioning the company may occur as well. From the construction of symmetrical schemes evolves the leaving out of 'branches', that is the application of short-cuts.

Reflection

The symbol for the situation functions as a metonym and serves as a building block for the process of schematisation. The imagined process of arranging tables as one of the possible actions within the context of a restaurant also supports the process of schematisation with meaning. It serves as a context—or situation—model.

The schematisation process develops progressively. The first curtailments to be applied by the pupils are justified by contextual arguments, expressed in considerations of symmetry, for instance: if two identical 'tables' $\frac{9}{12}$ occur in a schema, then table-arrangements with 'branches' for one of them can be left out, that is, schematising can proceed in a more simplified way. Gradually the pupils' focus of attention will shift from the contextual meaning of the schematisation to its mathematical properties, that is the numbers involved and their potential for division. A provisional formal stage will be attained when the greatest common divisor of both numbers involved directs the schematisation process from the start.

The ratio-table evolves from the schematisation process in a natural manner as has been shown. Together with the shift from contextual to mathematical meaning it will make the time ripe yet for the establishing and formulating of rules by the pupils themselves, like the unit-ratio or the cross-products rule.

DEALING WITH THE COURSE OF FAIR SHARING

Let us start with an example:

> Divide 3 bars of chocolate among 4 children. Each child will get three fourths (or three quarters) of a bar, providing the sharing is done fairly. [First the learners estimate their answers.] Does each person get more or less than half a bar?

Upon deciding that it is more than half a bar, the pupils can begin to distribute half bars and then figure out what to do with the rest. What finally might result after individual work and negotiation in the classroom afterwards, is (a) First two, then one (Fig. 14.12).

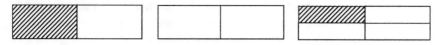

FIG. 14.12.   Showing first two, then one.

Everyone gets: half a bar (of chocolate) and later a quarter of a bar more. This might be gradually symbolised:

$1/2$ of a bar + $1/4$ of a bar
$1/2$ bar + $1/4$ bar
$1/2$ b + $1/4$ b

One by one (Fig. 14.13):

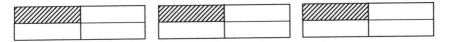

FIG. 14.13. Sharing one by one.

Everyone gets:

¹/₄ bar + ¹/₄ bar + ¹/₄ bar
¹/₄b + ¹/₄b + ¹/₄b, which is
3 times ¹/₄ bar, 3 × ¹/₄b, ³/₄b

(b) All three at once (Fig.14.14). Two children get:

1 bar − ¹/₄ bar or 1b − ¹/₄b

and two children get:

¹/₂b + ¹/₄b or ¹/₄b + ¹/₂b

(see also Bidwell, 1982)

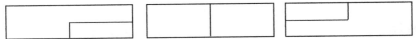

FIG. 14.14. Sharing three at once.

This example illustrates that fair sharing is a compound process of division and portioning, of composing portions from parts, which finds ways of informal operations with fractions and streamlining actions leading to shortcuts. The following expressions show this symbolically:

¹/₄b + ¹/₄b + ¹/₄b = 3 × ¹/₄b = ³/₄b = ¹/₄b + ¹/₄b + ¹/₄b
¹/₂b + ¹/₄b = ³/₄b = ¹/₂b+ ¹/₄b
¹/₂b + ¹/₄b = ³/₄b = ¹/₄b +¹/₂b
1b − ¹/₄b = ³/₄b = 1b − ¹/₄b

Comparison of the first and the second line in the example shows that two fourths of a bar are hidden in one half bar and so on. The material drawn has already showed this. It now can become anchored mentally and symbolically that ¹/₂b is what might be called a *pseudonym* for ¹/₄b + ¹/₄b or ²/₄ and vice versa ('*schuilnaam*' in Dutch sounds less learned).

While discussing their findings on the fair-sharing tasks the children can make inventories of all the different expressions found and later on produce their own expressions based on assignments like. "Tell your own stories of ⁵/₆." Following on from this can be:

- exploration of situations like 'Divide 6 bars of chocolate among 8 children' and '5 bars among 4 children' and so on with an eye to equivalent outcomes and outcomes to be described with mixed numbers.

Consider the first example. Children might apply strategies like:

- referring to '3 bars, 4 children', but 'now it is doubled';
- sharing one by one;
- sharing out halves and quarters and so on (cf. Streefland, 1991).

It will be obvious that this kind of activity will lead to the production of a variety of equivalencies, like $3/4b = 6/8b$, $5/4b = 1 1/4b$ and so on, due to varying distribution in situations with larger numbers.

It should be clear that all sorts of issues of reconstructing having to do with the performance of distribution activities might arise. For instance, determining the course of the division from the numerical portions is also a possible situation.

Example: 5 bars are divided among 8 children; each child gets $1/4b + 1/4b + 1/8b$. How were the bars shared? Make a drawing of it.

Comments

It is striking that in fair sharing as a varied source for the production of fractions, the concept of fraction and the *informal operating* with fractions are directly related to each other, although it must be said that from the very beginning the portions are described by means of linguistic tools that will still have to acquire their meaning as fractions during the course of learning.

The fractions $3/4b$ came into being in many ways. In this kind of approach it is impossible to constitute mentally the *part–whole aspect* of a fraction without becoming involved in insightful or informal or rule-anticipating operations because the many (de)compositions in which they evolve from fair sharing. Fair sharing probably provides a blueprint for fractions, the part–whole concept related to equivalence, mixed numbers and operational relations.

However, it must be admitted that just a tip of the veil has been raised and many questions were left unanswered. What about:

- the operator-quality of fractions, or, better, the behaviour of fractions *in* operations?
- the role of a unit fraction as a building block for the constitution of a more general idea of fraction?
- What about the main operations?
- What about the rules for the four main operations? Will they still have to be imposed on the learners?

We are progressing steadily into the domain of fractions but some patience is needed, because we are entering a field of genuine complexity. Before proceeding, some further reflection is still needed.

Reflection

Besides referring to fair sharing it is also necessary to refer here to the idea of table arrangements and the connected process of schematisation once more. First we should consider the question of the fractional language. Fractions as part–whole describers do indeed refer to something; bars of chocolate, pizzas and so on. What needs to be done is to convert the objects to be shared into objects of reference in the notation afterwards. The children cannot learn to think of ¼ as the mathematical object 'rational number' unless its 'rationalness' is understood in a variety of situations. That is why it is necessary to keep open the connection with the concrete source where the fractions were provoked by fair sharing. This is why in the notation the objects will maintain their presence, either written in full terms or abbreviated, unless the context makes it clear what the applied fractions are referring to. Although much more could be said about the processes of abstraction, generalisation and unification, at this stage it is sufficient to consider only this need to keep the referred situations present in the pupils' minds.

My second reflective note concerns the intertwinement of learning strands for both fractions and ratio and proportion. The schematisation process based on the situation-model of table arrangements can be interwoven with the fair-sharing branch of the course on fractions. Schematising aims at bringing sharing down to situations with lower terms; that is, at generating situations where portions are equivalent although numbers are smaller. That means that the pupils can shift to varying the factual fair sharing at any stage of the schematisation process in order to decide the outcome of the original situations. Thus a close conceptual connection between $\frac{x}{y}$ and outcome 'x/y of....', describing everyone's individual portion, will be constructed mentally.

ON THE WAY TO FORMAL OPERATIONS

The famous German author and poet Goethe (1749–1832) once wrote a very small poem on whole and fractional numbers. His conclusion at the end of it, was (cf. Streefland, 1993a):

> Whole numbers won't bear a secret for you
> But fractions a big one, sure they do!'

A famous anecdote reflects this secret, or so it seems. It is about Anwar's last will:

> An old Arab, Anwar was his name, decreed before he died that the eldest son inherit one-half, his second one-fourth and his younger son one-fifth of all his

camels. He died leaving 19 camels and his three sons could not agree on how to divide them. A dervish—passing by on his camel—observed the disagreement, dismounted and stated helpfully: 'I will loan you my camel'. Each son now took his share of the twenty camels. The dervish then remounted his beast of burden and continued along his way, leaving all three heirs contented. And so did come to pass the last will of Anwar.

How did the dervish avoid the threatening conflict between Anwar's sons while they tried in vain to divide their inheritance? As Anwar's story shows, the presence of either a *non fitting* quantity (value of magnitude or number) or a *fitting* one decides the solvability of the problem. From the 19 camels, the first son would receive $9\frac{1}{2}$' the second $4\frac{3}{4}$; the third son would receive $3\frac{4}{5}$ if their number of 19 remained unchanged.

Anwar's heritage could be shared after the dervish loaned his camel. Moreover the differences between the subsequent shares for the three sons can be determined very easily and expressed in either different numbers of camels (10, 5 and 4 respectively) or in different parts of the herd of 20 camels (of 20 camels = 10 camels and so on). The dervish's wisdom shows how we need to analyse mediating quantities, as he did with the number of camels, by converting it from a non-fitting into a mediating quantity.

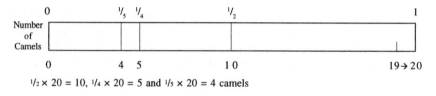

$\frac{1}{2} \times 20 = 10$, $\frac{1}{4} \times 20 = 5$ and $\frac{1}{5} \times 20 = 4$ camels

FIG. 14.15. The sharing of Anwar's heritage.

An experiment (with 9–10-year-olds) carried out by A. Lek (1992) in the Netherlands stressed the use of mediating quantities for learning operations with fractions. Before discussing an example I will sum up some introductory activities:

- the exploration of situations of fair sharing with bars of chocolate, counting different numbers of smaller blocks, like 4,6,8,12 ... and so on and representing them visually;
- the description of the results in fractional language with notations reflecting the objects of reference, that is 'bar' or 'b' in the present case;
- thinking of fitting numbers of sharers for different bars; for instance a bar of 24 pieces can be shared with 4 kids, with 6, and so on, and their visual representations;
- determining and comparing different parts like $\frac{1}{4}b$, $\frac{2}{3}b$, $\frac{3}{5}b$, $1\frac{1}{4}b$, and so on, when the numbers of pieces in the subsequent bars are known. For

instance: suppose 2/3b and 3/5b must be taken from bars of 15 pieces. Will that be possible? In the case of 3/4b, 5/6b and 15 pieces the pupils will say 'no', due to experiences from outside the classroom, because it is difficult, if not impossible, to break the small blocks into smaller pieces.

Example: looking for a fitting bar of chocolate.
Problem: Koeno gets 3/4 of a bar, Marja gets 5/6 of a bar. Who will get more? How much all together? How much will remain from a whole bar, when Koeno has got his share?

$$\text{Koeno gets } \frac{3}{4} \text{ of a bar}$$

$$\text{Marja gets } \frac{5}{6} \text{ of a bar}$$

How much do they get altogether?
How much is left from Koeno's bar?

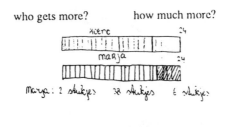

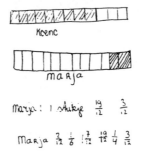

What is striking in the solutions are the differences in level. There were children who described the outcome by means of 'so many pieces'. But fractions were also applied, even equivalent fractions and converting an improper fraction into a mixed number. What is important, too, is the use of different numbers of blocks in the bars, 12 and 24, reflecting different ways of reasoning. For example: Koeno 3/4 of a bar. A bar of four pieces would fit, but since Marja will get 5/6 of a bar it would be necessary to break the pieces. This is too difficult, so I will try 6 pieces . . ., 12 pieces or 4 times 6 pieces. The children are free to find their numbers of pieces. Afterwards there will be a discussion of what the most efficient methods are.

The children in the experiment showed a preference for 'striplike' bars that is with the pieces in a row. This kind of representation acts in the discussion too, while considering the different approaches.

On the blackboard might appear, for instance:

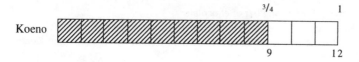

that is: the parts of the bar on top and the numbers of pieces at the bottom. This is a pre-stage to the use of the number-line with two scales.

The comparison is easy now and can be described in different ways as the example showed.

Later one can shift to weights and prices of the bars. Then the numbers for the weights or the prices will be at the bottom of the visual models. For instance: suppose a bar costs 60 cents. How many cents did Koeno's portion cost?

There are several possibilities for the children to find the answer. For instance, by making use of the numbers of pieces, or by partitioning the amount of cents.

Two final remarks on this question will be emphasised:

1. As far as the mediating quantities are concerned, the use of so-called natural magnitudes like hour, day, week, year, dozen, metre and so on, is important here.

2. The present approach can be characterised by the gradual shift that is made from a fitting number of pieces in the context of bars of chocolate to the determination of the least common multiple of the denominators involved.

The shift is enacted in rather a natural manner along the following sequence (just for the bars);

- problems with given numbers of blocks in the bars;
- the pupils find the numbers of blocks themselves;
- the pupils are encouraged to find bars with the least possible numbers of blocks;

- the denominators of the given fractions are compared with the least numbers of block as found. For instance

2/3 and 3/4 → 12 pieces

and 2/3 and 5/6 → 6 pieces.

Why?

Comments

From the activity of fair sharing we moved to formal operations with fractions. In doing so, some important things happened. At the same time it must be admitted that operating with fractions at a formal level is far away yet or so it seems.

Let me first consider in more detail 'the important things' that happened. Exploring the sharing of chocolate bars and representing them visually are important activities. Why? Well, the bars—and many different goodies to be shared—embody shape and content. What were the bars' shapes? Rectangles and strips. As soon as partionings have been both carried out in the visual material and symbolised, one more shift can be made to the bars' content—that is, to number of pieces, price, or weight of the bars.

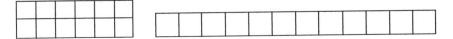

The objects, represented in the notation $1/2b + 1/4b$, can now be replaced by the different content numbers—that is the values of the different magnitudes. The *part–whole* character of the fractions undergoes a decisive change: they become fractions in *operators* (halving 12 or taking one quarter of 12).

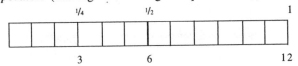

$$1/2b + 1/4b = 1/2(12) + 1/4(12) = 6 + 3 = 3/4\,(12)$$

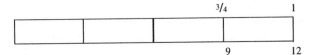

which means $3/4b$.

Or, provided the bar costs 40 cents

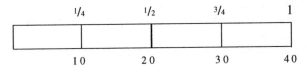

$$1/2b + 1/4b = 1/2\,(40) + 1/4(40) = 20 + 10 = 30 = 3/4(40) = 3/4b$$

The shift from the description of situations of division to operational situations with fractions is a rather complicated one because this shift concerns:

- converting part–whole descriptions into fractions in operators;
- converting the objects into visual representations connected with the values of magnitude that describe the content of the objects.

Visual models can evolve from the visual representations as was shown. Procedures for the remaining main operations can be developed in the same manner. For instance, subtraction evolves in a natural manner for the (additive) comparison of two (or more) situations of fair sharing and their outcomes. An example of comparison has already been given. Similarly, multiplication and division can be treated by starting with multiplicative comparisons. For instance:

Koeno got ³/₄ of a bar and Marja ⁵/₆. How many times does Koeno's ³/₄ of a bar fit into Marja's ⁵/₆ of a bar or vice-versa?

The way in which both portions can be made comparable more easily has been shown in detail already. We need the same measures for both of them, that is strips of 12, 24, . . . pieces

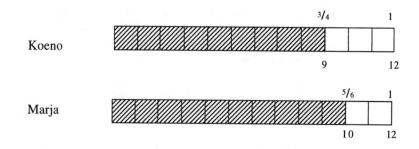

It turns out that it is either 1 and ¹/₉ time(s) or ⁹/₁₀ time(s)

Problems of multiplicative comparison of two different quantities or magnitudes can be prepared in this way. The example shows that shifting from a particular unit to a new one during the solution is decisive for the correctness of the final outcome.

The following example shows that this shift from one unit to another is not self-evident at all, especially when two different magnitudes are involved. Thus multiplicative comparison necessarily needs to be met in the course on fractions.

Somebody went to Paris in his car with a full tank of petrol. After about ²/₃ of the way he noticed that a quarter of the tank was still left.
Will he get there with the petrol he has left?

This is a question of multiplicative comparison, because two different, although related, magnitudes are involved. So how can we expect the pupils to consider such situations from a ratio (that is a multiplicative) point of view, if the programme they went through did not contain situations of comparison and order?

The children might fall into the trap of an additive point of view, as Leila did (Fig. 14.16). Her approach to the problem is promising indeed—and very dervish-like because she succeeded in coping with mediating quantities. But at the crucial stage of comparison she fell into the trap of additive comparison. Or is it the course designer who should be blamed for overlooking teaching the recommended way of comparison?

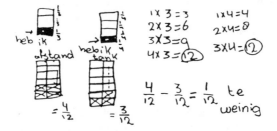

FIG. 14.16.   Leila's solution.

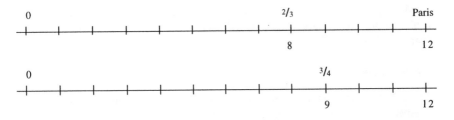

After all, as the number lines show, 9 parts of the tank were used up for 8 parts of the distance. Since the complete distance needs to be covered, the question is how many times do the 8 parts (of the distance) fit into the 9 parts (of the petrol used)? The diagram above shows the outcome: 1¹/₈ times. Hence, the remaining petrol will not be sufficient to reach Paris without refilling the tank, because 1¹/₈ tank will be needed to cover the whole distance. As Anthony showed (Fig.14.17) taking a ratio- or multiplicative standpoint was very important here.

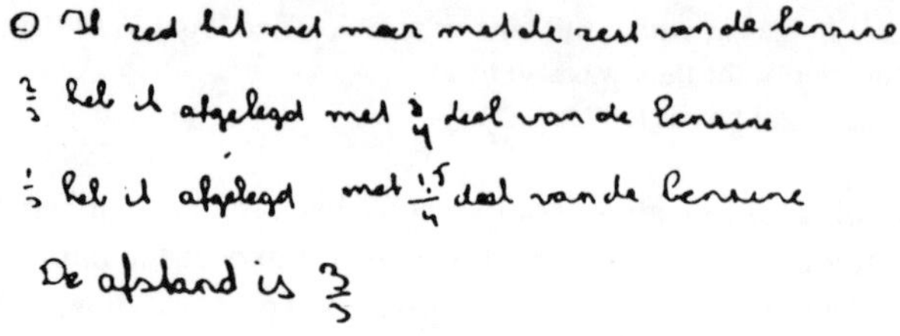

O Ik red het niet maar met de rest van de benzine

⅔ heb ik afgelegd met ¾ deel van de benzine

⅓ heb ik afgelegd met 1.5/4 deel van de benzine

De afstand is ⅗

I won't get there with the rest of the petrol
I've travelled 2/3 with 3/4 of the petrol
I've travelled 1/3 with 1.5/4 of the petrol
The distance is 3/3.

FIG. 14.17. Anthony's solution.

The phenomenon of the multiplicative standpoint (comparison, ordering) needs to be considered not only in the study of fractions but also in the teaching of ratio and percent. Moreover, the courses need to be linked with each other and at some stages even interwoven with the course on fractions. Some advantages of my proposal are:

- a conceptual connection will be established between the multiplication and division of fractions;
- the problems to be raised are rather natural in character, and
- can be solved at different levels, varying from context-bound to more abstract.

Much preparatory work can be done in the fair-sharing stage of the course. It is also important to start with comparisons that are natural from a multiplicative point of view—for instance, the comparison of $3^1/_4b$ and $3/_4b$.

Reflection

The previous section leads to four questions of major importance from the perspective of long-term learning, namely:

(a)   the model function of bars of chocolate;
(b)   the part played by measurement;
(c)   the question of abstraction, and
(d)   the question of generalisation.

These are briefly considered below.

Bar model.   The bar of chocolate functions as an important context or situation model. This is not only due to the fact that the bar unites in itself both discrete and continuous quantities but also that the discreteness is experienced by the children: 'You cannot break the pieces of a bar easily, so I will go in search for a better fitting bar'.

For instance $3/4 \times 5/6 = 5/6$ reminds one of a bar of 6 pieces from which 5 need to be taken; this in turn does not fit very well to take $3/4$ from, so it is necessary to try a bar of 12 pieces, and so on.

Measurement.   The example of the way to Paris and petrol-consumption showed that situations of measurement are also important. In general, the number of participants in a division situation determines how to 'measure' the portions; the units change depending on the situation. In contrast, conventional measures have pre-established (standard) units.

Measurement of length, for instance, provides a clear case.

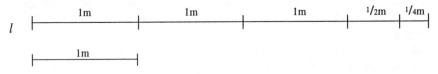

Let length or path l be measured with a unit of 1m. After pacing 1m three times the process ceases. To continue the measurement in metres 1m needs to be refined; taking $1/2$m will help.

Then the process continues but ceases again. The refined unit ($1/2$m) needs another refinement $1/2$ of $1/2$ of 1m = $1/4$m. The length l equals 3m and $1/2$m and $1/4$m. If the first refinement of the unit 1m were $1/4$m then the process would have resulted in $l = 3m + 3/4m = 33/4m$. This means that equivalent fractions (and operational connections) can also be produced by means of measurement. Shifting from the unit metre to the submeasure centimetre opens the door to operating via this mediating submeasure.

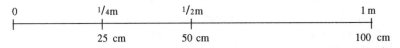

All kinds of connections can be established and investigated in this manner. Moreover the transition of a fraction as a part–whole description into an operator can be experienced in this way time and again. Needless to say, measuring time with its various submeasures (day, hours, minutes and so on) is a wealthy source of shifting from fractions to whole numbers and not only for that (see the chapter by Magina and Hoyles in this book).

In measurement, the existence of different units provides for a variety of submeasures, which can act as mediating quantities to carry out the shift from fractions to whole numbers as a framework for solving the problems with fractions. This is a more suitable level for the learners in their initial approach to fractions as operators.

From this course of thought about fractions, learners develop operational control over part–whole and operator-aspects of fractions. This means that both the language of fractions and other tools, like visual models, can be mastered.

The questions of abstraction and generalisation will be addressed in the discussion below.

DISCUSSION

At a certain stage, as was shown, the children learned what $\frac{1}{2}$b, $\frac{1}{4}$b, $\frac{1}{2}$b + $\frac{1}{4}$b, and so on (with b = bar) mean or represent. The b will receive new values like 100 grammes or 200 cents. In the terms of Van den Brink (1989) the pupils are given the opportunity to 'decorate' $\frac{1}{2}$b + $\frac{1}{4}$b and so on, together with their subsequent visualisations, with new, context-restricted meanings. Or, to express it differently, the same fractions appear in varying situations, time and again, only the way they are named and the quantities and magnitudes they refer to, differ each time. As a consequence the learner will observe that $\frac{1}{2}$b + $\frac{1}{4}$b are not different due to these new 'decorations'. The fractions remain what they are, and thus in time become what they are to the pupils, i.e. formal fractions, mathematical objects or noöumena (cf. Freudenthal, 1983, ch.2), gradually freed from their context-restrictedness and at the same time remaining operational. The process of abstraction in this sense is not carried out by 'taking away from' but rather by 'adding to', due to the shifting of (context) environment to environment. As other context environments are assigned to the same models, notations and operations, a more formal fraction construction results in the written representation as well as in the minds of the learners. During this process of 'abstracting by addition' there is at the same time a movement from the concrete, contextual content into mathematical form. This process is reflected in the way notations, schematisation and visual models develop. There is a gradual exchange of concrete, contextual meaning and form into mathematical meaning and form. It is a process of formalisation, not by imposing mathematical formalism on the learners, but by enabling them to formalise phenomena from reality in a mathematical manner, shaping them mathematically. The learner who gets stuck in the context, nevertheless can follow the course to some extent, albeit still at the level where the mental object fraction is constituted but not formalised.

Some snapshots of a new course on fractions have been given, from a mathematical-didactical point of view most of the time. In retrospect, however, this is more than a sketch of a course. It is also a sketch of a framework for courses on fractions, because many different elaborations are still possible. I mentioned, for instance, 'time' as a theme for fractions; 'time' with its dial as a dynamical model for pizzas or pancakes; a dial that can be 'unrolled' as a time line on which fractions and the numbers of the different submeasures can go hand in hand to solve all kind of problems via mediating quantities. It is possible to develop a coherent approach to fractions and even to support the teaching-learning process by means of computer-environments for fractions (Zuidema & Van der Gaag 1993), provided these are justified sufficiently in a mathematical-didactical manner.

Although there is already some evidence in support of the approach suggested here, some aspects of this proposal need further investigation. This need for more evidence does not detract from the scientific status of this chapter, because provoking questions and raising hypotheses about how to promote children's understanding are important activities in the science of mathematics education.

15 Didactic Engineering

Régine Douady
IREM, Université PARIS 7, France

INTRODUCTION

In this chapter, we are concerned with the relation between what the teacher intends to teach in mathematics, and what the pupils are likely to learn. The verbs *to teach, to learn, to know* can carry various meanings and we shall clarify the sense in which we use them here.

Didactical engineering denotes a set of classroom sequences which are conceived, linked together and organised in time by an *engineer-teacher* in order to carry out a learning project for a population of pupils.

In the course of exchanges between the teacher and the pupils, the project evolves under the reaction of the pupils, and also under the choices and decisions of the teacher. Didactical engineering is both a *product*, resulting from an *a-priori* analysis—and a *process*, resulting from an adaptation to the implementation of the product in the dynamic conditions of a classroom. We are concerned with the various factors that govern the elaboration of didactical engineering and their interdependence.

Didactical engineering also refers to a research method which is especially useful in dealing with the complexity of the classroom. This method is widespread in French research. (We refer the interested reader to Douady, 1987; Artigue & Perrin-Glorian, 1991a; Artigue, 1992.)

This chapter is not a report of a research project. Its aim is to reflect on proposals for teaching specific aspects of mathematics, based on didactical choices which are analysed, argued and justified by existing research about the

373

mathematical topics from the cognitive (and classroom) point of view. We also consider the social aspects of teaching by analysing the didactical contract—that is, the implicit or explicit agreement between teachers and pupils about what it means to learn mathematics and what role this learning plays in their relationship—because this didactical contract can sometimes get in the way of learning. In analysing the didactical contract, we discuss the constraints to which teachers are subject, their possible choices, and the decisions they can come to in order to obtain a balance between accepting the constraints in the situation and fulfilling their own aspirations.

We focus on the relation between *the building of meaning* and *the capitalisation of knowledge* by the pupils. We also consider the importance of these processes for the teachers and on the role that they want to assign to the processes in the classroom.

However, there is an even more basic question of sociological order, which constrains the direction of possible didactical actions: What is the place of knowledge in school for the teacher and for the pupils? Is it at stake in the didactical relation? In the first part of the chapter, we consider how the choices and decisions of the teachers vary according to whether mathematical knowledge is or is not an issue, for themselves or for their pupils. We can then turn to examples of didactical engineering, where the teaching of specific mathematics topics is considered: this will be described in the second part of the chapter. In the conclusion, we summarise the elements that we consider as essential for the progression of the knowledge of the pupils.

A. MATHEMATICAL KNOWLEDGE IN THE DIDACTIC RELATION

1. What is it to Know Mathematics? What is it to Learn?

When a teacher and students come together in a class, the expectation is that the teacher is there in order to teach some knowledge, and that the students are there in order to learn this same knowledge. I shall say what meaning I give here to the verbs 'to know, to teach, to learn'.

To know mathematics has a double aspect. On the one hand it is to have available, at a functional level, certain concepts and theorems that can be used to solve problems and interpret information, and also to be able to *pose* new questions ... The situations or problems are generators of relations between concepts, whether these are expressed in problem statements, or are mobilised for dealing with the problem. Concepts and relations can therefore be partially external to the mathematics, or entirely internal to its subject area. The concepts and theorems have the *status of tool*. The tools are set in a *context*, under the action and control of a *person* (or of a group) at a *given moment of time*. This aspect of knowing leads to a *semantic dimension* of meaning.

To know mathematics, is also to be able to identify concepts and theorems as elements of a scientifically and socially recognised corpus of knowledge. It is also to be able to formulate definitions, and to state theorems belonging to this corpus and to prove them. That is why I maintain that the concepts and the theorems concerned have the *status of object*. They are *decontextualised, depersonalised* (even if they are designated by a proper noun) and *atemporal*.

The work involved in the process of decontextualisation and depersonalisation contributes to the capitalisation of knowledge. *The work involved in recontextualisation, and in handling problems which this entails, contributes to deepening and extending meaning.* Such activity does not preclude the acquisition of particular techniques or facts, which may be provisional.

Concepts, like theorems, can be worked on, modified according to the situations where they are called upon to be used, and this can cause new concepts to emerge, which in their turn can be worked on, interpreted, modified, generalised. For theorems, we can explore the domain for which they are *valid*: imagine variations, construct proofs, or consider constructing counter-examples to assure ourselves that they are not possible. Analysing situations that produce impossibilities, or have to be rejected, forms part of the meaning of the situation under study. It contributes to giving a meaning to the mathematical tools. In all cases, we are led to set up relationships between different concepts, possibly across them, from different frameworks of study.

This is notably the case when the problem requires us to set up a symbolic space within which the problem is translated into a form that is acceptable for study. This process, which is very powerful and common in mathematics, provides the opportunity *for creating something new from what is already known*.

Setting up these relations is also a *source of meaning for those who do it*. This work can be carried out on the tools adapted for use with a problem, as well as on the objects, so as to enlarge their significance, without necessarily leading to a complete understanding or their precise (and aesthetic) formulation. It requires respect for a set of *internal rules* of mathematics and recourse to *different modes of expression*.

Conformity to rules permitted for written mathematics, and in mathematical argument, is another component of meaning, which we refer to as the *syntactic dimension*. *To teach*, for a teacher, is to create those conditions that will, in the end, enable the students to come to know. *To learn*, for a student, is to become involved in an intellectual activity, whose consequence is to have at one's disposal some knowledge, with its double aspect of tool and object. In order for teaching and learning to take place, there must therefore be some *knowledge*, that is *an object that is important, indeed essential, as part of the exchange between teacher and students*, and this knowledge has to be something that is at stake as part of the school experience.

However, reality may be something completely different from this ideal situation, where knowledge is the core of the relationship between teachers and pupils in school. The role that knowledge plays for teachers and pupils constrains the type of didactical contract that the teachers and the pupils can develop in their classroom. Different possibilities besides the ideal situation must be considered, depending on whether the teacher views mathematical knowledge as central or not and whether the pupils view mathematical knowledge as central or not.

1. Knowledge can be at stake for the teacher, but not at all for some of the pupils.   Then, two elements influence the teachers' decisions, or at least shape their expectations: (a) What does it mean for these pupils to go to school? What do they expect from the school? What does it mean for them to learn? and (b) What is the proportion of pupils in the class for whom knowledge is not at stake in school?

These pupils may just want to go from one grade to the next, and go as far as possible in the system so as to get a good job. They may go to school to learn about life, to make friends, and to manage in life. It makes no difference to them whether they learn mathematics there or anything else. Whatever their intentions may be when entering the school, pupils succeed or fail more or less in their personal projects.

Teachers, on the other hand, may in this situation try to defend their convictions about mathematics or simply try to survive (their only option in some cases!), depending on their personal histories, their own representations and knowledge of mathematics, their will to convince and the strength of the constraints to which they are subject in the situation.

When knowledge is central to the teacher but not to the pupils, there are two possibilities for the teacher, which may be followed according to the circumstances:

- either the teachers give up, in which case there is nothing to consider seriously about mathematics teaching and learning;
- or they maintain their requirement that knowledge should be at the core of their relationship with the pupils.

If they maintain their commitment to teaching, there are two possibilities, at least at the beginning of the school year:

- The teacher enters into conflict with the pupils straight away (and only some students will learn and pass);
- The teacher agrees to enter the pupils' logic, at least temporarily and tries to make the didactic contract evolve progressively. The teacher's aim is to change the relation of most pupils in the class towards mathematics. This will be an extreme challenge for the teacher who gets involved, through mathematics, in a process of changing pupils' attitudes to school, teacher–pupil relations, and the relations between pupils in school. This requires that

the teacher puts the pupils in a position to make choices, to test effects, to control their own learning, and possibly give up on the first choices and make new choices. The teacher must make sure that the pupils have at their disposal the minimum means in order to play this role. With respect to the didactical contract, this implies that the pupils agree to enter the role of actors and not take refuge in a passive role. In this learning context the teacher must play what Brousseau (1988, p.325) has called the *devolution game*: "devolution is an act by which the teacher makes the pupil accept the responsibility of an (a-didactical) learning situation, and him/herself accepts the consequences of that transfer". An example of such a situation in the form of a short chronicle will be presented in the second part of this chapter.

However, this situation is hard to manage, as well as the pupils who refuse the mathematical game. The teacher may attempt to play with the affective dimension. This will work for a while, possibly for a year, but there is not enough stability to ensure the building of a critical mass of knowledge that could create a new relation towards mathematics. The temptation is then great for the teacher to give up on knowledge and make do with the techniques or algorithms, more or less accurately memorised, which will lead pupils away from whatever could make sense for them.

2. Knowledge is at stake neither for the teacher nor for the pupils. In this case, in order for teachers to do their job as teachers and for the pupils to do their job as pupils, the class will have to perform a didactical fiction. The teacher will teach and the pupils will "learn", they will be evaluated, and most of them will get satisfactory grades.

But what about the mathematics that they were supposed to teach and learn? Well, teachers' usual response is to ask pupils to perform tasks that are fragmented into elementary subtasks, algorithmised until a reasonable percentage of the pupils can answer in a satisfactory way.

The consequence of such a choice is that the meaning of the mathematical activity is sacrificed. The pupils have no way of controlling their production, except to re-do work in the same way. The lack of reliability of knowledge developed in this way is well known. Within this lack of commitment to knowledge, there is no reason for pupils to control their own learning. Evaluation is the business of the teacher, and the teacher is more and more appealed to in order to check whether answers are correct, with no way for pupils to structure their own knowledge. Resort to repetitive exercises becomes unavoidable. Pupils understand less and less why they have to do mathematics. But the teacher succeeds in getting the course delivered. If the assessment tests are well chosen—small questions in keeping with habits—enough pupils will pass their examinations. For the teacher and also for the pupils, survival is ensured.

3. Knowledge is at stake for some pupils but not for the teacher. There is a risk that pupils who come to school in order to learn something, who are interested in mathematics when it is the object of teaching, may be disappointed. Such pupils might then reject the mathematics lessons and also the school as a whole, if they feel that it does not fulfil its role. Then, they may look for knowledge or another centre of interest elsewhere or start a conflict with their teachers. This situation is not an improbable one and it occurs in heterogeneous classes where, even if teachers are able to detect that there is a problem, they do not really grasp the situation.

4. Knowledge is at stake for the teacher and for the pupils. This is the most favourable situation as far as mathematics is concerned. However the construction of meaning does not automatically imply the capitalisation of knowledge.

The theory of conceptual fields (Vergnaud, 1991), the theory of situations (Brousseau, 1987, 1990), the tool–object dialectic, the interplay between frameworks and conceptual windows (Douady, 1987b, 1991, 1992), metacognitive representations (Bautier & Robert, 1988; Robert & Robinet, 1989) are efficient tools for understanding and organising the relationship of the various actors of the didactical system towards mathematics, and helping the pupils to conceptualise reality.

B. EXAMPLES OF DIDACTICAL ENGINEERING

In this section we first recount an example of changes in the relationship towards mathematics in a class of 10–11-year-old pupils. Later we give one example of didactical engineering. It is centred on algebraic calculus and deals mainly with the meaning of certain algebraic writing. It is micro-engineering organised around a problem where several notions coming under various frameworks interact. It lasts for three classes of one and a half hours each. Interplay between frameworks acts as a motor of the didactical progression.

1. Mental Arithmetic in CM2: A Chronicle

The fifth year of elementary school, pupils 10–11 years old.

1.1. Circumstances

The setting is an area with brand new blocks of flats inhabited for the most part by large families who typically are in difficult social or economic situations. The teacher is recently appointed to the school. But he is an experienced teacher, and he has been a member of our research team in the didactics of mathematics for several years.

He meets his new class in September and addresses his 24 pupils in his usual manner. He soon notices that 11 among the 24 pupils cannot read a rather simple text. They are no better in writing. In these circumstances, how can he engage them in doing mathematics?

A good starting point is possible: mental arithmetic. This is an essential mathematical activity. In fact, it is an authentic process which evolves with time. Its expression is mainly oral, with little room for writing. The teacher has good experience of it as a method for conceptualising numbers and their operational properties. The sessions are usually short and periodical (about 10 minutes daily). This is an approach that seems to us to be very appropriate to the difficulties of this class, according to our experience.

1.2. The Method

- The teacher asks the pupils to perform a mathematical operation.
- The pupils listen to the question and memorise it. They do the operation mentally.
- At the teacher's signal, they write the answer on a slate and lift it so the teacher can read every answer. Some are correct, others are wrong.
- The teacher questions several pupils in turn (with correct or wrong answers) on the calculating procedure.
- Each pupil must be able to describe the sequence of his or her calculations. Pupils might actually detect an error and correct it orally, and the correction is accepted provided that they can explain what was wrong and why. The other pupils are listening, ready to join in any controversy.
- The teacher asks the pupils who have solved the problem in a different way to raise their hands and describe their method.
- The pupils, through collective oral exchanges regulated by the teacher, compare the advantages and disadvantages (their speed and the possibility of control) of the different methods.

Many properties of numbers and operations—order, compatibility with operations—are explicitly in use during this activity, but not at a theoretical level. These properties work within their tool-status to guide calculation and to make choices, justify answers or detect inconsistencies. Explicit practices for computing develop. For instance: "I am sure his answer is wrong because 12×11 is greater than 12×10, and he gets less than 120".

These sessions involve intense attention and mutual listening, as well as memory, but work well for short periods usually not exceeding 10 or 15 minutes.

1.3. The Realisation

In fact, this admirable programme failed at the first step. For many pupils, listening to the teacher when he was talking to them was not part of their contract. The only relationship that they could conceive with the teacher was a relationship based on the authority of the teacher and the obedience—actually *the disobedience*—of the pupils. Faced with such a situation, the teacher had three choices:

- to accept their logic and engage in a test of strength with them based on the authority given to him by his institutional position;
- to try to convince them with the argument—based on his representation of the school as a place of knowledge—that school can give them something and that they would do better by changing their logic;
- to accept the pupils' logic and to make didactical choices aimed at making their relationship with the school evolve.

The first course would probably have led to a conflict that the teacher could only have won at the cost of jeopardising all learning for most of pupils and of high stress for himself. For many reasons, the second course undoubtedly would also have led to failure. In the end, the teacher decided to take the third track. It was the only way to communicate with most of the pupils.

1.4. The Objectives

Globally speaking, the teacher's aim was to transform the stake that the pupils had in what they were doing and to change what they implicitly sought at school. His ambition was to make mathematics the main object of communication between the pupils and himself and the centre of interest in the exchanges between the pupils themselves during the time institutionally devoted to that discipline.

For the members of our didactics engineering team, the aim was to detect the factors that influence such a change. More precisely, the objectives of the teacher were the following:

- *To develop an attitude of attention and respect* in the relationship between the teacher and the pupils, or in the relationship between the pupils themselves: when the teacher talks to the pupils, or when a pupil talks to the others, those who are not talking listen and try to understand;
- *The context of the exchanges* should be essentially mathematical.

Because the theme is mental arithmetic, numbers and operations were the context for work.

The *knowledge presumed* available to the pupils—which would be sufficient at first—was the *names* of numbers and operations.

The tasks reflected the teacher's intention to change the pupils' stake in mathematics, to increase their numerical knowledge and their skill in using symbols and in practical reasoning, and to foster a certain responsibility concerning the product.

The *knowledge expected* as a result was concerned with the conceptual aspect of numbers—with their properties, ways of writing and representing them. In particular, the pupils were expected to be able to represent numerically problems that were initially posed in a geometric language, and to deal with them either entirely or only partially by calculation, possibly with the help of Cartesian graphics.

1.5. The Tasks

First task: dealing with the issue of teacher's authority.

T(the teacher): I shall give you sums, and I will ask some of you to *repeat* what I have said. I am not asking you to calculate or find a result: just repeat the sums exactly.

Any pupil can do this, unless they refuse to play the school game. Indeed there is hubbub and protest among some pupils. The teacher persists.

T: 14 times 4, Pierre? 5 times 22, Paul? 40 divided by 8, Marie?

Similar requests are repeated over several days but the sums become slightly more complex on each occasion.

The variables that are at the teacher's disposal here are: For mathematics:

- The domain of numbers involved (between 0 and 100 at the beginning).
- The nature of numbers: integers or not.
- The operations: familiar or less familiar.
- The complexity of the statement (one operation, or several).

For class management:

- The number of pupils questioned.
- The time-length of the activity.
- The number of class-meeting.

Second task: change of contract.

T: I will give you some sums, and I will ask some of you *to repeat them in another way*. For instance, for 15×3, you can propose $5 \times 3 \times 3$, or $(10 + 5) \times 3$ . . . or any other expression which would give the same result if one would make the calculation, but we shall not calculate. You must not repeat the same expression twice.

The person who is questioned may be helped by another pupil if s(he) has no idea. The others must listen carefully in order to tell if the proposed expression is acceptable or not.

A new variable is at the teacher's disposal: whether or not to suggest that the pupils write their proposal or not.

So, after a few lessons under the total control of the teacher, those who have some numerical knowledge have an opportunity to express it in a relatively constraint-free context. They have enough choice within a well established framework. On the other hand, they have to respond to the teacher's demand, so that they will not be taken for "a little teacher" and rejected by their peers who are less able mathematically. This work should last for two or three weeks.

Third task: devolution of responsibility to the pupils and moving to a new object of study.

T: Same game as before, but each one may propose an answer. The only condition is that it has not been given before. I want a new one each time.

The teacher wants to direct the pupils towards writing, and also towards the explicit study of properties of numbers and operations. In order to do that, he relies on an evolution of the game *from an oral to a written one*, and on an interaction between the two modes. He has therefore to organise this evolution.

Oral expression is sufficient as long as the information that the pupils have to collect does not surpass their memory capacity. In order for the written expression to be necessary, the oral expression must fail, and so the children's memory capacity must be overstretched.

Thus, in order to obtain the intended evolution, the teacher plays with the variable "number of pupils questioned". He makes it *jump* by changing the rule of the game: *each one may propose an answer*. He counts on the familiarity already developed in this practice of mental arithmetic to obtain *many* propositions.

On the pupils' side, the expected reaction takes place after two or three classes:

"We cannot remember everything, we have to write."
"We have to agree on which propositions are the same and which are new."

The operational properties are here *implicit tools* for classification, expressed in terms of action, in a given context.

The oral *explanation* required from each pupil in the condition of "active listening" by the others tends to favour the *depersonalisation* of processes and to advance the conceptualisation of underlying properties.

Fourth task: change of problems.

T: Find rules to discriminate between propositions that are similar and those that are different.

From the mathematical point of view, the pupils still work within the numerical framework. However the properties of the operations are now the objects of study, and not numbers and relations between numbers and operations.

Review

The *devolution* of mental arithmetic as conceived by the teacher and the interplay oral/writing took two months or so to be set up, with 10 to 30 minutes per day, five days a week. This practice took place all through the year.

Several factors combined to make both the social relationship within the class and the relationship towards knowledge change. Among these factors was the appointment of two teachers to work with the class, who co-operated effectively, especially in the work on symbolisation: these were a male teacher for science and a female teacher with a psychological training and experience with pupils who have reading problems. A special role was played by the activity of mental arithmetic.

1.6. Mental Arithmetic and Problem Solving

We have observed in our research that regular practice in mental arithmetic in the fashion described earlier leads to an increased speed in calculation in almost every pupil. This helps them on several occasions when facing a problem.

In the beginning of a task, mental arithmetic can be used in order to collect enough information to answer the task. One example of a task was:

Given a rectangle, find another rectangle with a greater perimeter and a smaller area.

The first method that the pupils used in order to answer this question consisted of choosing several rectangles with a greater perimeter and computing the area, or several rectangles with a smaller area and computing the perimeter, before they could consider simultaneous variations. The possibility of computing many cases mentally and quickly was an asset in this task.

In the course of solving the task, mental arithmetic is used in order to simplify operations in order to calculate more quickly, such as using successive multiplications or divisions by 2, or else in order to optimise numerical choices in situations of framing.

At the end of tasks, mental arithmetic is used in order to verify the result of an algorithm. For instance, after solving an equation using an algorithm, students can check the result by substituting it in the equation.

Issues for reflection: Could the calculator be used in place of mental arithmetic? If not, what is specific to each of the computing modes (mental, written, with calculator), and how can the different modes be combined in a task where the numerical relations are important?

2. Algebraic Calculus

A class at the end of secondary school (pupils 14–15 years old).

2.1. Role of Algebra in School and College

An important, and even essential, role of *algebra* for pupils in *school* and *college* is that algebra can be a *framework* for solving and also for asking various questions, both in but also outside of mathematics.

In algebra, letters are used to designate unknown but also known quantities, fixed or variable according to the situation. We can calculate with literal expressions—involving letters and numbers—according to certain rules. Depending on which situations are the object of study, letters may denote numbers, vectors, values of various magnitudes, functions, and all of these are elements on which operations can be performed. Because of this versatility, algebra allows us both to create and at the same time to solve many types of problems. By representing situations through algebra, one can situate the problems better, understand them better, and thus adapt the solutions to new situations, some of which are pointed out in the next paragraphs.

Throughout their school years, pupils face the problem of extending the field of numbers that they know to include other numbers. At first the extension might simply be from small natural numbers to larger natural numbers but this extension may later on be from natural to rational, real and possibly also complex numbers. The reason for these extensions might be in the scientific reasoning involved in a non-numerical task: measuring lengths that are smaller than the unit chosen or when the length lies between two consecutive multiples of the unit. The use of literal representation can be a support in this process of extension. Literal representation can also be used for the convenience of reasoning:

- in order to have an infinite field of numbers available, where all operations are possible without worrying whether the result corresponds to an actual measure;
- or when using numbers that are defined through their relations to each other (for example, x and $x - 1$), for instance, to be able to make a valid argument for many cases.

The issue may be whether to establish links between magnitudes, for instance between lengths to get the perimeter, the area or the volume. In the case of spatial magnitudes, the geometric objects involved are polygons, polyhedra, spheres, and cylinders. In order to model and answer the questions that arise, an algebraic calculus is developed. The elements are expressions in which known and unknown quantities are combined. *Writing* and *solving* equations are *essential working tools* for modelling questions and answers about the relationships between magnitudes. For instance, in the process of extending the domain of numbers, from natural to rational numbers, rational numbers appear as solutions of equations $a.x = b$, where a and b are positive natural numbers and b is smaller than a. Similarly, searching for the side of a square with a given area n boils down to solving the equation $x^2 = n$. Although such equations are formulated with integers, other numbers are needed in order to solve them. Pupils in *secondary school* who do not have the adequate knowledge can still understand the problem and formulate it in an equation. While trying to solve such equations, they are led to change their viewpoint, and possibly to shift to a function viewpoint, an approximation or an inequation viewpoint. Thus, they are led to create new numbers (Douady, 1985).

Using algebra in this way produces a dialectic between the objects that one wants to study and the tools being used to deal with them. The objects and the tools involved are expressed under various forms within a framework. According to the form of the expression, properties are more or less visible. This is the case with polynomials of degree n (n = 2 or 3 in the cases concerned here) in the variable x: they are objects of the algebraic framework which may possibly be written as products of factors of degree 1 or 2. The zeros and the sign can be found easily. The expression as a sum of monomials, or of terms each of which is a product of factors, may be the first form obtained when the problem is set in an equation. So these objects and tools are not necessarily situated in the same framework. One cannot avoid relating different registers of expression, as well as different frameworks: numerical, algebraical, graphical, geometrical.

This analysis leads us to include in learning, and therefore in teaching, sequences focused on transformations of writing, on changes of register, changes of framework. This requires specific thought and proposals on the conditions for these changes to happen, at some point in the training, under the responsibility and the control of the pupils themselves.

2.2. The Traditional School Context

A salient characteristic of traditional teaching is the separation of frameworks in which algebra is used, a practice that is quite the opposite of what we have come to suggest. There are several explanations for this separation in traditional teaching. First, the separation is an answer to institutional constraints: it is a good way of cutting up the knowledge that must be transmitted to the pupils and of organising the pupils' tasks in order to evaluate their skills. Second, it denotes a certain conception of the way in which the pupils learn and how their task can be made easier (to teach one new thing at a time).

This separation of frameworks poses a serious problem about the representation of knowledge: how can the teachers relate *new* and *old* knowledge? How can they relate mathematical domains that are different? Which relation do the teachers themselves consider?

The implicit or explicit answers to these questions will have consequences for the choices of the content of the teaching, the expectations of the teacher concerning the skill and the achievements of the pupils and thus for the work that they ask the students to do.

In France, according to the official syllabus, literal calculus, i.e. calculation with expressions including letters and numbers, is introduced cautiously in *"5ème"* (second year, secondary school, age 12). The learning of solutions for first degree equations with one unknown starts in *"4ème"* (third year secondary school, age 13). The introduction of *remarkable identities* [typically $a^2 - b^2 = (a+b)(a-b)$], the practice of *developments* and *factorisation* takes place progressively in *"4ème"*, *"3ème"* and *"2ème"* (third to fifth year secondary, age 13–15).

From the mathematical point of view, the objects are expressions of polynomials in one numerical variable as linear combinations of monomials with real coefficients or as products of factors. Naturally these mathematical terms are not part of the teachers' classroom discourse, nor *a-fortiori* of the pupils.'

In the traditional classroom, the work is mainly on written problems, divorced from the problems that motivate their interest to the pupils and could provide the written expressions with meaning. It is literal calculus, not algebraic calculus. It is presented and treated as an extension of numerical calculation: the pupils are led to believe that "it is the same, but with letters". This is how teachers integrate the new with the old: they solve (or rather think that they have solved) the problem of the new–old relation. But by doing so, they deprive themselves of *the possibility of using algebra as a tool*, for instance, to extend the numerical field. On the other hand, they know pretty well that algebraic calculus is *not exactly like* numerical calculus. For instance $5^2 + 5 = 30$ but $x^2 + x$ cannot be written in a more reduced form. However, reassembling it as $3x$ is a common mistake of pupils.

Thus in the traditional classroom the teacher will state the rules of algebraic calculus, and require the pupils to learn them and apply them in specific literal expressions. The pupils will learn algorithms for solving equations—initially first-degree with one unknown, usually with small integers as coefficients, later systems of two first-degree equations with two unknowns, then equations of second degree. They will learn to use remarkable identities such as $a^2 - b^2 = (a+b)$ $(a-b)$, or expressions that can easily be converted to these, so as to transform well chosen literal expressions: products into sums, sums into products, in cases where there is a *visible common factor*. Usually, this is a formal training that takes the form of solving many similar exercises. It takes a lot of the teachers' and the pupils' time and effort.

This description may seem to be a sort of caricature but, except for some circles involved in didactical or pedagogical reflection, it is a rather accurate description.

On the pupils' side, persistent and recurrent mistakes are observed. Let us mention some of them in the school practice of solving equations, of transforming products into sums or sums into products:

- replace in a computation A^n by $A + \ldots + A$ (n terms);

- shift numbers, according to the "needs" of the computation, from coefficient position to exponent position (or vice-versa), with the effect of grouping terms of various degrees in one term;
- wrong management of parentheses;
- change sign systematically in the transfer of an expression (possibly just one letter or number) from one side to the other of an equation, even in case of multiplying or dividing.

One of the reasons is that the pupils have at their disposal no control tool exterior to the calculus register. In order to check a computation, they can only do it again.

Let us give two examples, concerning "ordinary" pupils in "ordinary" classes.

(1) There is no relation between

- *solving an equation* in the sense of implementing an algorithm, and
- *replacing the unknown by the numerical solution found* in order to check the expected equality.

There is in any case a noticeable drop in performance if, rather than asking to solve an equation, one asks whether a given number is a solution of the equation.

(2) There is no relation between

- *factorising a given algebraic expression as a product*, and
- *checking whether the given expression and the transformed one take the same value for a given value of x, in particular if they vanish for the same values of x*, these values being easily found in the factorised form.

Establishing a meaning-link between the two actions mentioned in each of the above examples requires a consideration of algebraic expressions as functions, with the unknown taking the status of variable. Such a link is essential if algebra is to fulfil its role as a tool framework.

From the viewpoint of the teacher or of the "didacticien", one may ask whether such a formal training on specific algebraic objects within the algebraic framework can represent a stage towards the availability of this calculus in a functional viewpoint. One may also ask whether the knowledge acquired by the pupils at a high cost is at their disposal when they need to solve problems that require transformation of the expression or where a significant part of the work is to isolate the appropriate unknowns, denote them, write the relations between known and unknown quantities, and choose the appropriate way to deal with them.

In view of the above analysis, we very clearly answer NO, in so far as most of the pupils are concerned. Acquiring the technique is essential, but not just under any condition.

If one deprives the pupils of the work that allows them to become familiar with relating various viewpoints, domains, registers, and frameworks, one ends up by creating an *obstacle* to the mastering of algebra as a working framework. For many pupils, the result is just the same as that of other work done from time to time without an official position in the "didactical contract".

2.3. About Meaning

Like other researchers, we attribute great importance to the building of *meaning* for the availability of mathematical concepts when the pupils have to deal with new situations.

As we observed earlier, meaning has at least two components: semantic and syntactic. In order to take into account the semantic component, we need to stress the tool status of concepts, and the relations between various conceptions inside or outside mathematics. In order to take into account its syntactic component, we must emphasise the system of symbolic relations, the way in which the different systems work and are dealt with by the pupils. The work on algebraic modelling provides a particularly good opportunity for the teacher and the pupils to achieve a fruitful interaction between the semantic and the syntactic components of meaning.

However, at least in so far as algebra is concerned, meaning is not enough. The efficiency of an algebraic treatment is based precisely on *forgetting* the initial context. Thus, one has to take into account how meaning can influence the building of algorithms and at the same time how to grow apart from it. The learning of algebraic calculus can be analysed in terms of *balance and interaction* between *the building of meaning* and *technical familiarity with algorithms*.

Question: Taking the above remarks as hypotheses, how does one translate them into didactical engineering?

Let us state some obvious facts: in order for pupils to have at their disposal a well-mastered competence in algebra, one problem or even several problems are not enough. It is a long and exacting business which requires non-stop intellectual watchfulness. For instance, the interconnections between different frameworks or the changes of viewpoint within a given framework which occur while going through a problem provide opportunities for confronting ideas, looking for consistencies and controlling results. However, what must be done in order to activate such a process is not obvious. Authentic training is required. We shall come back later (3.2) to conditions that allow for this process to develop.

3. Elaboration of a Problem in Algebra

We now consider the case where the teacher and the pupils meet in class essentially in order to do mathematics. In our example, the class is about algebra.

We first describe the school context and the aims of the didactical sequence. Afterwards we propose a problem constructed so that the objects of study need to be used in the solution. We will present a mathematical and didactical analysis of the text of the problem, in which we try to identify the variables with which the teacher can play, the choices made, the reasons for these choices, and finally what we expect from the pupils.

3.1. The School Context

We are concerned here with pupils entering the *"lycée"* (age 16). The majority of the pupils have had earlier opportunities of handling algebraic expressions, mostly of a low level. They have had to transform expressions according to the rules of literal calculation: expansions (from the product form to the sum form), and a few cases of factoring. They have already solved some first-degree equations with one unknown. The equations were either formulated directly in the algebraic framework, or resulted from writing equations for simple problems in geometry, measurement, or everyday life. The pupils are used to calculators. They also have experience in marking points in a plane framed with two orthogonal graded axes.

The mathematical objects with which we are concerned here are mainly polynomial functions in one variable, of low degree: degree 1 for solving equations, degree 2 or 3 (rarely more) for factoring or expansion of algebraic expressions.

3.2. Didactical Choices

3.2.1 The Objects of Study.   In an algebraic framework, the object of study is factoring and expansion of polynomials, relating the various forms of writing the problem to be solved (zeroes of a polynomial, solutions of equations). In a graphical framework, the object is graphic representation and the identification of some properties.

3.2.2 Presentation.   The pupils are asked to carry out investigations in the context of a problem where certain conditions must be satisfied (for example, to identify points in a plane when the coordinates satisfy specific relations, or to verify if there are points on the horizontal or on the vertical axis etc.). Here we state the most important conditions.

- *With his/her previous knowledge, a pupil can understand the text.* This means that (s)he can give a certain meaning to the words and to the sentences used. Moreover (s)he has some ideas about tackling the problem.
- *With his/her knowledge, the pupil is unable to solve the problem completely.* However, it is not just an application of the known notions or methods. It may be that the pertinent mathematical notions are explicitly not part of the pupils' knowledge. This is what happens in parts (A), and (B) question (2), where the pertinent notion is that of function.

It may happen that the pupils have these notions but in another context, and they may have difficulties in adapting them to the new context. This is what occurs in part (C), where the factoring of both members of the equations is the adapted tool for solving it.

- *The objects of teaching, which the teacher wants the pupils to learn and remember, are the tools adapted to the solution of the problem.* Here the object is factorisation as a tool for solving equations of second degree.
- *The problem can be expressed in at least two frameworks.* This hypothesis takes into account the fact that a *mathematical notion* involved in the problem *is not involved alone but in relation to others.* The pupils' difficulty in managing and exploiting each of the frameworks and the relation between them varies with the frameworks involved and with the familiarity that the pupils have with them.

When the framework is changed, the objective is not to search for what is common in the different formulations of the problem in order to stress that common part as object of study. It is rather to look for new questions, which are significant intermediate steps in the problem. It is also to have at one's disposal different tools which are well adapted to the new formulation of the problem but which did not seem intuitively connected at the beginning.

The common structure in the frameworks acts as a relay in the transfer. Here the graphical and the algebraic frameworks interact to advance the study and to suggest procedures.

3.2.3 Objectives for the Choice of the Problem.   A first objective is to *combine* subjects that have been approached and treated separately and which, from the mathematical viewpoint, are related in terms of meaning. The starting point is the following: written expression is the main means to communicate mathematics, but it is also the means to progress. Here the factored expression and the expanded expression give access to different properties of polynomials. The problem itself makes this fact clear. This will give the pupils the means of providing the algebraic expressions with some meaning, and advancing in the comprehension and the knowledge of the properties that they convey.

In order to satisfy this requirement, we choose to use the objects of study as *tools adapted* for solving the problem. This leads us to widen the mathematical field in which the problem will lie. In particular, the studies that take place in the algebraic framework and in the graphic framework; these frameworks will have to interact and not just to be juxtaposed, and we shall introduce here a "function" view-point.

A second objective is to give the pupils *scientific means of control.*

A third objective is to create new objects. The solution should lead to *new knowledge which makes sense for the pupils and which the teacher can institutionalise in class.*

The objectives that we have just formulated are centred on *factoring* and *expanding* in algebra. In fact, the work towards them will lead to a widening of the didactical situation in such a way that lots of mathematical elements— notions, methods—in various frameworks, will be studied in terms of meaning and technique. Interplay between frameworks and changes of framework will play a key role in this work.

3.2.4 Mathematical Choices and Reasons for Them. *In algebraic terms*, in order to make a polynomial of degree 2 vanish, it is better to have it expressed as a product of factors of degree 1 since, by making one of the factors vanish, one makes the product vanish. So we shall ask a question outside the algebraic framework, but in such a way that in order to answer it one will have to make a polynomial expression vanish. In order to compute the numerical value of such an expression, the expanded form is often the most convenient.

In order to solve an equation of degree 2 with one part written in expanded form and another part factored, one has to homogenise the writing: all of it must be expanded or all of it factored. If the technique of solving with the discriminant is not available, factoring is the only route for solving the equation.

To solve an equation $A(x) = 0$, [for instance $ax + b = 0$, or $(ax + b)(cx + d) = 0$, or $ax^2 + bx + c = 0$] is to find the values of the unknown x for which *the expression* $A(x)$ equals 0, or find the values for the unknown x for which *the function* $x \to A(x)$ vanishes. Implicitly or explicitly, we use these two viewpoints in the different parts of the problems.

In graphical terms, making a polynomial vanish, or solving an equation, is a matter of finding the point where the curve representing the function intersects the horizontal axis. We shall pose the questions in a graphical framework, but to answer them we will have to work in an algebraic framework, either by computing, after having chosen a numerical value for x, or by solving equations—and here the choice of the expression may be crucial.

3.2.5 Statement of the Problem and A-priori Analysis. Propose a problem that almost all pupils should be able to tackle with their present knowledge, without imposing a procedure.

The problem:

The plane is provided with two orthogonal axes.
(A) We consider the points in the plane whose coordinates (x, y) satisfy the relation
$y = (x + 3)(8 - x/2)$. We denote by E the set of such points.
(1) Give 5 pairs of coordinates corresponding to points in E and 5 pairs of coordinates corresponding to points of the plane not in E.
(2) Represent graphically as many points of E as possible.

(3) Are there points of E on the horizontal axis? On the vertical axis?
If yes, give the coordinates of these points.
If no, say why.

(4) Can there be two points of E with the same abscissa? With the same ordinate?
If yes, give examples. If no, say why.

(B) We are now interested in the set F of points in the plane whose coordinates (x,y) satisfy the relation

$$y = x^2 - 9$$

Answer the same questions as in (A).

(C) Are there points which lie both in E and F?
If yes, give if possible the coordinates of these points.

A-priori *analysis of the situation:*

Various frameworks are involved in this problem, and in order to deal with them, it is in the pupils' interest *to make them interact.* This requires the pupils to have *enough* skill in each framework. These prerequisites are listed below, according to the reference frameworks. On the other hand, a question regularly occurs to the teacher who has chosen or built a problem: does it actually bring into play the concepts to be treated, and in the conditions that he or she wants (learning, familiarisation, test of knowledge or skill)? Moreover the teacher needs to know on which variable he or she can play and what is the range of such choices for the pupils. These are important elements in the teacher's room for manoeuvre and therefore require explicit consideration.

(a) *The skills*: Assumed knowledge of the pupils.

(1) Prerequisite to tackling the problem.

In the *graphic framework:*

- draw axes and graduate them;
- plot points with given coordinates;
- read the coordinates of marked points;
- vocabulary supposed to be known with its meaning: framework, axes, orthogonal, graduation, coordinates, abscissa, ordinate.

In the *algebraic framework:*

Substitute numerical values for letters in an algebraic expression and calculate its value.

In the *numerical framework:*

- compute correctly with natural integers;
- a certain mastery of computations with relative integers, decimals, and fractions;
- use a calculator to solve problems.

(2) Algebraic skills likely to be available, which can help but can also sometimes hinder problem solving:

- expand algebraic expressions of degree 1 or 2 involving products of factors;
- factor in some particular cases;
- solve an equation of degree 1 with one unknown.

(b) The frameworks of the problem.
The questions are asked in the graphic framework, but the data points are selected according to a specified algebraic relation [for example, in (A), the relation is $y = (x + 3)(8 - x/2)$]. The numerical framework is a background.

(c) The tools.
The (conceptual) tools:

- conceptions underlying the prerequisite explicit tools, such as factoring;
- the theorem "a product of factors vanishes if one of the factors vanishes" as an implicit tool.

A technological tool:
A calculator, programmable if possible: once the method of work has been decided (substituting numerical values for the letters in the algebraic expressions and computing their values), the calculator may then be programmed in order to give a great number of points in E and F and provide a geometrical view of these sets.

(d) The variables of the problem.

Concerning *the algebraic relations:*

- The degree: 2 or 3
- The written expression: factored or expanded
- The order of monomials
- The numerical coefficients: integers or not, positive or negative
- The values of the zeroes.

Concerning *the graphic framework:*

- The number of points to be marked: finite or infinite
- The position of points to select: arbitrary, on one axis within the limits of the material support, outside these limits, outside the axes but satisfying a particular condition.

Concerning *the numerical data:*
- Collecting and treating pertinent numerical information
- Allow or do not allow the use of a calculator.

(e) The didactical choices that fix the variables and the expectations of the teacher.

In part (A) of the problem above, *the first expectation* of the teacher is that the pupils give meaning to the expression "x and y satisfy the relation". In order to test that, they are asked to place 5 points satisfying the relation and 5 points not satisfying it. If there is a difficulty, the teacher can open a discussion in the class about what meaning to give to such an expression.

The second expectation concerns the more or less accurate knowledge of the points of E. Once the working method has been decided (to substitute numerical values for the letters in the algebraic expressions and compute their value), a calculator can be programmed to provide the co-ordinates of a great number of points of E, and later of F. It is thus possible to get a geometrical picture of these sets. This will make it possible later to view the points that are common to E and F as intersection points of two curves.

By choosing two parabolas whose concavities are of opposite sense and whose summits (vertices) are not too far, one facilitates the conviction of the geometrical existence of the points of intersection. Some technical work will still have to be done with algebraic tools, namely computing the coordinates of these points in order to demonstrate their existence concretely.

We have just described what we call an *interplay between frameworks*, between algebraic and graphic frameworks, exploiting, in each of them, that which is easy to do and can be transferred to the other one so as to solve the problem. We shall come back later to this didactical tool.

The third expectation is that the pupils relate the elements:

"this point is on the horizontal axes" and "its ordinate $y = 0$"
"search the values of x which make y vanish" and "solve the equation $y = 0$",

finding from there a way to identify the points of E on the horizontal axes.

The chosen algebraic relation has been written as a product of two factors of degree 1 so as to facilitate the search of values of x which make y vanish. However, in view of the pupils' familiarity with expanded expressions, one may think that a number of them will have a tendency to expand the product. But these pupils do not know how to solve an equation of second degree. The expanded expression leads them into a dead end (they will get out by some amalgamation; "the end justifies the means").

The coefficients have been chosen in such a way that:

- one of the roots is a small integer and so it can be found after a few tests of integer values for x;

- the other is great enough to escape the tests and is outside the bounds of the sheet that supports the graphic framework. Then one has to solve a first-degree equation explicitly.

The fourth expectation is that the pupils will transform a method: "I choose a value for x, any one, just one I like, I compute according to the formula and I find the value of y" into a property of the relation: "to each value of x corresponds a unique value of y". And later into a feature of the set E: "to each value of x corresponds a point in E".

In part (B) the problem is analogous to the previous one, but with an algebraic relation that is a remarkable identity "difference of squares". The teacher expects a rather quick solution of this part. Its interest is twofold:

- To test the pupils on what they have learned in part (A), giving them an opportunity to ask the same questions again and possibly to understand them better; and
- To prepare part (C), the actual purpose of the problem.

In part (C), the pupils are asked to find the points common to the two sets described in parts (A) and (B) respectively. Graphically, a common point of E and F has coordinates (x, y), where y can be expressed in two ways in terms of x according to whether it is considered as belonging to E or F (let us denote them by y_E and y_F). The previous work is expected to lead the pupils to the algebraic translation of the question. But, algebraically, the sign "=" will have to take another meaning than the one that it has taken in the previous parts. There, the ordinate y was the result of a calculation and the sign "=" had the meaning "results in". The graphical reference—a point has a unique pair of coordinates—suggests writing $y_E = y_F$ in order to express that the ordinate of a point common to E and F can be expressed in two ways, which has nothing to do with the result of a calculation. On the other hand, the equality holds only for the points that are common to E and F. In other words, there are as many common points as values of x which realise the equality.

Algebraically, this is equivalent to the solution of an equation of second degree involving x on both sides of the equal sign. This poses a difficulty, widely recognised by teachers and researchers, to pupils even when they have to solve first-degree equations. In order to make the task easier, we have chosen one of the points on the horizontal axis, so that it belongs to the points already marked in the two sets. It corresponds to x + 3 = 0. In view of the choices described above concerning the relative position of the two parabolas, the other point is graphically visible.

$$y_E = (x+3)(8-x/2)$$
$$y_F = x^2 - 9$$

In order to make the algebraic solution necessary, one has to choose the coordinates of this point—and therefore the coefficients of the equations—in such a way that it cannot be found after a few empirical tests.

So, in order to solve the equation $x^2 - 9 = (x + 3) (8 - x/2)$, expanding and grouping the terms of the same degree leads to a dead end, at least if the rules of algebra are respected. It is necessary to express the left hand member as $(x - 3) (x + 3)$. Factoring is a tool. Solving $x - 3 = 8 - x/2$ is another tool. The value $x = 22/3$ cannot be found by chance.

(f) On the pupils' side.

In the course of the work, the pupils can make many mistakes. For instance, they can produce calculations that are mathematically invalid, such as grouping terms of different degrees, if this leads them to an answer. This is where the graphic reference is profitable, if the pupils are *used to* looking for consistency between the results of different procedures for the same question.

Indeed, looking for consistencies may take a lot of time. If a pupil gets involved and does not obtain a convincing result, and if the work (s)he has produced is not officially recognised by the teacher, this pupil will not be inclined to do it again. However, the transfer of responsibility (at least partially) and of the control of the production to the pupils themselves can be a promotor of the progress of learning. Such a task requires mathematical skill. It also needs to be a part of the didactical contract.

Graphical knowledge of the situation can act as a *guide*, but it can also act as a *control* of the algebraic situation. One of the points common to E and F is already known and it should be found also through the algebraic solution. The other point can be found by solving an equation of first degree with small coefficients: $x - 3 = 8 - x/2$ for the computation of x. It remains to compute the corresponding value of y. The coordinates must correspond to values that are graphically acceptable.

(g) On the teacher's side.

By varying the coefficients of the polynomials the teacher can change the goals of the task. If the objective is mainly conceptual, (s)he can make the technical task of the pupils easier and still preserve the strength and the significance of the concepts involved. This can be accomplished either by making appropriate choices in the data of the problem, or by making available technology (calculators, computer) which helps the pupils to master the technical difficulties, or by using both resources as in the problem above.

If the goal of the task is rather to create familiarity or test the possibility of reinvesting the knowledge of what has just been learned in more complex situations, where this knowledge is only one element of the situation, then the issue may be technical.

3.2.6 A Realisation that Illustrates the Tool–Object Dialectic. The problem chosen above is proposed to the pupils.

Step 1: Mobilising *objects as working tools.* The issue is to bring into play *known* material to start the research.

Step 2: Bringing into play *implicit tools, interpretation, change of framework.* The point is to *adapt* the knowledge in case there is trouble or one is stuck, to question and possibly to reconsider the choices made (perhaps it was not good to develop the given expression: it might have been better to treat it in the factored form), and to exploit the information provided by the interpretation in another framework, for example, in a graphic framework.

Step 3: Local institutionalisation, linked to context. Explication of some tools. After all the pupils' work on the problem, the teacher must select what has been meaningful to the pupils and what is mathematically interesting and can be reinvested. By doing this the teacher explicitly organises the pupils' knowledge. If this knowledge is linked to classroom activities, we speak of *local institutionalisation.* If it is relatively decontextualised and depersonalised, and therefore in the condition of being communicated and understood outside the classroom, without knowledge of the history of its production, the knowledge involved is in its object status and we shall speak of *institutionalisation.* Briefly, we say that the teachers gives a lecture.

The present case is concerned mainly with local institutionalisation:

Vocabulary: $y = (x + 3)(8 - x/2)$ is called the *equation* of E, $y = x^2 - 9$ is the equation of F. These equations are of *second degree* (explaining where 2 comes from).

Relating graphs and algebra:

- The points of E on the horizontal axis are the points with coordinates $(x, 0)$. Therefore x is solution of $(x + 3)(8 - x/2) = 0$.
- The points of F on the horizontal axis are the points $(x, 0)$ where x is solution of $x^2 - 9 = 0$.

New knowledge in algebra:

- There are cases where equations of second degree can be solved: When there is no term in x as in the equation of F.

  When it can be written as a product of factors, for instance by noticing a common factor or a remarkable identity.

  Then, if one of the factors vanishes, the product vanishes. Conversely if a product $AB = 0$, then either $A = 0$ or $B = 0$.
- *A method:* in order to solve an equation of degree 2 of the form $A.B = 0$, one

solves the two equations of first degree A = 0 and B = 0. Each of these equations has a solution which is a solution of the given equation of degree 2.

Step 4: Institutionalisation. Some tools, after sufficient depersonalisation and decontextualisation, take another status: that of elements in an organised mathematical knowledge, which can be reinvested in situations or problems different from the ones used to introduce them. Their status then becomes one of object/potential tool. At the moment when it is proposed, the problem described above does not involve such a step.

For the teacher, institutionalisation is a *process* that begins with the choice of a certain problem, with the decisions that organise the didactical situation. The instruction given by the teacher concerning the object of teaching is just a step in the process.

But on the pupils' part, the process cannot be viewed as such, i.e. as a set of steps organised in a consistent way in view of a learning objective. In particular, the teacher may find difficulties which some populations of pupils in realising the situation that (s)he has conceived for a given didactical end. The pupils have to be in scientific interaction with the problem for a while, without the mediation of the teacher to tell them what is allowed. This means, moreover, that the pupils are conscious that the (a-didactical) situation conceived by their teacher builds up the meaning of what will later be institutionalised.

M.J. Perrin-Glorian (1993) in her research on working-class pupils makes it clear that most of them make no connection between the work done to solve a problem given by the teacher and the lecture that the teacher gives later on. This is one of our reasons for introducing the example of mental arithmetic.

Reminding situations. In the course of our didactical experiments with M.J. Perrin, we have spotted situations that are particularly useful in favouring the decontextualisation and the depersonalisation of certain tools involved in the mathematical work. We called them *reminding situations*.

By this, we mean a moment at the beginning of the class where the teacher asks pupils to *recall* the essential points of the previous sessions on a given theme that is still under study.

The report, which lasts about 10 to 15 minutes, is placed under the pupils' control. The teacher echoes the questions, possibly asks some, repeats the information given but does not introduce any him/herself. The *time* that pupils have to complete the report, *linked to the constraint* of reminding them of all the essential points, is a didactical variable.

This is a very important phase for selecting and memorising important events, for putting them in relation with further lessons, for the decontextualisation and depersonalisation of what the teacher intends to institutionalise later on. It is profitable to make the practice of reminders the responsibility of the pupils because, at nearly every class meeting, the work requested is situated with respect to the previous work, whether they were questions posed or results obtained in solving problems.

So each pupil knows that he/she has to remember the main points of the development of a class in anticipation of the next one. In fact, the situation is often complex and a pupil is unable to fulfil the contract by him/herself. But often the class as a whole can do it.

Note that if the teacher himself/herself reminds the class of what happened, no essential point will be forgotten but the teacher's reminding does not play its didactical role in the process of conceptualisation.

Step 5: Familiarisation with the objects *and reinvestment*. Even if the learning situation develops according to the expectations of the teacher, one is still left with the question of what the pupils will have actually learned and what they will be able to reinvest in the problems that come up in a more complex version of the same context or in a different context with a similar or greater complexity.

In fact, before they are able to reinvest their knowledge, the pupils need to familiarise themselves with their new knowledge. One way is first to give them problems that are close to the problem already studied. For instance:

- Solve the equation $x^2 - 4 + (x + 2)(2x - 5) = 0$. [Here factoring is the adapted tool, but the text does not say anything about that. However $x^2 - 4$ is visibly a difference of squares];
- Solve other similar questions;
- Systematically, transform products into sums and convenient sums into products.

Step 6: Reinvestment using the knowledge as tool *in more complex problems*. Questions where factoring is less obvious and where the graphical representation will be of great help:

- Are there common points to the two sets with equations
  $y = x^2 - x - 6$ and $y = (x + 2)(8x - 7)$
- Same question with
  $y = 5x^2 + x - 18$ and $y = (x + 2)(8x - 7)$

Here the context has not changed.

Through these last two questions, a new problem is approached. *How can an expression that does not show a visible or quasi-visible "common factor"* [such as $(x + 2)$ in the first equation] be factorised?

The adequate tool, unknown to the pupils, is the following theory:

If the expression vanishes for $x = a$, then $(x - a)$ is one of the factors in the factoring.

The converse has been used in the precise exercises on solving second-degree equations which the students have done. In order to advance, it is necessary to make explicit the relation between first-degree factors in the factoring and solutions found for the equation. Then a method may be derived:

If you want to factor an expression of second degree, try to find by any means (computing, graphic) values of x that make it vanish. If you find two, you can write the two factors. (Multiplying them you will find the initial expression up to a constant factor.)

If you find one, you can write the factor corresponding to this value and then manage to find another one such that by multiplying you recover the initial expression. If you don't find any, then you are stuck.

Note that this thought process spreads out over a long period—probably a few months. During this period, the question is studied, left to rest, and resumed in different problems. What is aimed at is the further study of polynomials, an important object in mathematics. In view of such a study, the work proposed allows us to set milestones that make sense for the pupils.

We have just described the unfolding of the *tool–object dialectic* with *interplays* (Douady, 1991) between the graphic and the algebraic frameworks.

The *conceptual windows* that the pupils activate are different from one pupil to the next. We note in this way the parts of the framework that a pupil lets interact or which s/he combines in order to solve a problem. Here they include graphical representations constituted by sets of points, elements of the algebraic framework (some remarkable identities, equations, various algebraic expressions, a few operating rules), numbers and ways of computing, some linear or similar functions. For a given pupil, the window evolves during the work according to the questions or the methods suggested by his/her knowledge. The windows also constitute the support of the interplay between frameworks.

A set of elements of a given framework can also be pertinent with respect to the problem studied by a pupil or a group of pupils at a given moment, and can make various ranges or various viewpoints within this framework. Some examples are the range of equations and their solutions, that of numerical variations of an algebraic expression and of its zeroes, and that of factoring.

CONCLUSION

The engineering that we have presented fits well with the tool–object dialectic. It is organised around a problem that provides meaning to the mathematical conceptions studied. It involves contextualisation, changes of context, reformulation of problems, decontextualisation, and also the personalisation and transmission of procedures and of personal knowledge as well as depersonalisation.

In other words, the teacher must organise the transformation of tool status into object and vice-versa. The goal is to put the pupils in a position to capitalise on the knowledge available in situations that have meaning for them.

All this requires the teacher to be in a situation that allows him/her to carry out the devolution of the problem and thus requires that the pupils enter into a direct interaction with the problem; this excludes the teacher as an authority but not as a scientific partner. Clearly such conditions are not always realised.

The work of A. Robert and other researchers around her shows the importance of instituting and of using "metaknowledge", of speaking *about* mathematics in order to facilitate the access to certain concepts or certain domains of mathematics. This also helps when the problem chosen does not fit well with the conditions that we have outlined above.

Now, suppose that this stage has been reached, and that the pupils have actually worked on the problem and produced the results attached to the problem. The teacher still has to start the decontextualisation and depersonalisation of some elements that he/she chooses for reasons related to his/her teaching intentions and to the behaviour of the pupils while dealing with the proposed problem. In other words, the teacher has to institutionalise certain notions, methods and practices, taking advantage of the pupils' solutions. Here again there are types of pupil for whom this is by no means obvious. To work on a problem does not imply to them that this work will be used later on. However, if solving a problem is to have an effective learning function for the pupil, then the pupil must establish a connection between what was learned and the conditions of use of the knowledge later on (Perrin-Glorian, 1993).

References

Abelson,. & diSessa, A. (1980). *Turtle geometry: The computer as a medium for exploring mathematics.* Cambridge, MA: MIT Press.

Abreu, G. de., Bishop, A.J. & Pompeu, G. (1992). Approaches into cultural conflicts in mathematics learning. *Proceedings of PME XVI.* University of New Hampshire, USA.

Abreu, G. de, Bishop, A.J., & Pompeu, G. (1997). *What children and teachers count as mathematics.* This volume.

Ackerman, E. (1990). From decontextualised to situated knowledge: revisiting Piaget's water-level experiments. In I. Harel, (Ed.), *Constructionist Learning.* Cambridge, MA: MIT Press.

Acredolo, C., Adams, A., & Schmid, J. (1984). On the understanding of the relationships between speed, duration, and distance. *Child Development, 55,* 2151–2159.

Acredolo, C., O'Connor, J., Banks, L., & Horobin, K. (1989). Children's ability to make probability estimates: Skills revealed through application of Anderson's functional measurement methodology. *Child Development, 60,* 933–945.

Allport, G.W. (1973). Attitudes in the history of social psychology. In N. Warren & M. Jahoda, *Attitudes: Selected Readings* (pp. 19–25) (second edition). London: Penguin Books.

Alves-Martins, M., Carvalho Neto, F. (1990). A influência dos factores sociais contextuais na resoluçaon de problema. *Anàlise Psicològica, 8,* 3, 265–274.

Amaiwa, S. (1987a). Transfer of subtraction procedures from abacus to paper and pencil. *Japanese Journal of Educational Psychology, 35,* 41–48. (in Japanese with English summary)

Amaiwa, S. (1987b). Strategies for multi-digit mental multiplication and division by experienced and non-experienced abacus operators. In G. Hatano (Ed.), *The acquisition of conceptual knowledge and belief system through expertise.* Report of Research Project, Grant-in-Aid for Scientific Research (c) 1984–86. (in Japanese)

Amaiwa, S. (1987c). *Transferring abacus skills to 6- and 12-base systems.* Paper presented at the 29th Annual Convention of the Japanese Association of Educational Psychology, Tokyo. (in Japanese)

Amaiwa, S., & Hatano, G. (1983, September). *Comprehension of subtraction procedures by intermediate abacus learners.* Paper presented at the 47th Annual Convention of the Japanese Psychological Association, Tokyo. (in Japanese)

Amaiwa, S. & Hatano, G. (1989). Effects of abacus learning on 3rd-graders' performance in paper-and-pencil tests ofcalculation. *Japanese Psychological Research, 31,* 161–168.

Anderson, J.R. (1980). *Cognitive psychology and its implications.* San Francisco: Freeman.

Anderson, J.R. (1982). Acquisition of cognitive skills. *Psychological Review, 89,* 369–406.

Anderson, N., & Butzin, C. (1978). Integration theory applied to children's judgments of equity. *Developmental Psychology, 14,* 593–606.

Anderson, N., & Cuneo, D. (1978). The height + width rule in children's judgments of quantity. *Journal of Experimental Psychology: General, 107,* 335–378.

Arbeiter, S. (1984). *Profiles, college-bound seniors, 1984.* NY: College Entrance Examination Board.

Are, B. (1988). *Significations sociales contextuelles et résolution de problème: influence sur l'élaboration et la gestion de stratégies comportementales et cognitives.* Mémoire de D.E.A Université de Provence. U.E.R. de Psychologie, Département des Sciences de l'Education.

Artigue, M. (1992). Didactic engineering. *Recherches en Didactique des Mathématiques,* Special book ICME VII.

Artigue, M. & Perrin-Glorian M.J. (1991). Didactic engineering, research and development tool: some theoretical problems linked to this duality. *For the learning of Mathematics, 11,* 13–17.

Artigues, M. (1988). Ingéniérie didactique. *Recherches en didactique des mathématiques, 9,* 3, 281–308.

Arzarello, F. (1992). Pre-algebraic problem solving. In J.P. Ponte, J.F. Matos, J.M. Matos, & D. Fernandes (Eds.), *Mathematical problem solving and new information technologies* (NATO ASI Series F, Vol. 89, pp. 155–166). Berlin: Springer-Verlag.

Ascher, M. (1991). *Ethnomathematics: A Multicultural View of Mathematical Ideas.* Pacific Grove, CA: Cole Brooks.

Assessment of Performance Unit. (1980). *Mathematical development, secondary survey, report no.1.* London: HMSO.

Baddeley, A.D. (1986). *Working memory.* Oxford, UK: Clarendon Press.

Barnes, B. (1982). *T.S. Kuhn and Social Science.* New York: Columbia University Press.

Balacheff, N. (1990). Towards a problematique for research on mathematics teaching. *Journal for Research in Mathematics Education, 21,* 258–272.

Baroody, A.J. (1987). *Children's Mathematical Thinking.* NY: Teachers College Press.

Baroody, A.J. (1992). The development of preschoolers' counting skills and principles. In J. Bideaud, C. Meljac, J.P. Fischer (Eds.) *Pathways To Number* (pp. 99–126). Hillsdale, NJ: Lawrence Erlbaum Associates Inc.

Bateson, G. (1972). *Steps to an ecology of mind.* London: Jason Aronson Inc.

Bautier E. & Robert A. (1988). Réflexions sur le rôle des représentations métacognitives dans l'apprentissage des mathématiques. *Revue Française de Pedagogie, 84,* 13–19, INRP, Paris.

Bebout, H. (1990). Children's symbolic representations of addition and subtraction word problems. *Journal for Research in Mathematics Education, 21,* 123-131.

Behr, M., Harel, G., Post, T., & Lesh, R. (1992). Rational number, ratio, and proportion. In D.A. Grouws (Ed.), *Handbook of research on mathematics and teaching and learning.* New York: MacMillan Publishing.

Bell, A. (1980). Developmental studies in the additive composition of number. *Recherches en Didactique des Mathematiques, 1,* 113–141.

Bell, A. (1995). Purpose in school algebra. In C. Kieran (Ed.), New perspectives on school algebra: Papers and discussions of the ICME-7 algebra working group (special issue). *Journal of Mathematical Behavior, 14,* 41–73.

Bell, A., Greer, B., Grimison, L., & Mangan, C. (1989). Children's performance on Multiplicative Word Problems: Elements of a Descriptive Theory, *Journal of Research in Mathematics Education 20*, 5, 434–449.

Bell, A., & Janvier, C. (1981). The interpretation of graphs representing situations. *For the Learning of Mathematics, 2* (1), 34–42.

Bell, A., Malone, J.A., & Taylor, P.C. (1987). *Algebra—an exploratory teaching experiment.* Nottingham, UK: Shell Centre for Mathematical Education.

Bempechat, J., Nakkula, M.J., Wu, J., & Ginsburg, H.P. (1993). *Attributions as predictors of mathematics achievement.* Unpublished manuscript.

Bidwell, J.K. (1982). Share Five Chocolate Bars among Six Children, *Mathematics Teaching 99*, 4–8.

Bill, V., Leer, M., Reams, L., & Resnick, L. (1992). From cupcakes to equations: The structure of discourse in a primary mathematics classroom. *Verbum, 1*, 63–85.

Binet, A. (1969). The perception of lengths and numbers. In R.H. Pollack & M.W. Brenner (Eds.), *The experimental psychology of Alfred Binet* (pp. 79–92). New York: Springer Publishing Co.

Bishop A.J. (1988). *Mathematical Enculturation. A cultural perspective on Mathematics Education.* Dordrecht, Boston, London: Kluwer Academic Publishers.

Bishop, A.J. (1991). Mathematical values in the teaching process. In Alan J. Bishop et al. (Eds) *Mathematical Knowledge: Its Growth Through Teaching* (pp. 195–214). Dordrecht: Kluwer.

Bishop, A.J. & Abreu, G. de., (1991). Children's use of outside-school knowledge to solve mathematics problems in-school, *Proceedings of PME XV, vol. 1* (pp.128–135) Assisi, Italy.

Boero, P. (1989). Mathematical literacy for all experiences and problems. *Actes du colloque, PME. 13*, Paris, 62–76.

Booth, L.R. (1984). *Algebra: Children's strategies and errors.* Windsor, UK: NFER-Nelson.

Braunfeld, P. & M. Wolfe (1966). Fractions for low achievers. *The Arithmetic Teacher, 13*, (8), 647–655.

Briars, D.J., & Larkin, J.H. (1984). An integrated model of skill in solving elementary word problems. *Cognition and Instruction, 1*, 245–296.

Briars, D.J., & Siegler, R.S. (1984). A featural analysis of preschoolers' counting knowledge. *Developmental Psychology, 20*, 607–618.

Brissiaud, R. (1988). De l'âge du capitaine à l'âge du berger. Quel est le contrôle de la validité d'un énoncé de problème au CE2? *Revue Française de Pédagogie, 82*, 23–31.

Brossard, M. (1994). *Ecole et adaptation.* Bordeaux: Stablon.

Brousseau G. (1987). Fondements et méthodes de la didactique. *Recherches en Didactique des Mathématiques, 7*, 33–115.

Brousseau, G. (1988). Le contrat didactique: le milieu. *Recherches en Didactique des Mathématiques, 7*, 2, 33–115.

Brown, J.S., Collins, A., & Duguid, P. (1989). Situated Cognition and the Culture of Learning. *Educational Researcher, 18* (1), 32–42.

Brownell, W.A. (1956). Meaning and skill—Maintaining the balance. *Arithmetic Teacher, 3*, 129–136

Brun, J. (1979). Pédagogie des mathématiques et psychologie, analyse de quelques rapports. In J. Brun & F. Conne ((Eds.) Approches en psychopédagogie des mathématiques, *Cahiers de la Section des sciences de l'education* Université de Genève, *12*, 1–24.

Brun, J., & Conne, F. (1979). Approches en psychopédagogie des mathématiques. *Cahiers de la Section des sciences de l'éducation*, Université de Genève, *12*.

Brun, J., & Conne, F. (1990). Analyses didactiques de protocoles d'observation du déroulement des situations. *Education et recherche, 3*, 261–286.

Brun, J., & Schubauer-Leoni, M.L. (1981). Recherches sur l'activité de codage d'opérations additives en situation d'interaction sociale et de communication. *Cahiers IMAG*, Université de Grenoble.

Bruner, J. (1990). *Acts of Meaning*. Cambridge, MA: Harvard University Press.

Bryant, P.E. (1989). Unevenness in mathematical and cognitive development: A discussion of the five papers. *The Quarterly Newsletter of the Laboratory of Comparative Human Cognition, 11*, 34–38.

Bryant, P.E. & Kopytynska, H. (1976). Spontaneous measurement by young children. *Nature, 260*, 773.

Bryant, P.E., Morgado, L. & Nunes, T. (1992). Children's understanding of multiplication. *Proceedings of the Annual Conference of the Psychology of Mathematics Education, Tokyo*, August.

BSY: (1986). *Brazilian Statistics Year-book–1986*. Rio de Janeiro, Brazil: IBGE.

Burns, R.B. (1979). *The Self-concept: Theory, Measurement, Development and Behaviour*. London: Longman.

Butlen D. & Pezard M. (1992). Calcul mental et résolution de problèmes multimplicatifs, une experimentation du CP au CM2. *Recherches en Didactique des Mathématiques, 12*, 2–3.

Campbell, J., & Graham, D. (1985). Mental multiplication skill: Structure, process and acquisition. *Canadian Journal of Psychology, 39*, 338–366.

Carpenter, T.P., Corbitt, M.K., Kepner, H. S. Jr., Lindquist, M.M., & Reys, R. E. (1981). *Results from the second mathematics assessment of the National Assessment of Educational Progress*. Reston, VA: National Council of Teachers of Mathematics.

Carpenter, T.P. Fennema, E., Peterson, P.L., Chiang, C., & Loef, M. (1989). Using knowledge of children's mathematical thinking in classroom teaching: An experimental study. *American Educational Research Journal, 26*, 449–531.

Carpenter, T.P., Lindquist, M.M., Matthews, W., & Silver, E.A. (1983). Results of the third NAEP mathematics assessment: secondary school. *Mathematics Teacher, 76*, 652–659.

Carpenter, T.P., & Moser, J.M. (1982). The development of addition and subttraction problem solving skills. In T.P. Carpenter, J.M. Moser, & T. Romberg (Eds.) *Addition and subtraction: A cognitive perspective* (pp. 9–24). Hillsdale, NJ: Lawrence Erlbaum Associates Inc.

Carpenter, T.P., & Moser, J.M. (1983). The Acquisition of Addition and Subtraction Concepts. In R. Lesh & M. Landau (Eds.), *The Acquisition of Mathematics Concepts and Processes*. New York: Academic Press.

Carpenter, T.P., & Moser, J.M. (1984). The Acquisition of Addition and Subtraction Concepts in Grades One Through Three, *Journal for Research in Mathematics Education, 13* (3), 179–202.

Carpenter, T.P., Moser, J.M. & Romberg, T.A. (Eds.) (1982). *Addition and subtraction: A cognitive perspective*. Hillsdale, NJ: Lawrence Erlbaum Associates Inc.

Carraher, D.W. (1991). Mathematics Learned In and Out of School: A Selective Review of Studies from Brazil. In M. Harris (Ed.), *School Mathematics and Work* (pp. 169–201). London: The Falmer Press.

Carraher, T.N. (1985). The decimal system: understanding and notation. *Proceedings of the 9th International Conference for the Psychology of Mathematics Education, 11* 288–303. Utrecht: Research Group on Mathematics Education and Educational Computer Centre, State University of Utrecht.

Carraher, T.N. (1988). Street mathematics and school mathematics, *PMEXII, 1*, 1–23, Hungary.

Carraher, T.N., Carraher, D.W., & Schliemann, A.D., (1985). Mathematics in the Streets and in Schools. *British Journal of Developmental Psychology, 3*, 21–29.

Carraher, T.N., Carraher, D.W. & Schliemann, A.D. (1987). Written and oral mathematics, *Journal for Research in Mathematics Education, 18*, 2, 83–97.

Carraher, T.N., Carraher, D.W. & Schliemann, A.D. (1988a) *Na Vida dez, na Escola Zero,* Brazil: Cortez editora, S. Paulo.

Carraher, T.N. & Meira, L. (1990). Learning Computer Languages and Concepts In D. Clements, & M. Battista, (1989) *Learning of Geometric Concepts in a Logo Environment, Journal for Research in Mathematics Education, 20,* 450–467.

Carraher, T.N., Schliemann, A.D. & Carraher, D.W. (1988b). Mathematical Concepts in Everyday Life. In G.B. Saxe & M. Gearhart, (Eds.) *Children's Mathematics.*

Carry, L.R., Lewis, C., & Bernard, J. (1980). *Psychology of equation solving: An information processing study* (Final Technical Report). Austin: University of Texas at Austin, Department of Curriculum and Instruction.

Carvalho Neto, F. (1990). *L'influence des situations sociales contextuelles dans la résolution de problèmes: mécanismes d'élection de représentations, règles et algorithmes résolutifs.* Mémoire de D.E.A. Université de Provence, UER de Psychologie et de Sciences de l'Education.

Case, R. (1982). General developmental influences on the acquisition of elementary concepts and algorithms in arithmetic. In T.P. Carpenter, J.M. Moser, & T.A. Romberg (Eds.), *Addition and subtraction: A cognitive perspective* (pp. 156–170). Hillsdale, NJ: Lawrence Erlbaum Associates Inc.

Chaiklin, S. (1989). Cognitive studies of algebra problem solving and learning. In S. Wagner & C. Kieran (Eds.), *Research issues in the learning and teaching of algebra* (pp. 93–114). Reston, VA: National Council of Teachers of Mathematics; Hillsdale, NJ: Lawrence Erlbaum Associates Inc.

Chalouh, L., & Herscovics, N. (1988). Teaching algebraic expressions in a meaningful way. In A.F. Coxford, (Ed.), *The ideas of algebra, K-12* (1988 Yearbook of the National Council of Teachers of Mathematics, pp. 33–42). Reston, VA: NCTM.

Charlot, B. & Bautier, E. (1993). Rapport a l'école, rapport au savoir et enseignement des mathématiques *Repères IREM, 10,* Topiques Editions, Pont à Mousson, France.

Chevallard, Y. (1985). *La transposition didactique. Du savoir savan au savoir enseigne.* Grenoble: La pensee sauvage.

Chevallard, Y. (1988). Sur l'analyse didactique. Deux études sur les notions de contrat et de situation. *Publications de l'IREM d'Aix-Marseille, 14*

Chevallard, Y. (1989). Le concept de rapport au savoir. Rapport personnel, rapport institutionnel, rapport officiel. *Cahiers du Seminaire de didactique des mathematiques et de l'informatique* 1988–89, Université Joseph Fournier- Grenoble I.

Chevallard, Y. (1992). Concepts fondamentaux de la didactique: perspectives apportées par une approche anthropologique, *Recherches en Didactique des Mathématiques, 12,* 1, 73–112. Grenoble: La Pensée Sauvage.

Chevallard, Y., & Conne, F. (1984). Jalons à propos d'algèbre. *Interactions Didactiques, 3,* 1–54 (Universités de Genève et de Neuchâtel).

Chi, M.T.H., Glaser, R., & Rees, E. (1982). Expertise in problem solving. In R.J. Sternberg (Ed.), *Advances in the psychology of human intelligence* (Vol. 1, pp. 7–75). Hilldale, NJ: Lawrence Erlbaum Associates Inc.

Clement, J. (1985). Misconceptions in graphing. In L. Streefland (Ed.), *Proceedings of the Ninth International Conference for the Psychology of Mathematics Education* (Vol. 1, pp. 369–375). Utrecht, The Netherlands: State University of Utrecht.

Clements, D., & Battista, M. (1990). Learning of geometry concepts in a logo environment. *Journal for Research in Mathematics Education, 20,* 450–467.

Close, G.S. (1982). *Children's Understanding of Angle at the Primary/Secondary Transfer Stage.* External paper, Polytechnic of South Bank, London.

Cobb, P. (1987). Information-processing Psychology and Mathematics Education—A Constructivist Perspective. *The Journal of Mathematical Behaviour, 6,* 1, 4–40.

Cobb, P. (1990). The tension between theories of learning and instruction in mathematics education. In V. Lee (Ed.) *Children's Learning in School*, (pp. 137–151) Milton Keynes, UK: The Open University.

Cobb, P., Perlwitz, M., & Underwood, D. (1992b). *Individual Construction, Mathematical Acculturation, and the Classroom Community.* Paper presented at the Nuffield Enquiry into Primary Mathematics, Children's learning in Mathematics, Exeter, Great Britain.

Cobb, P., Yackel, E., & Wood T. (1992a). A Constructivist Alternative to the Representational View of Mind in Mathematics Education, *Journal for Research in Mathematics Education, 23,* 1, 2–33.

Cole M. (1991). Conclusion. In L.B. Resnick, J.M. Levine & S.D. Teasley (Eds) *Socially shared cognition.* Washington D.C.: American Psychological Association, pp.398–417.

Cowan, R. & Daniels, H. (1989). Children's use of counting and guidelines in judging relative number. *British Iournal of Educational Psychology, 59,* 200–210.

Cummins, D. (1991). Children's interpretations of arithmetic word problems. *Cognition and Instruction, 8,* 261–289.

Cummins, D., Kintsch, W., Reusser, K., & Weimer, R. (1988). The role of understanding in solving word problems. *Cognitive Psychology, 20,* 405–438.

D'Ambrosio, U. (1985a). *Socio-cultural Bases for Mathematics Education.* Campinas, Brazil: Unicamp.

D'Ambrosio, U. (1985b). Ethnomathematics and its place in the history and pedagogy of mathematics. *For the Learning of Mathematics, 5,* 1, 44–48.

De Corte, E. (1992). On the learning and teaching of problem-solving skills in mathematics and Logo programming. *Applied Psychology: An International Review, 20,* 317–331.

De Corte, E., Greer, B., & Verschaffel, L. (1996). Mathematics. In D. Berliner & R. Calfee (Eds.) *Handbook of Educational Psychology* (pp. 491–549). New York: MacMillan.

De Corte, E., & Somers, R. (1982). Estimating the outcome of a task as a heuristic strategy in arithmetic problem solving: A teaching experiment with sixth-graders. *Human Learning, 1,* 105–121.

De Corte, E., & Verschaffel, L. (1983). *Beginning first graders' initial representation of arithmetic problems.* Paper presented at the Annual Meeting of American Educational Research, Montréal.

De Corte, E., & Verschaffel, L (1985a). Beginning first graders' initial representation of arithmetic word problems. *Journal of Mathematical Behavior, 4,* 3–21.

De Corte, E., & Verschaffel, L. (1985b). Writing number sentences to represent addition and subtraction word problems. In S. Damarin & M. Shelton (Eds.) *Proceedings of the Seventh Annual Meeting of the North American Chapter of the International Group for the Psychology of Mathematics Education, Columbus, Ohio, 2-5 October 1985* (pp. 50–56) Columbus OH: Department of Psychology, Ohio State University.

De Corte, E., & Verschaffel, L. (1985c). Working with simple word problems in early mathematics instruction. In L. Streefland (Ed.) *Proceedings of the Ninth International Conference for the Psychology of Mathematics Education. Vol. l. Individual contributions* (pp. 304–309) Utrecht, The Netherlands: Research Group on Mathematics Education and Educational Computer Center, Subfaculty of Mathematics, University of Utrecht.

De Corte, E., & Verschaffel, L. (1987a). The effect of semantic structure on first graders' strategies for solving addition and subtraction word problems. *Journal for Research in Mathematics Education, 18,* 363–381.

De Corte, E., & Verschaffel, L. (1987b). First graders' eye movements during elementary addition and subtraction word problem solving. In G. Lüer & U. Lass (Eds.), *Fourth European Conference on Eye Movements. Vol 1: Proceedings* (pp.148–150) Toronto/ Göttingen: C.J. Hogrefe, Inc.

De Corte, E., & Verschaffel, L. (1988). Computer simulation as a tool in research on problem solving in subject-matter domains. *The International Journal of Educational Research, 12*, 49–69.

De Corte, E., & Verschaffel, L. (1989). Teaching word problems in the primary school. What research has to say to the teacher. In B. Greer & G. Mulhern (Eds.) *New Developments in Teaching Mathematics* (pp.85–106) London: Routledge.

De Corte, E., Verschaffel, L., & De Win, L. (1985a). The influence of recording verbal problems on children's problem representations and solutions. *Journal of Educational Psychology, 77*, 460–470.

De Corte, E., Verschaffel, L., Janssens, V., & Joillet, L. (1985b). Teaching word problems in the first grade: A confrontation of educational practice with results of recent research. In T.A. Romberg (Ed.) *Using research in the professional life of mathematics teachers* (pp. 186–195) Madison, WI: Center for Education Research, University of Wisconsin.

De Corte, E., Verschaffel, L., & Van Coillie, V. (1988). Influence of number size, problem structure and response mode on children's solutions of multiplication word problems. *Journal of Mathematical Behavior, 7*, 197–216.

d'Espagnat B. (1979). *A la recherche du réel. Le regard d'un physicien.* Paris: Gauthier-Villars.

DES (1987). *APU—Secondary survey report.* London, UK: HMSO.

Desforges, A. & Desforges, G. (1980). Number-based strategies of sharing in young children, *Educational Studies, 6* 97–109.

Desforges, Ch. & Cockburn A. (1987). *Understanding the Mathematics Teacher, A Study of Practice in First School.* London: The Falmer Press.

Diário de Noticias (5 October, 1990). *Com of proprios numeros do governo PS relembra problemas cronicos no escolar.* Madeira, Portugal, p.6.

Dick, T. (1988). *Student use of graphical information to monitor symbolic calculations.* Unpublished manuscript, Department of Mathematics, Oregon State University.

diSessa, A. (1990). Social niches for future software. In A. diSessa, M. Gardner, J. Greeno, A. Schoenfeld, & E. Stafe (Eds.), *Towards a scientific practice of science education.* Hillsdale, NJ: Lawrence Erlbaum Associates Inc.

diSessa, A.A., Abelson, H. & Ploger, D. (1991). An Overview of Boxer. *Journal of Mathematical Behavior, 10*, 1, 3–15.

Doise, W., Mugny, G., & Perret-Clermont, A.-N. (1975). Social interaction and the development of cognitive operations. *European Journal of Social Psychology, 5*, 367–383.

Dolk, M., & Uittenboogaard W. (1989). De ouderavond, *Willem Bartjens, 9*, 1, 14–20.

Donaldson M. (1978). *Children's minds.* New York: W.W. Norton.

Douady R. (1985). The interplays between different settings. *Proceedings of 9th PME Conference,* Vol 2, 33–52, Norwickerhoot, Pays Bas.

Douady R. (1987a). L'ingénierie didactique: une méthodologie privilégiée de la recherche. *Proceedings of 11th PME Conference,* Vol 3, 222–228, Montréal, Canada.

Douady R. (1987b). Jeux de cadres et Dialectique outil-objet. *Recherches en Didactique des Mathématiques, 7*, 5–32.

Douady R. (1991). Tool, object, setting, window: elements for analysing and constructing didactical situations in mathematics.. In Bishop A., Mellin-Olsen S. & van Dormolen, J. (Eds) *Mathematical knowledge: its growth through teaching*, 109–129. Dordrecht, Boston, London: Kluwer Academic Publishers.

Douady R. (1992). Des apports de la didactique des mathématiques à l'enseignement. *Repères—IREM, 6*, 132–158, Topiques Edition, Pont à Mousson.

Douady R. (1994). Ingénierie didactique et évolution du rapport au savoir. *Repères—IREM, 15*, 37–61, Topiques Edition, Pont à Mousson.

Douady R. & Perrin-Glorian M.J. (1989). Un processus d'apprentissage du concept d'aire de surface plane, *Educational Studies in Mathematics, 20*, 387–424.

Douwen, L. (1983). *Kwalitatief-psychologische analyse van het probleemoplossend denken bij leerlingen van het vierde leer-jaar: een constaterend individueel onderzoek met vraagstukken over vermenigvuldigen en delen.* [A qualitative psychological analysis of children's solutions of multiplication and division word problems.] (Unpublished master's thesis.) Leuven, Belgium: Center for Instructional Psychology and Technology, University of Leuven.

Dreyfus, T., & Eisenberg T. (1987). On the deep structure of functions. In J.C. Bergeron, N. Herscovics, & C. Kieran (Eds.), *Proceedings of the Eleventh International Conference for the Psychology of Mathematics Education* (Vol. I, pp. 190–196). Montréal: Université de Montréal.

Dreyfus, T., & Halevi, T. (1988, July–August). *Quadfun—a case study of pupil computer interaction.* Paper presented to the theme group on Microcomputers and the Teaching of Mathematics at the Sixth International Congress on Mathematical Education, Budapest, Hungary.

Ebeling, K., & Gelman, S. (1988). Coordination of size standards by young children. *Child Development, 59,* 888–896.

Edwards, D. & Mercer, N. (1987). *Common Knowledge: The Development of Understanding in the Classroom.* London: Methuen.

Entwisle, D.R., & Alexander, K.L. (1990). Beginning school math competence: Minority and majority comparisons. *Child Development, 61,* 454–471.

Ernest, P. (1991). *The Philosophy of Mathematics Education.* Hampshire: The Falmer Press.

Evans, J.T. (1991). Cognition, Affect, Context in Numerical Activity Among Adults, *PME XV,* 33–39, Italy.

Ezaki, S. (1980, April). On interiorized activity in abacus-derived mental arithmetic. *Nihon-Shuzan [Abacus in Japan],* Serial No.*314,* 2–5 (in Japanese).

Fey, J.T. (Ed.). (1989). *Computer-intensive algebra.* College Park: University of Maryland.

Fischbein, E. (1987). *Intuition in Science and Mathematics.* Dordrecht: Reidel.

Fischbein, E., Deri, M., Nello, M., & Marino, M. (1985). The role of implicit models in solving verbal problems in multiplication and division. *Journal for Research in Mathematics Education, 16,* 3–17.

Forman, E. (1989). The role of peer interaction in the social construction of mathematical knowledge. *International Journal of Educational Research, 13,* 55–70.

Forman, E.A. (1992). Discourse, intersubjectivity and the development of peer collaboration: a Vygotskian approach. In L.T. Winegard & J. Valsiner (Eds), *Children's development within social contexts: metatheoretical, theoretical and methodological issues.* Hillsdale, NJ: Lawrence Erlbaum Associates Inc.

Freire, P. (1972). *Pedagogy of the Oppressed.* Harmondsworth, UK: Penguin Books.

Freudenthal, H. (1971). Geometry Between the Devil and the Deep Sea. *Educational Studies in Mathematic 3,* 413–435.

Freudenthal, H. (1973). *Mathematics as an Educational Task.* Dordrecht, The Netherlands: Reidel.

Freudenthal, H. (1982). Variables and functions. In G. van Barneveld & H. Krabbendam (Eds.), *Proceedings of Conference on Functions* (pp. 7–20). Enschede, The Netherlands: National Institute for Curriculum Development.

Freudenthal, H. (1983). *Didactical Phenomenology of Mathematical Structures.* Dordrecht: Reidel.

Freudenthal, H. (1991). *Revisiting Mathematics Education.* Dordrecht: Kluwer Academic Publishers.

Frydman, O. & Bryant, P.E. (1988). Sharing and the understanding of number equivalence by young children. *Cognitive Development, 3,* 323–339.

Frye, D., Braisby, N., Lowe, J., Maroudas, C. & Nicholls, J. (1989). Young children's understanding of counting and cardinality. *Child Development, 60*, 1158–1171.

Furth, G. (1969). *Piaget and Knowledge: Theoretical Foundations* London: Prentice-Hall Inc.

Furth, G. (1977). The Operative and Figurative Aspects of Knowledge in Piaget's Theory. In B. Geber (Ed.), *Piaget and Knowing: studies in Genetic Epistemology*. London: Routledge & Kegan Paul.

Fuson, K. (1992). Research on whole number addition and subtraction. In D.A. Grouws (Ed.) *Handbook for Research on Mathematics Teaching and Learning* (pp.243–275). New York: Macmillan.

Fuson, K.C. (1988). *Children's counting and concepts of number*. New York: Springer Verlag.

Fuson, K.C., & Kwon, Y. (1992). Effects on children's addition and subtraction of the system of number words and other cultural tools. In J. Bideaud, C. Meljac, & Fischer, J.-P. (Eds.), *Pathways to number* (pp. 283–306). Hillsdale, NJ: Lawrence Erlbaum Associates Inc.

Gagné, R.M. (1965). *The Conditions of Learning*. New York: Holt, Rinehart & Winston.

Galen, F. van, Gravemeijer, K., Kraemer, J-M., Meeuwisse, A., & Venneulen, W. (1985). *Rekenen in een tweed* (Mathematics in a second language). Enschede: Institute for Curriculum Development, SLO.

Garançon, M., Kieran, C., & Boileau, A. (1990). Introducing algebra: A functional approach in a computer environment. In G. Booker, P. Cobb, & T.N. de Mendicuti (Eds.), *Proceedings of the Fourteenth International Conference for the Psychology of Mathematics Education* (Vol. II, pp. 51–58). Mexico City: PME Program Committee.

Garofalo, J., & Lester, F. (1985). Metacognition, cognitive monitoring and mathematical performance. *Journal for Research in Mathematics Education, 16*, 163–176.

Gay, J. & Cole, M. (1967). *The New Mathematics and an Old Culture: a study of learning among the Kpelle of Liberia*. New York: Holt, Rinehart & Winston.

Gelman, R. (1979). Preschool thought. *American Psychologist, 34*, 900–905.

Gelman, R. & Gallistel, C.R. (1978). *The Child's Understanding of Number*. Cambridge, MA: Harvard University Press.

Gelman, R. & Meck, E. (1983). Preschoolers' counting: principles before skill. *Cognition, 13*, 343–360.

Gelman, S., & Ebeling, K. (1989). Children's use of nonegocentric standards in judgments of functional size. *Child Development, 60*, 920–932.

Gerdes, P. (1988). On culture, geometrical thinking and mathematics education. *Educational Studies in Mathematics, 19*, 137–162.

Ghiglione, R. (1986). *L'homme communiquant*. Paris: Armand Colin.

Ghiglione, R. (1987). Questionner. In A. Blanchet, R. Ghiglione, J. Massonat & A Trognon, (Eds) *Les techniques d'enquête en sciences sociales*. Paris: Dunod.

Gibson, J. (1979). *The ecological approach to visual perception*. Boston: Houghton Mifflin.

Gilly, M. (1989). A propos de la théorie du conflit sociocognitif et des mécanismes psycho sociaux des constructions cognitives: perspectives actuelles et modèles explicatifs. In N. Bednarz & C. Garnier (Eds) *Construction des savoirs: obstacles et conflits*. Ottawa: Cirade.

Ginsburg, H. (1977). *Children's arithmetic: The learning process*. New York: Van Nostrand.

Ginsburg, H.P. (1989). *Children's arithmetic*. (2nd Edn.). Austin, TX: Pro-Ed.

Ginsburg, H., & Allardice, B. (1984). Children's difficulties with school mathematics. In B. Rogoff & J. Lave (Eds.), *Everyday cognition: Its development in social context* (pp. 194–219). Cambridge, MA: Harvard University Press.

Ginsburg, H.P., & Baroody, A.J. (1983). *The test of early mathematics ability*. (1st Edn.). Austin, TX: Pro-Ed.

Ginsburg, H.P., & Baroody, A.J. (1990). *The test of early mathematics ability*, (2nd Edn.). Austin, TX: Pro-Ed.

Ginsburg, H.P., Bempechat, J., & Chung, Y.E. (1992a). Parent influences on children's mathematics. In T. Sticht & B. MacDonald (Eds.), *Intergenerational transfer of cognitive skills, Volume II: Theory and research in cognitive science* (pp. 91–121.) Norwood, NJ: Ablex.

Ginsburg, H.P., Lopez, L.S., Mukhopadhyay, S., Yamamoto, T.A., Willis, M., & Kelly, M.S. (1992b). Assessing Understandings of Arithmetic. In R. Lesh & S. Lamon (Eds.), *Assessment of Authentic Performance in School Mathematics* (pp. 265–289). Washington, DC: American Association for the Advancement of Science.

Ginsburg, H.P., Posner, J.K., & Russell, R.L. (1981). The development of mental addition as a function of schooling and culture. *Journal of Cross-Cultural Psychology, 12*, 163–168.

Ginsburg, H.P., & Russell, R.L. (1981). Social class and racial influences on early mathematical thinking. *Monographs of the Society for Research in Child Development, 46*, Serial no. 193.

Giosuè, F. (1992). *Quanti anni hanno la maestra e il capitano? Approccio psicosociale alla costruzione della risposta a problemi assurdi in contesto scolastico.* Doctorat de recherche en psychologie. Dipartimento di Scienze dell'Educazione, Université de Bologne (Italy).

Glaser, R., & Pellegrino, J. (1982). Analyzing aptitudes for learning: Inductive reasoning. In R. Glaser (Ed.), *Advances in instruction psychology* (Vol 2, pp. 269–345). Hillsdale, NJ: Lawrence Erlbaum Associates Inc.

Goldenberg, E.P. (1988). Mathematics, metaphors, and human factors: Mathematical, technical, and pedagogical challenges in the educational use of graphical representation of functions. *Journal of Mathematical Behavior, 7*, 135–173.

Goodnow J.J. (1989). *The acquisition of cognitive and other values.* Paper presented at the Biennial meeting of the International Society for the Study of Behavioral Development, University of Jyvaskyla, Finland, July 1989.

Goodstein, H.A., Cawley, J.F., Gordon, S., & Helfgott, J. (1971). Verbal problem solving among educable mentally retarded children. *American Journal of Mental Deficiency, 76*, 238–241.

Gravemeijer, K. (Ed.) (1983). *Rekenen & Wiskunde.* Baarn: Bekadidact.

Gravemeijer, K. (1993). The empty number line as an alternative means ofrepresentation for addition and subtraction. In De Lange, J., I. Huntley, Ch. Keitel & M. Niss (Eds.) *Innovation in Mathematics Education by Modelling and Applications* (pp. 141–149).

Gravemeijer, K. (1994). Modelling two digit addition and subtraction problems with an empty number line. In T. Breiteig, G. Kaiser-Messmer & I. Huntley (Eds), *Mathematics works— Mathematical Modelling in the Classroom* (pp. 51–61). London. Ellis Horwood/Simon & Schuster.

Greco, P. (1962). Quantité et quotité. In P. Greco & A. Morf (Eds), *Structures numeriques elementaires*. Paris: P.U.F.

Greeno, J. G. (1978). *Significant basic research questions and significant applied questions.* Paper presented at the Annual Meeting of the American Educational Research Association, Toronto, Ontario.

Greeno, J.G. (1982, March). *A cognitive learning analysis of algebra.* Paper presented at the annual meeting of the American Educational Research Association, Boston, MA.

Greer, B. (1992). Multiplication and division as models of situations. In D.A. Grouws (Ed.) *Handbook of Research on Mathematics Teaching and Learning* (pp. 276–295). New York: Macmillan.

Greer, B. (1993). The modelling perspective on wor(1)d problems. *Journal of Mathematical Behavior, 12*, 239–250.

Grossen, M. (1988). *L'intersubjectivité en situation de test.* Cousset (Fribourg) DelVal.

Grossen, M., Iannacone, A., Liengme Bessire, M.J., & Perret-Clermont, A.N. (1996). Actual and perceived expertise: the role of social comparison in the mastery of right and left recognition in novice-expert dyads. *Swiss Journal of Psychology, 55,* 176–187.

Grossen, M., Liengme Bessire, M.J., & Perret-Clermont, A.N. (1997). Construction de l'interaction et dynamiques socio-cognitives. In M. Grossen, & B. Py (Eds.) *Pratiques sociales et médiations symboliques.* Bern: P. Lang.

Grossen, M., & Perret-Clermont, A.-N. (in press). Psycho-social perspective on cognitive development: construction of adult-child intersubjectivity in logic tasks. In R. Maier & W.J de Graaf (Eds.) *Processes of sociogenesis.* New York: Springer Verlag.

Gudmundsdottir S. (1991). Story-maker, story-teller: narrative structures in curriculum. *Journal of Curriculum Studies, 23,* 33, 207–218.

Hanna, G., & Winchester, I. (Eds.). (1990). Creativity, thought, and mathematical proof. *Interchange, 21* (1).

Harré R. (1986). The step to social constructionism. In M. Richards & P. Light (Eds.), *Children of Social Worlds,* (pp. 287–296). Cambridge: Polity Press.

Harris, P.L. (1989). *Children and Emotion: The Development of Psychological Understanding* Oxford: Basil Blackwell.

Hart, K. (1986). *The step to formalisation.* Institute of Education, University of London: Proceedings of the 10th International Conference of the Psychology of Mathematics Education, pp. 59–164.

Hart, K. (1988). Ratio and proportion. In J. Hiebert & M. Behr (Eds.), *Number concepts and operations in the middle grades* (pp. 198–219). Hillsdale, NJ: Lawrence Erlbaum Associates Inc.

Hart, K.M. (1981). *Children's Understanding of Mathematics: 11–16.* London: Murray.

Harvey, B. (1985). *Computer Science Logo Style.* Cambridge, Massachusetts: MIT Press.

Hatano, G. (1988a). Social and motivational bases for mathematical understanding. In G.B. Saxe & M. Gearhart (Eds.), *Children's mathematics* (pp. 55–70). San Francisco: Jossey-Bass.

Hatano, G. (1988b). Becoming an expert in mental abacus operation: A case of routine expertise. *Advances in Japanese Cognitive Science (1,* 141–160). Tokyo: Kodansha Scientific. (in Japanese with English summary)

Hatano, G., Amaiwa, S. & Shimiu, K. (1987). Formation of a mental abacus for computation and its use as a memory device for digits: A developmental study. *Developmental Psychology, 23,* 832–838.

Hatano, G. & Inagaki, K. (1986). Two courses of expertise. In H. Stevenson, H. Azuma, & K. Hakuta (Eds.), *Child development and education in Japan* (pp. 262–272). New York: Freeman.

Hatano, G., Miyake, Y., & Binks, M.G. (1977). Performance of expert abacus operators. *Cognition, 5,* 47–55.

Hatano, G. & Osawa, K. (1983). Digit memory of grand experts in abacus-derived mental calculation. *Cognition, 15,* 95–110.

Hatta, T., & Ikeda, K. (1988). Hemisphere specialization of abacus experts in mental calculation: Evidence from results of time-sharing tasks. *Neuropsychologia, 26,* 877–893.

Hegarty, M., Mayer, R.E., & Green, C.E. (1992). Comprehension of arithmetic word problems: Evidence from students' eye fixations. *Journal of Educational Psychology, 84,* 76–84.

Heid, M.K. (1988). *"Algebra with Computers": A description and an evaluation of student performance and attitudes* (Report to the State College Area School District Board of Education). State College: Pennsylvania State University.

Heid, M.K., Sheets, C., Matras, M.A., & Menasian, J. (1988). *Classroom and computer lab interaction in a computer-intensive algebra curriculum.* Paper presented at the annual meeting of the American Educational Research Association, New Orleans, LA.

Herschkowitz, R. (1990). Psychological aspects of learning geometry. In P. Nesher, & J. Kilpatrick (Eds.) *Mathematics and Cognition: A research synthesis by the International Group for the Psychology of Mathematics Education* (pp. 31–52). Cambridge, UK: Cambridge University Press.

Herscovics, N. (1989). Cognitive obstacles encountered in the learning of algebra. In S. Wagner & C. Kieran (Eds.), *Research issues in the learning and teaching of algebra* (pp. 60–86). Reston, VA: National Council of Teachers of Mathematics; Hillsdale, NJ: Lawrence Erlbaum Associates Inc.

Hertzig, M.E., Birch, H.G., Thomas, A., & Mendez, O.A. (1968). Class and ethnic differences in the responsiveness of preschool children to cognitive demands. *Monographs of the Society for Research in Child Development, 33*, Serial no. 117.

Hiele, P.M. van (1985). *Structure and Insight, A Theory of Mathematics Education.* New York.

Hilton, P. (1983). Do we still need to teach fractions? In M. Zweng (Ed.) *Proceedings of the Fourth International Congress on Mathematical Education.* Boston: Birkhäuser Verlag.

Howson, A.G., Keitel, C. & Kilpatrick, J. (1981). *Curriculum Development in Mathematics.* London: Cambridge University Press.

Hoyles, C. (1993). Microworlds/Schoolworlds: The transformation of an innovation. In W. Dörfler, C. Keitel, & K. Ruthven (Eds.), *Learning from Computers: Mathematics Education and Technology* (pp. 1–17). Berlin: Springer-Verlag.

Hoyles, C., & Noss, R. (1987). Children working in a structured logo environment: From doing to understanding. *Recherches en Didactique des Mathématiques, 8* (1.2), 131–174.

Hoyles C. & Noss R. (1988). Children working in a Structured Logo Environment: From Doing to Understanding. *Recherches en Didactique des Mathématiques, 8,* 131–174.

Hoyles C. & Noss R. (1992). A pedagogy for mathematical microworlds. *Educational Studies in Mathematics 23,* 31–57.

Hoyles, C. & Noss, R. (1993). Out of the cul-de-sac? In J. Becker, & B. Pence, (Eds) *Proceedings of the Fifteenth Annual Meeting of the North American Chapter of the International Group for the Psychology of Mathematics Education,* (invited lecture) 1-83-90 San José State University.

Hoyles, C. & Sutherland, R. (1989). *Logo Mathematics in the Classroom.* London: Routledge.

Hoyles, C., Noss, R. & Sutherland, R. (1991). *The Ratio and Proportion Microworld. Final Report of the Microworlds Project Vol. 3.* Institute of Education, University of London.

Hoz R., & Harel, G. (1989). The facilitating role of table forms in solving algebra speed problems: Real or imaginary? In G. Vergnaud, J. Rogalski, & M. Artigue (Eds.), *Proceedings of the Thirteenth International Conference for the Psychology of Mathematics Education* (Vol. II, pp. 123–130). Paris: G.R. Didactique, CNRS.

Hughes, M. (1981). Can preschool children add and subtract? *Educational Psychology, 1,* 207–219.

Hughes M. (1986). *Children and number: Difficulties in learning mathematics.* Oxford: Blackwell Publishers.

Hundeide, K (1981). Contractual congruence or logical consistency, *The Quarterly Newsletter of the Laboratory of Comparative Human Cognition, 3,* 4, 77–79.

Hundeide, K. (1985). The tacit background of children's judgements. In J.V. Wertsch (Ed.) *Culture communication and cognition: Vygotskian perspectives,* Cambridge: Cambridge University Press.

Hunter, I.M.L. (1968/1977). Mental Calculation. In P.N. Johnson-Laird & P.C. Wason (Eds.), *Thinking.* Cambridge, UK: Cambridge University Press.

Iannaccone, A., & Perret-Clermont, A.N. (1993). Qu'est-ce qui s'apprend? Qu'est-ce qui se développe? In J. Wassmann & P.R. Dasen (Eds.) *Les savoirs quotidiens. Les approaches cognitives dans le dialogue interdisciplinaire.* Presses Universitaires de Fribourg (Suisse).

Inhelder, B., & Piaget, J. (1958). *The growth of logical thinking from childhood to adolescence.* New York: Basic Books.

IREM de Grenoble (1980). Quel est l'âge du capitaine? *Bulletin de l'APMEP, 323*, 235–243.

Janvier, C. (1978). *The interpretation of complex Cartesian graphs—studies and teaching experiments.* Unpublished doctoral dissertation, University of Nottingham, England.

Jaspers, M. (1991). *Prototypes of computer-assisted instruction for arithmetic word-problem solving* (Unpublished doctoral dissertation). Nijmegen, The Netherlands: Department of Special Education, University of Nijmegen.

Johnson, D.C. (Ed.) (1989). *Children's Mathematical Frameworks 8–13: A Study of Classroom Teaching.* Windsor: NFER-Nelson.

Johnson, M. (1987). *The body in the mind: The bodily basis of meaning, imagination, and reason.* Chicago: University of Chicago Press.

Jordan, N.C., Huttenlocher, J., & Levine, S.C. (1992). Differential calculation abilities in young children from middle- and low-income families. *Developmental Psychology, 28*, 644–53.

Kaput, J.J. (1985). *Multiplicative word problems and intensive quantities. An integrated software response* (Technical report 85–19). Cambridge, MA: Educational Technology Center, Harvard Graduate School of Education.

Kaput, J.J. (1989). Linking representations in the symbol systems of algebra. In S. Wagner & C. Kieran (Eds.), *Research issues in the learning and teaching of algebra* (pp.167–194). Reston, VA: National Council of Teachers of Mathematics; Hillsdale, NJ: Lawrence Erlbaum Associates Inc.

Karplus, R., Pulos, S., & Stage, E. (1983). Proportional reasoning of early adolescents. In R. Lesh & M. Landau (Eds.), *Acquisition of mathematical concepts and processes* (pp.45–91). New York: Academic Press.

Kegan, R. (1982). *The evolving self.* Cambridge, MA: Harvard University Press.

Kerslake, D. (1977). The understanding of graphs. *Mathematics in School, 6*(2), 22–25.

Kerslake, D. (1981). Graphs. In K.M. Hart (Ed.), *Children's understanding of mathematics: 11–16* (pp.120–136). London: John Murray.

Kieran, C. (1979). Children's operational thinking within the context of bracketing and the order of operations. In D. Tall (Ed.), *Proceedings of the Third International Conference for the Psychology of Mathematics Education* (pp.128–135). Coventry, UK: Warwick University, Mathematics Education Research Centre.

Kieran, C. (1981). Concepts associated with the equality symbol. *Educational Studies in Mathematics, 12*, 317–326.

Kieran, C. (1982, March). *The learning of algebra: A teaching experiment.* Paper presented at the annual meeting of the American Educational Research Association, New York. (ERIC Document Reproduction Service No. ED 216 884).

Kieran, C. (1984). A comparison between novice and more-expert algebra students on tasks dealing with the equivalence of equations. In J.M. Moser (Ed.), *Proceedings of the Sixth Annual Meeting of PME-NA* (pp. 83–91). Madison: University of Wisconsin.

Kieran, C. (1989). The early learning of algebra: A structural perspective. In S. Wagner & C. Kieran (Eds.), *Research issues in the learning and teaching of algebra* (pp.33–56). Reston, VA: National Council of Teachers of Mathematics; Hillsdale, NJ: Lawrence Erlbaum Associates Inc.

Kieran, C. (1992). The learning and teaching of school algebra. In D.A. Grouws (Ed.), *Handbook of research on mathematics teaching and learning* (pp. 390–419). New York: Macmillan.

Kieran, C. (1993). Functions, graphing, and technology: Integrating research on learning and instruction. In T.A. Romberg, E. Fennema, & T.P. Carpenter (Eds.), *Integrating research on the graphical representation of function* (pp.189–237). Hillsdale, NJ: Lawrence Erlbaum Associates Inc.

Kieran, C. (Ed.) (1995). New perspectives on school algebra: Papers and discussions of the ICME-7 Algebra Working Group. *Journal of Mathematical Behavior, 14*, 1–162.

Kieran, C., Boileau, A., & Garançon, M. (1989). Processes of mathematization in algebra problem solving within a computer environment: A functional approach. In C.A. Maher, G.A. Goldin, & R.B. Davis (Eds.), *Proceedings of the Eleventh Annual Meeting of PME-NA* (pp. 26–34). New Brunswick, NJ: Rutgers University.

Kieran, C., Garançon, M., Boileau, A., & Pelletier, M. (1988). Numerical approaches to algebra problem solving in a computer environment. In M.J. Behr, C.B. Lacampagne, & M.M. Wheeler (Eds.), *Proceedings of the Tenth Annual Meeting of PME-NA* (pp. 141–149). DeKalb: Northern Illinois University.

Kirk, G.E., Hunt, J.M., & Volkmar, F. (1975). Social class and preschool language skill: V. Cognitive and semantic mastery of number. *Genetic Psychology Monographs, 92*, 131–153.

Klein, A., & Starkey, P. (1988). Universals in the development of early arithmetic cognition. In G.B. Saxe & M. Gearhart (Eds.), *Children's mathematics* (pp. 5–26). San Francisco: Jossey-Bass.

Kohn, A. (1993). Preschooler's knowledge of density: Will it float? *Child Development, 64*, 1637–1650.

Kornilaki, E. (1994). *The understanding of the numeration system among preschool children.* London: Unpublished MSc thesis, Department of Child Development and Primary Education, University of London.

Kouba, V. (1989). Children's solution strategies for equivalent set multiplication and division word problems. *Journal for Research in Mathematics Education, 20*, 147–158.

Kozol, J. (1991). *Savage Inequalities: Children in America's schools.* NY: Crown Publishers.

Kun, A. (1977). Development of the magnitude-covariation and compensation schemata in ability and effort attributions of performance. *Child Development, 48*, 862–873.

Kun, A., Parsons, I., & Ruble, D. (1974). Development of integration processes using ability and effort information to predict outcome. *Developmental Psychology, 5*, 721–732

Kynigos, C. (1989). *From Intrinsic to Non-intrinsic Geometry: A Study of Children's Understandings in Logo-based Microworlds.* Doctoral thesis, Institute of Education, University of London.

Labinowitcz, E. (1985). *Learning from Children.* Amsterdam: Addison-Wesley.

Laborde, C. (1993). Microworlds/Schoolworlds: The Transformation of an Innovation. In C. Keitel, & K. Ruthven (Eds.) *Learning from Computers: Mathematics Education and Technology.* Berlin: Springer-Verlag.

Laborde, C., & Laborde, J.M. (1995). What about a learning environment where Euclidean concepts are manipulated with a mouse? In A. diSessa, C. Hoyles, & R. Noss (Eds.), *Computers for Exploratory Learning.* Berlin: Springer Verlag.

Lakatos, I. (1976). *Proofs and Refutations.* Cambridge: Cambridge University Press.

Lampert, M. (1986). Knowing, doing, and teaching multiplication. *Cognition and Instruction*, 305–342.

Lampert, M. (1989). Choosing and Using Mathematical Tools in Classroom Discourse. In J. Brophy (Ed.), *Advances in Research on Teaching*, Volume 1. Greenwich: JAI Press Inc, CT, 233–264.

Lampert M. (1992). Practices and problems in teaching authentic mathematics. In F.K. Oser, A. Dick & J.L. Patry (Eds.), *Effective and responsible teaching.* San Francisco: Jossey-Bass Publishers, pp. 295–314.

Lancy, D.F. (1983). *Cross-cultural studies in cognition and mathematics.* New York: Academic Press.

Lave, J. (1988). *Cognition in practice: Mind, mathematics and culture in everyday life.* Cambridge, UK: Cambridge University Press.

Lave, J. (1989). *Cognition in Practice*. Cambridge University Press.

Lave, J., Murtaugh, M. & de la Rocha, O. (1984). The dialectic of arithmetic grocery shopping. In B. Rogoff & J. Lave (Eds.), *Everyday cognition: Its development in social context* (pp. 95–116). Cambridge MA: Harvard University Press.

Lazar, I. (1983). Discussion and implication of the findings. In The Consortium for Longitudinal Studies. *As the Twig is Bent... Lasting Effects of Preschool Programs*, Hillsdale, NJ: Lawrence Erlbaum Associates Inc.

League of Japan Abacus Associations. (1989). *Soroban*. Tokyo: The Japan Chamber of Commerce and Industry.

Lee, L., & Wheeler, D. (1987). *Algebraic thinking in high school students: Their conceptions of generalisation and justification* (Research Report). Montreal: Concordia University, Mathematics Department.

Lei no46/86 (14 October, 1986). Lei de Bases do Sistema Educativo. In *Diário da Republica*, Lisboa, Portugal.

Leinhardt, G., Zaslavsky, O., & Stein, M.K. (1990). Functions, graphs, and graphing: Tasks, learning, and teaching. *Review of Educational Research, 60*, 1–64.

Lek, A. (1992). *Met repen begrepen* [Understood with bars]. Utrecht, Faculty of Social Sciences.

Leron, U., & Zazkis, R. (1992). Of Geometry, Turtles, and Groups. In C. Hoyles & R. Noss, (Eds.) *Learning Mathematics and Logo* (pp. 319–352). Cambridge, MA: MIT Press.

Lesh, R. (1985). Conceptual Analysis of Mathematical Ideas and Problem Solving Processes. In L. Streefland (Ed.), *Proceedings of the Ninth International Conference for the Psychology of Mathematics Education, Vol. 2*. Utrecht: Freudenthal Institute, 73–97.

Lesh, R. & Landau, M. (1983). *Acquisition of mathematics concepts and processes*. New York: Academic Press.

Lesh, R., Post, T., & Behr, M. (1987). Dienes revisited: Multiple embodiments in computer environments. In I. Wirszup & R. Streit (Eds.), *Developments in school mathematics education around the world* (pp. 647–680). Reston, VA: National Council of Teachers of Mathematics.

Lewis, A., & Mayer, R. (1987). Students' miscomprehension of relational statements in arithmetic word problems. *Journal of Educational Psychology 79*, 363–371.

Lewis, C. (1981). Skill in algebra. In J.R. Anderson (Ed.), *Cognitive skills and their acquisition*. Hillsdale, NJ: Lawrence Erlbaum Associates Inc.

Linchevski, L., & Sfard, A. (1991). Rules without reasons as processes without objects—the case of equations and inequalities. In F. Furinghetti (Ed.), *Proceedings of the Fifteenth International Conference for the Psychology of Mathematics Education* (Vol. II, pp. 317–324). Assisi, Italy: PME Program Committee.

Lovett, S., & Singer, J. (1991, April). *The development of children's understanding of probability: Perceptual and quantitative conceptions*. Poster presented at the biennial meeting of the Society for Research in Child Development, Seattle, WA.

Luria, A.R. (1976). *Cognitive development, its cultural and social foundations*. Cambridge, MA: Harvard University Press.

Luria, A.R. (1979). *Curso de Psicologia Geral*. [A general psychology course]. Rio de Janeiro: Civilizacao Brasileira, Vol. 1.

Lynn, R. (1982). IQ in Japan and in the United States shows a growing disparity. *Nature, 297*, 222–223.

Lynn, R., & Hampson, S. (1987). Further evidence of the cognitive abilities of the Japanese: data from the WPPSI. *International Journal of Behavioral Development, 10*, 23–36.

Markovits, Z., Eylon, B.-S., & Bruckheimer, M. (1986). Functions today and yesterday. *For the Learning of Mathematics, 6*, 2, 18–24.

Marshall, S., Barthuli, K.E., Brewer, M.A., & Rose, F.E. (1989). *Story problem solver: A schema-based system of instruction* (Technical report no. 89–01). San Diego, CA: Center for Research in Mathematics and Science Education, San Diego State University.

Mason, J. (1996). Expressing generality and roots of algebra. In N. Bednarz, C. Kieran, & L. Lee (Eds.), *Approaches to algebra: Perspectives for research and teaching* (pp. 65–86). Dordrecht, The Netherlands: Kluwer.

Mason, J., Graham, A., Pimm, D., & Gowar, N. (1985). *Routes to/roots of algebra.* Milton Keynes, UK: The Open University Press.

Mason, J. & Pimm, D. (1984). Generic examples: seeing the general in the particular. *Educational Studies in Mathematics 15,* 277–289.

Matz, M. (1979). *Towards a process model for high school algebra errors* (Working Paper 181). Cambridge, MA: Massachusetts Institute of Technology, Artificial Intelligence Laboratory.

Mayer, R.E. (1980). *Schemas for algebra story problems* (Report No. 80–3). Santa Barbara: University of California, Department of Psychology, Series in Learning and Cognition.

McLeod, D.B. (1992). Research on affect in mathematics education: A reconceptualisation. In D.A. Grouws (Ed.) *Handbook of research on mathematics teaching and learning* (pp.575–596). New York: Macmillan.

McKnight, C.C., Crosswhite, F.J., Dossey, J.A., Kifer, E., Swafford, J.O., Travers, K.J., & Cooney, T.J. (1987). *The underachieving curriculum: Assessing U.S. school mathematics from an international perspective.* Champaign, IL; Stipes Publishing Co.

McLloyd, V. (1990). The impact of economic hardship on Black families and children: Psychological distress, parenting, and socioemotional development. *Child Development, 61,* 311–346.

Mevarech, Z.R., & Yitschak, D. (1983). Students' misconceptions of the equivalence relationship. In R. Hershkowitz (Ed.), *Proceedings of the Seventh International Conference for the Psychology of Mathematics Education* (pp.313–318). Rehovot, Israel: Weizmann Institute of Science.

Mellin-Olsen, S. (1987). *The Politics of Mathematics Education.* Dordrecht, Holland: Kluwer.

Michie, S. (1984). Why preschoolers are reluctant to count spontaneously. *British Journal of Developmental Psychology, 2,* 347–358.

Miller, K. (1984). The child as the measurer of all things: measurement procedures and the development of quantitative concepts. In C Sophian (Ed). *Origins of Cognitive Skills,* pp. 93–228. Hillsdale, NJ: Lawrence Erlbaum Associates Inc.

Miller, K., & Gelman, R. (1983). The child's representation of number: A multidimensional scaling analysis. *Child Development, 54,* 1470–1479.

Miller, K.F., & Stigler, J.W. (1987). Counting in Chinese: Cultural variation in a basic cognitive skill. *Cognitive development, 2,* 279–305.

Miller, K., & Stigler, J. (1991). Meanings of skill: Effects of abacus expertise on number representation. *Cognition and Instruction, 8,* 29–67.

Miura, I.T. (1987). Mathematics achievement as a function of language. *Journal of Educational Psychology, 79,* 79–82.

Miura, I.T., Kim, C.C., Chang, C.-M., & Okamoto, Y. (1988). Effects of language characteristics on children's cognitive representation of number: cross-national comparisons. *Child Development, 59,* 1445–1450.

Miura, I.T., & Okamoto, Y. (1989). Comparisons of American and Japanese first graders' cognitive representation of number and understanding of place value. *Journal of Educational Psychology, 81,* 109–113.

Mordkowitz, E.R., & Ginsburg, H.P. (1987). Early academic socialization of successful Asian-American college students. *Quarterly Newsletter of the Laboratory for Comparative Human Cognition, 9,* 85–91.

Moschkovich, J. (1990). Students' interpretations of linear equations and their graphs. In G. Booker, P. Cobb, & T.N. de Mendicuti (Eds.), *Proceedings of the Fourteenth International Conference for the Psychology of Mathematics Education* (Vol. II, pp. 109–116). Mexico City: PME Program Committee.

Moschkovich, J., Schoenfeld, A.H., & Arcavi, A. (1993). Aspects of understanding: On multiple perspectives and representations of linear relations, and connections among them. In T.A. Romberg, E. Fennema, & T.P. Carpenter (Eds.), *Integrating research on the graphical representation of function* (pp. 69–100). Hillsdale, NJ: Lawrence Erlbaum Associates Inc.

Moscovici, S. (1988). Notes Towards a Description of Social Representations. *European Journal of Social Psychology, 18,* 211–250.

Mugny, G., Perret-Clermont, A.N. & Doise, W. (1981). Interpersonal coordinations and sociological differences in the construction of the intellect. In G.M. Stephenson & J.M. Davis (Eds), *Progress in Applied Social Psychology*,Vol 1. Chichester, UK: John Wiley & Sons.

Mulligan, C.H. (1988). Using polynomials to amaze. In A.F. Coxford (Ed.), *The ideas of algebra, K-12* (1988 Yearbook of National Council of Teachers of Mathematics, pp. 206–211). Reston, VA: NCTM.

Mulligan, J. (1992, August). *Children's solutions to multiplication and division word problems: A longitudinal study.* Paper presented at the Seventh International Conference on Mathematics Education, Quebec, Canada, August 1992.

Mundy, J. (1984). Analysis of errors of first year calculus students. In A. Bell, B. Low, & J. Kilpatrick (Eds.), *Theory, research, and practice in mathematics education.* Nottingham, UK: Shell Centre for Mathematical Education.

Murray, H., Olivier, A., & Human, P. (1992, August). *The development of young students' division strategies.* Paper presented at the Seventh International Conference on Mathematics Education, Quebec, Canada.

National Center for Education Statistics. (1990). *Digest of Education Statistics.* Washington, DC: U.S. Department of Education, Office of Educational Research and Improvement.

Natriello, G., McDill, E.L., & Pallas, A.M. (1990). *Schooling disadvantaged children: racing against catastrophe.* NY: Teachers College Press.

Neisser, U. (Ed.). (1986). *The school achievement of minority children: new perspectives.* Hillsdale, NJ: Lawrence Erlbaum Associates Inc.

Nesher, P. (1980). The stereotyped nature of school word problems. *For the Learning of Mathematics, 1,* 41–48.

Nesher, P. (1982). Levels of description in the analysis of addition and subtraction. In T.P. Carpenter, J.M. Moser & T. Romberg (Eds.), *Addition and subtraction: A cognitive perspective* (pp. 25–38). Hillsdale NJ: Lawrence Erlbaum Associates Inc.

Nesher, P. (1988). Multiplicative school word problems. Theoretical approaches and empirical findings. In J. Hiebert & M. Behr (Eds.) *Number concepts and operations in the middle grades* (pp. 19–40). Hillsdale, NJ: Lawrence Erlbaum Associates Inc.

Nesher, P., & Teubal, E. (1975). Verbal cues as an interfering factor in verbal problem solving. *Educational Studies in Mathematics, 6,* 41–51.

Noelting, G. (1980). The development of proportional reasoning and the ratio concept: Part 1— Differentiation of stages. *Educational Studies in Mathematics, 11,* 217–253.

Noss, R. (1986). Constructing a Conceptual Framework for Elementary Algebra through Logo Programming. *Educational Studies in Mathematics, 17*(4) 335–357.

Noss, R. (1988). The Computer as a Cultural Influence in Mathematical Learning. *Educational Studies in Mathematics, 19,* 2, 251–268.

Noss, R. (1991). The Social Shaping of Computing in Mathematics Education. In D. Pimm & E. Love (Eds.) *The Teaching and Learning of School Mathematics.* London: Hodder & Stoughton.

Noss, R. & Hoyles, C. (1992). Logo and the Learning of Mathematics: Looking Back and Looking Forward. In C. Hoyles & R. Noss (Eds) *Learning Logo and Mathematics*. Cambridge MA: MIT Press

Noss, R. & Hoyles, C. (1995). The Dark Side of the Moon. In J. Mason, & R. Sutherland (Eds.) *Exploiting Mental Imagery with Computers in Mathematics Education*. Berlin: Springer Verlag.

Noss, R. & Hoyles, C. (1996). *Windows on mathematical meanings: Learning cultures and computers*. Dordrecht: Kluwer Academic Publishers.

Nunes, T. (1988). Street Mathematics and School Mathematics. In *Proceedings of the PME Xll, Vol 11–24*. Veszprem, Hungary.

Nunes T. (1992a). Cognitive invariants and cultural variation in mathematical concepts. *International Journal of Behavioral Development, 15*, 4, 433–453.

Nunes, T. (1992b). Ethnomathematics and everyday cognition. In D.A. Grouws (Ed.) *Handbook of research on mathematics teaching and learning* (pp. 557–574) New York: Macmillan.

Nunes, T. (1992c). *Social and personal constructions in learning mathematics*. Paper presented at the Nuffield Enquiry into Primary Mathematics, 'Children's learning in Mathematics', Exeter, Great Britain.

Nunes, T. (1993). Learning mathematics. Perspectives from everyday life. In R. Davis & C. Maher (Eds.), *Schools, mathematics, and the world of reality* (pp. 61–78). Needham Heights (MA): Allyn & Bacon.

Nunes T. (in press). Ethnomathematics and everyday cognition. In *Handbook for Research in Mathematics Education*, NCTM, USA.

Nunes, T. & Bryant, P. (1992, August). *Rotating candy bars and rearranging oranges. A study of children's understanding of commutativity*. Paper presented at the Seventh International Conference on Mathematics Education, Quebec, Canada.

Nunes, T. & Bryant, P.E. (1996). *Children doing mathematics* Oxford: Blackwell.

Nunes, T., Light, P., & Mason, J. (1993a). Tools for thought: The measurement of length and area. *Learning and Instruction, 3*, 39–54.

Nunes, T., Light, P., Mason, J., & Allerton, M. (1994). *Children's understanding of the concept of area*. London: Institute of Education, Research Report presented to the ESRC.

Nunes, T., Schliemann, A.-L. & Carraher, D. (1993b). *Street mathematics and school mathematics*. New York: Cambridge University Press.

Oakes, J. (1990). *Multiplying inequalities: The effects of race, social class, and tracking on opportunities to learn mathematics and science*. Santa Monica, CA: The RAND Corporation.

Ogbu, J. (1986). The Consequences of the American Caste System. In U. Neisser (Ed.)., *The school achievement of minority children: new perspectives*. Hillsdale, NJ: Lawrence Erlbaum Associates Inc.

Otte, M. (1990). Intuition and logic. *For the Learning of Mathematics, 10*(2), 37–43.

Overtoom, R. (1991). *Informatieverwerking door hoogbegaafde leerlingen bij het oplossen van wiskundeproblemen* [Information processing by gifted students in solving mathematical problems, with a summary in English]. De Lier, The Netherlands: Academisch Boeken Centrum.

Papert, S. (1972). Teaching Children to be Mathematicians versus Teaching about Mathematics. *International Journal of Mathematics Education in Science and Technology, 3*, 249–262

Papert, S. (1980). *Mindstorms. Children, Computers and Powerful Ideas*, New York: Basic Books.

Papert, S. (1987). Computer Criticism vs. Technocentric Thinking. *Educational Researcher, 16*, 1, 22–30.

Papert, S. (1992). Foreword. In C. Hoyles & R. Noss (Eds.), *Learning Mathematics and Logo* (pp. ix-xi). Cambridge, Massachusetts: MIT Press.

Pateson, G. (1972). *Steps to an ecology of mind: A revolutionary approach to man's understanding of himself.* New York: Ballantine.

Pea, R. & Kurland, M. (1984). On the Cognitive Effects of Learning Computer Programming. *New Ideas in Psychology, 2,* 137–168.

Perret-Clermont A.N. (1976). *L'interaction sociale comme facteur du développement cognitif.* Thèse de doctorat. Faculté de Psychologie et des Sciences de l'Education, Université de Genève.

Perret-Clermont, A.N. (1980). *Social interaction and cognitive development in children.* London: Academic Press.

Perret-Clermont, A.N. (1982). Approaches in the social psychology of learning and group work. In P. Stringer (Ed) *Confronting social issues* (pp.97–122). London: Academic Press.

Perret-Clermont A.N. (1992a). Les implicites dans les situations d'apprentissage. *Cahiers de l'Institut Supérieur de Pedagogie, Université de Paris,19,* 20–53.

Perret-Clermont, A.N. (1992b). Transmitting knowledge: implicit negotiations in the teacher-student relationship. In F.K. Oser, A. Dick & J.L. Patry (Eds) *Effective and responsible teaching* (pp.329–341). San Francisco: Jossey-Bass.

Perret-Clermont, A.-N., Brun, J., Saada, E.H., Schubauer-Leoni, M.L. (1984). Learning, a social actualization and reconstruction of knowledge, In H. Tajfel (Ed.) *The social dimension* (pp. 52–68). London: Academic Press.

Perret-Clermont, A.-N., & Nicolet, M. (Eds.) (1988). *Interagir et connaître.* Cousset (Fribourg): DelVal.

Perret-Clermont, A.-N., Perret, J.F. & Bell, N. (1991a). The social construction of meaning and cognitive activity in elementary school children. In L.B. Resnick, J.M. Levine & S.D. Teasley (Eds) *Perspectives on socially shared cognition* (pp. 41–62). Washington D.C.: American Psychological Association.

Perret-Clermont, A.-N., & Schubauer-Leoni, M.L. (1981). Conflict and cooperation as opportunities for learning. In P. Robinson (Ed.) *Communication in Development* pp. 203–233. London: Academic Press.

Perret-Clermont, A.-N., & Schubauer-Leoni, M.L. (1989). The social construction of meaning in math class interactions. In C. Keitel (Ed.) *Mathematics, education, and society , Science and Technology Education,* Document Series no 35 (pp.121–122). Paris: Unesco, Division of Science, Technical and Environmental Education.

Perret-Clermont, A.-N., & Schubauer-Leoni, M.L. (1992). *Is a "mathematical task" more than a mathematical task?* Paper presented at the XXVth International Congress of Psychology, Brussels, 19–24 July 1992.

Perret-Clermont, A.-N., Schubauer-Leoni, M.L. & Grossen M. (1990). Contexte social du questionnnement et modalités d'explication. *Cahiers d'acquisition et de pathologie du langage, 7/8,* 37–53.

Perret-Clermont, A.-N., Schubauer-Leoni, M.L. & Grossen M. (1991b). Interactions sociales dans le développement cognitif: nouvelles directions de recherche. *Cahiers de Psychologie Université de Neuchâtel, 29,* 17–39.

Perret-Clermont, A.-N., Schubauer-Leoni, M.L., & Trognon, A. (1992). L'extorsion des réponses en situation asymétrique. *Verbum, 1–2,* 3–32.

Perret J.F. (1981). Evaluation et modalités de recherches empiriques. Contribution au débat sur l'élargissement des méthodes d'évaluation pédagogique. *Education et Recherche, 1,* 65–75.

Perrin-Glorian M.J. (1993). Questions didactiques soulevées à partir de l'enseignement des mathématiques dans des classes "faibles". *Recherches en Didactique des Mathématiques, 13,* 5–119.

Piaget, J. (1947). *The Psychology of Intelligence.* [Trans. M. Piercy & D.E. Berlyne, 1972]. Totowa, NJ: Littlefield, Adams, & Co.

Piaget, J. (1952). *The child's conception of number.* London: Routledge & Kegan Paul.

Piaget, J. (1965). *The child's conception of number.* New York: Norton.

Piaget, J., Grize, J., Szeminska, A., & Bang, V. (1977). *Epistemology and psychology of functions.* Boston: D. Reidel.

Piaget, J. & Inhelder, B. (1966). *Mental Imagery in the Child.* London: Routledge & Kegan Paul.

Piaget, J., Inhelder, B., & Sinclair, H. (1968). *Mémoire et Intelligence.* Universitaire de France Press.

Piaget, J., Inhelder, B., & Szeminska, A. (1960). *The Child's Conception of Geometry,* London: Routledge & Kegan Paul Ltd.

Piaget, J., Inhelder, B., & Szeminska, A. (1966). *The child's conception of geometry.* London (or *La géometrie spontanée de l'enfant.* Paris 1948).

Pickert, G. (1968). Die Bruchrechnung als Operieren mit Abbildungen. *Mathematisch-Physikalische Semesterberichte, Band XV, 32–47.*

Pimm, D. (1987). *Speaking Mathematically.* London: Routledge & Kegan Paul.

Pompeu, G. Jr, (1992). *Bringing ethnomathematics into the school curriculum: An investigation of teachers' attitudes and pupils' learning* (unpublished). PhD Thesis, Cambridge University.

Ponte, J.P. M. (1984). Functional reasoning and the interpretation of Cartesian graphs (Doctoral dissertation, University of Georgia, 1984). *Dissertation Abstracts International, 45* (6), 1675A. (University Microfilms No. 8421144).

Pontecorvo C. (1990). Social context, semiotic mediation and forms of discourse in constructing knowledge at school. In H. Mandel, E. De Corte, N. Bennett, H. Friederich (Eds), *Learning and Instruction.* A publication of the European Association for Research on Learning and Instruction, volume 2.1, pp.1–27. Oxford: Pergamon Press.

Pontecorvo C., Ajello A.M. & Zucchermaglio C. (1991). *Discutendo si impara. Interazione e sociale e conoscenza a scuola.* Roma: La Nuova Italia.

Prigogine I. & Stengers I. (1979). *La nouvelle alliance. Métamorphose de la science.* Paris: Gallimard.

Raz, I.S., & Bryant, P. (1990). Social background, phonological awareness and children's reading. *British Journal of Developmental Psychology, 8,* 209–225.

Reed H.J. & Lave I. (1981). Arithmetic as a tool for investigating relations between culture and cognition. In R.W. Casson (Ed.) *Language, culture and cognition: anthropological perspectives.* pp.437–455. New York: Macmillan.

Reed, S.K. (1987). A structure-mapping model for word problems. *Journal of Experimental Psychology: Learning, Memory and Cognition, 13,* 124–139.

Reed, S.K., Dempster, A., & Ettinger, M. (1985). Usefulness of analogous solutions for solving algebra word problems. *Journal of Experimental Psychology: Learning, Memory and Cognition, 11,* 106–125.

Rengering, J. (1983). *De staartdeling. Een geïntegreerde aanpak volgens het principe van progressieve schematisering.* Utrecht: OW&OC.

Resnick, L. (1992). From protoquantities to operators: Building mathematical competence on a foundation of everyday knowledge. In G. Leinhardt, R. Putnam, & R.A Hattrup (Eds.), *Analysis of arithmetic for mathematics teaching.* Hillsdale, NJ: Lawrence Erlbaum Associates Inc.

Resnick, L., & Greeno, J. (1990). *Conceptual growth of number and quantity.* Unpublished manuscript, University of Pittsburgh, Learning Research and Development Center.

Resnick, L., & Singer, J. (1993). Protoquantitative origins of ratio reasoning. In T.P. Carpenter, E. Fennema, & T.A. Romberg (Eds.), *Rational numbers: An integration of research* (pp. 107–130). Hillsdale, NJ: Lawrence Erlbaum Associates Inc.

Resnick, L. B. (1982). Syntax and semantics in learning to subtract. In T.P. Carpenter, J.M. Moser, & T.A. Romberg (Eds.), *Addition and subtraction: A cognitive perspective* (pp. 136–155). Hillsdale, NJ: Lawrence Erlbaum Associates Inc.

Resnick, L.B. (1986). The development of mathematical intuition. In M. Perlmutter (Ed.), *Minnesota symposia on child psychology* (Vol. 19, pp.159–194). Hillsdale, NJ: Lawrence Erlbaum Associates Inc.

Resnick, L.B. & Omanson, S.F. (1987). Learning to Understand Arithmetic. In R. Glaser (Ed.), *Advances in Instructional Psychology*, Vol. 3. London: Lawrence Erlbaum Associates Ltd.

Reston, VA. National Council of Teachers of Mathematics: Washington, DC.

Reusser, K. (1988). Problem solving beyond the logic of things: Contextual effects on understanding and solving word problems. *Instructional Science, 17*, 309–338.

Ricco, G. (1982). Les premiere acquisitions de la notion de fonction lineaire chez l'enfant de la 7 a 11 ans [Initial acquisitions of the linear function concept by children 7 to 11 years old]. *Educational Studies in Mathematics, 13*, 289–327.

Riley, M.S., Greeno, J.G., & Heller, J.I. (1983). Development of children's problem-solving ability in arithmetic. In H.P. Ginsburg (Ed.) *The development of mathematical thinking* (pp.153–196). New York: Academic Press.

Roazzi, A. & Bryant, P. (1992). Social class, context and cognitive development. In P. Light & G. Butterworth (Eds) *Context and cognition. Ways of learning and knowing*. Hemel Hempstead, UK: Harvester Wheatsheaf.

Robert, A. & Robinet, J. (1989). Représentations des enseignants de mathématiques sur les mathématiques et leur enseignement. *Cahier de DIDIREM, 1*. IREM PARIS 7.

Robert, A. & Tenaud, I. (1989). Une expérience d'enseignement de la géométrie en Terminale C (scientific section, 16–18 years old). *Recherches en Didactique des Mathématiques, 9*, 31–70.

Robitaille, D. & Dirks, M. (1982). Models for the mathematics curriculum. *For the Learning of Mathematics, 2*, 3, 3–21.

Rogalski, J. (1992). Acquisition de notions relatives à la dimensionalité des mesures spatiales (longueur, surface). Recherches en Didactique des Mathématiques. Grenoble: *La Pensee Sauvage, 3*, 3, 343–396.

Romberg, T.A. (Ed.), *Rational numbers: An integration of research* (pp.107–130). Hillsdale, NJ: Lawrence Erlbaum Associates Inc.

Romberg, T.A., & Carpenter, T.C. (1986). Research on teaching and learning mathematics. Two disciplines of scientific inquiry. In M.C. Wittrock (Ed.) *Handbook of research on teaching* (3rd edition) (pp.850–873). New York: Macmillan.

Rommetveit, R. (1974). *On message structure: a framework for the study of language and communication*. New York, London: John Wiley & Sons Ltd.

Rubio, G. (1990). Algebra word problems: A numerical approach for its resolution (a teaching experiment in the classroom). In G. Booker, P. Cobb, & T.N. de Mendicuti (Eds.), *Proceedings of the Fourteenth International Conference for the Psychology of Mathematics Education* (Vol. II, pp. 125–132). Mexico City: PME Program Committee.

Saada, E.H., & Brun, J. (1984). L'élaboration des formulations dans un jeu en arithmétique. *Recherches en didactique des mathématiques, 5*, 2, 141–185.

Säljö R. (1991). Learning and mediation: fitting reality into a table. *Learning and Instruction, 1*, 261–272.

Säljö R., & Wyndhamn, J. (1987). The formal setting as context for cognitive activities. An empirical study of arithmetic operations under conflicting premises for communication, *European Journal of Psychology of Education, 3*, 233–245.

Sawyer. W.W. (1969). *Aanschouwelijk Algebra*. Utrecht/Antwerpen.

Saxe, G. (1979). A developmental analysis of notational counting. *Child Development, 48*, 1512–1520.

Saxe, G.B. (1988). Candy selling and math learning. *Educational Researcher, 17*, 14–21.

Saxe, G.B. (1991). *Culture and Cognitive Development: Studies in Mathematics Understanding* Hillsdale, NJ: Lawrence Erlbaum Associates.

Saxe, G., Guberman, S.R. & Gearhart, M. (1987). Social processes in early number development. *Monographs of the Society for Research in Child Development, 52*, (2, Serial No. 216).

Schliemann, A., & Carraher, D. (1992). Proportional reasoning in and out of school. In P. Light & G. Butterworth (Eds.), *Context and cognition: Ways of learning and knowing* (pp. 47–73). Hillsdale, NJ: Lawrence Erlbaum Associates Inc.

Schliemann, A., & Nunes, T. (1990). A situated schema of proportionality. *British Journal of Developmental Psychology, 8*, 259–269.

Schmidt, S., & Weisser, W. (1992). *Structures of one-step word problems involving multiplication and division* (Internal report). Köln, Germany: Seminar for Mathematics Education, Faculty of Education, University of Köln.

Schoenfeld, A.H. (1982). Some thoughts on problem-solving research and mathematics education. In K.F. Lester & J. Garofalo (Eds.) *Mathematical problem solving: issues in research*. Philadelphia: Franklin Institute Press.

Schoenfeld, A.H. (1985). *Mathematical Problem Solving*. London: Academic Press.

Schoenfeld A.H. (Ed.) (1987). *Cognitive Science and Mathematics Education*. Hillsdale, NJ: Lawrence Erlbaum Associates Inc.

Schoenfeld, A.H. (1991). On mathematics as sense-making: An informal attack on the unfortunate divorce of formal and informal mathematics. In J.F. Voss, D.N. Perkins & J.W. Segal (Eds.), *Informal reasoning and education* (pp.311–343). Hillsdale: NJ. Lawrence Erlbaum Associates Inc.

Schoenfeld, A.H. (1992). Learning to think mathematically: problem solving, metacognition, and sense making in mathematics. In D.A. Grouws (Ed.) *Handbook of Research on Mathematics Teaching and Learning: A Project of the National Council of Teachers of Mathematics* (pp.334–370). New York: Macmillan.

Schoenfeld, A.H. (in press). Ideas in the air. *International Journal of Educational Research*.

Schoenfeld, A.H., Smith, J.P., & Arcavi, A. (1993). Learning—The microgenetic analysis of one student's evolving understanding of a complex subject matter domain. In R. Glaser (Ed.), *Advances in instructional psychology* (Vol. 4, pp. 55–175). Hillsdale, NJ: Lawrence Erlbaum Associates Inc.

Schubauer-Leoni, M.L. (1986a). *Maître-élève-savoir: analyse psychosociale du jeu et des enjeux de la relation didactique*. Thèse de doctorat présentée à la Faculté de Psychologie et des Sciences de l'Education. Université de Genève.

Schubauer-Leoni, M.L. (1986b). Le contrat didactique: un cadre interprétatif pour comprendre les savoirs manifestés par les élèves en mathématiques. *European Journal of Psychology of Education, 1/2*, 139–153.

Schubauer-Leoni, M.L. (1988). L'interaction expérimentateur-sujet à propos d'un savoir mathématique: la situation de test revisitée. In A.-N. Perret-Clermont & M. Nicolet (Eds.) *Interagir et connaître* pp.251–264. Cousset (Fribourg): Del Val.

Schubauer-Leoni, M.L. (1989). Problématisation des notions d'obstacle épistémologique et de conflit socio-cognitif dans le champ pédagogique. In N. Bednarz & C. Garnier (Eds) *Construction des savoirs, obstacles et conflits* pp. 350–363. Montréal: Agence d'Arc Inc. & CIRADE.

Schubauer-Leoni, M.L. (1990). Ecritures additives en classe et en dehors de la classe: une affaire de contexte. *Resonances. 6*, 16–18.

Schubauer-Leoni, M.L. (1991). L'évaluation didactique: une affaire contractuelle. In J. Weiss (Ed.) *L'évaluation: un problème de communication* pp.79–95, Cousset, Fribourg: Del Val & IRDP.

Schubauer-Leoni, M.L. (1993). Il problema della definizione della situazione: interazione didattica o interazione "sperimentale"? In C. Pontecorvo (Ed.) *La condivisione della conoscenza* (pp. 57–74). Milan: La Nuova Italia Editrice.

Schubauer-Leoni, M.L. (1994). Quatre élèves et un problème de distances: approche didactique de l'analyse des interactions. In A. Trognon, U. Dausendschön-Gay, U. Krafft, & C. Riboni (Eds.) *La construction interactive du quotidien*, Collection Forum de l'I.F.R.A.S. Presses Universitaires de Nancy.

Schubauer-Leoni, M.L., Bell, N., Grossen, M., & Perret-Clermont, A.-N. (1989). Problems in assessment of learning: the social construction of questions and answers in the scholastic context. *International Journal of Educational Research, 13*, 671–684.

Schubauer-Leoni, M.L., & Grossen, M. (1984). Formulations écrites de problèmes additifs et interactions sociales. Etablissement d'une typologie d'écritures et de leur contenu. *Interactions Didactiques.* Universités de Genève et de Neuchâtel, 5.

Schubauer-Leoni, M.L. & Grossen, M. (1993). Negotiating the meaning of questions in didactic and experimental contracts. *European Journal of Psychology of Education, 4*, 451–471.

Schubauer-Leoni, M.L., & Ntamakiliro, L. (1993). L' "algèbre" vue par des professeurs de mathématiques du secondaire inférieur: démarche comparative en fonction des contextes institutionnels. In J.F. Perret & E. Runtz-Christan (Eds) *Les manuels font-ils école?* (pp. 107–124). Cousset (Fribourg): Del Val.

Schubauer-Leoni, M.L., & Ntamakiliro, L. (1994). La construction de réponses à des problèmes impossibles, *Revue des Sciences de l'éducation, Vol. XX.I*, 87–114.

Schubauer-Leoni, M.L., & Perret-Clermont, A.-N. (1980). Interactions sociales et représentations symboliques dans le cadre de problèmes additifs. *Recherches en didactique des mathématiques, 1*, 3, 297–350.

Schubauer-Leoni, M.L., & Perret-Clerrnont, A.-N. (1985). Interactions sociales dans l'apprentissage de connaissances mathématiques chez l'enfant. In G. Mugny (Ed.) *Psychologie sociale du développement cognitif* pp. 225–250. Bern: P. Lang, Collection Exploration.

Schubauer-Leoni, M.L., & Perret-Clermont, A.-N. (1987). Représentations et significations de savoirs scolaires. In S. Ehrlich & A. Florin (Eds.) Le fonctionnement de l'enfant à l'école, *Journal Européen de Psychologie de l'Education. Special Issue*, pp.55–62.

Schubauer-Leoni M.L., Perret-Clermont, A.-N. & Grossen, M. (1992). The construction of adult child intersubjectivity in psychological research and in school. In M. von Cranach, W. Doise & G. Mugny (Eds.) *Social representation and the social bases of knowledge*, volume I, pp. 69–76. Berne and Lewiston: Swiss Psychological Society and Hogrefe & Huber Publishers.

Schwartz, J.L. (1988). Intensive quantity and referent transforming arithmetic operations. In J. Heibert & M. Behr (Eds.), *Research agenda for mathematics education: Number concepts and operations in the middle grades* (pp 41–53).

Schwartz, J., & Yerushalmy, M. (1992). Getting students to function in and with algebra. In G. Harel & E. Dubinsky (Eds.), *The concept of function: Aspects of epistemology and pedagogy (MAA Notes*, Vol. 25, pp. 261–289). Washington, DC: Mathematical Association of America.

Scribner, S. & Cole, M. (1981). *The Psychology of Literacy.* Cambridge, MA: Harvard University Press.

Semin G.R. (1989). On genetic social psychology: a rejoinder to Doise. *European Journal of Social Psychology, 19*, 401–405.

Sera, M., & Smith, L. (1987). Big and little: "Nominal" and relative uses. *Cognitive Development, 2*, 89–111.

Sera, M., Troyer, D., & Smith, L. (1988). What do two-year-olds know about the sizes of things? *Child Development, 59*, 1489–1496.

Seron, X. & Fayol, M. (1994). Number transcoding in children: A functional analysis. *British Journal of Developmental Psychology, 12*, 281–300.

Sfard, A. (1987). Two conceptions of mathematical notions: Operational and structural. In J.C. Bergeron, N. Herscovics, & C. Kieran (Eds.), *Proceedings of the Eleventh International Conference for the Psychology of Mathematics Education* (Vol. III, pp. 162–169). Montréal: Université de Montréal.

Sfard, A. (1991). On the dual nature of mathematical conceptions: Reflections on processes and objects as different sides of the same coin. *Educational Studies in Mathematics, 22*, 1–36.

Sfard, A. (1992). Operational origins of mathematical objects and the quandary of reification—the case of function. In G. Harel & E. Dubinsky (Eds.), *The concept of function: Aspects of epistemology and pedagogy (MAA Notes*, Vol. 25, pp.59–84). Washington, DC: Mathematical Association of America.

Sfard, A., & Linchevski, L. (1994). The gains and the pitfalls of reification—the case of algebra. *Educational Studies in Mathematics, 26*, 191–228.

Shuard, H., & Neill, H. (1977). *From graphs to calculus.* Glasgow: Blackie.

Siegel, S. (1956). *Nonparametric Statistics for the Behavioural Sciences.* New York: McGraw-Hill.

Sierpinska, A. (1992). On understanding the notion of function. In G. Harel & E. Dubinsky (Eds.), *The concept of function: Aspects of epistemology and pedagogy (MAA Notes*, Vol. 25, pp.25–58). Washington, DC: Mathematical Association of America.

Silva, Z.M.H. (1993). *A compreensao da escrita numerica ela crianca.* Paper presented at the ISSBD Conference, Recife (Brazil), July.

Silver, E.A. (1985). Research on teaching mathematical problem solving. Some underrepresented themes and needed directions. In E.A. Silver (Ed.), *Teaching and Learning Mathematical Problem Solving: Multiple research Perspectives* (pp.247–266). Hillsdale, NJ: Lawrence Erlbaum Associates Inc.

Silverman, I., & Paskewitz, S. (1988). Developmental and individual differences in children's area judgment rules. *Journal of Experimental Child Psychology, 46*, 74–87.

Simmons, M. & Cope, P. (1993). Angle and Rotation: Effects of Different Types of Feedback on the Quality of Responses. *Educational Studies in Mathematics 24*, 163–176.

Singer, J. (1992). *Reasoning about density: Evidence for two processes.* Unpublished doctoral dissertation: University of Pittsburgh.

Singer, J., Kohn, A., & Resnick, L. (under review). *More is not arbitrary: Children's reasoning about direct covariation.*

Sleeman, D.H. (1984). An attempt to understand students' understanding of basic algebra. *Cognitive Science, 8*, 387–412.

Sloan, D. (Ed.) (1984). *The computer in education: a critical perspective.* New York: Teachers College Press.

Smith, M. B. (1973). Attitude change. In N. Warren, & M. Jahoda (Eds.), *Attitudes: Selected Readings* (pp. 26–46) (second edition). Harmondsworth, UK: Penguin books.

Soloway, E., Lochhead, J., & Clement, J. (1982). Does computer programming enhance problem solving ability? Some positive evidence on algebra word problems. In R.J. Seidel, R.E. Anderson, & B. Hunter (Eds.), *Computer literacy.* New York: Academic Press.

Song, M.-J., & Ginsburg, H.P. (1987). The development of informal and formal mathematical thinking in Korean and American children. *Child Development, 58*, 1286–1296.

Sophian, C. (1988). Limitations on preschool children's knowledge about counting: using counting to compare two sets. *Developmental Psychology, 24*, 634–640.

Sowder, L. (1988). Children's solutions of story problems. *Journal of Mathematical Behavior, 7*, 227–238.

Spinillo, A., & Bryant, P. (1991). Children's proportional judgments: The importance of "half." *Child Development, 62*, 427–440.

Starkey, P., & Klein, A. (1991). *Economic and cultural influences on early mathematical cognition.* Paper presented at the conference New Directions in Child and Family Research: Shaping Head Start in the 90s. Alexandria, VA.

Starkey, P. & Gelman, R. (1982). The development of addition and subtraction abilities prior to formal schooling in arithmetic. In T.P. Carpenter, J.N. Moser, & T.A. Romberg (Eds.) *Addition and subtraction: A cognitive perspective.* Hillsdale, NJ: Lawrence Erlbaum Associates, Inc.

Starkey, P., Spelke, E.S. & Gelman, R. (1990). Numerical abstraction by human infants. *Cognition, 36,* 97–127.

Steffe, L. (1991). The Constructivist Teaching Experiment: Illustrations and Implications. In E. Vonglaserfed (Ed.) *Radical Constructivivism in Mathematics Education.* Dordrecht: Kluwer.

Steffe, L. (1994). Children's Multiplying Schemes. In G. Harel & J. Confrey (Eds.), *The Development of Multiplicative Reasoning in the Learning of Mathematics* (pp.3–40). Albany, New York: State University of New York Press.

Steffe, L.P., Thompson, P.W. & Richards, J. (1982). Children's Counting in Arithmetical Problem Solving. In T.P. Carpenter, J.M. Moser & T.A. Romberg (Eds.), *Additional and Subtraction: A Cognitive Perspective,* pp.83–96. Hillsdale, NJ: Lawrence Erlbaum Associates Inc.

Steinberg, R.M., Sleeman, D.H., & Ktorza, D. (1991). Algebra students' knowledge of equivalence of equations. *Journal for Research in Mathematics Education, 22,* 112–121.

Stern, E. (1993). What makes certain arithmetic word problems involving the comparison of sets so difficult for children? *Journal of Educational Psychology, 85,* 7–23.

Stevenson, H.W., & Azuma, H. (1983). IQ in Japan and the United States: methodological problems in Lynn's analysis. *Nature, 306,* 291–292.

Stevenson, H.W., Chen, C, & Uttal, D.H. (1990a). Beliefs and achievement: a study of Black, White, and Hispanic children. *Child Development, 61,* 508–523.

Stevenson, H.W., Lee, S., & Stigler, J.W. (1986). Mathematics achievement of Chinese, Japanese, and American Children. *Science, 233,* 696–699.

Stevenson, H.W., Lummis, M., Lee, S., & Stigler, J.W. (1990b). *Making the grade in mathematics: elementary school mathematics in the United States, Taiwan, and Japan.* Reston, VA: National Council of Teachers of Mathematics.

Stevenson, H.W., Stigler, J.W., Lee, S., & Lucker, W. (1985). Cognitive performance and academic achievement of Japanese, Chinese, and American children. *Child Development, 56,* 718–34.

Stigler, J. & Perry, M. (1989). Cross cultural studies of mathematics teaching and learning: Recent findings and new directions. In D. Grouws & T. Cooney (Eds.) *Effective Mathematics Teaching* (pp.194–223). Hillsdale, NJ: Lawrence Erlbaum Associates Inc.

Stigler, J.W. (1984). "Mental abacus": The effect of abacus training on Chinese children's mental calculation. *Cognitive Psychology, 16,* 145–176.

Stigler, J.W. (1988). Research into practice: The use of verbal explanation in Japanese and American classrooms. *Arithmetic Teacher, 36,* (2), 27–29.

Stigler, J.W. & Baranes, R. (1988). Culture and mathematics learning. In E.Z. Rothkopf (Ed.) *Review of Research in Education* (Vol. 15). Washington, DC: American Educational Research Association.

Stigler, J.W., Lee, S., & Stevenson, H.W. (1986). Digit memory in Chinese and English: Evidence for a temporally limited store. *Cognition, 23,* 1–20.

Stigler, J.W., & Perry, M. (1988). Mathematics learning in Japanese, Chinese, and American classrooms. In G. Saxe & M. Gearhart (Eds.), *Children's mathematics.* San Francisco: Jossey-Bass.

Streefland, L. (1978). Some Observational Results Concerning the Mental Constitution of the Concept of Fraction. *Educational Studies in Mathematics, 9*, 51–73.

Streefland, L. (Ed.), *Proceedings of the Ninth International Conference for the Psychology of Mathematics Education*, vol. II. Utrecht: OW&OC, 73–97.

Streefland, L. (1985). Wiskunde als activiteit en de realiteit als bron. *Nieuwe Wiskrant, 5*(1), 60–67.

Streefland, L. (1988). Reconstructive learning. In A. Borbas (Ed.) *Proceedings of the Twelfth International Conference for the Psychology of Mathematics Education* (Vol.1, pp. 75–91) Veszprem, Hungary: OOK Printing House.

Streefland, L. (1991). *Fractions in Realistic Mathematics Education. A Paradigm of Developmental Research.* Dordrecht: Kluwer Academic Publishers.

Streefland, L. (1993a). Fractions: A Realistic Approach. In T.P. Carpenter, E. Fennema, T.A. Romberg (Eds), *An Integration of Research*, 289–327 Hillsdale, NJ: Lawrence Erlbaum Associates Inc.

Streefland, L. (1993b). The design of a mathematics course. *Educational Studies in Mathematics, 25*(½), *Special Issue on The Legacy of Hans Freudenthal*, 109–135.

Street, B.V. (1984). *Literacy in theory and practice.* Cambridge, UK: Cambridge University Press.

Street, B.V. (1987). Literacy and social chance: The significance of social context in the development of literacy programmes. In D. Wagner (Ed.), *The future of literacy in a changing world* (pp. 48–64). Oxford: Pergamon Press.

Sue, S., & Okazaki, S. (1990). Asian-American educational achievements: a phenomenon in search of an explanation. *American Psychologist, 45*, 913–920.

Surber, C. (1980). The development of reversible operations in judgments of ability, effort, and performance. *Child Development, 51*, 1018–1029.

Sutherland, R. (1989). Providing a Computer-based Framework for Algebraic Thinking *Educational Studies in Maths, 20*, 3, 317–344.

Swan, M. (1982). The teaching of functions and graphs. In G. van Barneveld & H. Krabbendam (Eds.), *Proceedings of Conference on Functions* (pp. 151–165). Enschede, The Netherlands: National Institute for Curriculum Development.

Tall D. & Thomas M. (1991). Encouraging versatile thinking in algebra using the computer. *Educational Studies in Mathematics, 22*, 125–147.

Thomas, H.L. (1969). *An analysis of stages in the attainment of a concept of function.* Unpublished doctoral dissertation, Columbia University, New York.

Thompson, A.G. (1992). Teachers' beliefs and conceptions: A synthesis of the research. In D.A. Grouws (Ed.) *Handbook of Research on Mathematics Teaching and Learning: A Project of the National Council of Teachers of Mathematics*, (pp.127–146). New York: Macmillan.

Tobin, J.J., Wu, D.Y.H., & Davidson, D.H. (1989). *Preschool in three cultures: Japan, China, and the United States.* New Haven: Yale University Press.

Toole, B.A. (Ed.) (1992). *Ada, the Enchantress of Numbers.* California: Strawberry Press.

Tourniaire, F. & Pulos, S. (1985). Proportional reasoning: A review of the literature. *Educational Studies in Mathematics, 16*, 181–204.

Toyama, H., & Gimbayashi, H. (1971). *Calculation systems by the "Water supply method".* (Extended edition) Tokyo: Meiji-Tosho. (in Japanese).

Treffers, A. (1987). *Three Dimensions. A Model of Goal and Theory Description in Mathematics Education: The Wiskobas Project.* Dordrecht: Reidel.

Treffers, A. (1991). Didactical Background of a Mathematics Program for Primary Education. In L. Streefland, (Ed.), *Realistic Mathematics Education in Primary School.* Utrecht: CD-ß, 21–57.

Treffers, A., Moor, E. de & Feijs, E. (1989). *Proeve van een nationaal programma voor het reken-wiskundeonderwiis* [Specimen of a national program for mathematics education]. Tilburg: Zwijsen.

Trognon A. (1992). Psicologia cognitiva e analisi delle conversazioni. In C. Galimberti (Ed.) *La conversazione. Prospettive sull'interazione psico-social*, pp. 115–155. Milano: Edizioni Angelo Guerini e Associati.

Trognon, A., & Retornaz, A. (1989). Clinique du rationnel: psychologie cognitive et analyse des conversations. *Connexions. 53*, 69–91.

Tunes, T. (1992). *Using letters to represent unknown values.* London: Institute of Education. Unpublished research report.

Usiskin, Z.P. (1979). The future of fractions. *The Arithmetic Teacher, 26(5)*, 18–20

Usiskin, Z. (1989). Conceptions of school algebra and uses of variables. In A.F. Coxford (Ed.), *The ideas of algebra, K-12* (1988 Yearbook of National Council of Teachers of Mathematics, pp. 8–19). Reston, VA: NCTM.

Van den Brink, F.J. (1989). *Realistic mathematics education to young children.* Utrecht, The Netherlands: OW & OC, Utrecht University.

Van Essen, G. (1991). *Heuristics and arithmetic word problems.* (Unpublished doctoral dissertation). Amsterdam, The Netherlands: State University Amsterdam.

Van Hiele, P.M. (1986). *Structure and Insight: A Theory of Mathematics Education.* London: Academic Press Inc.

Van Lehn, K. & Brown, J.S. (1980). Planning net: A representation for formalizing analogies and semantic models of procedural skills. In R.E. Snow, P. Federico, & W.E. Montague (Eds.), *Aptitude, learning, and instruction. Vol. 2: Cognitive process analyses of learning and problem solving.* Hillsdale, NJ: Lawrence Erlbaum Associates Inc.

Vergnaud, G. (1981). *L'enfant la mathématique et la réalité.* Bern: Peter Lang, Collection Exploration.

Vergnaud, G. (1982). A classification of cognitive tasks and operations of thought involved in addition and subtraction. In T. Carpenter, J. Moser, & T. Romberg (Eds.), *Addition and Subtraction: A Cognitive perspective* (pp.39–59). Hillsdale, NJ: Lawrence Erlbaum Associates Inc.

Vergnaud, G. (1983a). Didactique et acquisition du concept de volume. Introduction. *Recherches en Didactique des Mathématiques.* Grenoble: La Pensée Sauvage, *4*, 1, 9–25.

Vergnaud, G. (1983b). Multiplicative structures. In R. Lesh & M. Landau (Eds.), *Acquisition of mathematics concepts and processes* (pp. 127–174). New York: Academic Press.

Vergnaud, G. (1984). *Didactics as a Content-Oriented Approach to Research on the Learning of Physics, Mathematics and Natural Language.* New Orleans: *AERA.*

Vergnaud, G. (1987). "Conclusion". In C. Javier (Ed.) *Problem of Representation in the Teaching and Learning of Mathematics.* Hove, UK: Lawrence Erlbaum Associates Ltd.

Vergnaud, G. (1988). Multiplicative structures. In J. Hiebert & M. Behr (Eds.), *Number concepts and operations in the middle grades* (Vol. 2, pp. 141–161). Hillsdale, NJ: Lawrence Erlbaum Associates Inc.

Vergnaud, G. (1990). Epistemology and psychology of mathematics education. In P. Nesher & J. Kilpatrick (Eds.), *Mathematics and cognition: A research synthesis by the International Group for the Psychology of Mathematics Education* (pp.14–30). Cambridge: Cambridge University Press.

Vergnaud G. (1991). La théorie des champs conceptuels. *Recherches en Didactique des Mathématiques, 10*, 133–171.

Vergnaud, G., & Durand, C. (1976). Structures additives et complexité psychogénétique. *Revue Française de Pédagogie, 36*, 28–43.

Verschaffel, L. (1984). *Representatie- en oplossingsprocessen van eersteklassers bij aanvankelijke redactie-opgaven over optellen en aftrekken.* [First graders' representations and solution processes on elementary addition and subtraction word problems]. (Unpublished doctoral dissertation). Leuven, Belgium: Center for Instructional Psychology, University of Leuven.

Verschaffel, L. (1994). Using retelling data to study elementary school children's representations and solutions of compare problems. *Journal for Research in Mathematics Education, 25,* 140–164.

Verschaffel, L., De Corte, E., & Lasure, S. (1994). Realistic considerations in mathematical modeling of school word problems. *Learning and Instruction, 4,* 273–294.

Verschaffel, L., De Corte, E., & Pauwels, A. (1992). Solving compare problems: An eye-movement test of Lewis and Mayer's consistency hypothesis. *Journal of Educational Psychology, 84,* 85–94.

Verstappen, P. (1982). Some reflections on the introduction of relations and functions. In G. van Barneveld & H. Krabbendam (Eds.), *Proceedings of Conference on Functions* (pp. 166–184). Enschede, The Netherlands: National Institute for Curriculum Development.

Vinh Bang & Lunzer, E. (1965). Conservations spatiales, *Etudes d'épistémologie génétique,* volume 19. Paris: Presses Universitaires de France.

Vinner, S. (1983). Concept definition, concept image and the notion of function. *International Journal of Mathematical Education in Science and Technology, 14,* 293–305.

Vinner, S. (1989). The avoidance of visual considerations in calculus students. *Focus on Learning Problems in Mathematics, 11* (1,2), 149–156.

Vygotsky, L.S. (1962). *Thought and language.* Cambridge, MA: MIT Press.

Vygotsky L.S., Luria, A.R. & Leontiev A.N. (1991). *Linguagem. Desenvolvimento e Aprendizagem.* São Paulo: Icone Ed.

Wagner, S., & Kieran, C. (Eds.). (1989). *Research issues in the learning and teaching of algebra.* Reston, VA: National Council of Teachers of Mathematics; Hillsdale, NJ: Lawrence Erlbaum Associates Inc.

Wagner, S., Rachlin, S.L., & Jensen, R.J. (1984). *Algebra Learning Project: Final report.* Athens: University of Georgia, Department of Mathematics Education.

Wahl-Luckow, A. (1993). *The evolution of the concept of algebraic expression in a problem-solving computer environment: A process-object perspective.* Unpublished doctoral dissertation, Université du Québec à Montréal, Canada.

Waits, B.K., & Demana, F. (1988, July–August). *New models for teaching and learning mathematics through technology.* Paper presented to the theme group on Microcomputers and the Teaching of Mathematics at the Sixth International Congress on Mathematical Education, Budapest, Hungary.

Walkerdine, V. (1988). *The Mastery of Reason.* London: Routledge.

Wang, Y-J. (1995). *A study of Chinese children's counting and their understanding of the numeration system.* Unpublished Masters Dissertation, Institute of Education, University of London.

Wenger, R.H. (1987). Cognitive science and algebra learning. In A.H. Schoenfeld (Ed.), *Cognitive science and mathematics education* (pp. 217–251). Hillsdale, NJ: Lawrence Erlbaum Associates Inc.

Wertsch, J.V. (1990). The voice of rationality in a sociocultural approach to mind. In L.C. Moll (Ed.), *Vygotsky and Education* (pp. 111–126). Cambridge: Cambridge University Press.

Wheeler, D. (1996). Backwards and forwards: Reflections on different approaches to algebra. In N. Bednarz, C. Kieran, & L. Lee (Eds.), *Approaches to algebra: Perspectives for research and teaching* (pp. 317–325). Dordrecht, The Netherlands: Kluwer.

Wilkening, F. (1979). Combining of stimulus dimensions in children's and adult's judgments of area: An information integration analysis. *Developmental Psychology, 15,* 25–33.

Wilkening, F. (1981). Integrating velocity, time, and distance information: A developmental study. *Cognitive Psychology, 13,* 231–247.

Wilkening, F., Becker, I., & Trabasso, T. (1980). *Information integration by children.* Hillsdale, NJ: Lawrence Erlbaum Associates Inc.

Willis, G.B., & Fuson, K.C. (1988). Teaching children to use schematic drawings to solve addition and subtraction word problems. *Journal of Educational Psychology, 80,* 192–201.

Wynn, K. (1990). Children's understanding of counting. *Cognition, 36,* 155–193.

Wynn, K. (1992). Addition and subtraction by human infants. *Nature, 358,* 749–750.

Yackel, E. (1992). *The Evolution of Second Grade Children's Understanding of What Constitutes an Explanation in a Mathematics Class.* Paper presented at ICM Yackel, 1–7, Quebec, Canada.

Zaslavsky, C. (1987). *Maths Comes Alive: Activities From Many Cultures.* Portland, USA: J. Weston Walch.

Zuideman, J.J. & van der Gaag, C. (Eds) (1993). *De volgende opgave van de computer,* [Next problem on the computer] Utrecht: DC-ß reeks n. 12.

Author Index

Subject Index